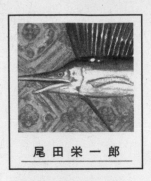

尾田栄一郎

Humans seem strong, but they're really weak.
They can drown in just two inches of water. Well,
basically that's what comes from only being able
to breathe through your nose and mouth. For
that reason, I think we should all master another
method of breathing. Breathe with your butt. All
right then, volume 37 is ~~farting~~ starting.

-Eiichiro Oda, 2005

Eiichiro Oda began his manga career at the age of 17, when his one-shot cowboy manga **Wanted!** won second place in the coveted Tezuka manga awards. Oda went on to work as an assistant to some of the biggest manga artists in the industry, including Nobuhiro Watsuki, before winning the Hop Step Award for new artists. His pirate adventure **One Piece**, which debuted in **Weekly Shonen Jump** in 1997, quickly became one of the most popular manga in Japan.

ONE PIECE VOL. 37
WATER SEVEN PART 6

SHONEN JUMP Manga Edition

STORY AND ART BY EIICHIRO ODA

English Adaptation/Jake Forbes
Translation/Taylor Eagle, HC Language Solutions
Touch-up Art & Lettering/HudsonYards
Design/Sean Lee
Supervising Editor/Yuki Murashige
Editor/Megan Bates

VP, Production/Alvin Lu
VP, Sales & Product Marketing/Gonzalo Ferreyra
VP, Creative/Linda Espinosa
Publisher/Hyoe Narita

ONE PIECE © 1997 by Eiichiro Oda. All rights reserved.
First published in Japan in 1997 by SHUEISHA Inc., Tokyo.
English translation rights arranged by SHUEISHA Inc.

Printed in the U.S.A.

Published by VIZ Media, LLC
P.O. Box 77010
San Francisco, CA 94107

10 9 8 7 6 5 4 3 2 1
First printing, March 2010

www.viz.com

PARENTAL ADVISORY
ONE PIECE is rated T for Teen and is recommended
for ages 13 and up. This volume contains fantasy
violence and tobacco usage.
ratings.viz.com

THE WORLD'S
MOST POPULAR MANGA

SHONEN JUMP

www.shonenjump.com

SHONEN JUMP MANGA

Vol. 37
TOM

STORY AND ART BY
EIICHIRO ODA

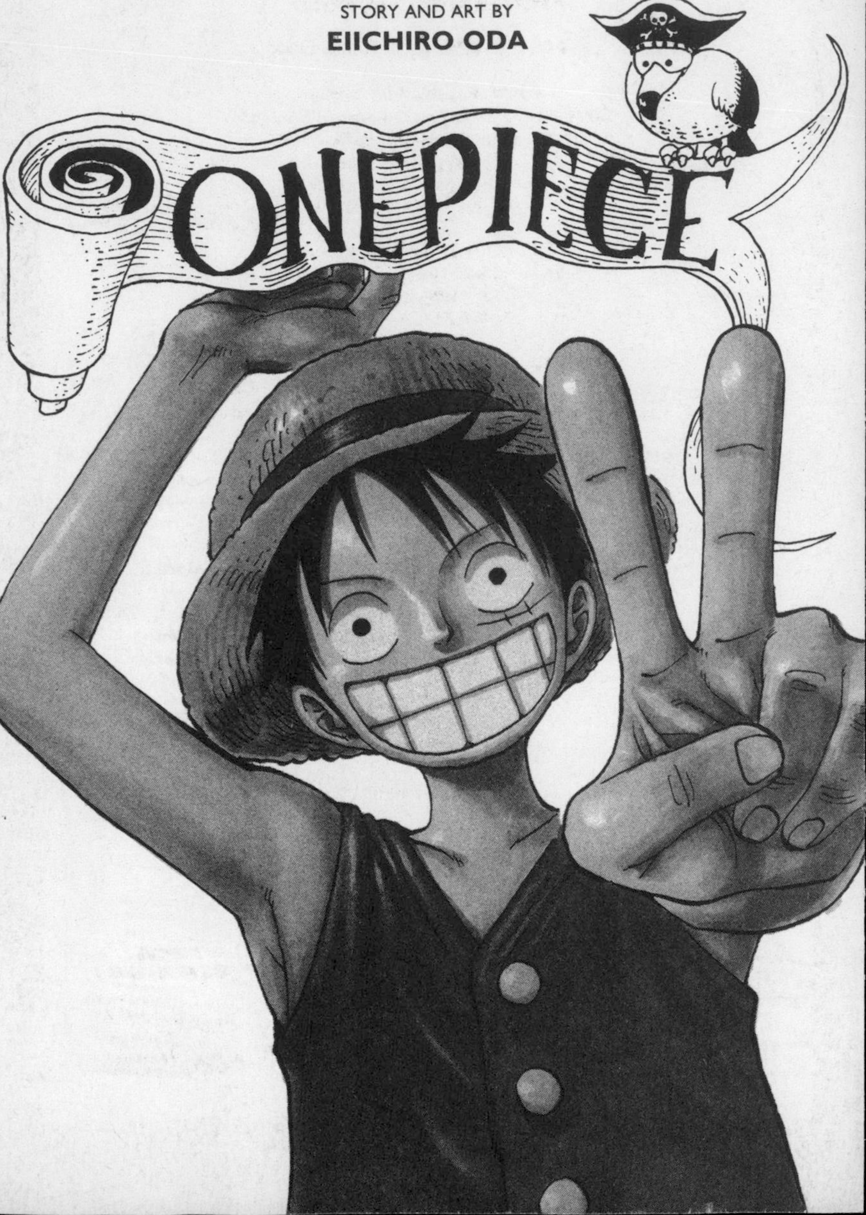
ONE PIECE

The Franky Family

Professional ship dismantlers, they moonlight as bounty hunters.

The master builder and an apprentice of Tom, the legendary shipwright.

Franky (Cutty Flam)

The Square Sisters

Kiwi & Mozu

Cipher Pol No. 9

A covert intelligence agency under the direct supervision of the World Government. They have been granted the license to kill uncooperative citizens.

Rob Lucci & Hattori

Kaku

Kalifa

Blueno

The Straw Hats

Boundlessly optimistic and able to stretch like rubber, he is determined to become King of the Pirates.

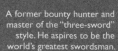

Monkey D. Luffy

A former bounty hunter and master of the "three-sword" style. He aspires to be the world's greatest swordsman.

Roronoa Zolo

A thief who specializes in robbing pirates. Nami hates pirates, but Luffy convinced her to be his navigator.

Nami

The bighearted cook (and ladies' man) whose dream is to find the legendary sea, the "All Blue."

Sanji

A blue-nosed man-reindeer and the ship's doctor.

Tony Tony Chopper

A mysterious woman in search of the Ponegliff on which true history is recorded.

Nico Robin

A village boy with a talent for telling tall tales. His father, Yasopp, is a member of Shanks's crew.

Usopp

THE STORY OF ONE PIECE

Volume 37

Monkey D. Luffy started out as just a kid with a dream—to become the greatest pirate in history! Stirred by the tales of pirate "Red-Haired" Shanks, Luffy vowed to become a pirate himself. That was before the enchanted Devil Fruit gave Luffy the power to stretch like rubber, at the cost of being unable to swim—a serious handicap for an aspiring sea dog. Undeterred, Luffy set out to sea and recruited some crewmates—master swordsman Zolo; treasure-hunting thief Nami; lying sharpshooter Usopp; the high-kicking chef Sanji; Chopper, the walkin' talkin' reindeer doctor; and the latest addition, Nico Robin, an archaeologist with a powerful physique!

After many adventures, the Straw Hats' ship, the *Merry Go*, is less than seaworthy. In order to get her repaired, they head to Water Seven, home of the best shipwrights. When told that *Merry* is damaged beyond repair, Luffy makes the agonizing decision to get a new ship. Furious at Luffy's decision, Usopp leaves the crew. And when Robin is linked to an assassination attempt on Mayor Iceberg, her betrayal and then desertion leave them flabbergasted. When the Straw Hats are blamed for the crime, they set out to learn the truth. But what they find out uncovers more deception—the other assassins are the agents of CP9, a covert agency working directly for the World Government! Their real motive is to secure the blueprints of the Pluton, the destructive ancient weapon believed to be in Iceberg's hands. But when they come up empty-handed, they focus their attention on another possibility—that Franky's got the blueprints!

Galley-La Company

A top shipbuilding company. They are purveyors to the World Government.

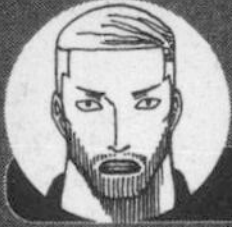

Mayor of Water Seven and president of Galley-La Company

Iceberg

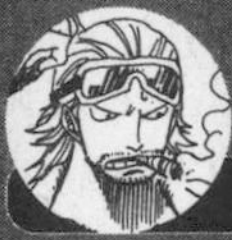

Rigging and Mast Foreman

Paulie

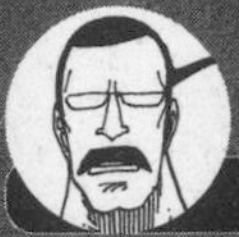

Pitch, Blacksmithing and Block-and-Tackle Foreman

Peepley Lulu

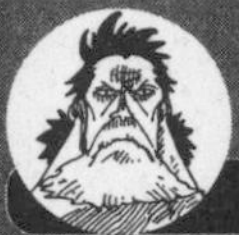

Cabinetry, Caulking and Flag-Making Foreman

Tilestone

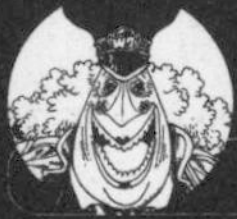

Stationmaster of Sea Train's Shift Station

Kokoro

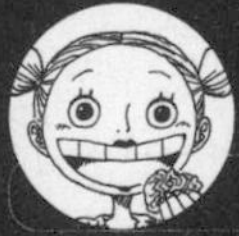

Kokoro's granddaughter

Chimney

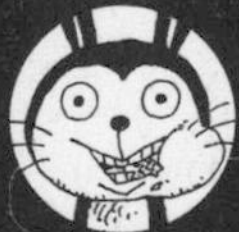

Cat (but actually a rabbit)

Gonbe

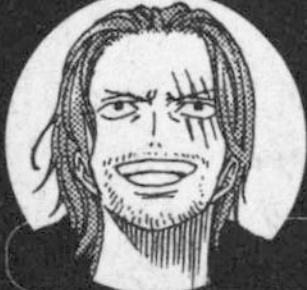

A pirate that Luffy idolizes. Shanks gave Luffy his trademark straw hat.

"Red-Haired" Shanks

WATER SEVEN

ONE PIECE

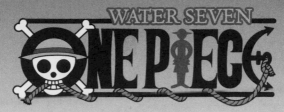

Vol. 37
Tom

CONTENTS

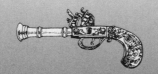

Chapter 347:
SIX POWERS

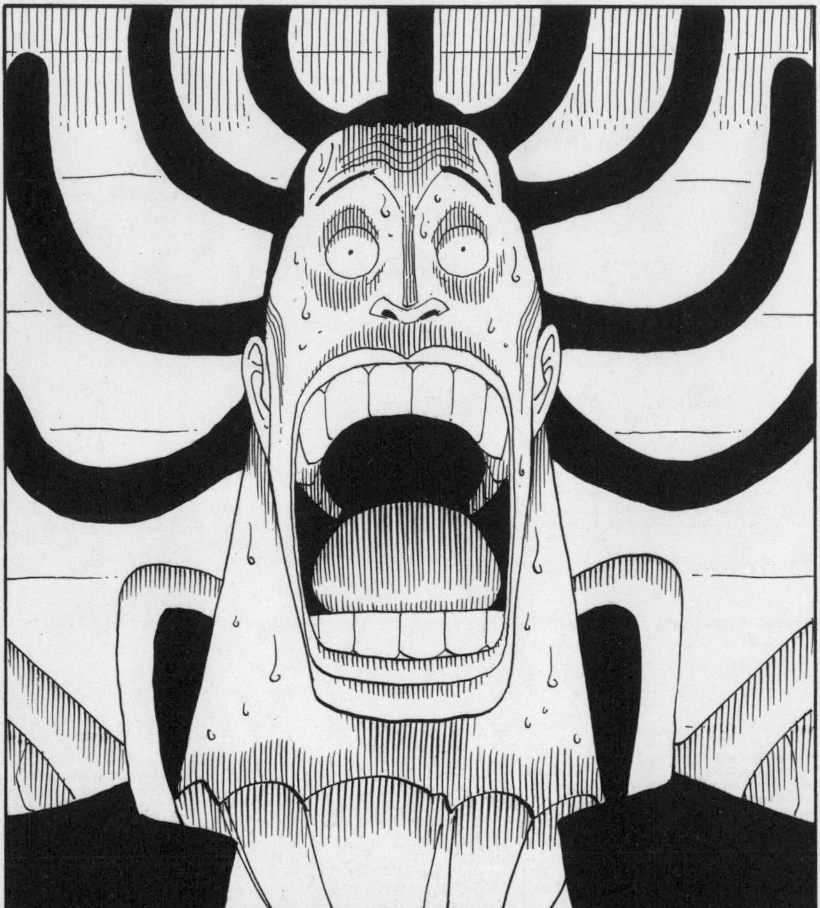

GEDATSU'S UNEXPECTED LIFE ON THE BLUE SEA, VOL. 31:
"THAT'S THE BATH ATTENDANT, MASTER GEDATSU"

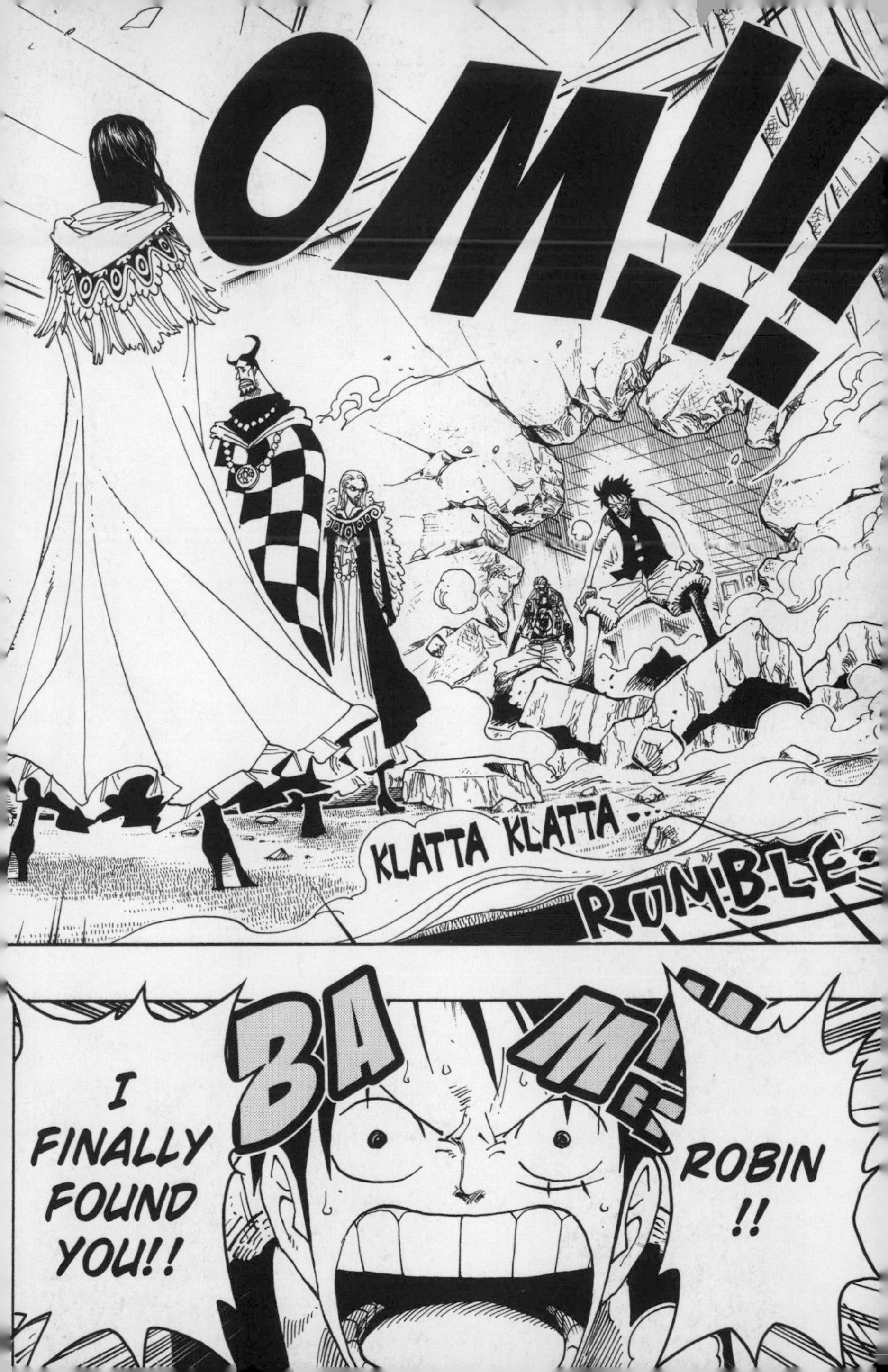
OM!!!
KLATTA KLATTA...
RUMBLE
BAM
ROBIN !!
I FINALLY FOUND YOU!!

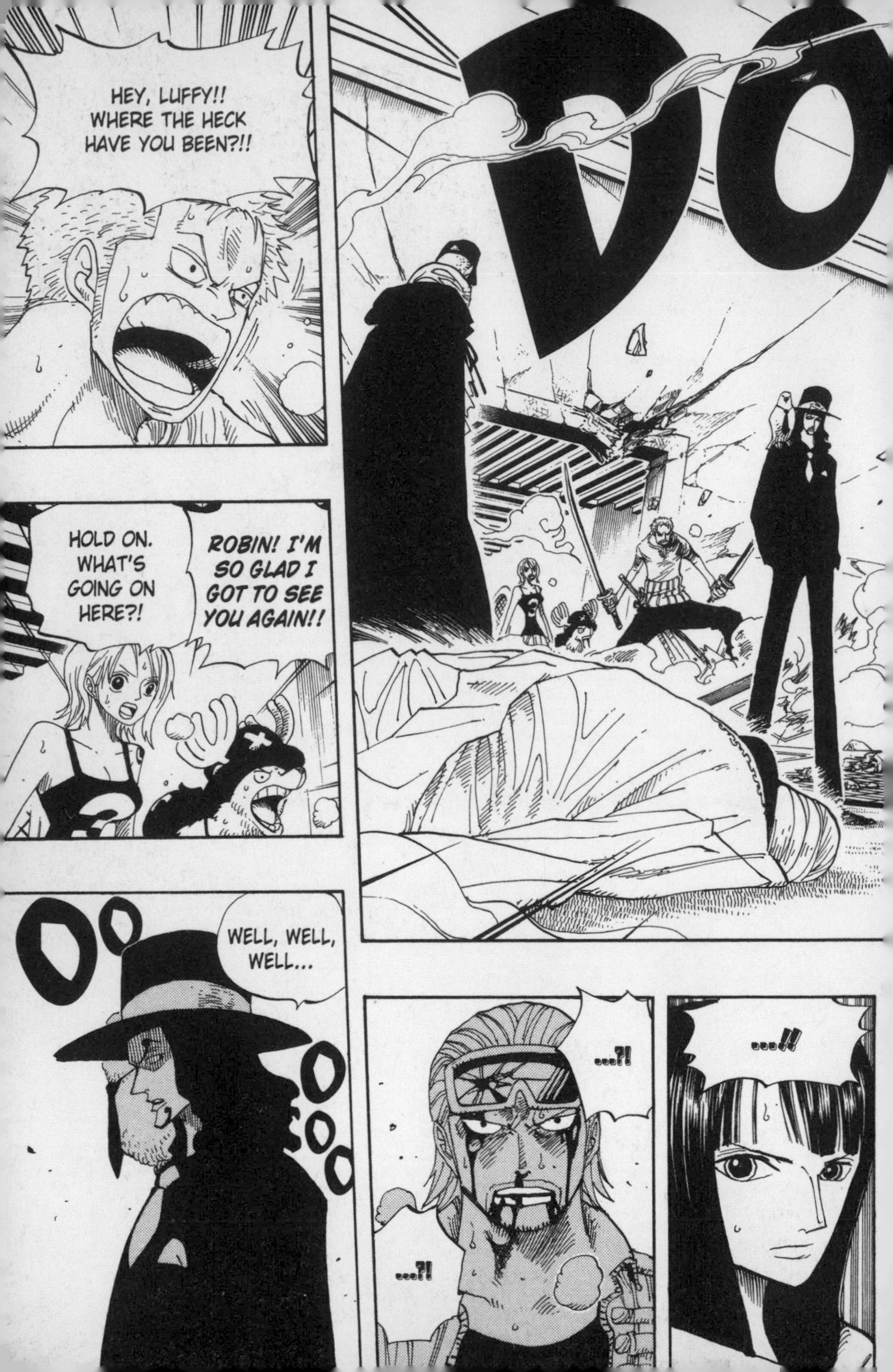
DO
HEY, LUFFY!!
WHERE THE HECK
HAVE YOU BEEN?!!
ROBIN! I'M SO GLAD I GOT TO SEE YOU AGAIN!!
HOLD ON. WHAT'S GOING ON HERE?!
...!!
...?!
...?!
WELL, WELL, WELL...
OO
OOO

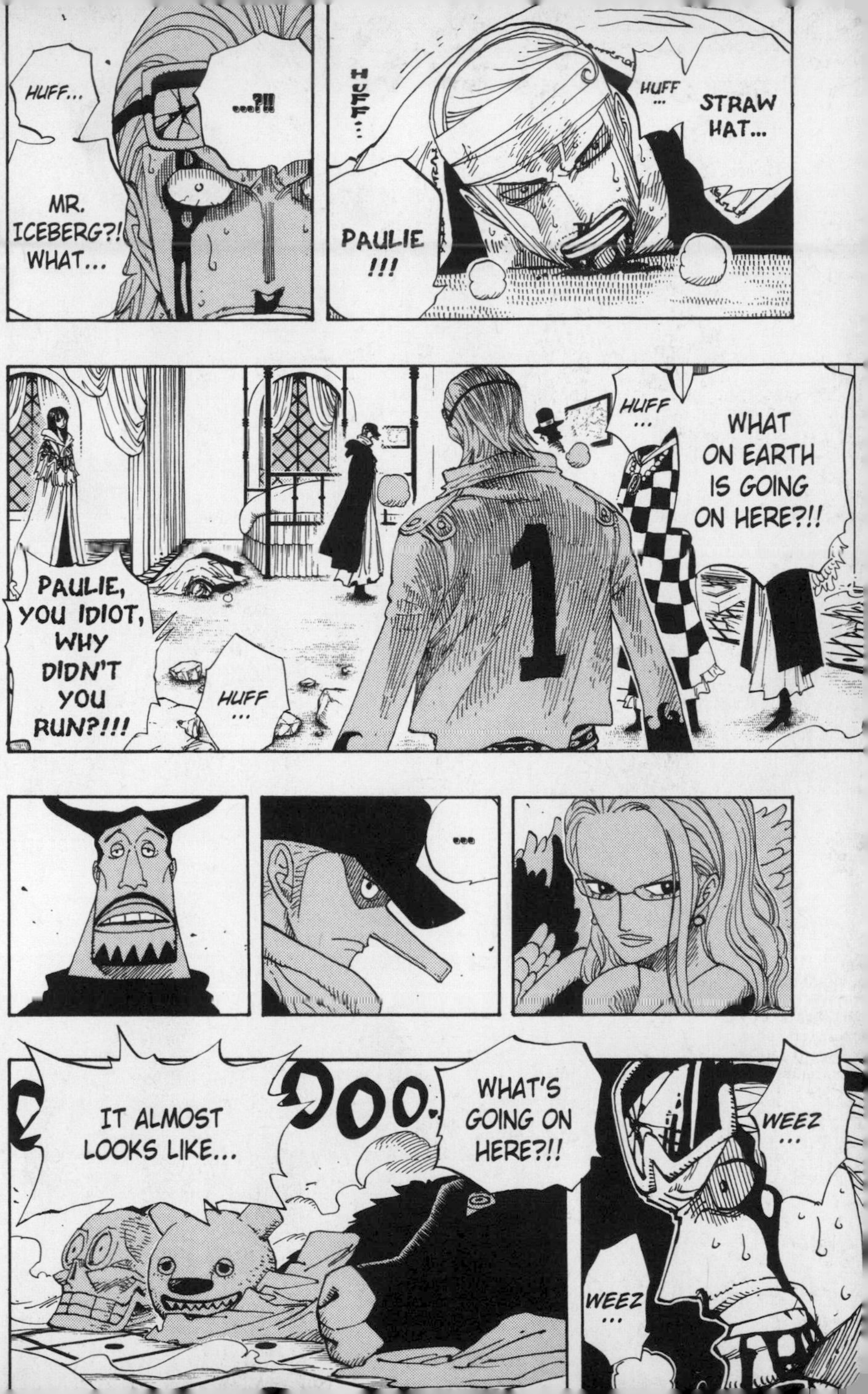
STRAW HAT...
HUFF ...
HUFF...
PAULIE !!!
...?!!
HUFF...
MR. ICEBERG?! WHAT...
HUFF ...
WHAT ON EARTH IS GOING ON HERE?!!
HUFF ...
PAULIE, YOU IDIOT, WHY DIDN'T YOU RUN?!!!
...
WEEZ ...
WEEZ ...
WHAT'S GOING ON HERE?!!
DOO
IT ALMOST LOOKS LIKE...

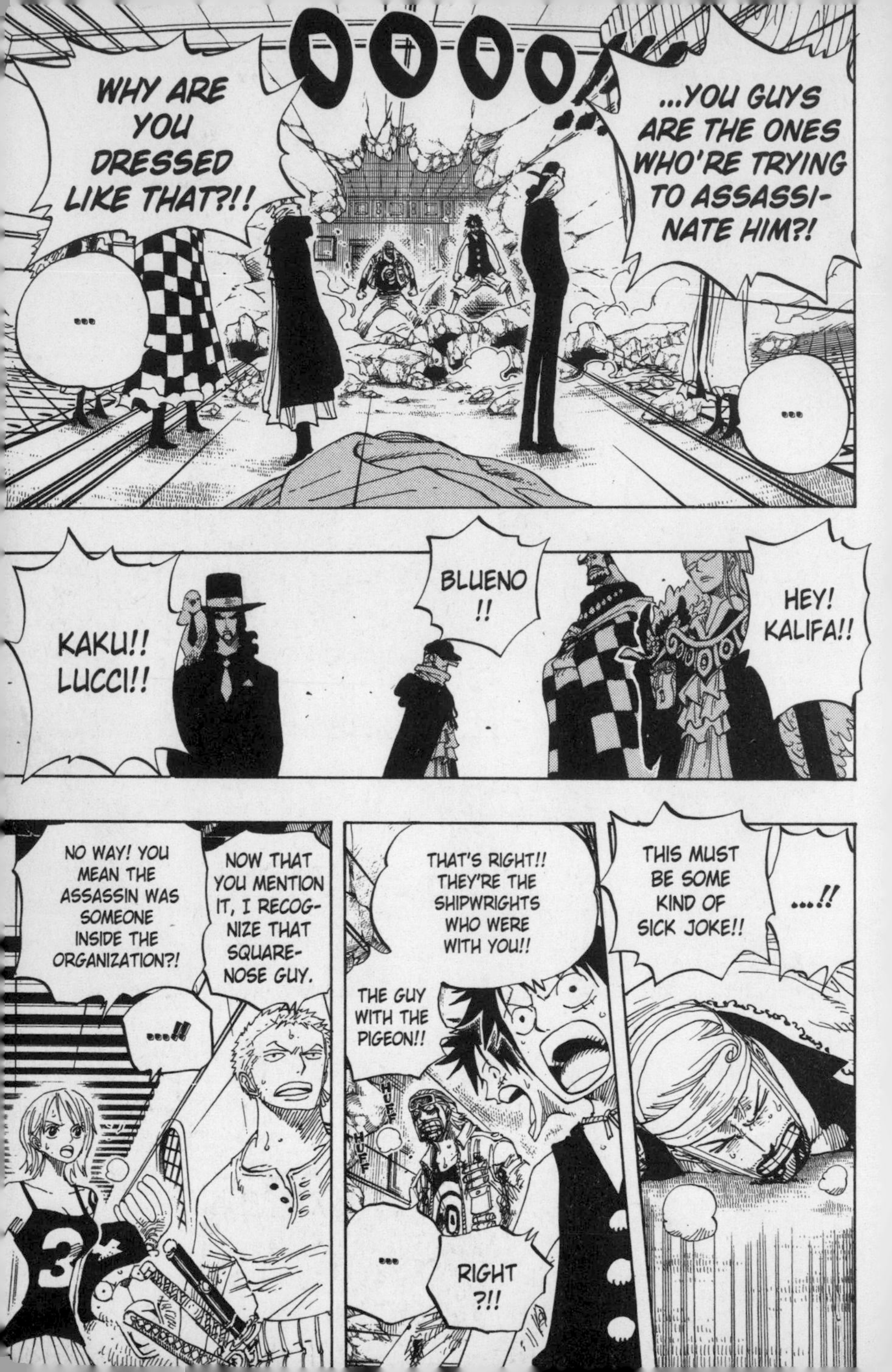
...YOU GUYS ARE THE ONES WHO'RE TRYING TO ASSASSINATE HIM?!
WHY ARE YOU DRESSED LIKE THAT?!!
...
...
HEY! KALIFA!!
BLUENO !!
KAKU!! LUCCI!!
...!!
THIS MUST BE SOME KIND OF SICK JOKE!!
THAT'S RIGHT!! THEY'RE THE SHIPWRIGHTS WHO WERE WITH YOU!!
THE GUY WITH THE PIGEON!!
HUFF HUFF
...
RIGHT ?!!
NOW THAT YOU MENTION IT, I RECOGNIZE THAT SQUARE-NOSE GUY.
NO WAY! YOU MEAN THE ASSASSIN WAS SOMEONE INSIDE THE ORGANIZATION?!
...!!

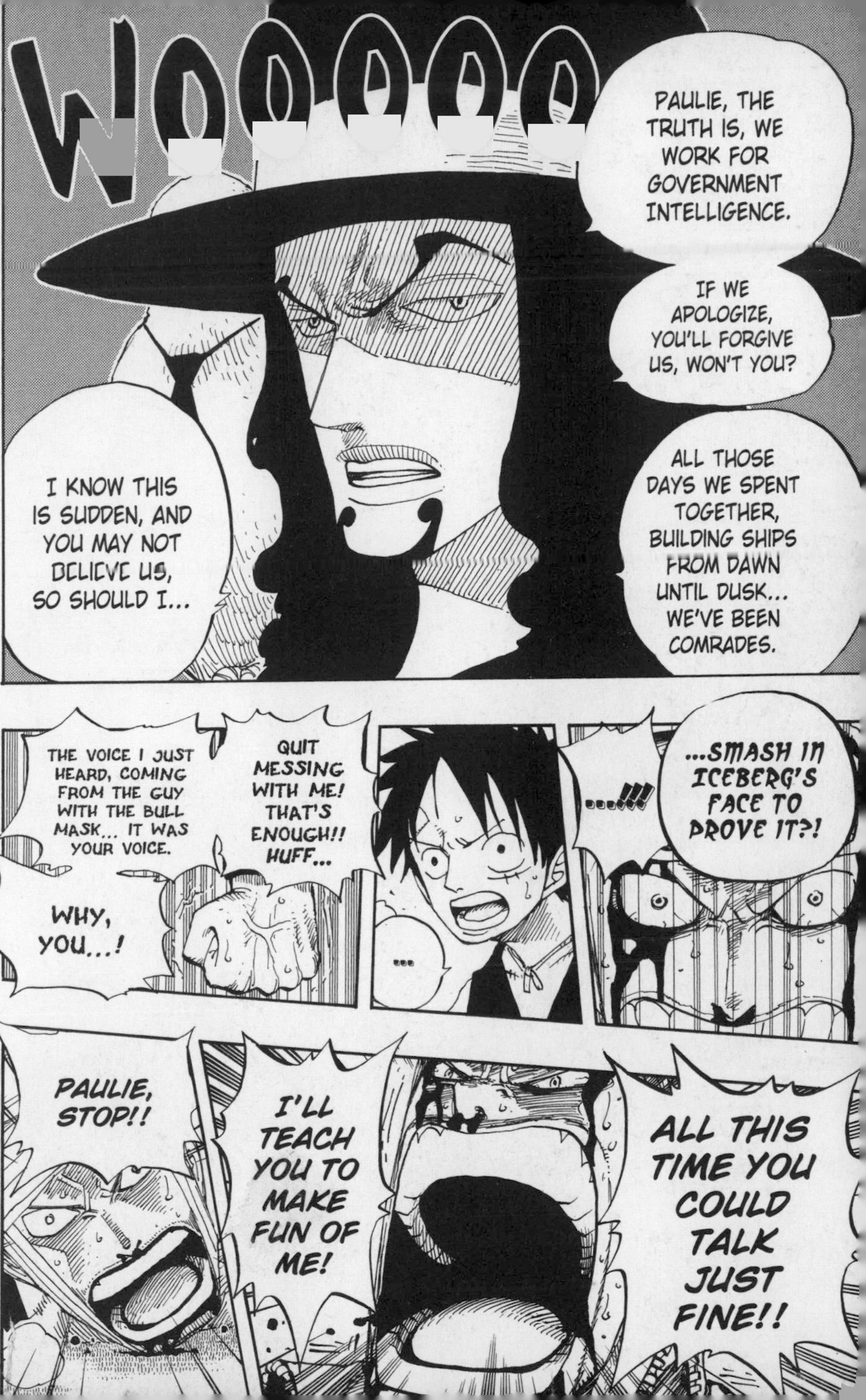
WOOOOO
PAULIE, THE TRUTH IS, WE WORK FOR GOVERNMENT INTELLIGENCE.
IF WE APOLOGIZE, YOU'LL FORGIVE US, WON'T YOU?
ALL THOSE DAYS WE SPENT TOGETHER, BUILDING SHIPS FROM DAWN UNTIL DUSK... WE'VE BEEN COMRADES.
I KNOW THIS IS SUDDEN, AND YOU MAY NOT BELIEVE US, SO SHOULD I...
...SMASH IN ICEBERG'S FACE TO PROVE IT?!
...!!!
...
QUIT MESSING WITH ME! THAT'S ENOUGH!! HUFF...
THE VOICE I JUST HEARD, COMING FROM THE GUY WITH THE BULL MASK... IT WAS YOUR VOICE.
WHY, YOU...!
ALL THIS TIME YOU COULD TALK JUST FINE!!
I'LL TEACH YOU TO MAKE FUN OF ME!
PAULIE, STOP!!

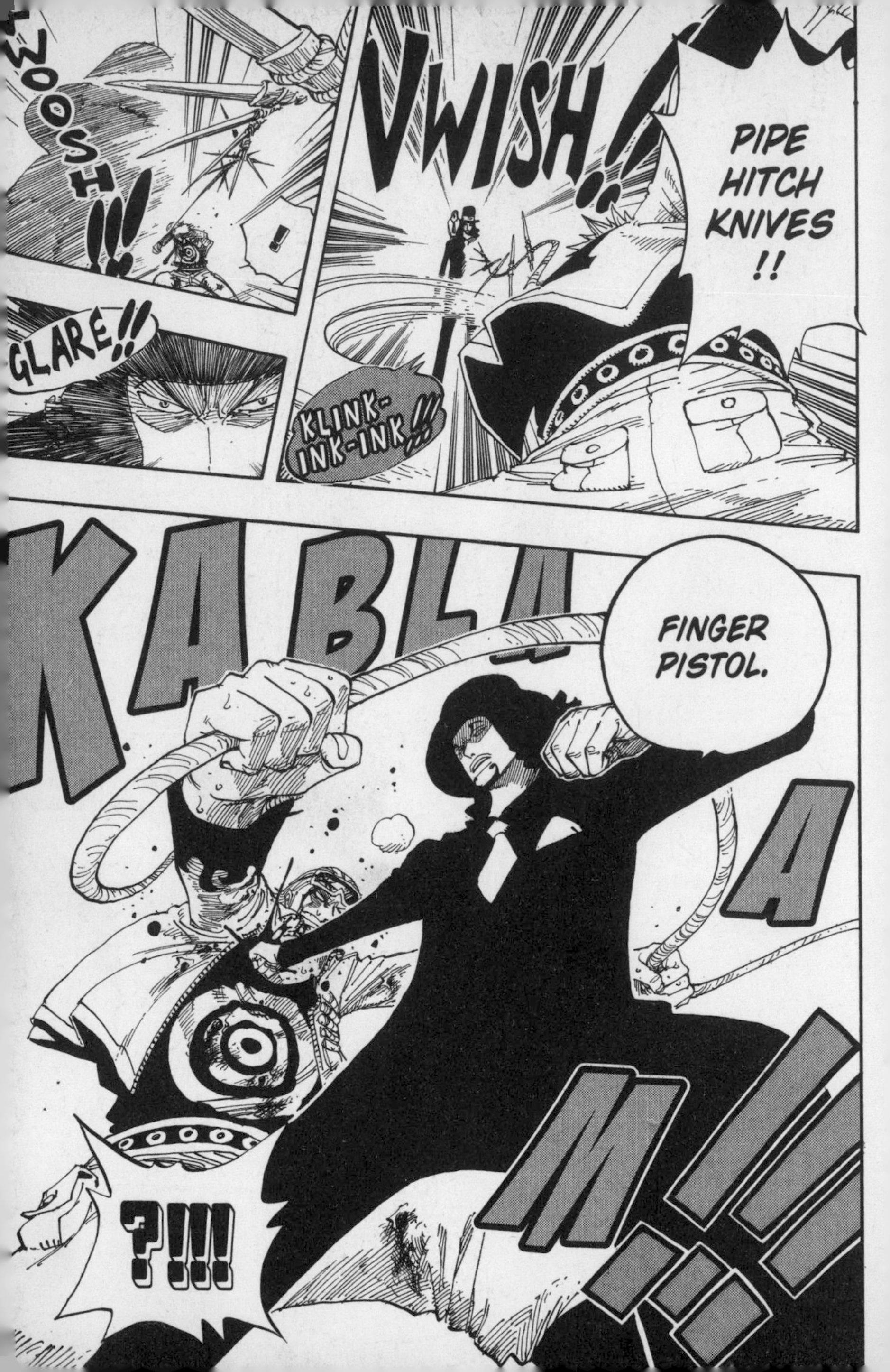
PIPE HITCH KNIVES !!
VWISH!!
KLINK-INK-INK!!!
WOOSH!!
!
GLARE!!
FINGER PISTOL.
KABLAAM!!!
?!!!

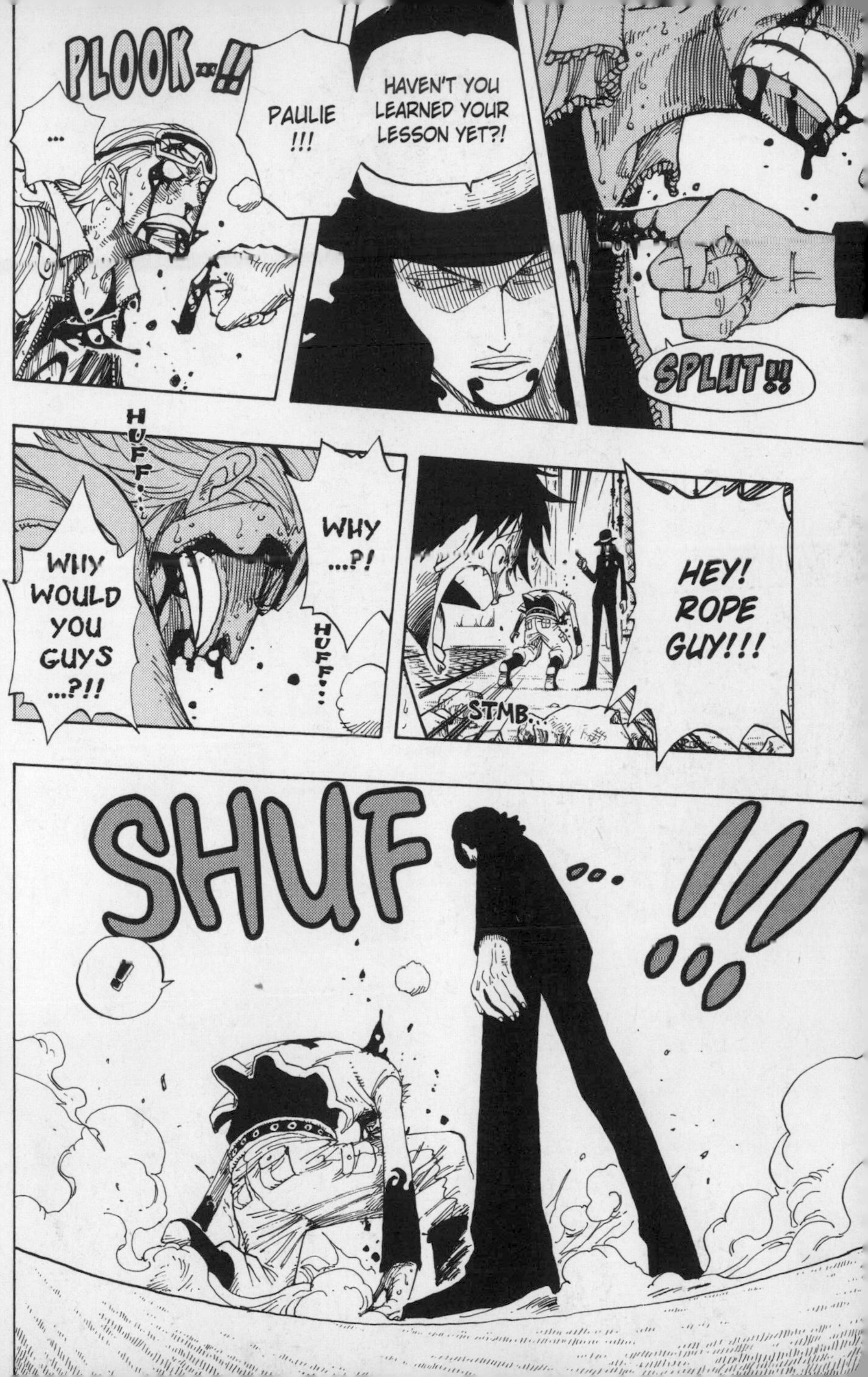

SPLUT!!
PAULIE !!!
HAVEN'T YOU LEARNED YOUR LESSON YET?!
PLOOK..!!
...
HEY! ROPE GUY!!!
STMB...
HUFF...
WHY ...?!
HUFF...
WHY WOULD YOU GUYS ...?!!
SHUF...!!!
!

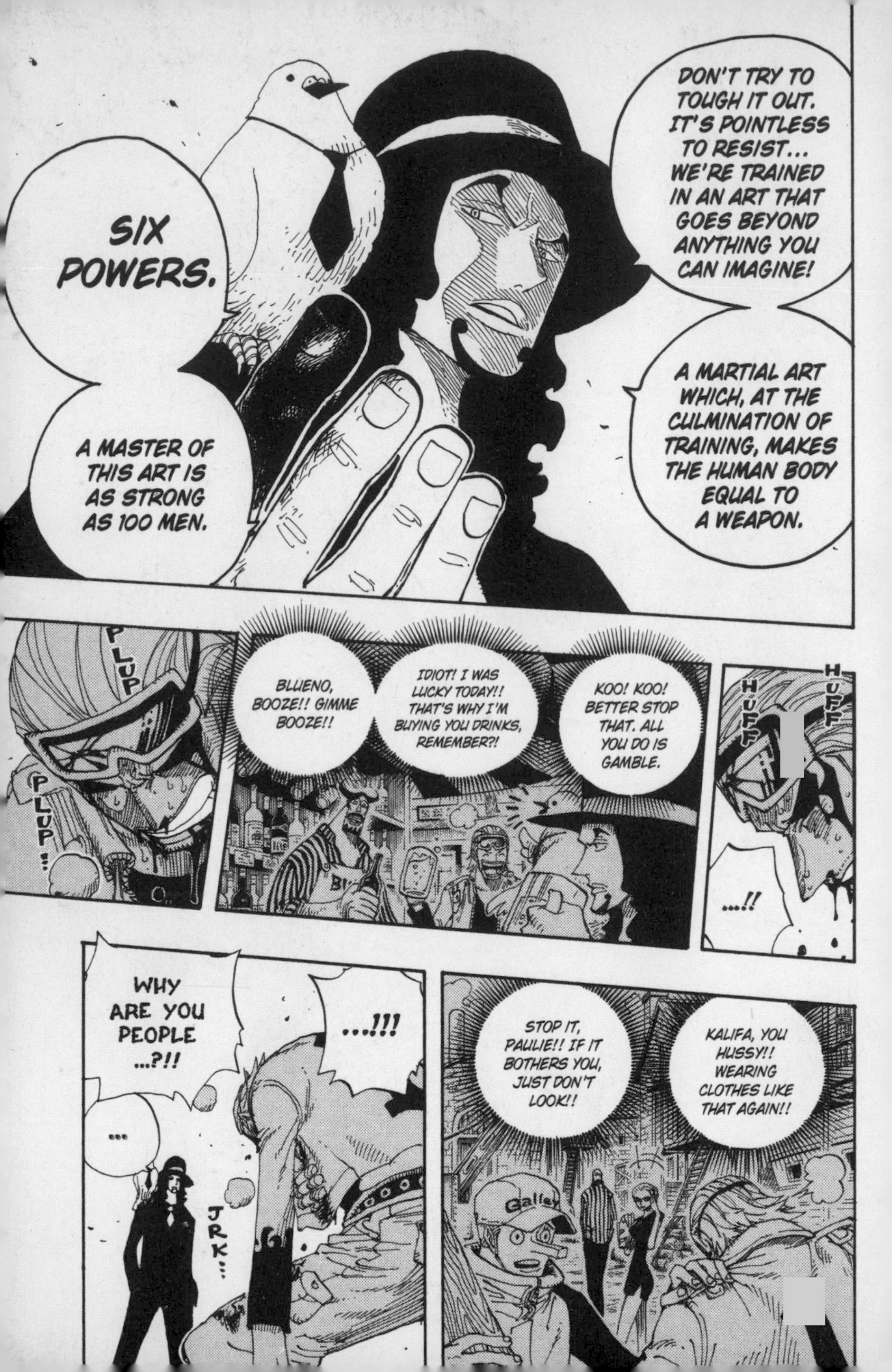
DON'T TRY TO TOUGH IT OUT. IT'S POINTLESS TO RESIST... WE'RE TRAINED IN AN ART THAT GOES BEYOND ANYTHING YOU CAN IMAGINE!
A MARTIAL ART WHICH, AT THE CULMINATION OF TRAINING, MAKES THE HUMAN BODY EQUAL TO A WEAPON.
SIX POWERS.
A MASTER OF THIS ART IS AS STRONG AS 100 MEN.
HUFF HUFF
...!!
KOO! KOO! BETTER STOP THAT. ALL YOU DO IS GAMBLE.
IDIOT! I WAS LUCKY TODAY!! THAT'S WHY I'M BUYING YOU DRINKS, REMEMBER?!
BLUENO, BOOZE!! GIMME BOOZE!!
PLUP
PLUP!!
KALIFA, YOU HUSSY!! WEARING CLOTHES LIKE THAT AGAIN!!
STOP IT, PAULIE!! IF IT BOTHERS YOU, JUST DON'T LOOK!!
...!!!
WHY ARE YOU PEOPLE ...?!!
...
JRK...

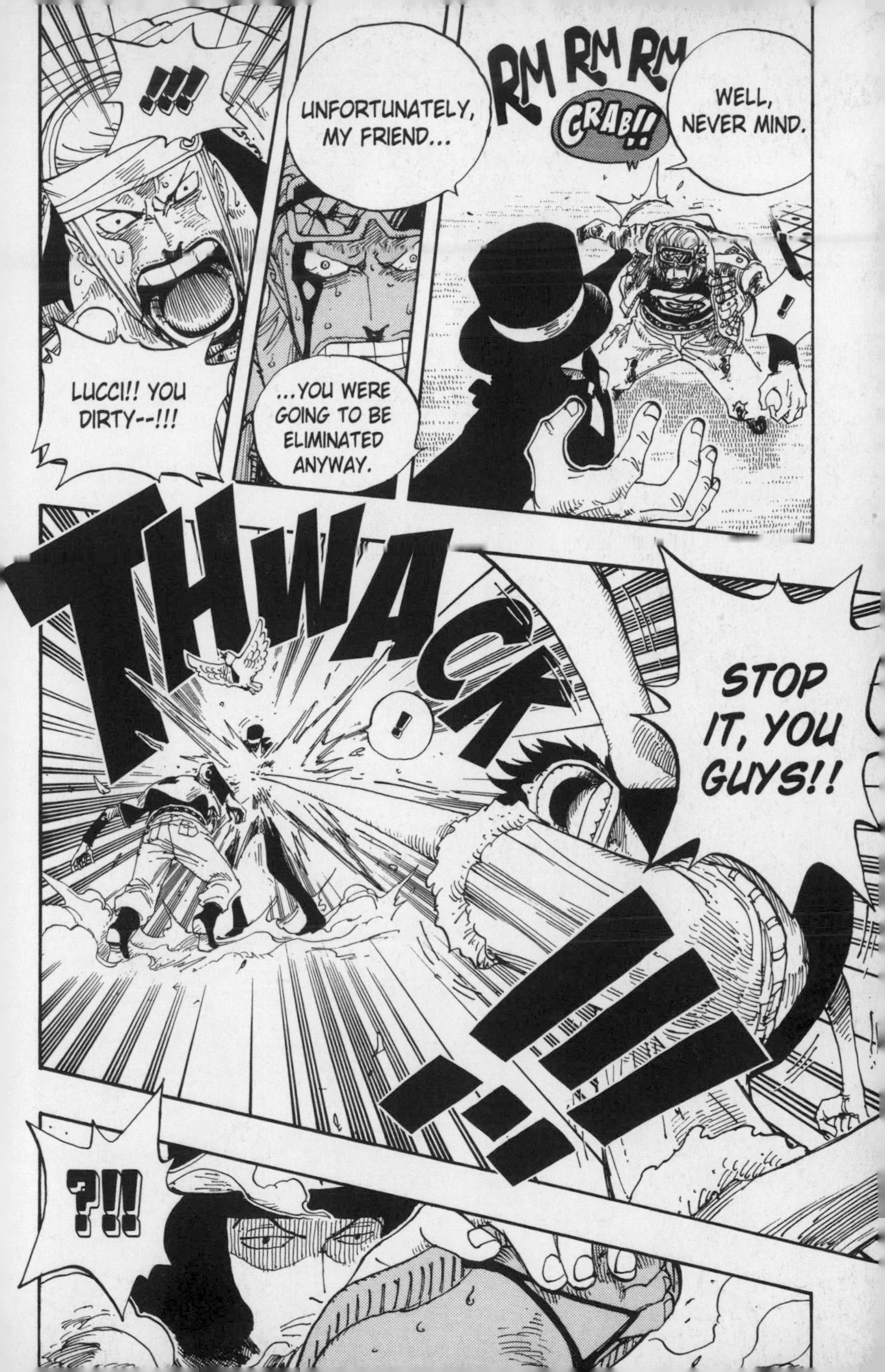
WELL, NEVER MIND.
RM RM RM
GRAB!!
UNFORTUNATELY, MY FRIEND...
...YOU WERE GOING TO BE ELIMINATED ANYWAY.
!!!
LUCCI!! YOU DIRTY--!!!
STOP IT, YOU GUYS!!
THWACK
!
?!!

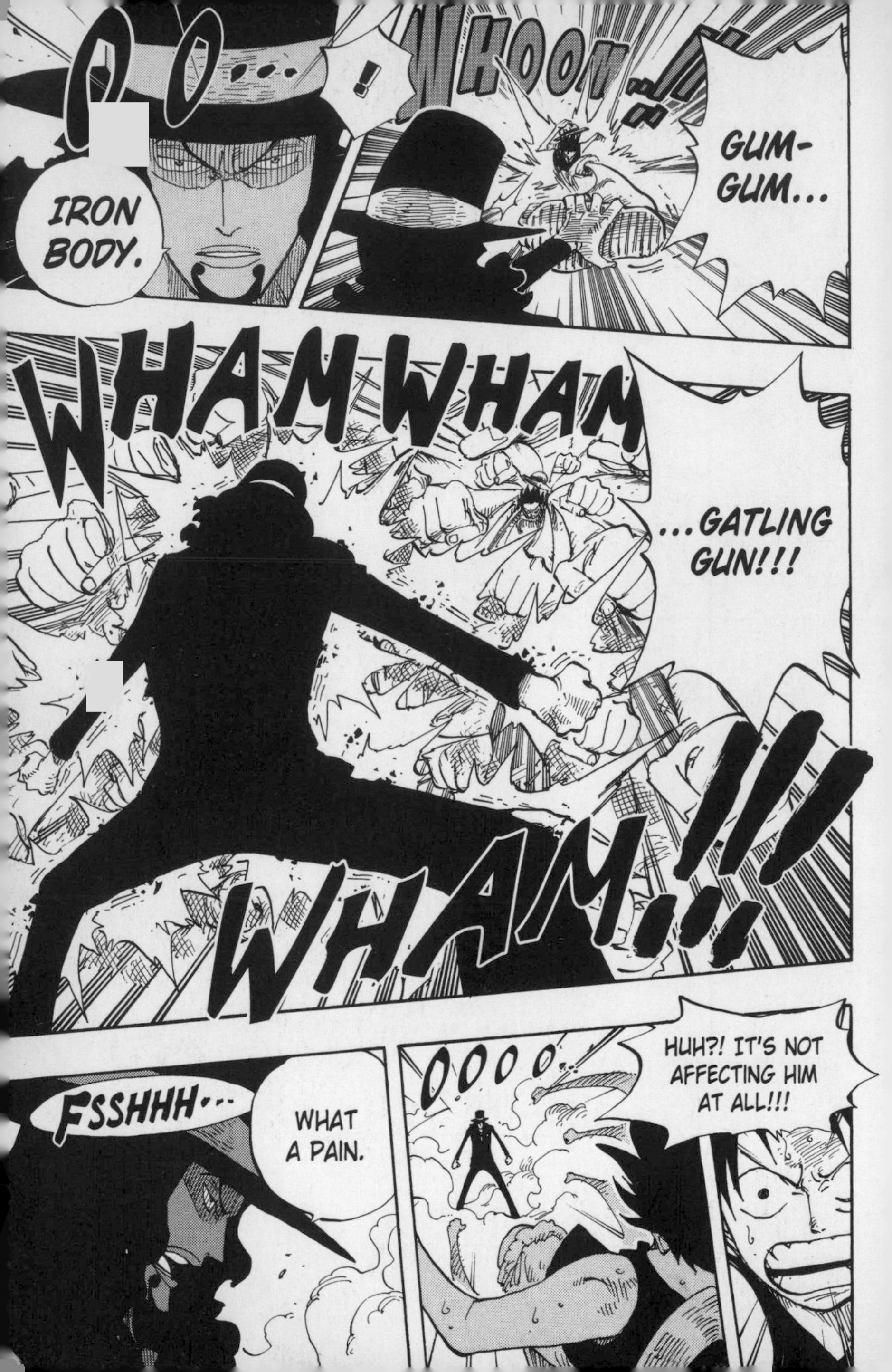
GUM-
GUM...
!
IRON
BODY.
WHAM WHAM
...GATLING
GUN!!!
WHAM!!!
HUH?! IT'S NOT
AFFECTING HIM
AT ALL!!!
FSSHHH...
WHAT
A PAIN.

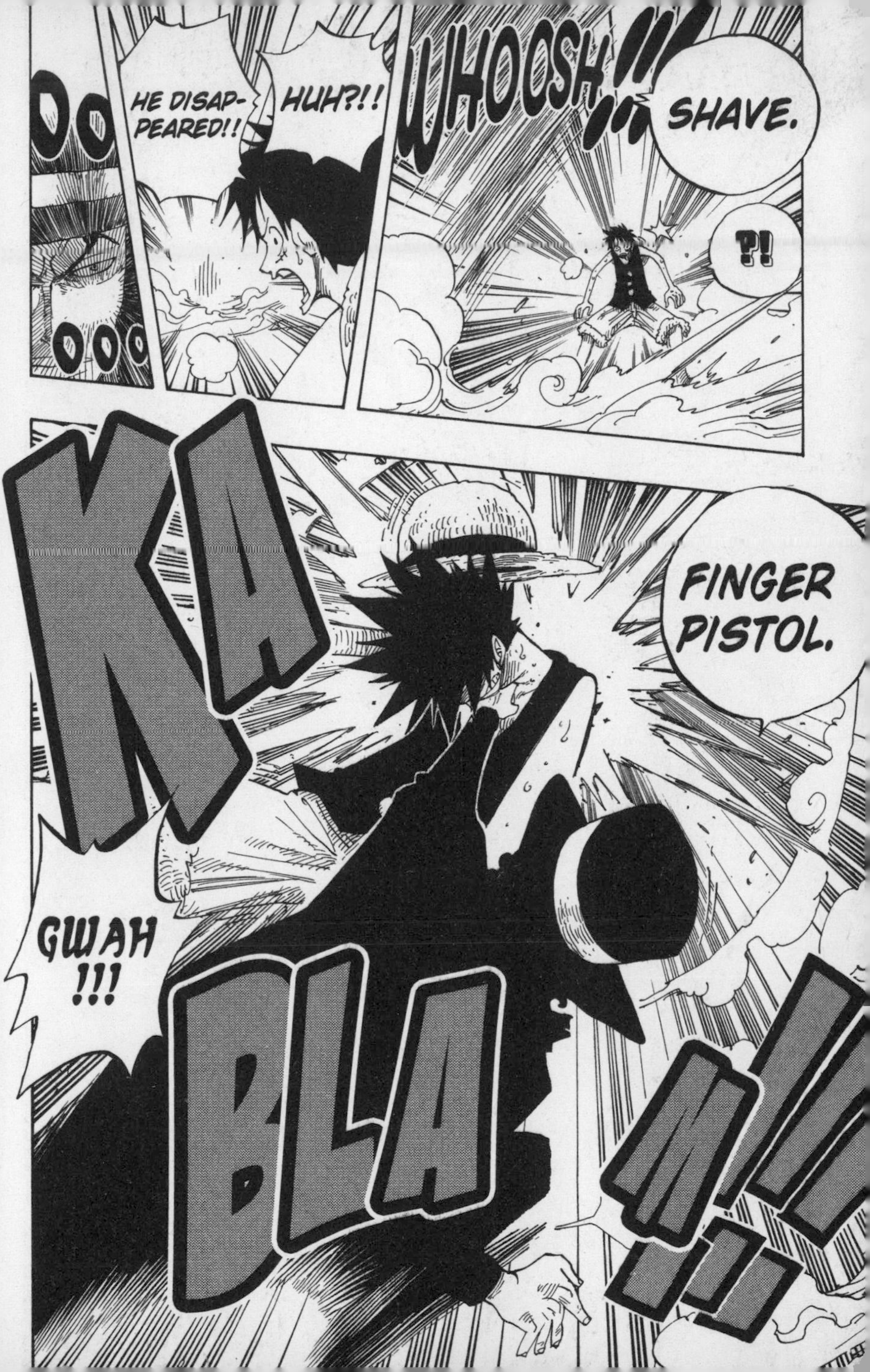
WHOOSH!!
SHAVE.
?!
HUH?!!
HE DISAP-
PEARED!!
FINGER
PISTOL.
KA
BLA
M!!
GWAH
!!!

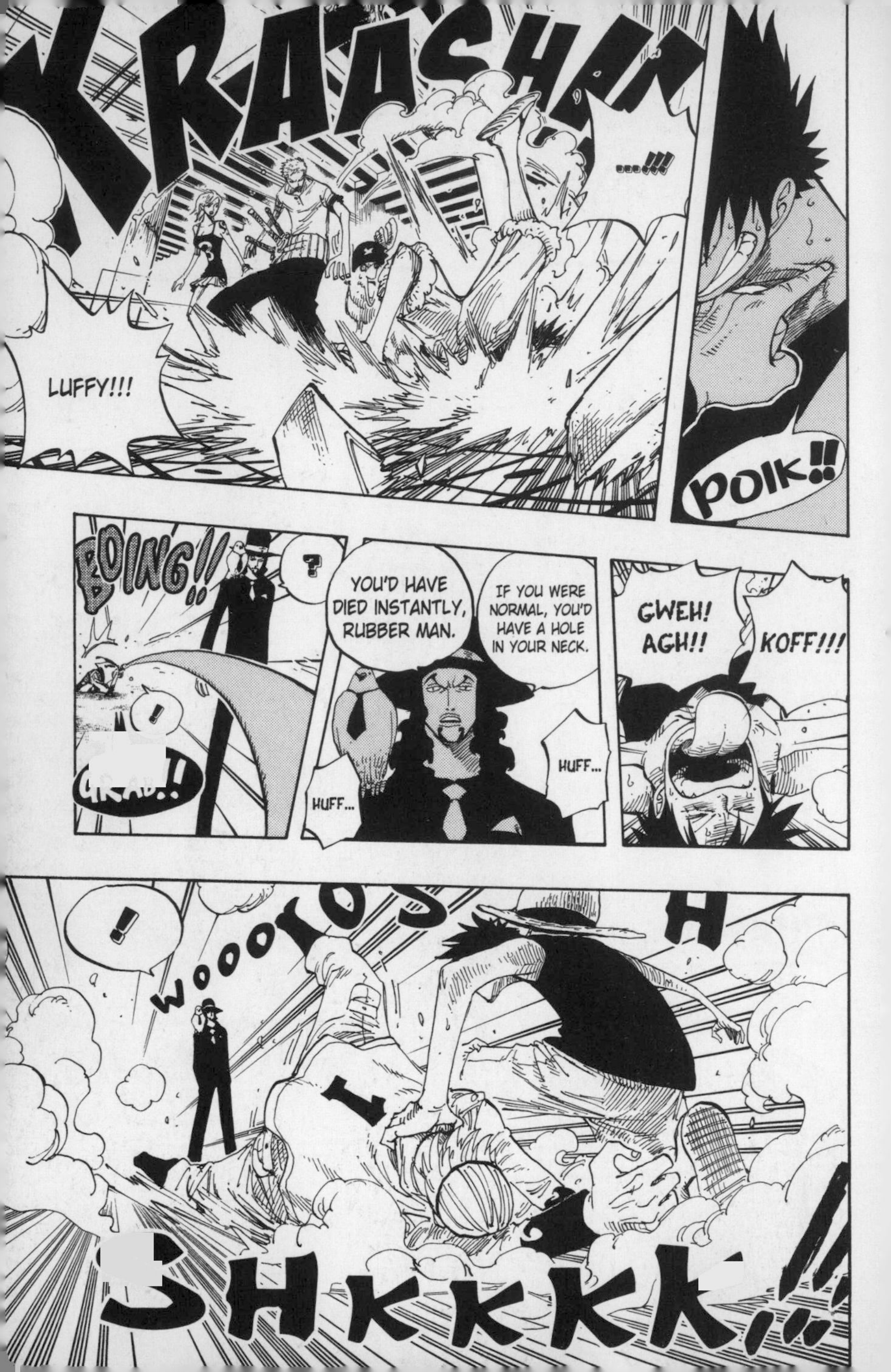
POIK!!
...!!!
LUFFY!!!
KOFF!!!
GWEH! AGH!!
IF YOU WERE NORMAL, YOU'D HAVE A HOLE IN YOUR NECK.
YOU'D HAVE DIED INSTANTLY, RUBBER MAN.
HUFF...
HUFF...
?
BOING!!
!
WOOOOSH
!

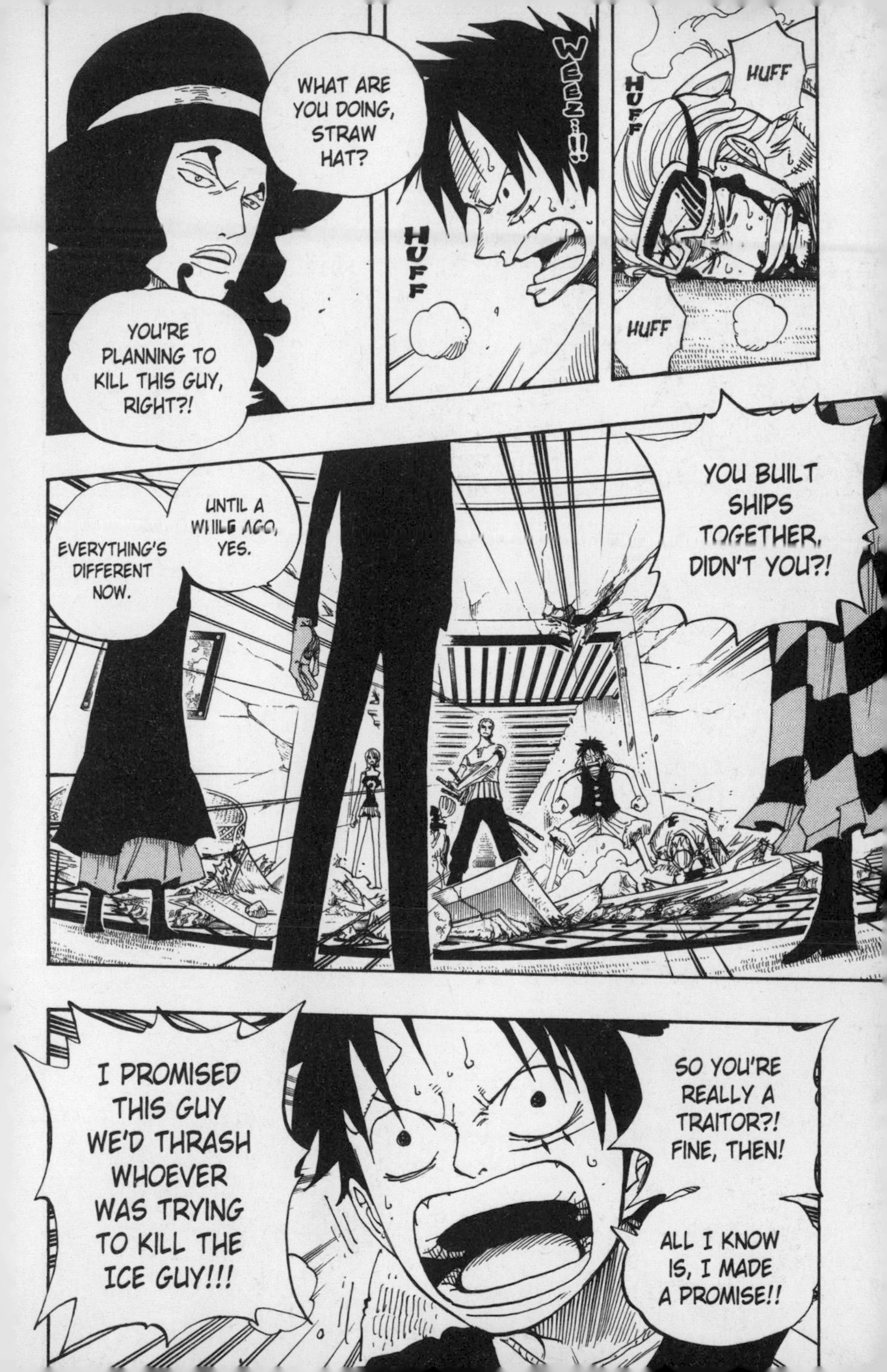
HUFF
HUFF
HUFF
WEEZ..!!
HUFF HUFF
WHAT ARE YOU DOING, STRAW HAT?
YOU'RE PLANNING TO KILL THIS GUY, RIGHT?!
YOU BUILT SHIPS TOGETHER, DIDN'T YOU?!
UNTIL A WHILE AGO, YES.
EVERYTHING'S DIFFERENT NOW.
SO YOU'RE REALLY A TRAITOR?! FINE, THEN!
ALL I KNOW IS, I MADE A PROMISE!!
I PROMISED THIS GUY WE'D THRASH WHOEVER WAS TRYING TO KILL THE ICE GUY!!!

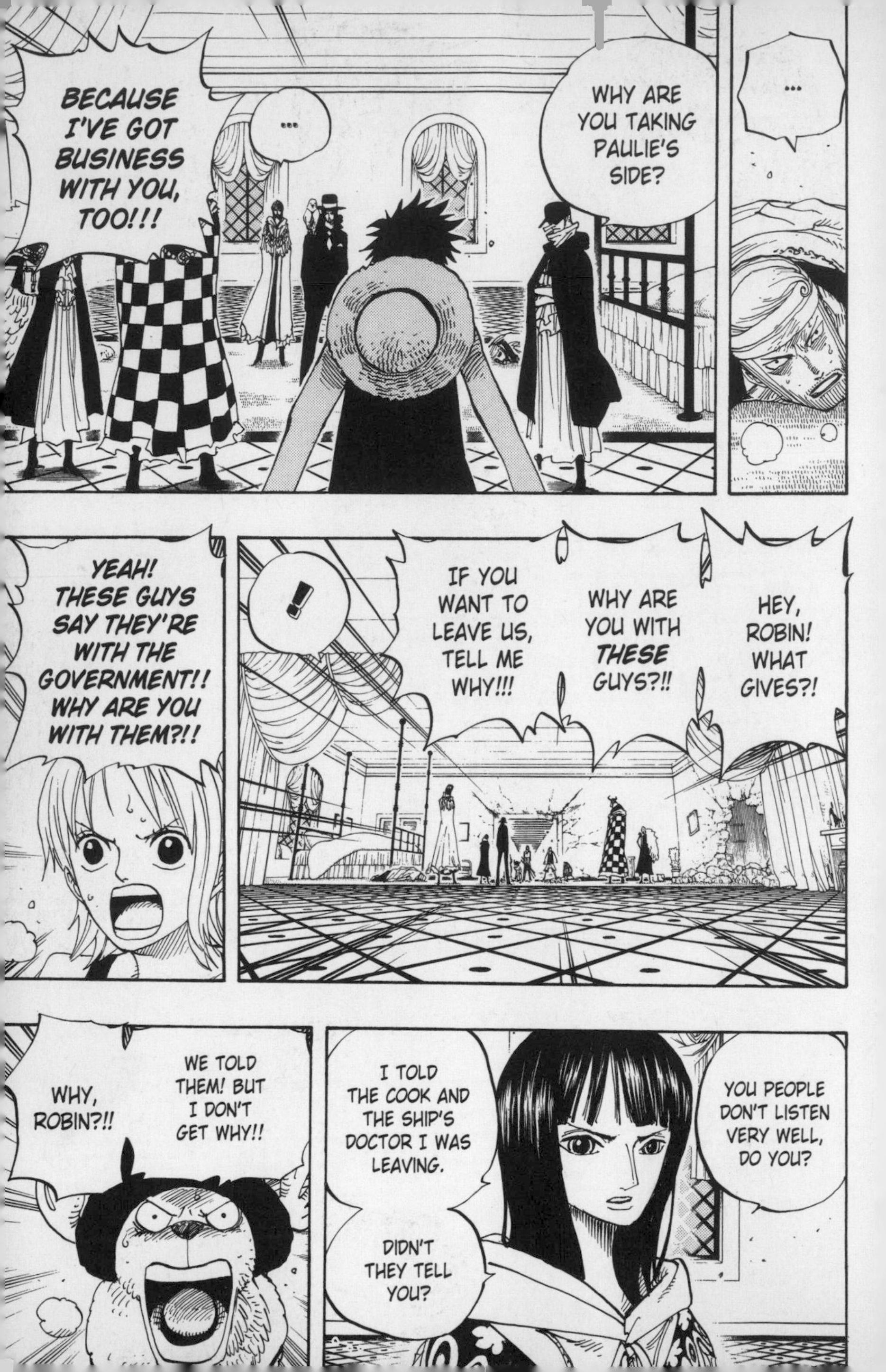

...
WHY ARE YOU TAKING PAULIE'S SIDE?
...
BECAUSE I'VE GOT BUSINESS WITH YOU, TOO!!!
HEY, ROBIN! WHAT GIVES?!
WHY ARE YOU WITH THESE GUYS?!!
IF YOU WANT TO LEAVE US, TELL ME WHY!!!
!
YEAH! THESE GUYS SAY THEY'RE WITH THE GOVERNMENT!! WHY ARE YOU WITH THEM?!!
YOU PEOPLE DON'T LISTEN VERY WELL, DO YOU?
I TOLD THE COOK AND THE SHIP'S DOCTOR I WAS LEAVING.
DIDN'T THEY TELL YOU?
WE TOLD THEM! BUT I DON'T GET WHY!!
WHY, ROBIN?!!

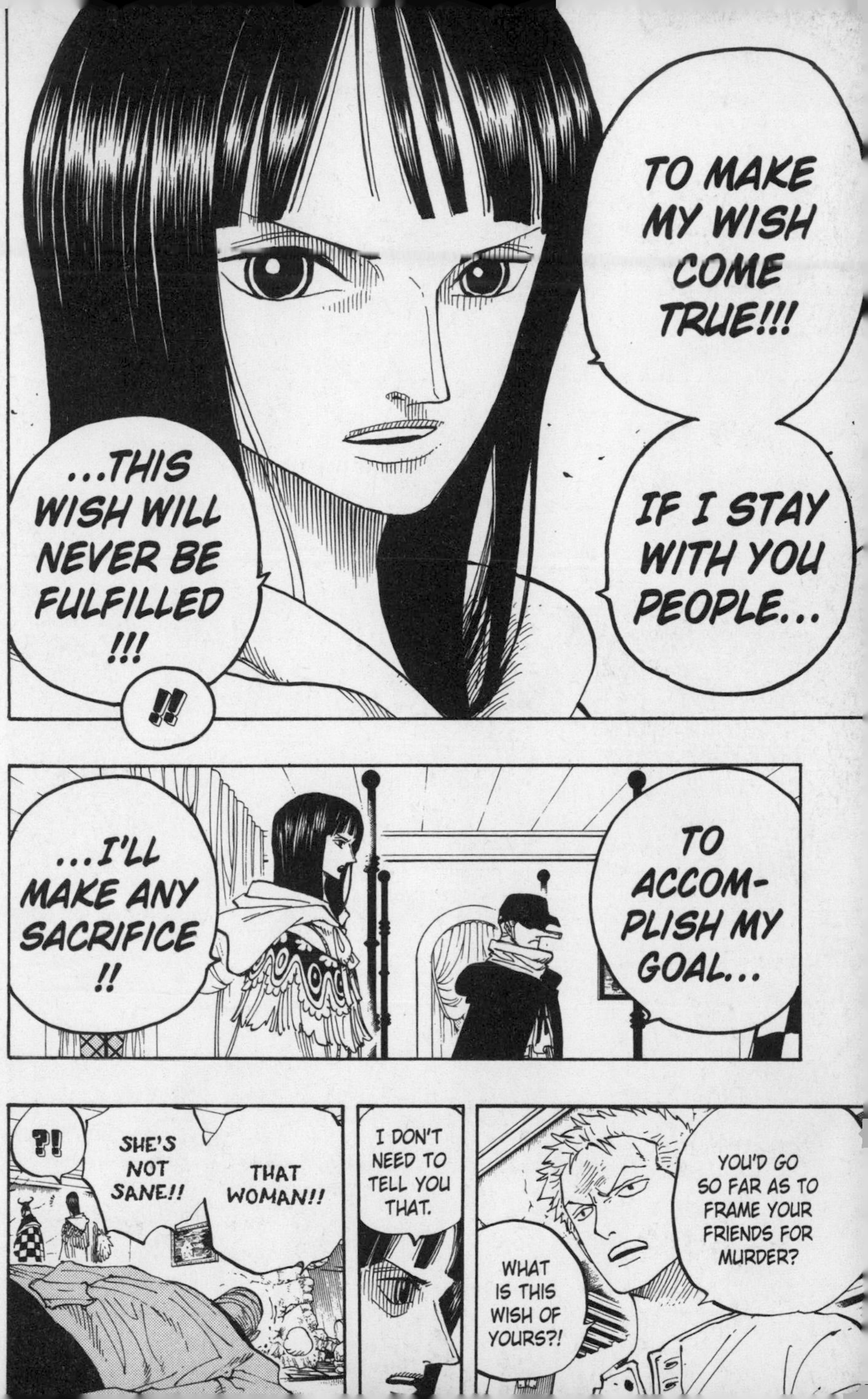

TO MAKE MY WISH COME TRUE!!!
IF I STAY WITH YOU PEOPLE...
...THIS WISH WILL NEVER BE FULFILLED!!!
!!
TO ACCOM-PLISH MY GOAL...
...I'LL MAKE ANY SACRIFICE!!
YOU'D GO SO FAR AS TO FRAME YOUR FRIENDS FOR MURDER?
WHAT IS THIS WISH OF YOURS?!
I DON'T NEED TO TELL YOU THAT.
?!
THAT WOMAN!!
SHE'S NOT SANE!!

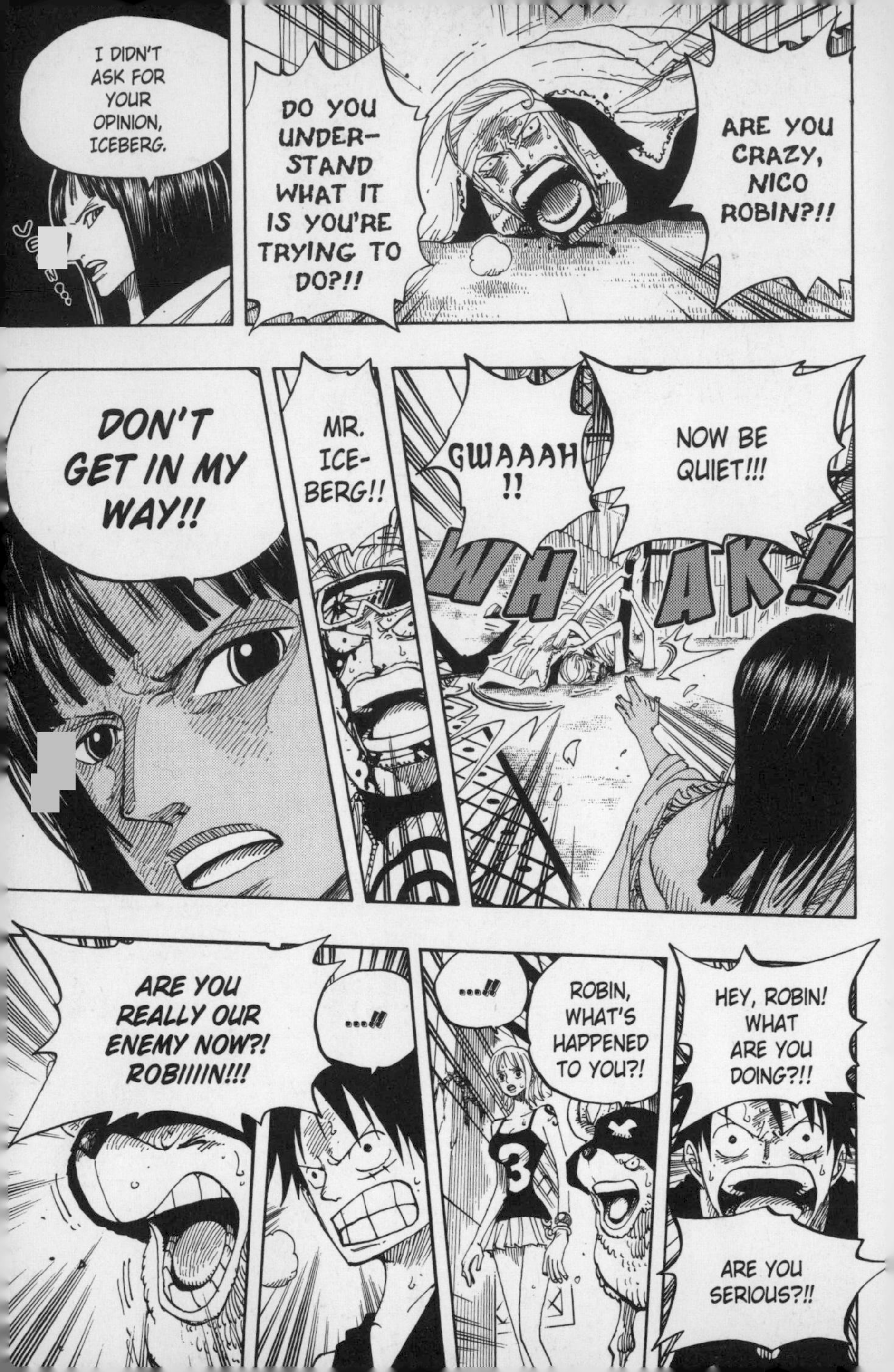
ARE YOU CRAZY, NICO ROBIN?!!
DO YOU UNDER-STAND WHAT IT IS YOU'RE TRYING TO DO?!!
I DIDN'T ASK FOR YOUR OPINION, ICEBERG.
NOW BE QUIET!!!
WH AK!!
GWAAAH!!
MR. ICE-BERG!!
DON'T GET IN MY WAY!!
HEY, ROBIN! WHAT ARE YOU DOING?!!
ARE YOU SERIOUS?!!
ROBIN, WHAT'S HAPPENED TO YOU?!
...!!
...!!
ARE YOU REALLY OUR ENEMY NOW?! ROBIIIIN!!!

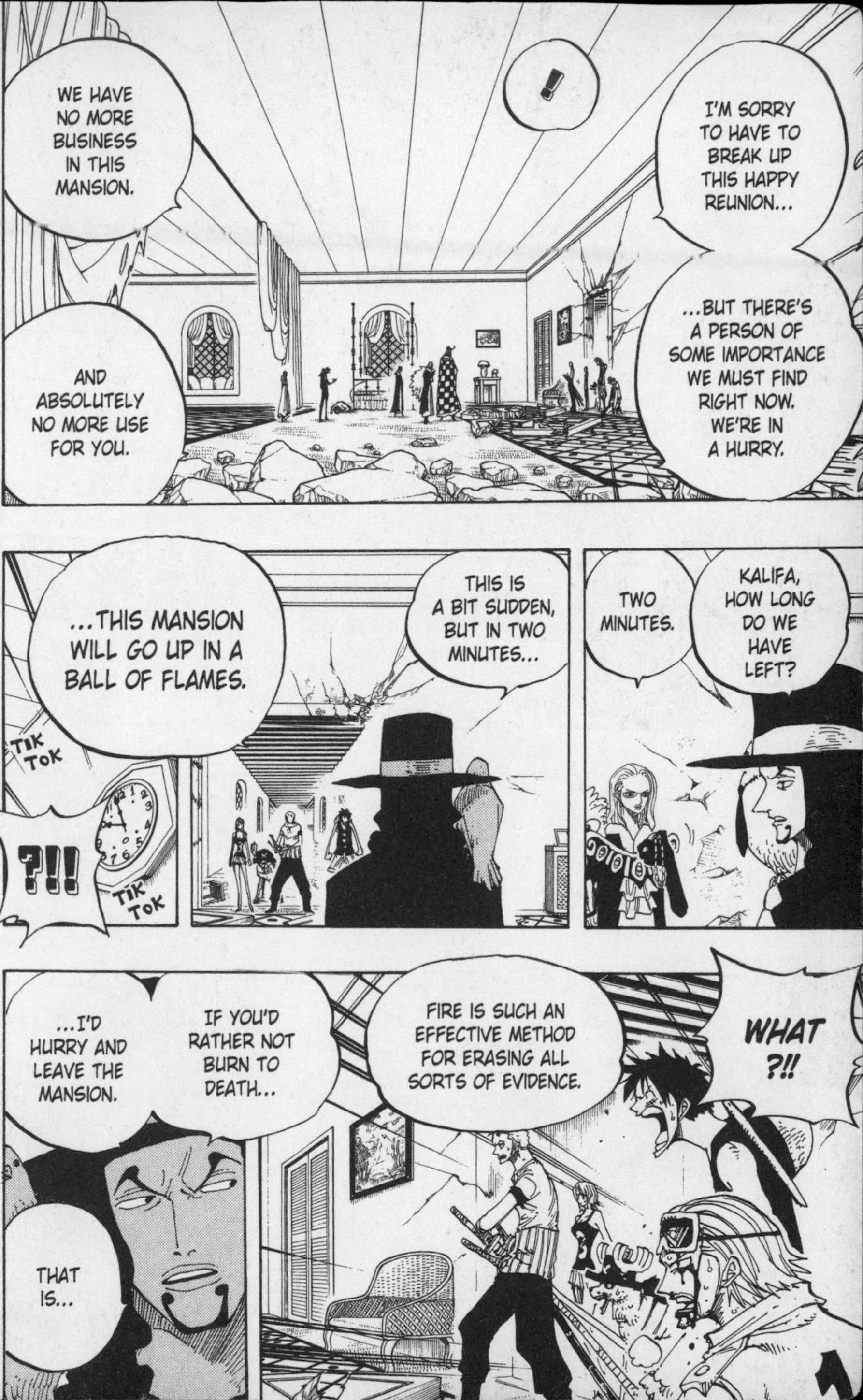
I'M SORRY TO HAVE TO BREAK UP THIS HAPPY REUNION...
...BUT THERE'S A PERSON OF SOME IMPORTANCE WE MUST FIND RIGHT NOW. WE'RE IN A HURRY.
!
WE HAVE NO MORE BUSINESS IN THIS MANSION.
AND ABSOLUTELY NO MORE USE FOR YOU.
KALIFA, HOW LONG DO WE HAVE LEFT?
TWO MINUTES.
THIS IS A BIT SUDDEN, BUT IN TWO MINUTES...
...THIS MANSION WILL GO UP IN A BALL OF FLAMES.
TIK TOK
?!!
TIK TOK
WHAT ?!!
FIRE IS SUCH AN EFFECTIVE METHOD FOR ERASING ALL SORTS OF EVIDENCE.
IF YOU'D RATHER NOT BURN TO DEATH...
...I'D HURRY AND LEAVE THE MANSION.
THAT IS...

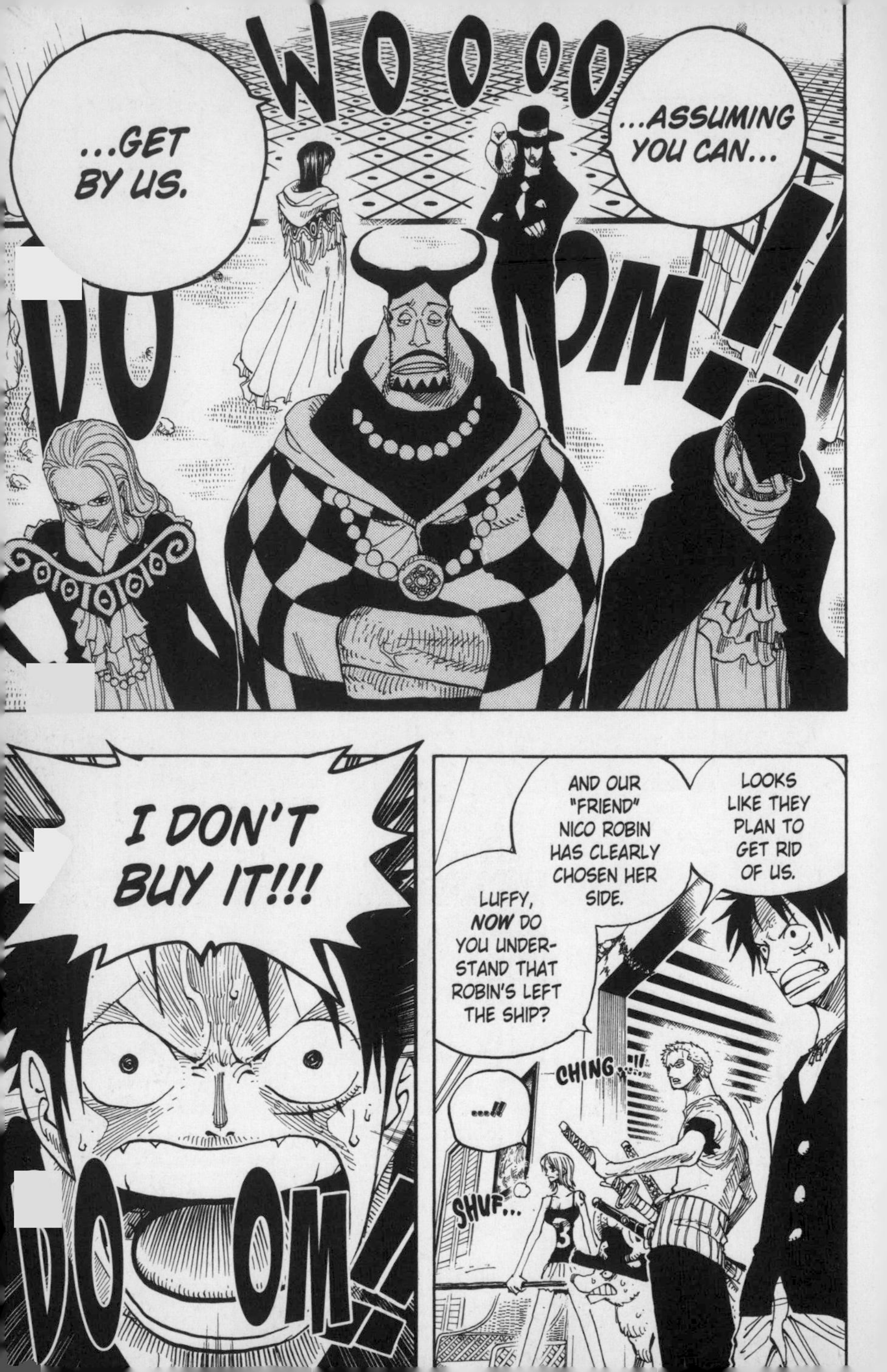
WOOOO
...ASSUMING YOU CAN...
...GET BY US.
DOOM!!
LOOKS LIKE THEY PLAN TO GET RID OF US.
AND OUR "FRIEND" NICO ROBIN HAS CLEARLY CHOSEN HER SIDE.
LUFFY, *NOW* DO YOU UNDERSTAND THAT ROBIN'S LEFT THE SHIP?
CHING...!!
...!!
SHUF...
I DON'T BUY IT!!!
DOOM!!

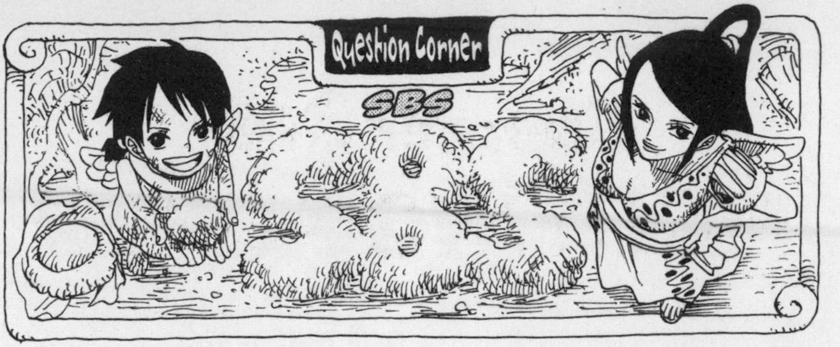
Question Corner
SBS

Reader: Just a minute, just a minute, Oda Sensei!! I didn't know you'd gotten married!! Why didn't you announce that earlier, huh?! And you told us you'd turned 30, but you said it late, and… Agh!! I don't have any presents ready—nothing at all. So just let me say a few words to you.

"The Question Corner is starting♡!"

Yaaay! Congratulations to you! Ah, I feel better now.

--Saitou

Oda: Thank you very much! Hey...

It started already! (Gasp!)

Well, all right, never mind, I'll forgive you just this once. I got a mountain of congratulatory messages from everybody, and it's put me in a good mood (grin, grin). It's so great to have such nice readers. Thank you. That said, not a single thing about my lifestyle has changed, so I'll keep running straight down the road of manga, the way I've always done!

Reader: Oda Sensei, I've got a question. Midway through the Skypiea arc (chapter 244), Luffy starts wearing a wristband and bracelet. Why is that? Is it just to look cool? When they come down from the sky, he isn't wearing them anymore.

--Gakkuri

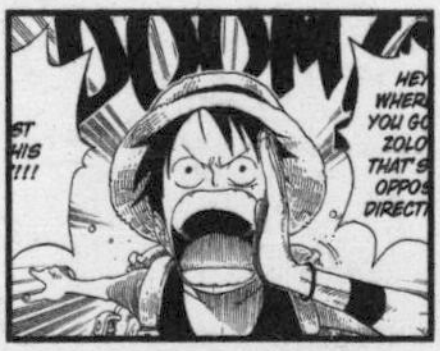
HEY
ZOLO
THAT'S

Oda: You're right. There's no meaning behind them. They're just there to look cool. Or rather, in that situation, Usopp and Sanji are there with him, remember? It seems as though when they changed into their adventure gear, Luffy spaced out while watching them and thought, "Hey! That looks adventure-ish, huh?" and borrowed a wristband from Usopp, and then Sanji said, "Okay, put this on too," and put a bracelet on him. Fundamentally speaking, Luffy, Zolo and Chopper are all incapable of dressing snappily. The only times they manage it are when Nami, Usopp, Sanji or Robin are around to help.

Chapter 348:
FIGHTING POWER

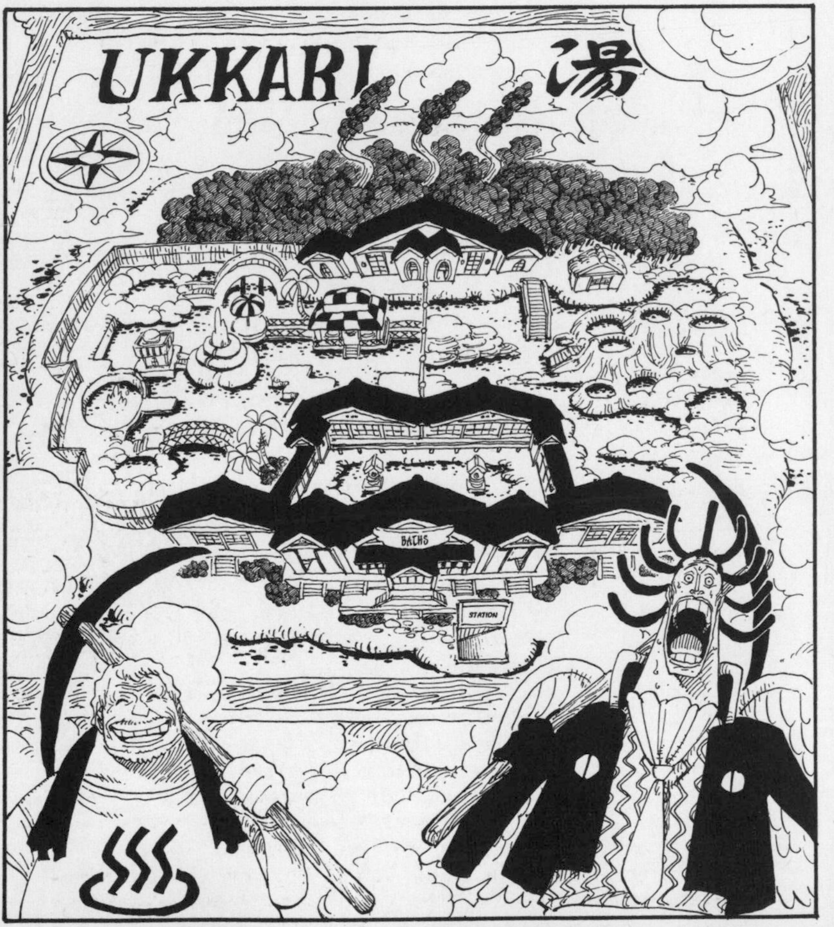

UKKARI
湯
BATHS
STATION

GEDATSU'S UNEXPECTED LIFE ON THE BLUE SEA, FINAL VOLUME:
"DROP BY ACCIDENTAL BATHS ON HOT SPRINGS ISLAND"

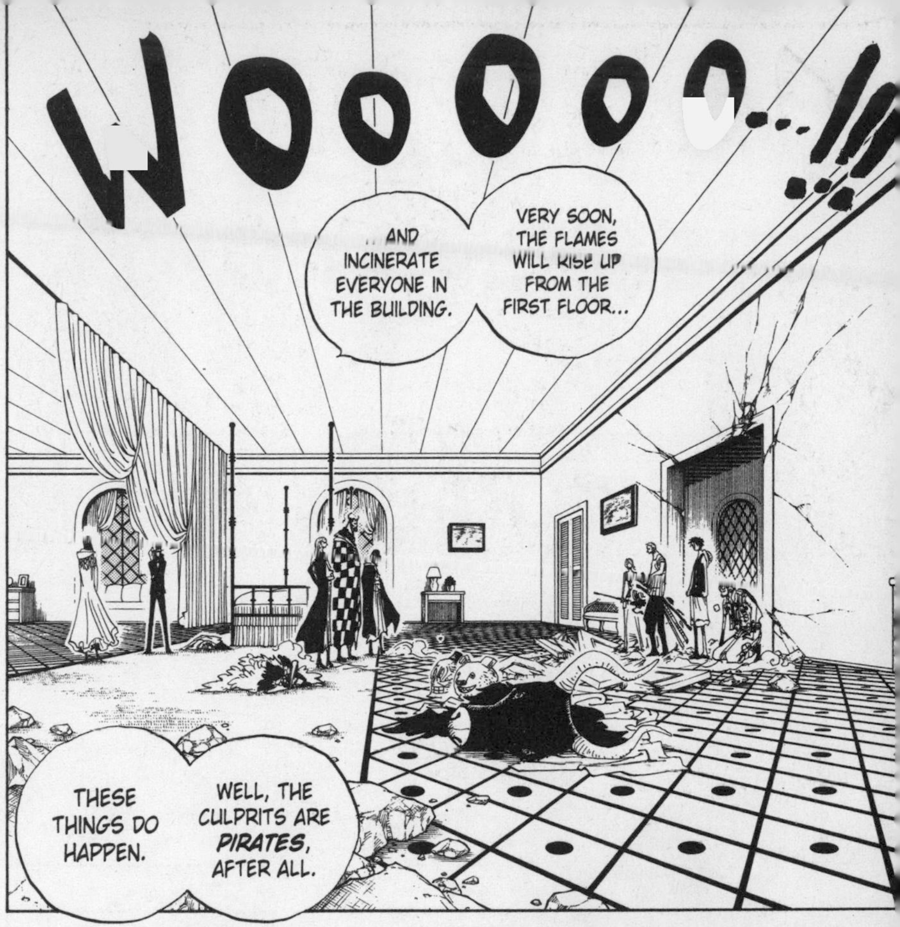
WOOOOO...!!!
VERY SOON, THE FLAMES WILL RISE UP FROM THE FIRST FLOOR...
...AND INCINERATE EVERYONE IN THE BUILDING.
WELL, THE CULPRITS ARE *PIRATES*, AFTER ALL.
THESE THINGS DO HAPPEN.

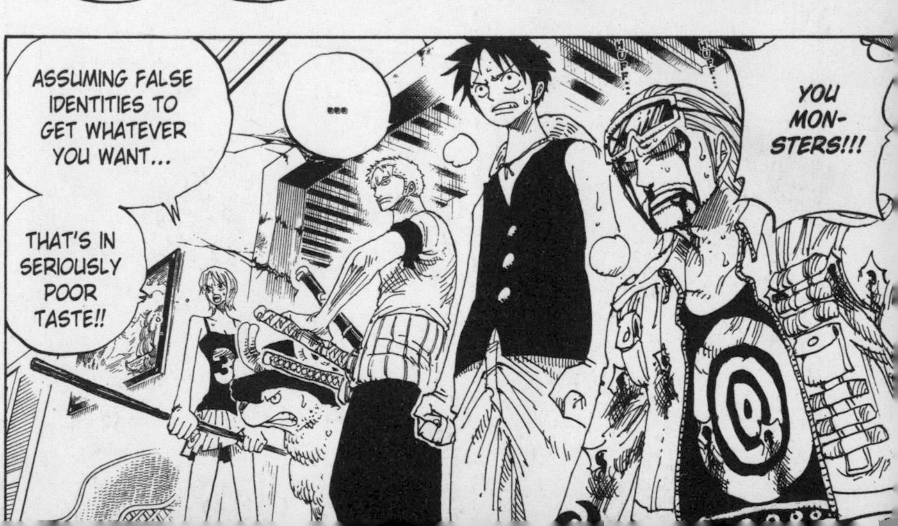
YOU MON-STERS!!!
HUFF...
HUFF...
...
ASSUMING FALSE IDENTITIES TO GET WHATEVER YOU WANT...
THAT'S IN SERIOUSLY POOR TASTE!!

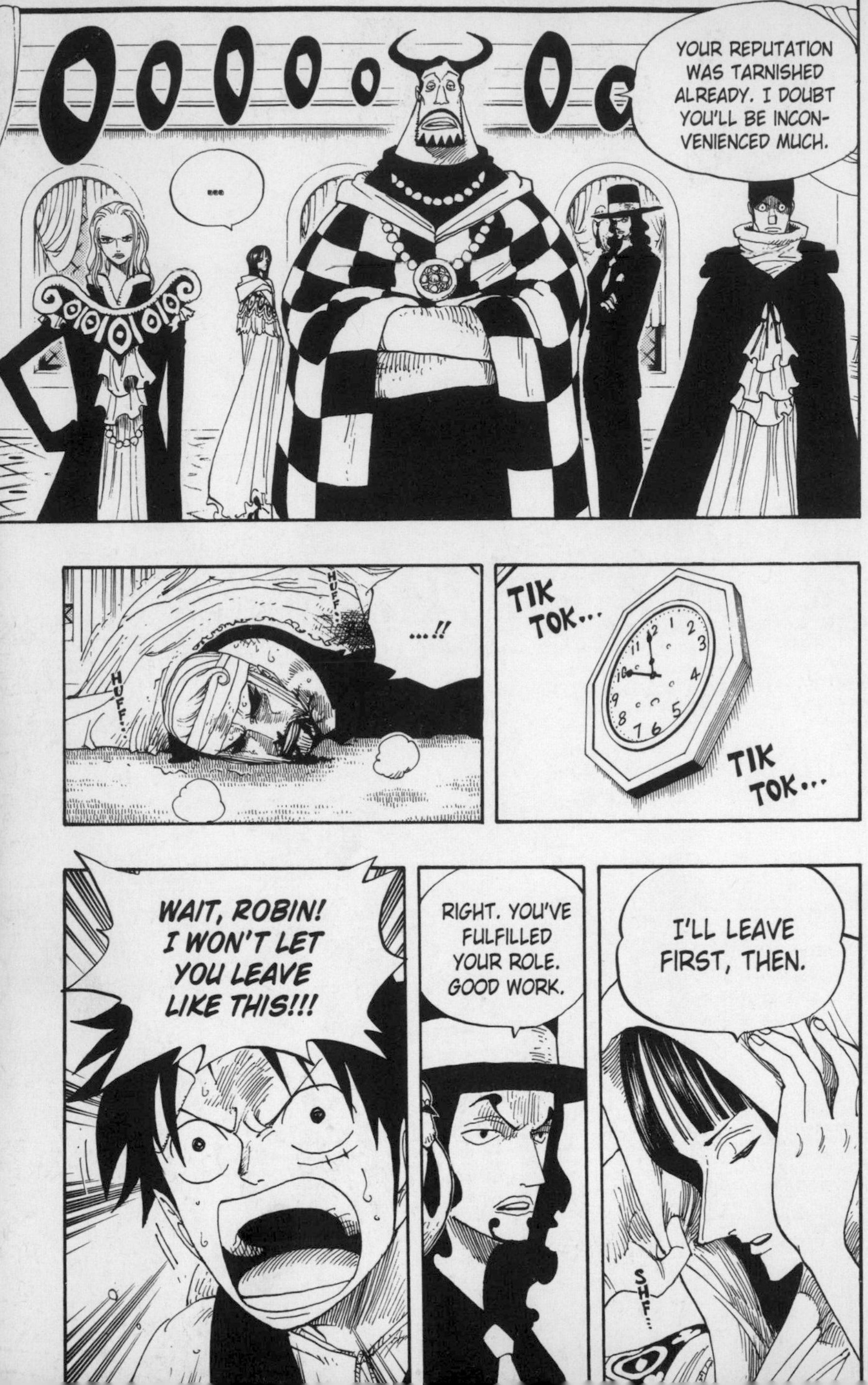
YOUR REPUTATION WAS TARNISHED ALREADY. I DOUBT YOU'LL BE INCONVENIENCED MUCH.
...
TIK TOK...
TIK TOK...
HUFF...
...!!
HUFF...
I'LL LEAVE FIRST, THEN.
SHF...
RIGHT. YOU'VE FULFILLED YOUR ROLE. GOOD WORK.
WAIT, ROBIN! I WON'T LET YOU LEAVE LIKE THIS!!!

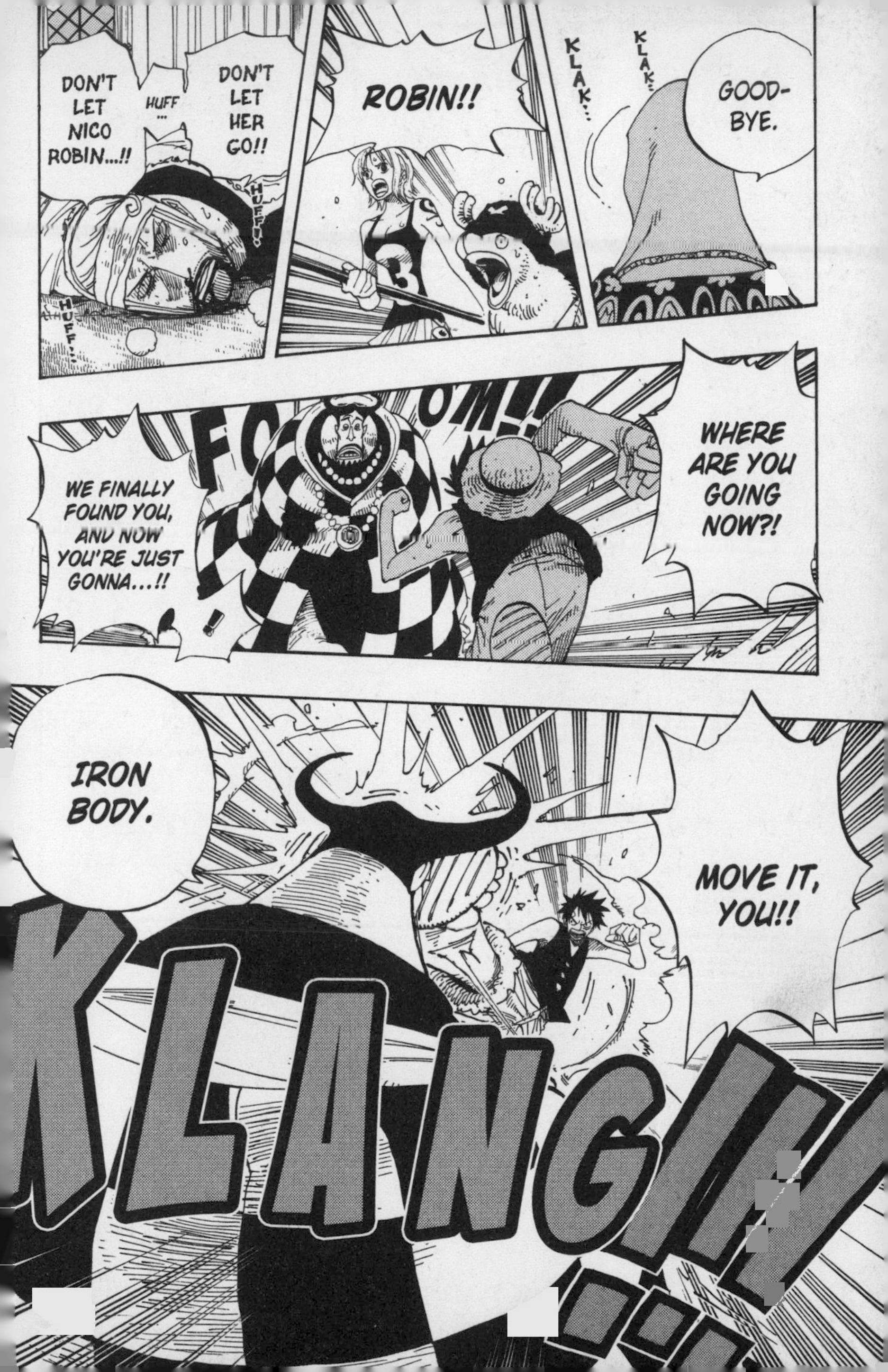
KLAK...
KLAK...
GOOD-BYE.
ROBIN!!
DON'T LET HER GO!!
HUFF...
DON'T LET NICO ROBIN...!!
HUFF!!
HUFF...
WHERE ARE YOU GOING NOW?!
WE FINALLY FOUND YOU, AND NOW YOU'RE JUST GONNA...!!
MOVE IT, YOU!!
IRON BODY.
KLANG!!

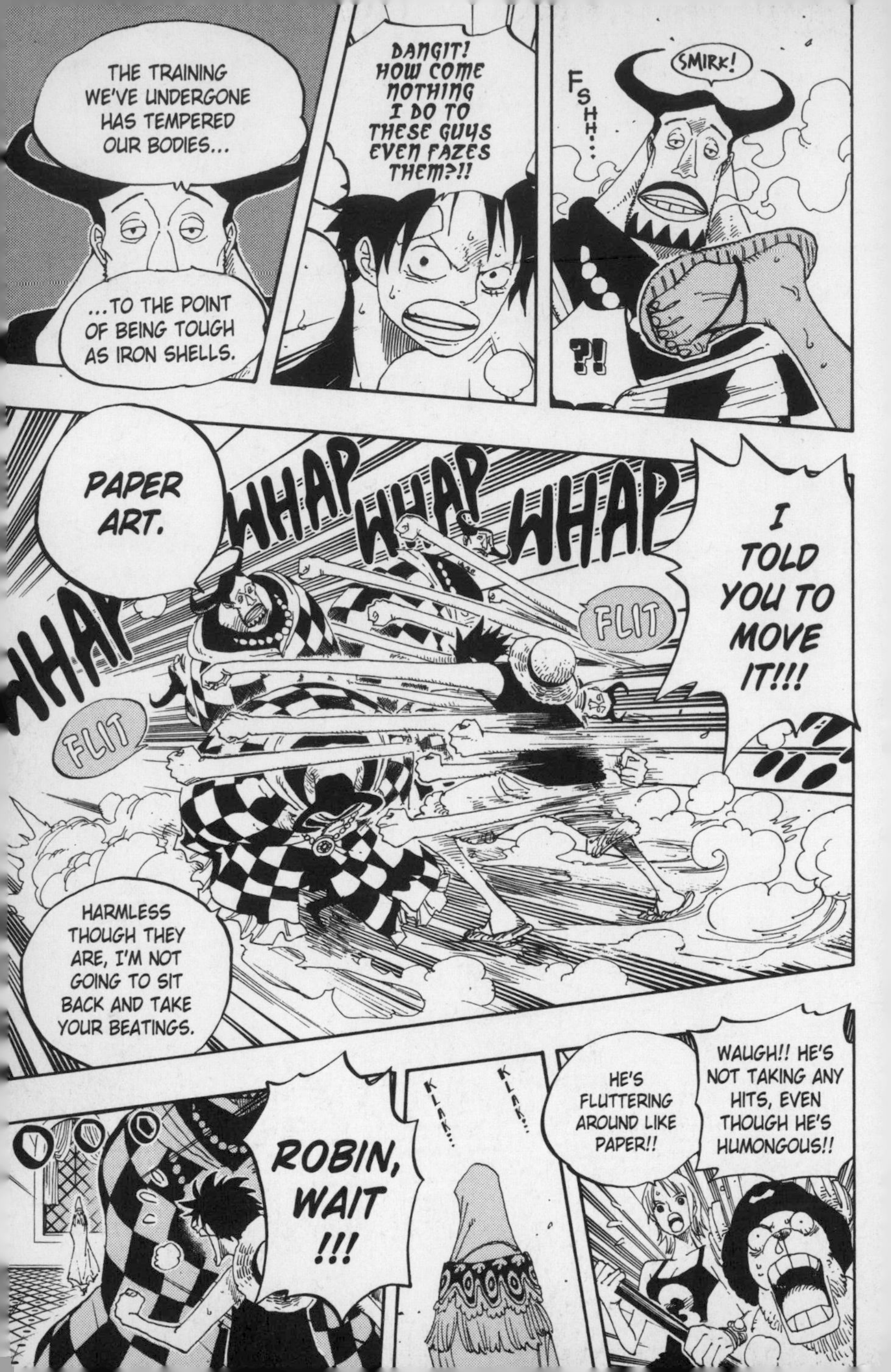
SMIRK!
FSHH...
?!
DANGIT! HOW COME NOTHING I DO TO THESE GUYS EVEN FAZES THEM?!!
THE TRAINING WE'VE UNDERGONE HAS TEMPERED OUR BODIES...
...TO THE POINT OF BEING TOUGH AS IRON SHELLS.
I TOLD YOU TO MOVE IT!!!
WHAP
WHAP
WHAP
FLIT
PAPER ART.
WHAP
FLIT
HARMLESS THOUGH THEY ARE, I'M NOT GOING TO SIT BACK AND TAKE YOUR BEATINGS.
WAUGH!! HE'S NOT TAKING ANY HITS, EVEN THOUGH HE'S HUMONGOUS!!
HE'S FLUTTERING AROUND LIKE PAPER!!
KLAK...
KLAK...
ROBIN, WAIT!!!

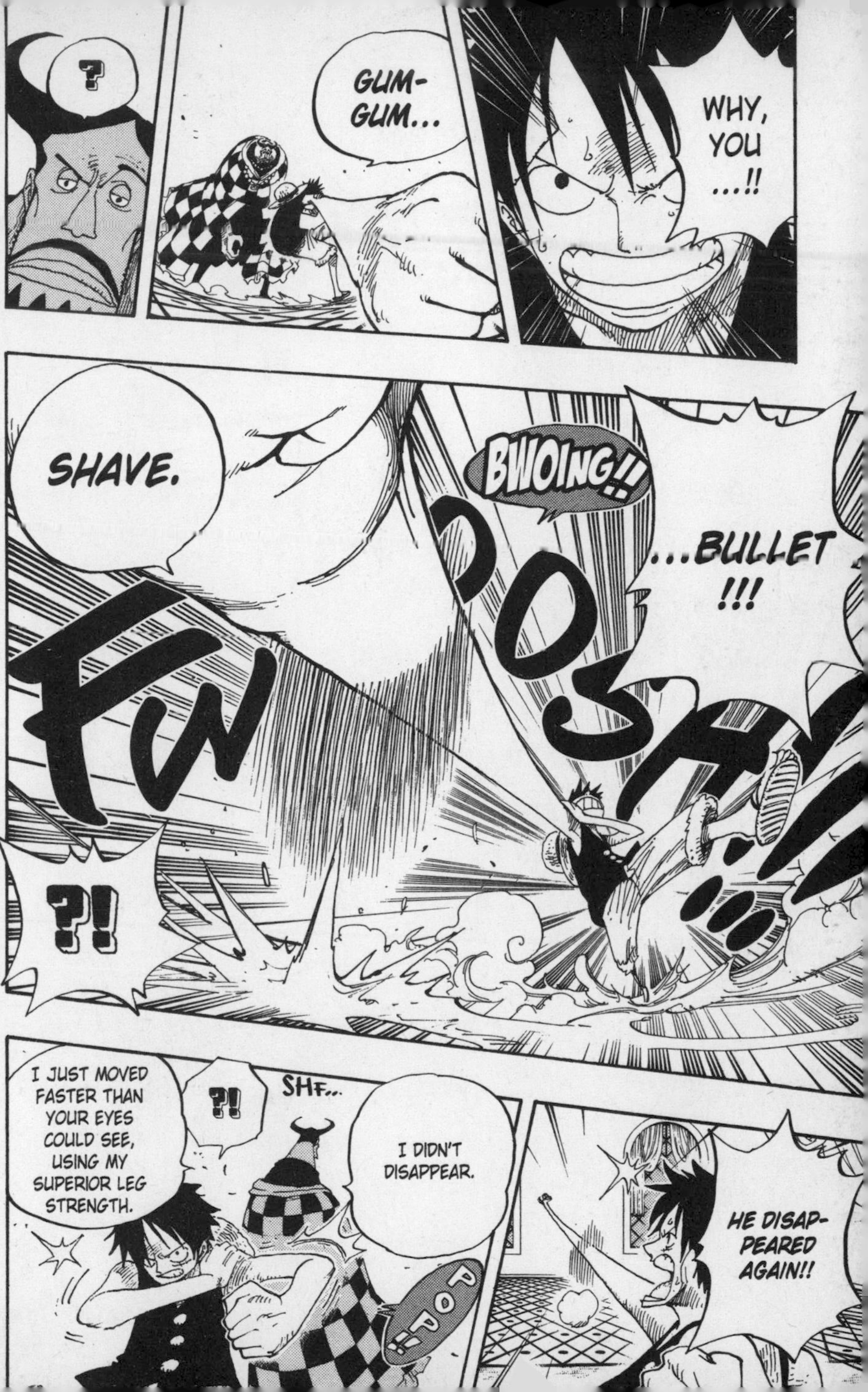
WHY, YOU ...!!
GUM-GUM...
?
...BULLET !!!
BWOING!!
DOSH...!!
SHAVE.
FW
?!
HE DISAP-PEARED AGAIN!!
I DIDN'T DISAPPEAR.
SHF...
?!
I JUST MOVED FASTER THAN YOUR EYES COULD SEE, USING MY SUPERIOR LEG STRENGTH.
POP!!

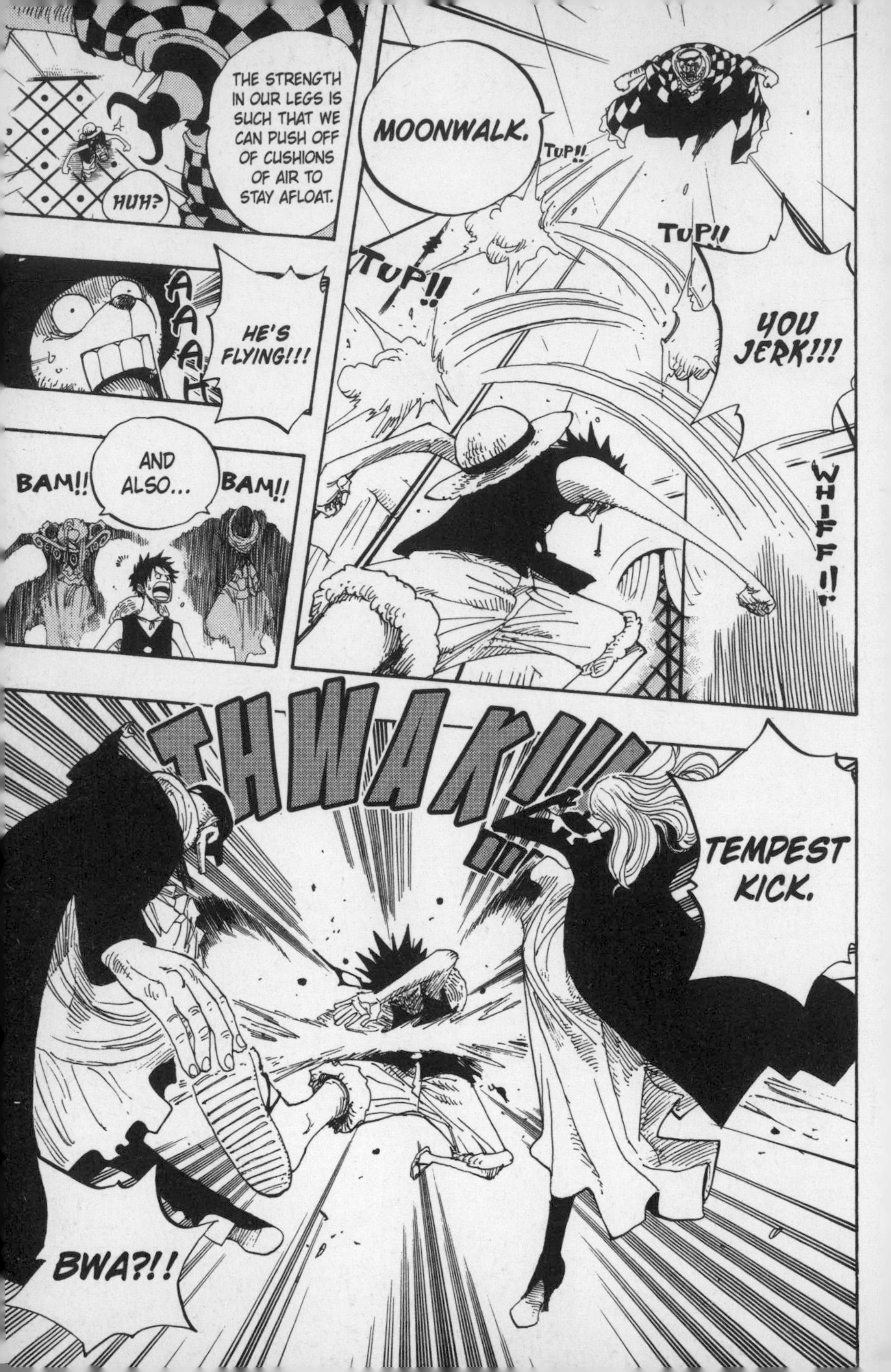
MOONWALK.
TUP!!
TUP!!
TUP!!
YOU JERK!!!
WHIFF!!
THE STRENGTH IN OUR LEGS IS SUCH THAT WE CAN PUSH OFF OF CUSHIONS OF AIR TO STAY AFLOAT.
HUH?
HE'S FLYING!!!
AAAAH
AND ALSO...
BAM!!
BAM!!
THWAK!!!
TEMPEST KICK.
BWA?!!

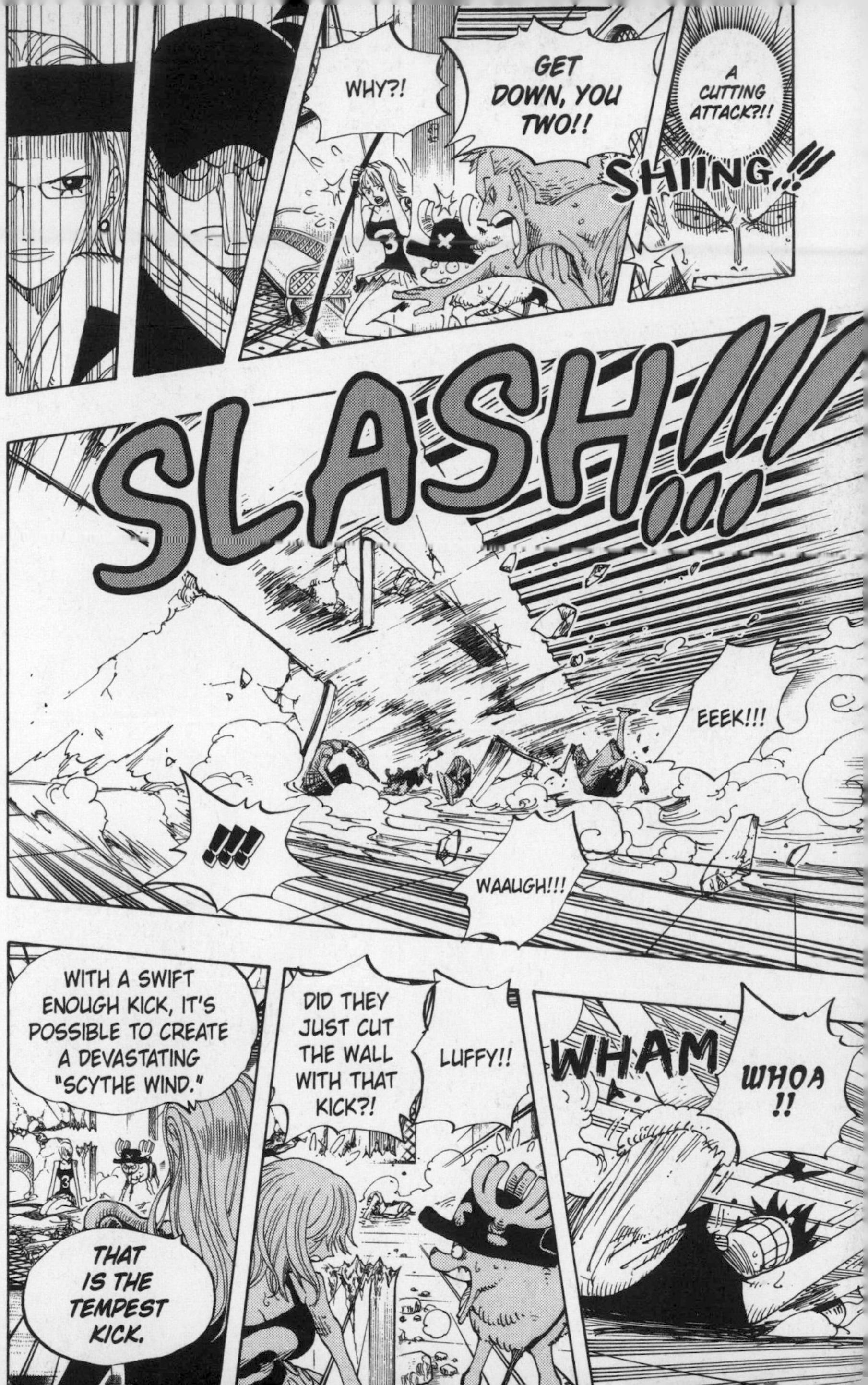
A CUTTING ATTACK?!!
SHIING..!!
GET DOWN, YOU TWO!!
WHY?!
SLASH!!!...
EEEK!!!
!!!
WAAUGH!!!
WHOA !!
WHAM
LUFFY!!
DID THEY JUST CUT THE WALL WITH THAT KICK?!
WITH A SWIFT ENOUGH KICK, IT'S POSSIBLE TO CREATE A DEVASTATING "SCYTHE WIND."
THAT IS THE TEMPEST KICK.

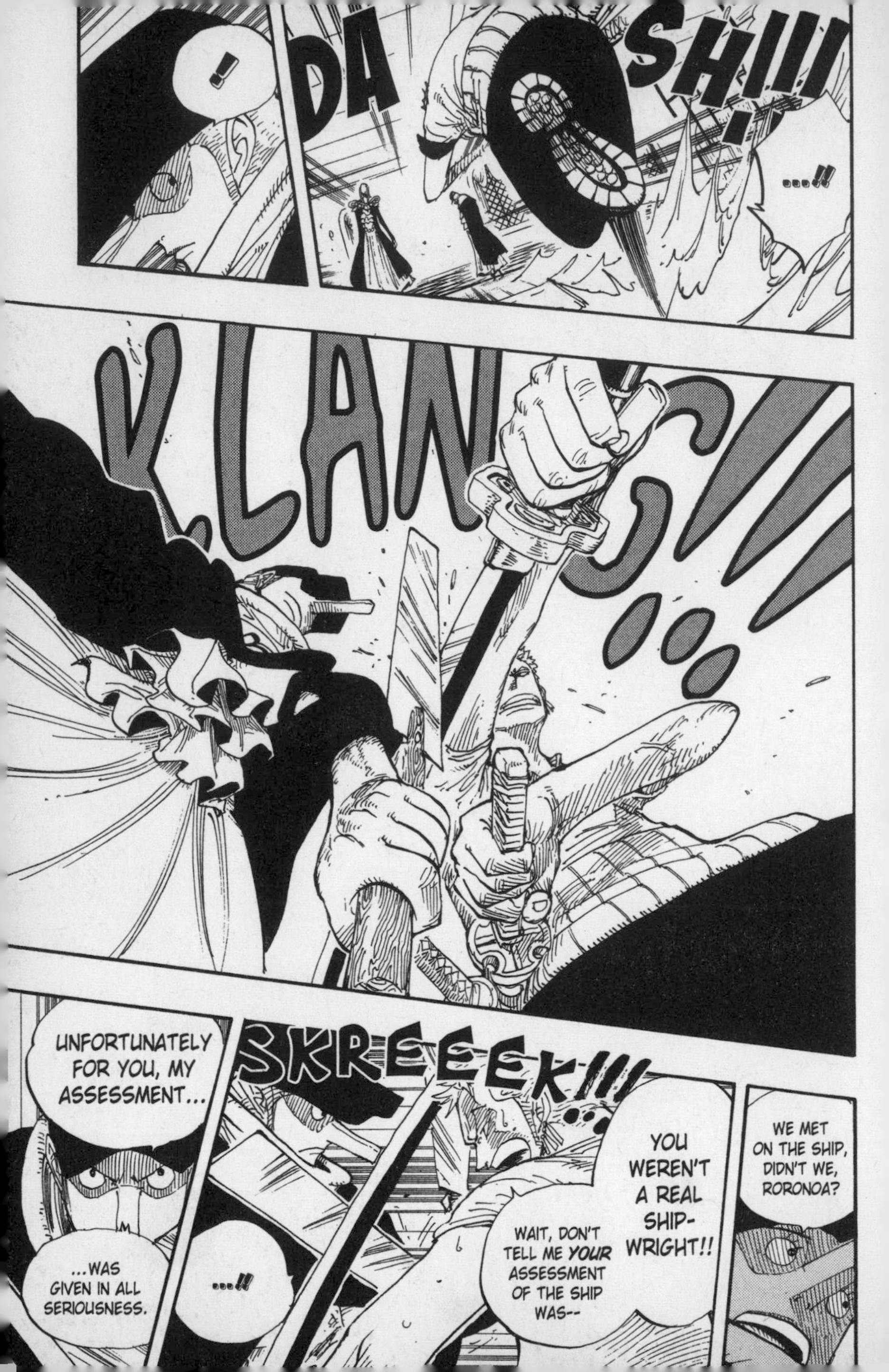
DASH!!!
...!!
!
KLANG!!...
WE MET ON THE SHIP, DIDN'T WE, RORONOA?
YOU WEREN'T A REAL SHIP-WRIGHT!!
WAIT, DON'T TELL ME *YOUR* ASSESSMENT OF THE SHIP WAS--
SKREEEK!!!
...!!
UNFORTUNATELY FOR YOU, MY ASSESSMENT...
...WAS GIVEN IN ALL SERIOUSNESS.

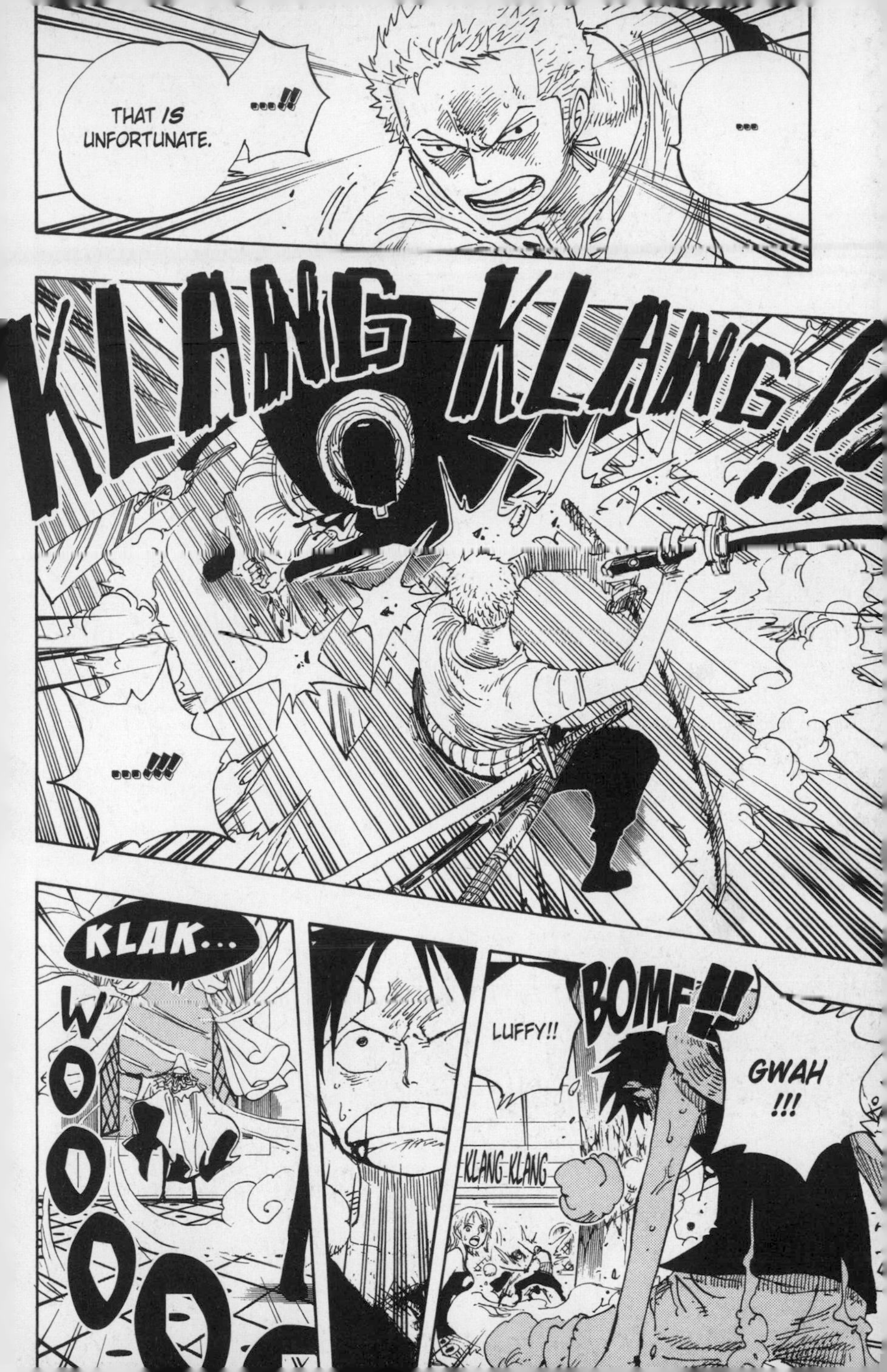
...
...!!
THAT IS UNFORTUNATE.
KLANG KLANG!!!
...!!!
BOMF!!
GWAH !!!
LUFFY!!
KLANG KLANG
KLAK...
WOOOO

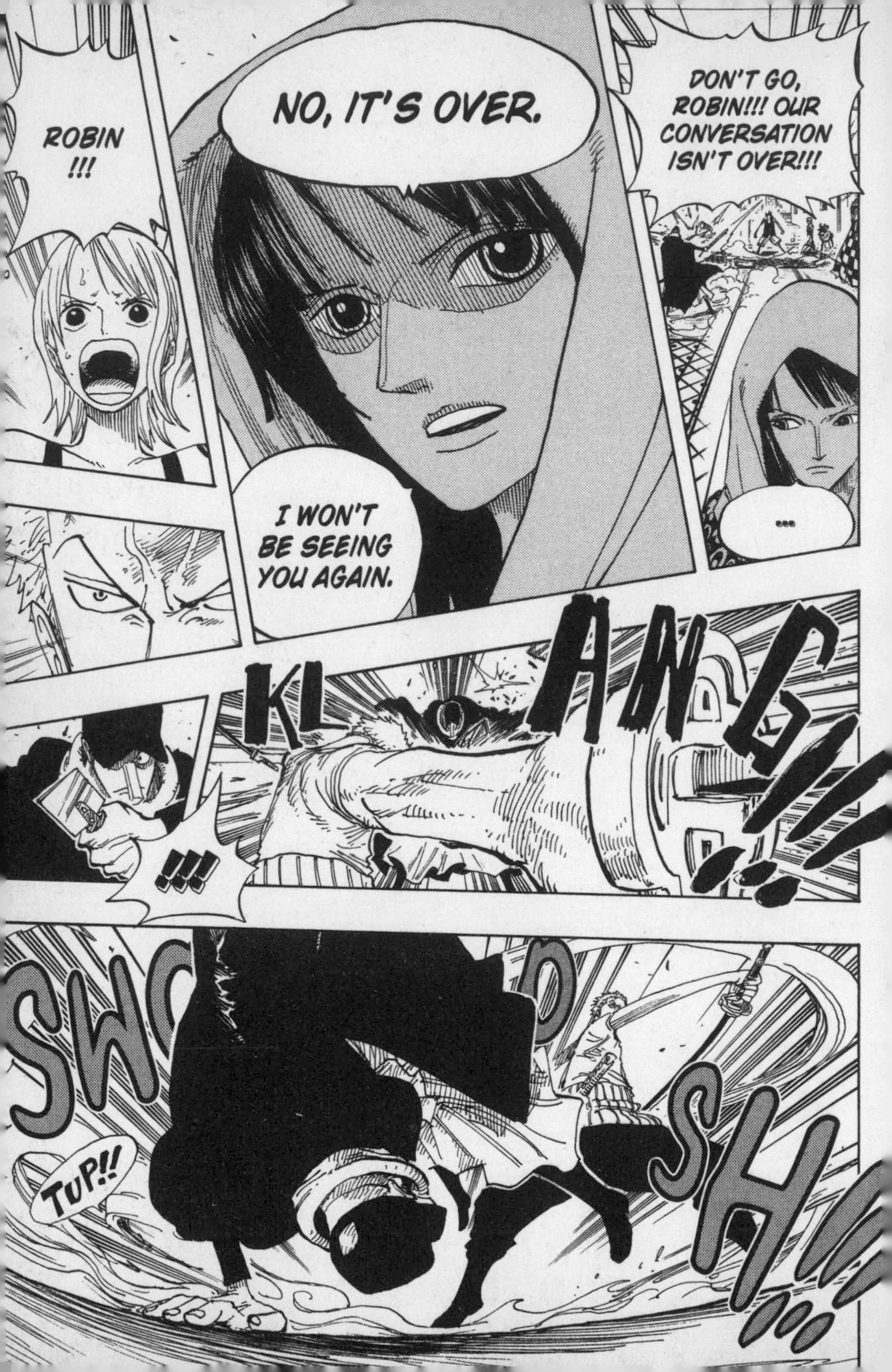
DON'T GO, ROBIN!!! OUR CONVERSATION ISN'T OVER!!!
...
NO, IT'S OVER.
I WON'T BE SEEING YOU AGAIN.
ROBIN !!!
KLANG!!!
!!!
SWOOSH!!!
TUP!!

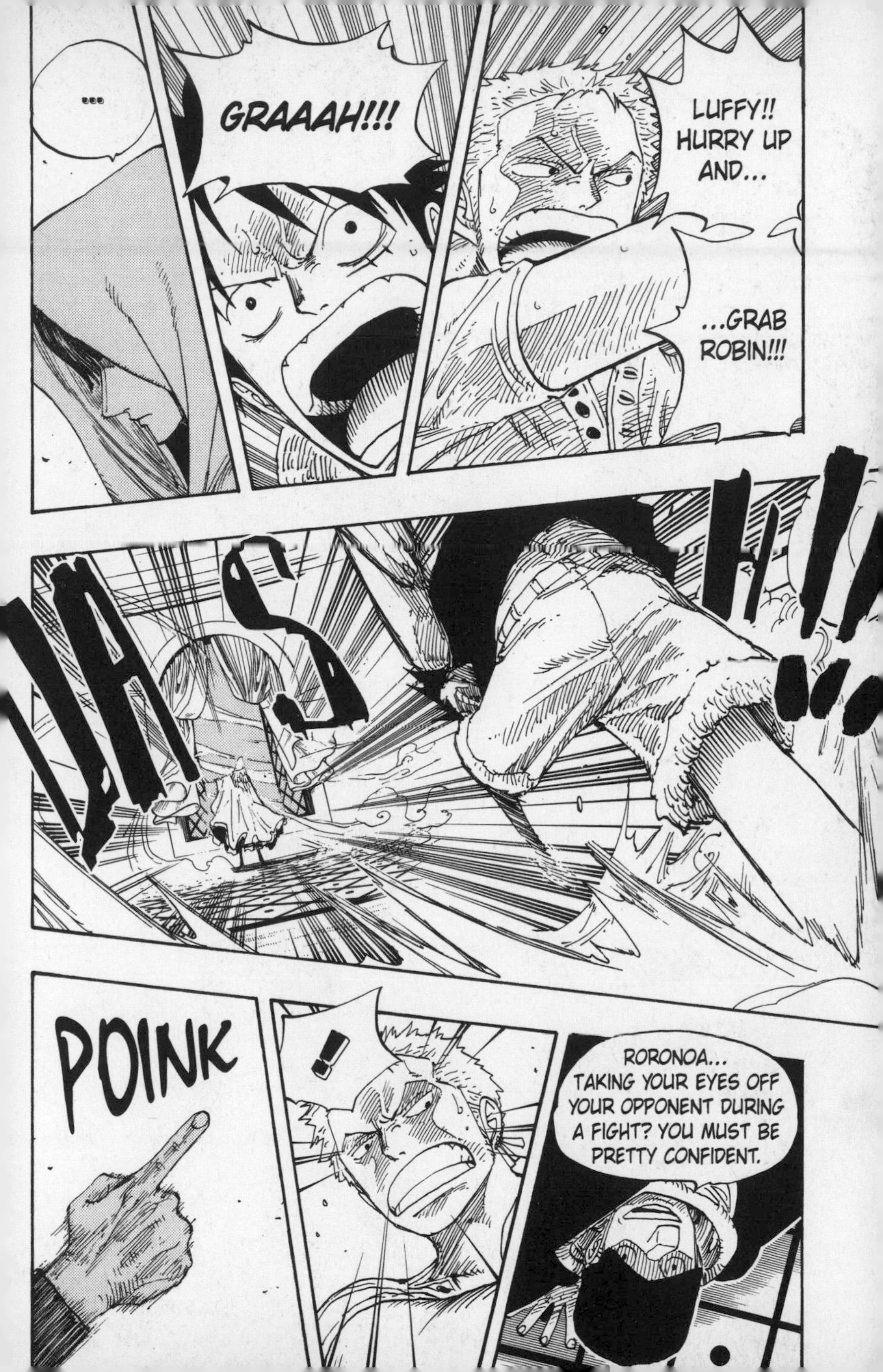
LUFFY!! HURRY UP AND...
...GRAB ROBIN!!!
GRAAAH!!!
...
DASH!!...
RORONOA... TAKING YOUR EYES OFF YOUR OPPONENT DURING A FIGHT? YOU MUST BE PRETTY CONFIDENT.
!
POINK

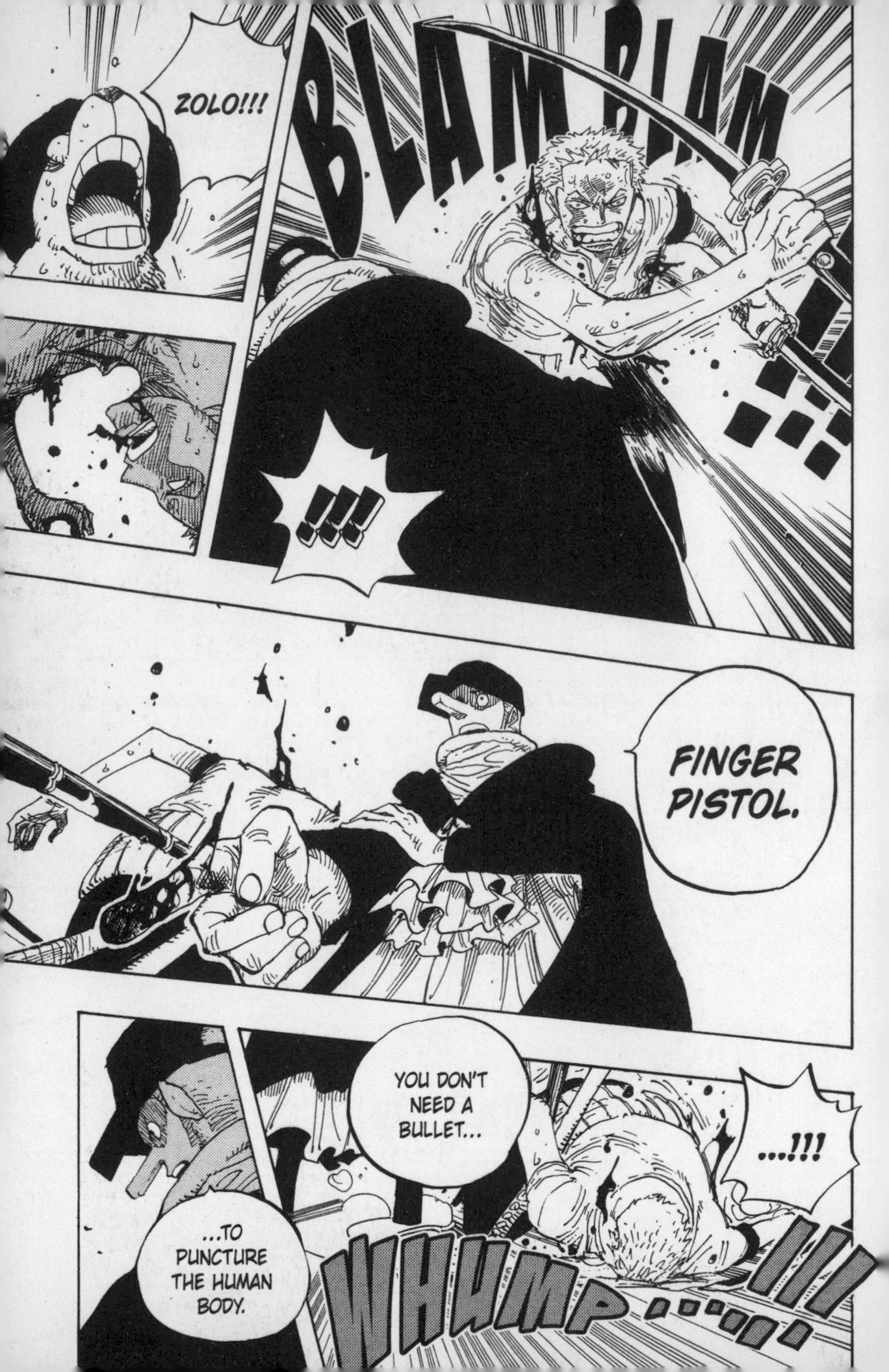
BLAM BLAM
!!!
ZOLO!!!
FINGER PISTOL.
...!!!
WHUMP...!!!
YOU DON'T NEED A BULLET...
...TO PUNCTURE THE HUMAN BODY.

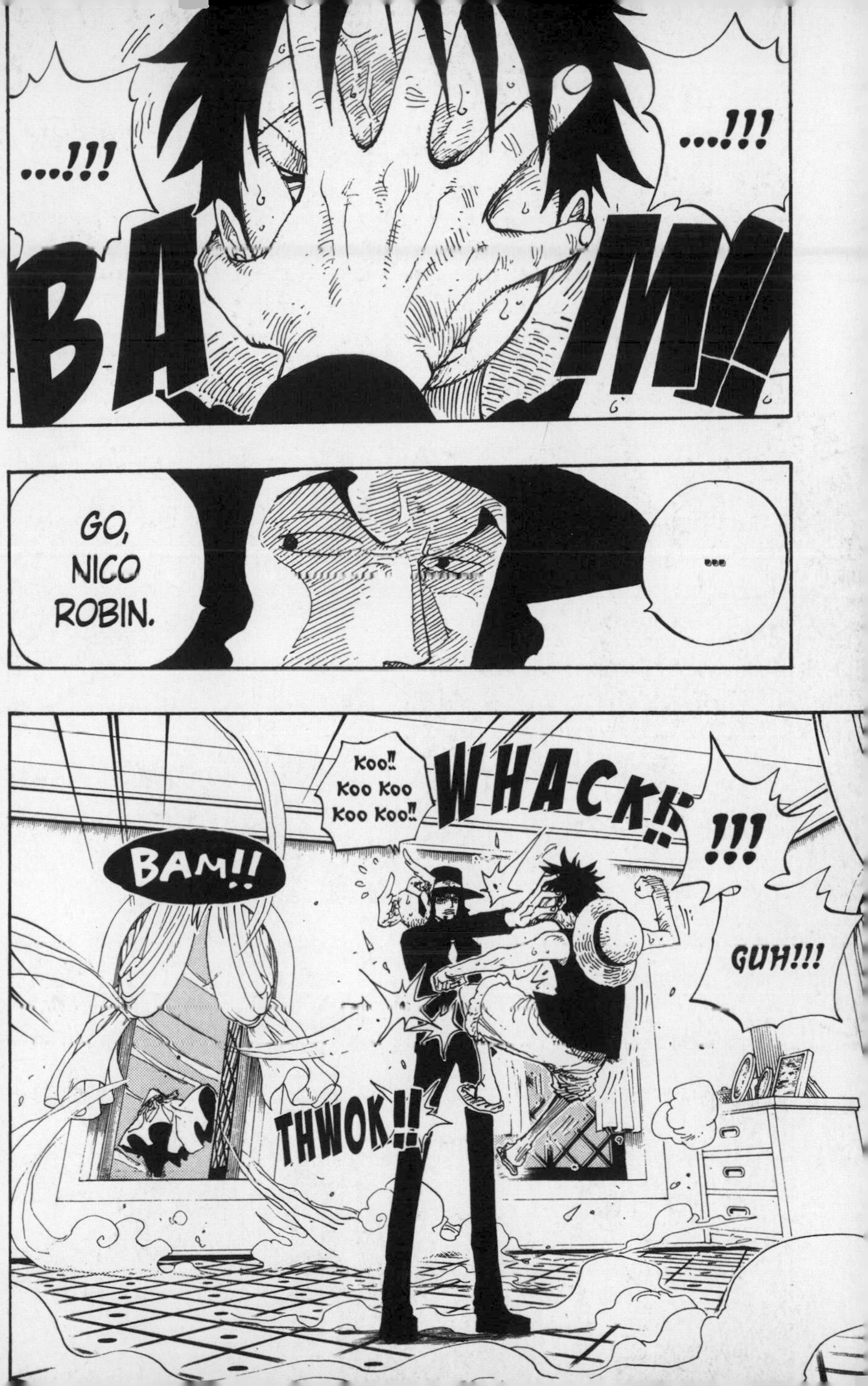
...!!!
...!!!
BAM!!
...
GO, NICO ROBIN.
!!!
GUH!!!
WHACK!!
Koo!! Koo Koo Koo Koo!!
BAM!!
THWOK!!

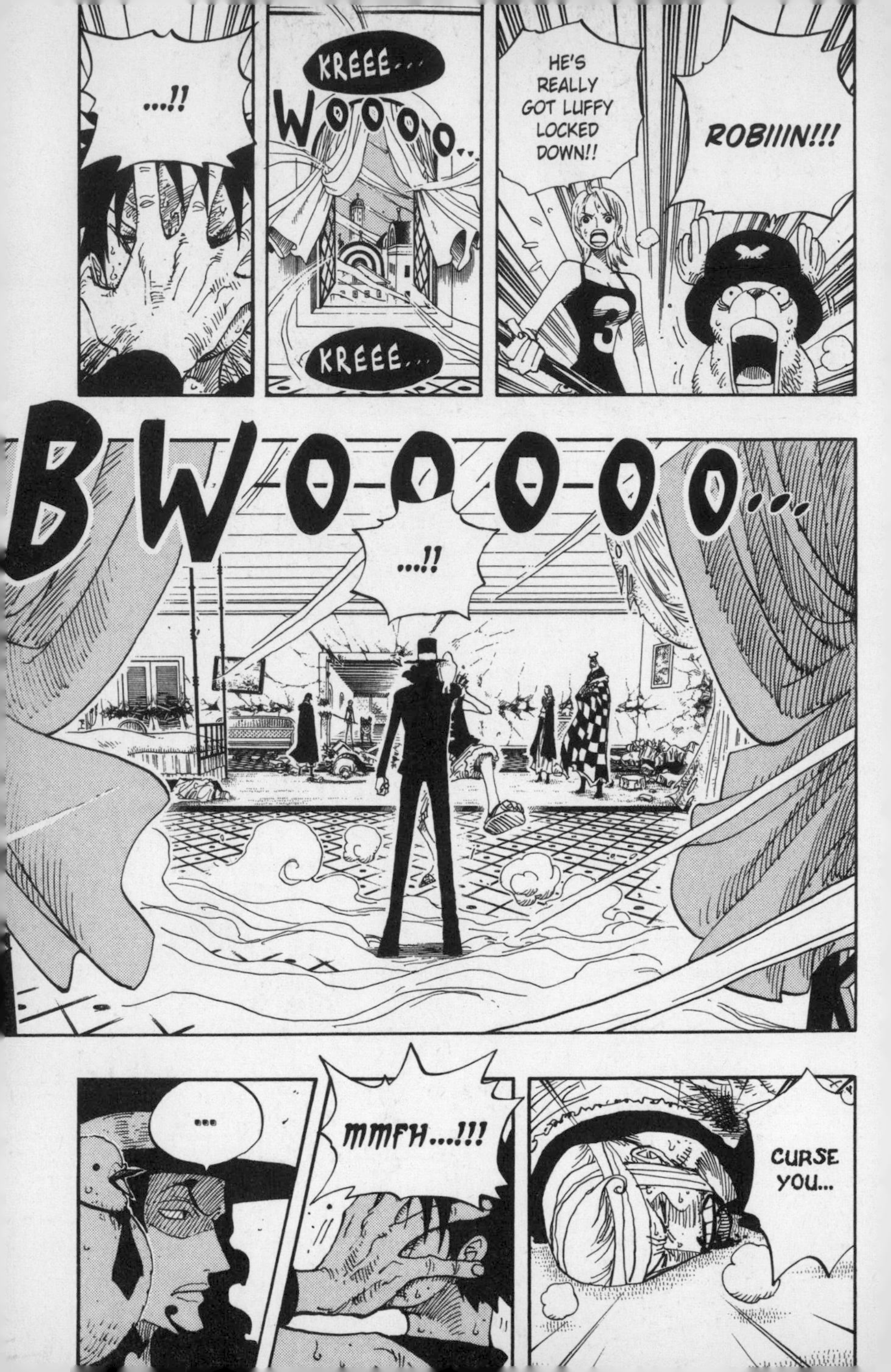
ROBIIIN!!!
HE'S REALLY GOT LUFFY LOCKED DOWN!!
KREEE...
WOOOO...
KREEE...
...!!
BWOOOOO...
...!!
CURSE YOU...
MMFH...!!!
...

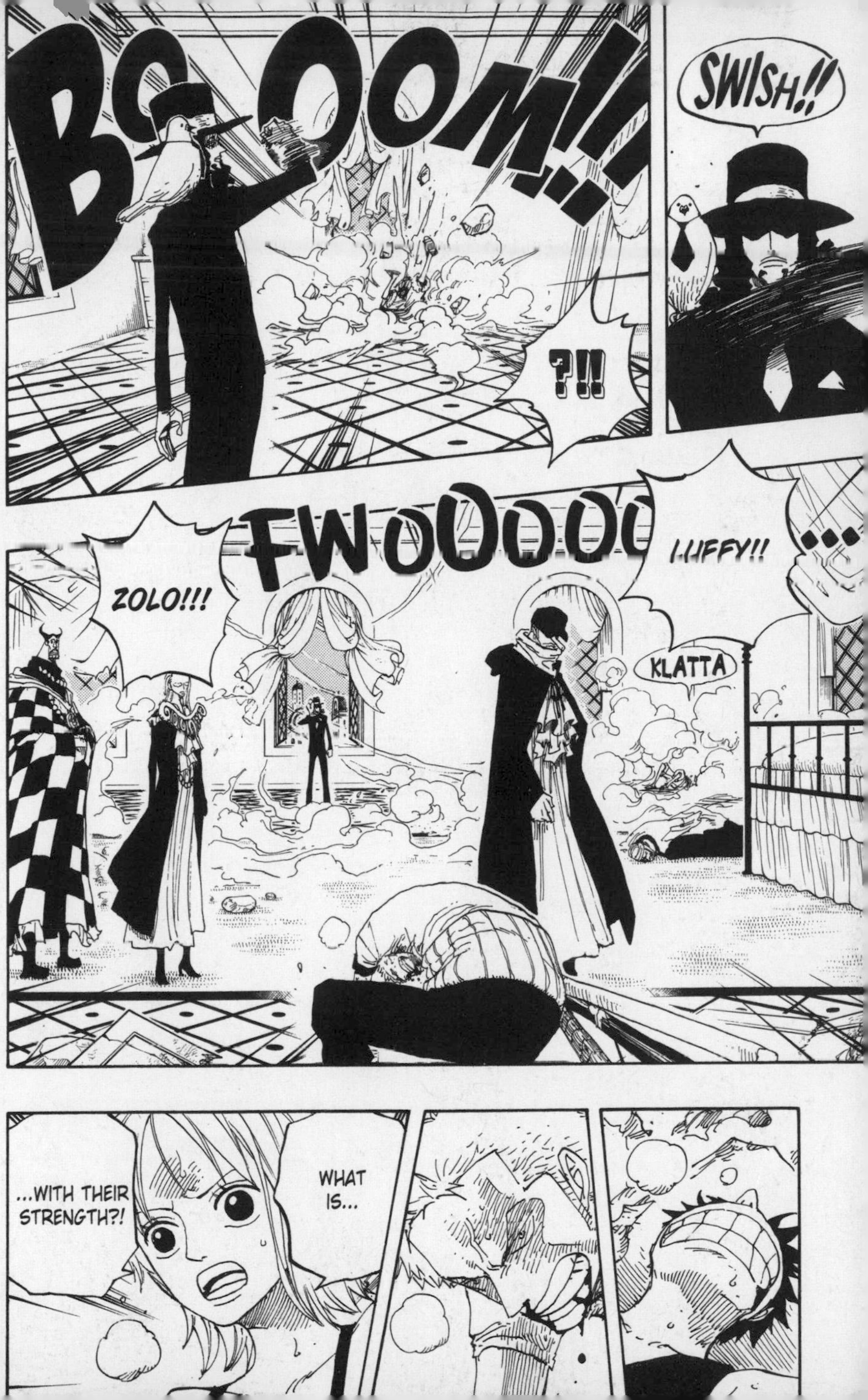
SWISH!!
BOOOM!!!
?!!
...
LUFFY!!
FWOOOOO
ZOLO!!!
KLATTA
WHAT IS...
...WITH THEIR STRENGTH?!

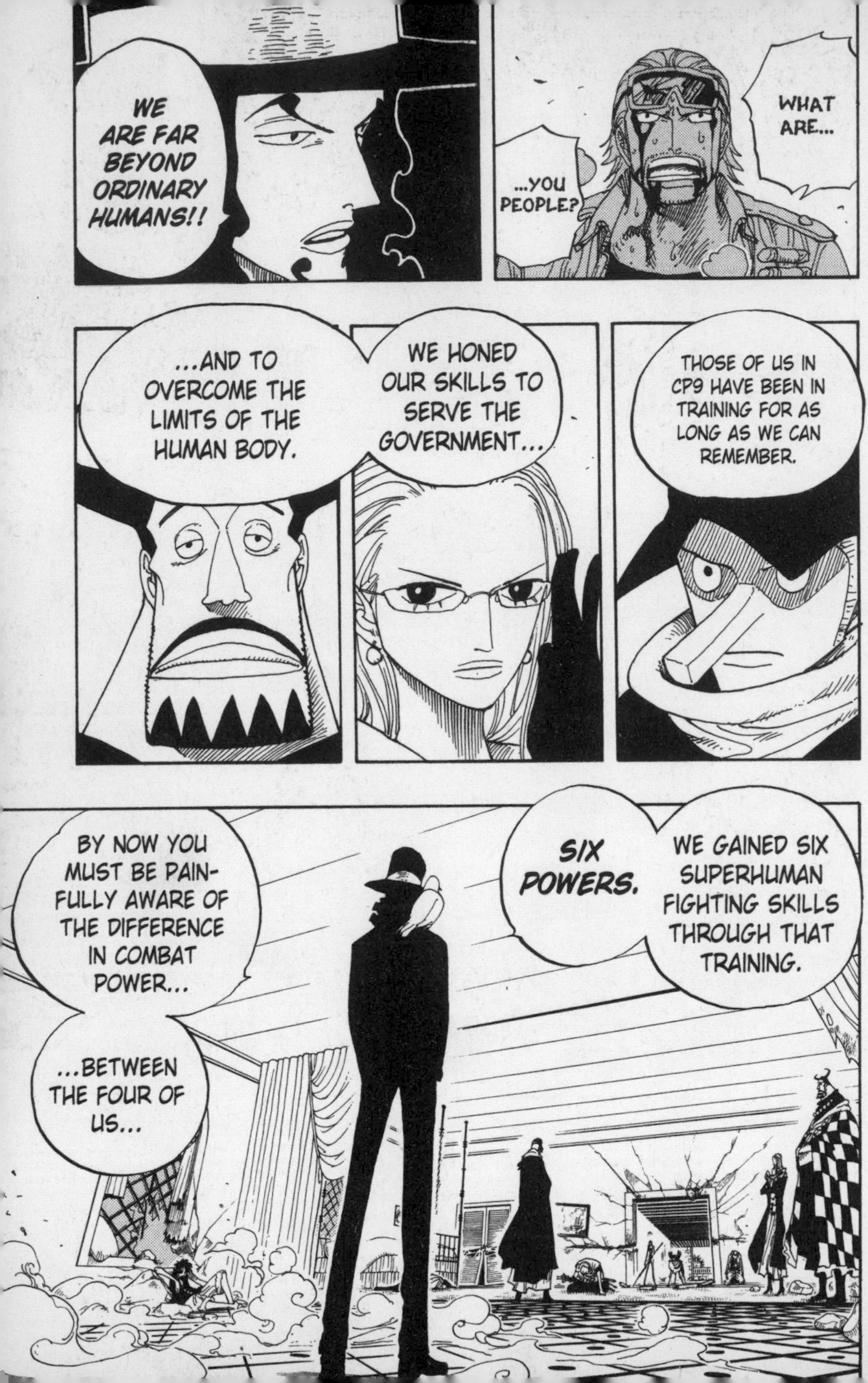
WHAT ARE...
...YOU PEOPLE?
WE ARE FAR BEYOND ORDINARY HUMANS!!
THOSE OF US IN CP9 HAVE BEEN IN TRAINING FOR AS LONG AS WE CAN REMEMBER.
WE HONED OUR SKILLS TO SERVE THE GOVERNMENT...
...AND TO OVERCOME THE LIMITS OF THE HUMAN BODY.
WE GAINED SIX SUPERHUMAN FIGHTING SKILLS THROUGH THAT TRAINING.
SIX POWERS.
BY NOW YOU MUST BE PAIN-FULLY AWARE OF THE DIFFERENCE IN COMBAT POWER...
...BETWEEN THE FOUR OF US...

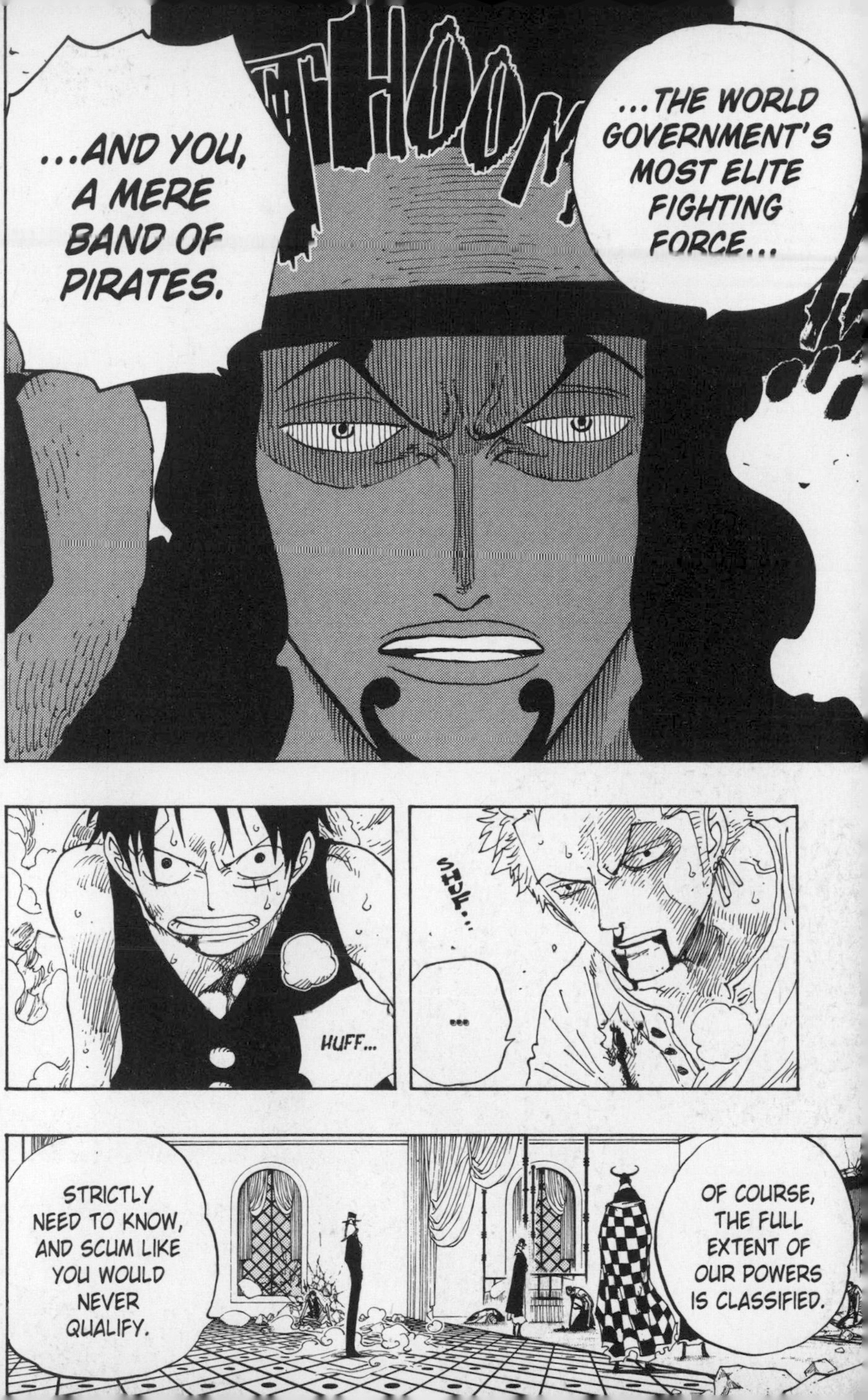
...THE WORLD GOVERNMENT'S MOST ELITE FIGHTING FORCE...
THOOM
...AND YOU, A MERE BAND OF PIRATES.
SHUF...
...
HUFF...
OF COURSE, THE FULL EXTENT OF OUR POWERS IS CLASSIFIED.
STRICTLY NEED TO KNOW, AND SCUM LIKE YOU WOULD NEVER QUALIFY.

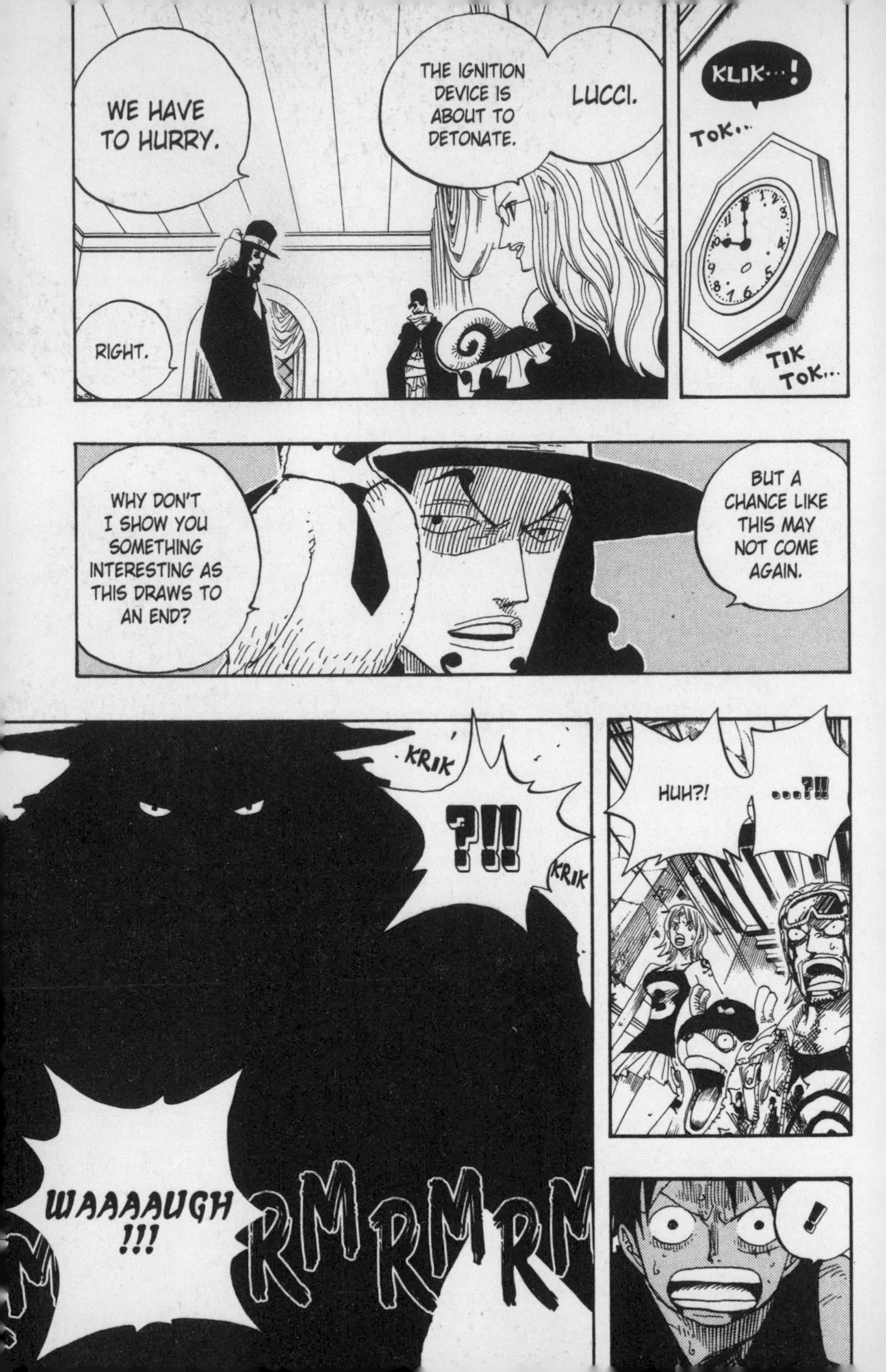
KLIK...!
TOK...
TIK TOK...
LUCCI.
THE IGNITION DEVICE IS ABOUT TO DETONATE.
WE HAVE TO HURRY.
RIGHT.
BUT A CHANCE LIKE THIS MAY NOT COME AGAIN.
WHY DON'T I SHOW YOU SOMETHING INTERESTING AS THIS DRAWS TO AN END?
...?!!
HUH?!
!
KRIK
?!!
KRIK
WAAAAUGH!!!
RMRMRM

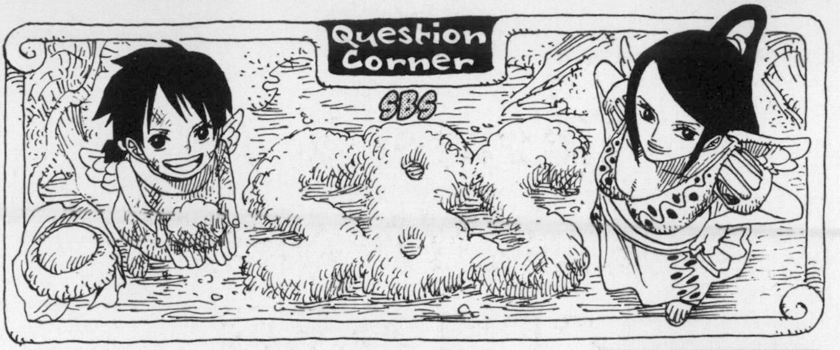
Question Corner
SBS

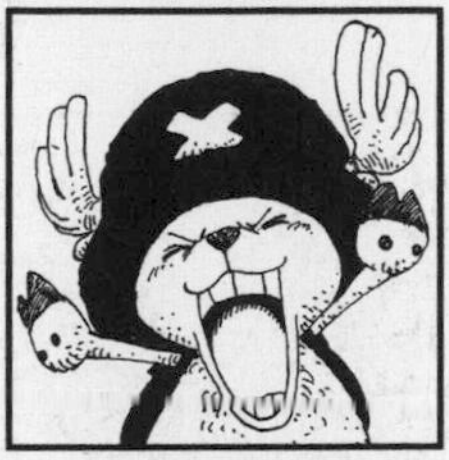

Reader: I just randomly thought of this. When Chopper's small (meaning, when he's his usual size), how does he carry things? Does he just pinch them up cleverly between his hooves? For some reason, this has really been bugging me.

--Midoringo

Oda: Let me show you with a picture.

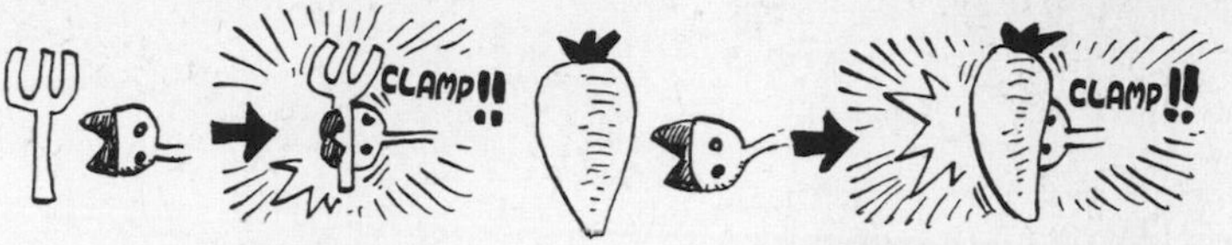
CLAMP!!
CLAMP!!

It's like this! He grabbed it!! (Persuasion by force.)

Reader: Oda! Question: Do you decide all the abilities provided by the Devil Fruits that appear in the anime and the movies? Please tell me.

--Matsutake

Oda: There are scriptwriters who create the original stories for the anime and movies, and whoever's writing the script at the time proposes the sort of fruit they want to use. My only role is granting or denying permission, telling them, "Oh, sure, that's fine" or "Oh, wait, I'm going to use that one later." That's all I do.

Reader: Oda Sensei, there's something that really, really bugs me right now. It's about Usopp's nose and the shipwright foreman Kaku's nose. Which one's longer? And, Oda Sensei, you're mean! You shouldn't mess with Kaku's nose. Still, it's real long.

--A Crew Member

Oda: Let's compare.

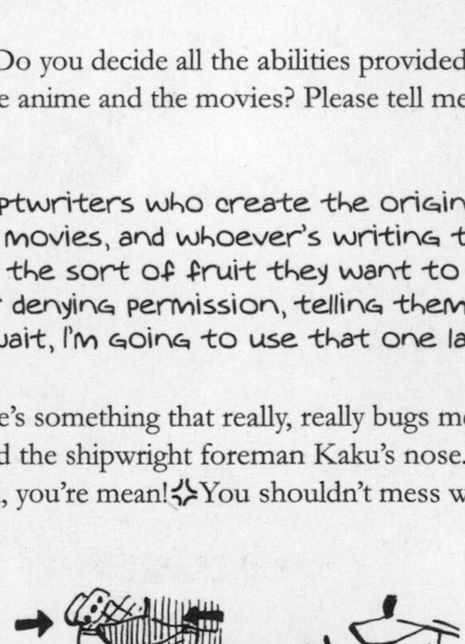

Ah! Thanks to the rounded bit at the end, Usopp's is longer!

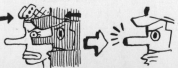

Chapter 349: ORDINARY CITIZENS

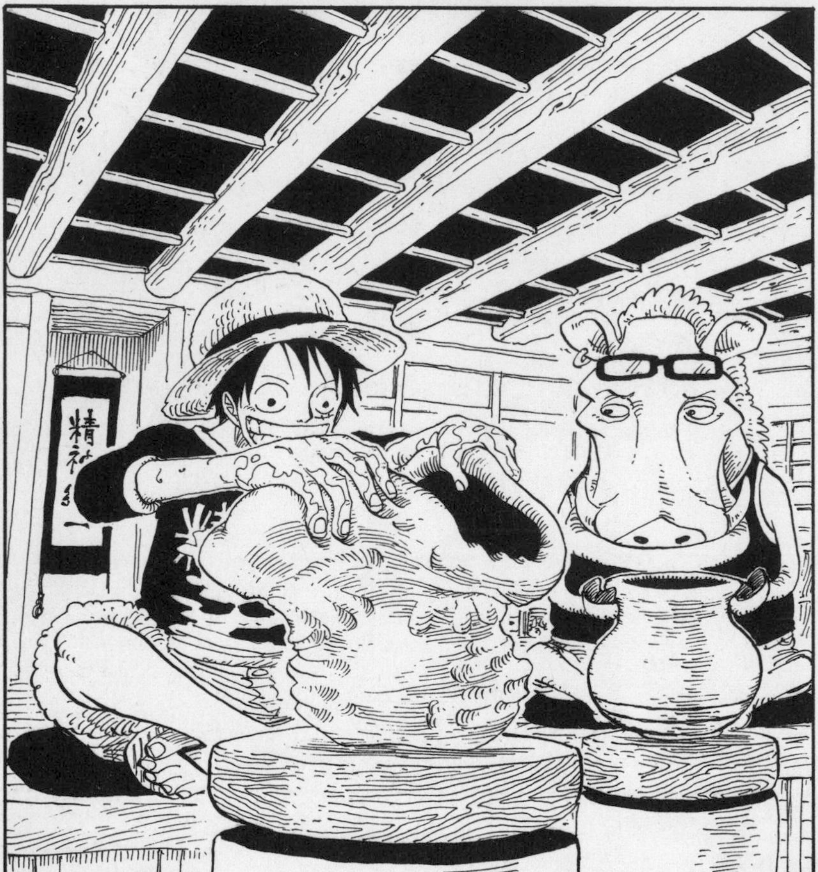

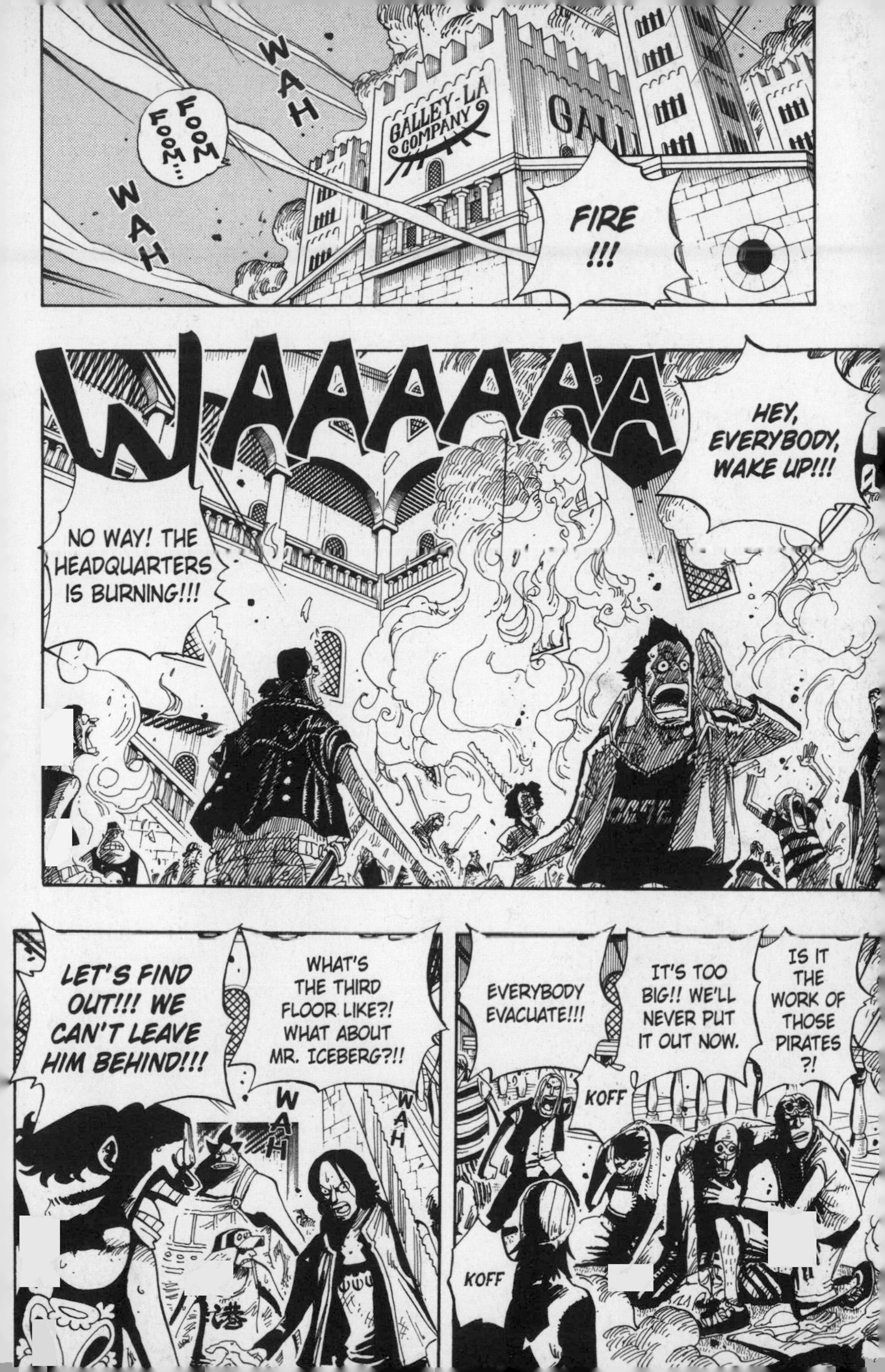
FIRE!!!
WAH
GALLEY-LA COMPANY
FOOM FOOM...
WAH
HEY, EVERYBODY, WAKE UP!!!
WAAAAAA
NO WAY! THE HEADQUARTERS IS BURNING!!!
IS IT THE WORK OF THOSE PIRATES?!
IT'S TOO BIG!! WE'LL NEVER PUT IT OUT NOW.
EVERYBODY EVACUATE!!!
KOFF
KOFF
WHAT'S THE THIRD FLOOR LIKE?! WHAT ABOUT MR. ICEBERG?!!
WAH
WAH
LET'S FIND OUT!!! WE CAN'T LEAVE HIM BEHIND!!!

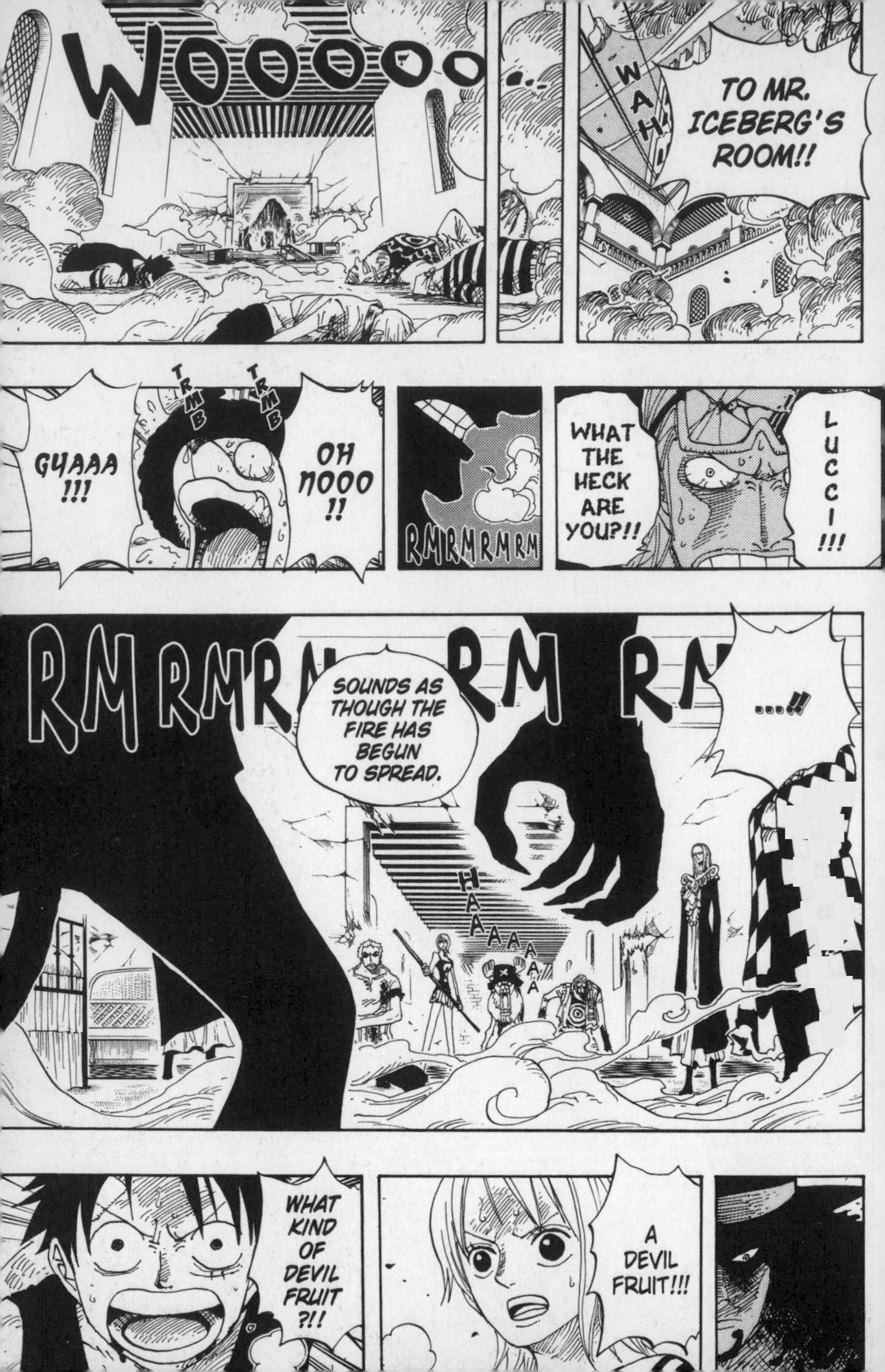
WAH
TO MR. ICEBERG'S ROOM!!
WOOOOO
LUCCI!!!
WHAT THE HECK ARE YOU?!!
RMRMRMRM
OH NOOO!!
TRMB
TRMB
GYAAA!!!
...!!
RM RM
SOUNDS AS THOUGH THE FIRE HAS BEGUN TO SPREAD.
RMRMRM
HAAAAAAA
A DEVIL FRUIT!!!
WHAT KIND OF DEVIL FRUIT?!!

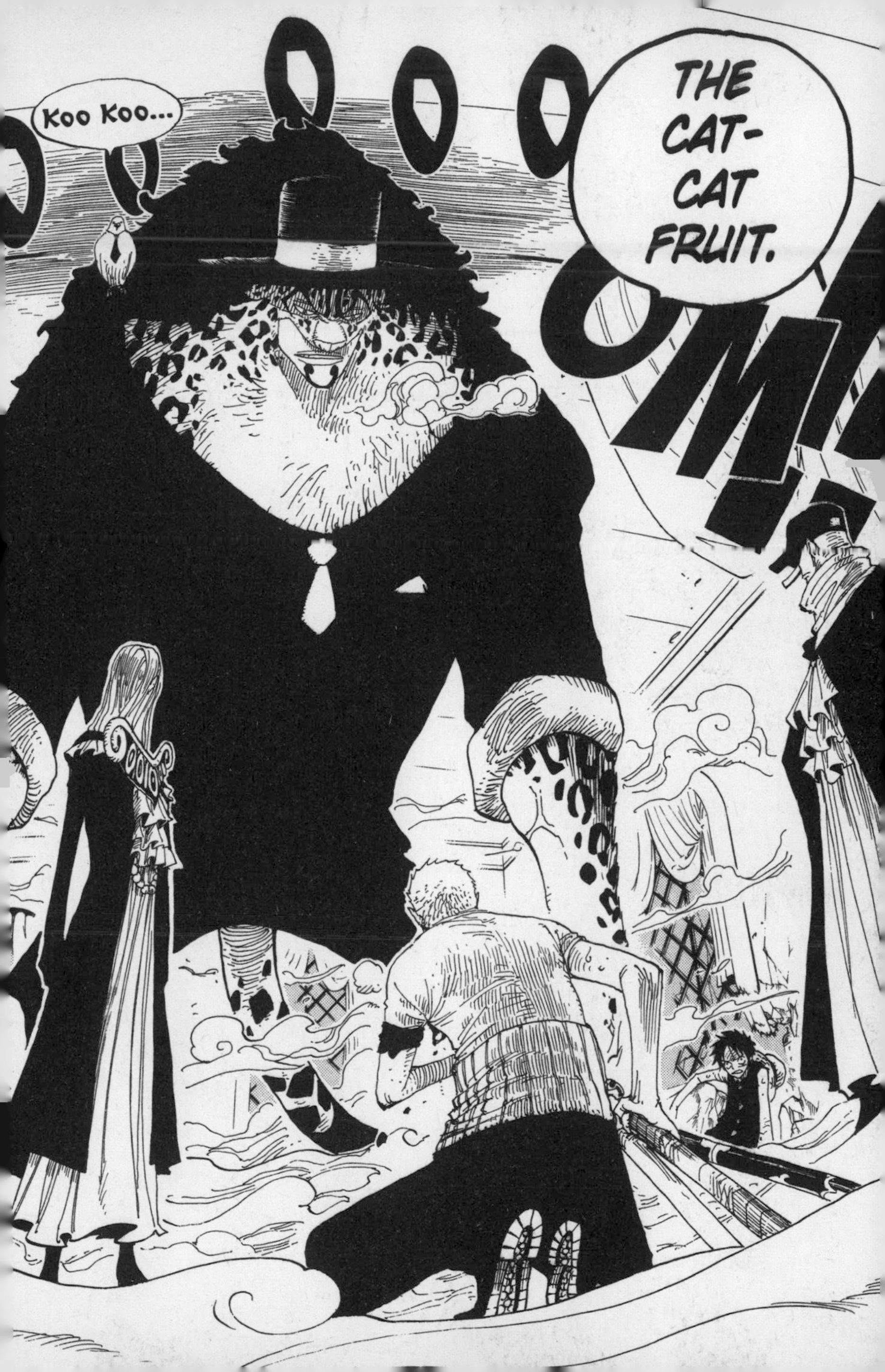
THE CAT-CAT FRUIT.
KOO KOO...

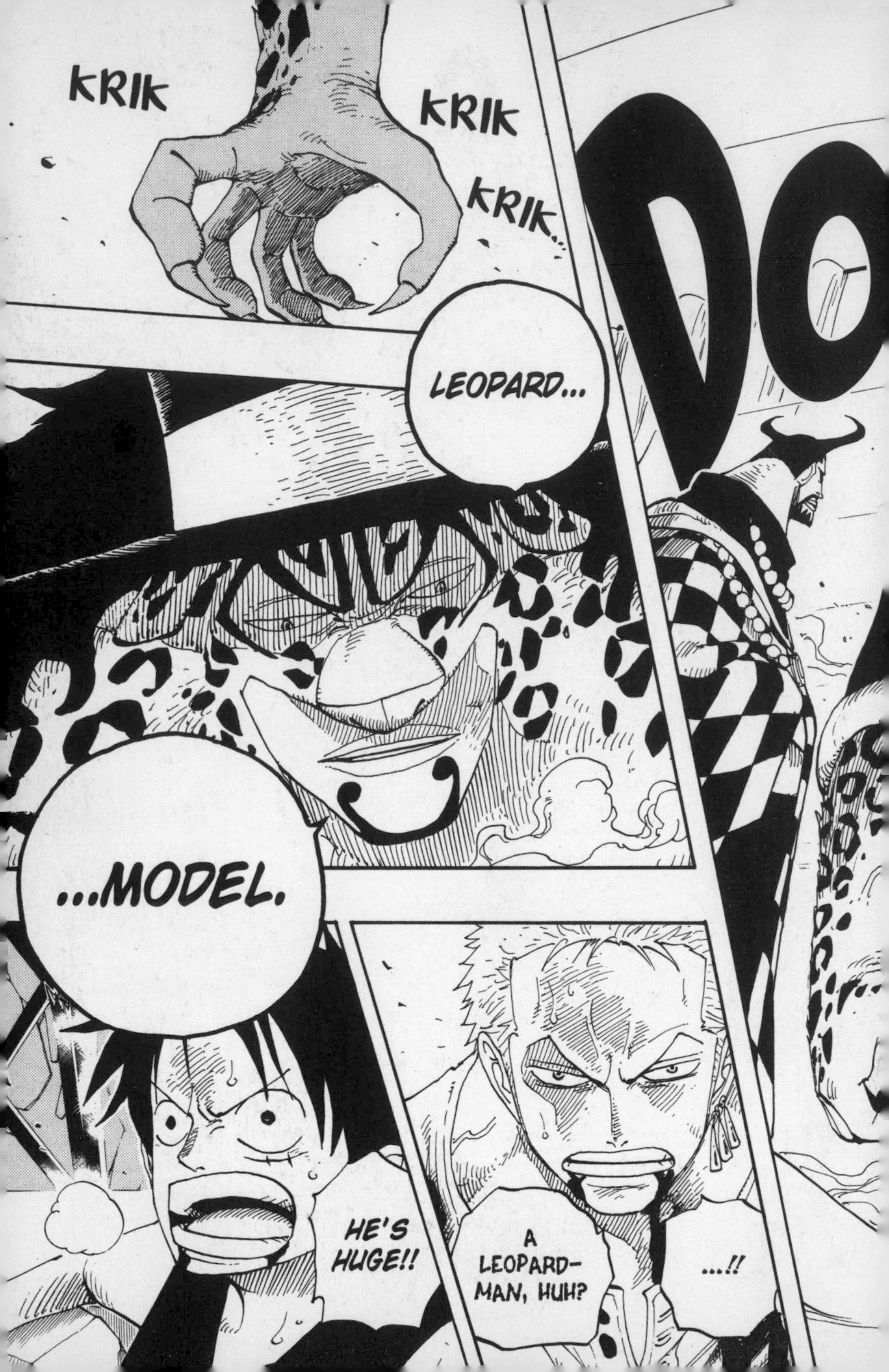
DO
KRIK
KRIK
KRIK...
LEOPARD...
...MODEL.
...!!
A LEOPARD-MAN, HUH?
HE'S HUGE!!

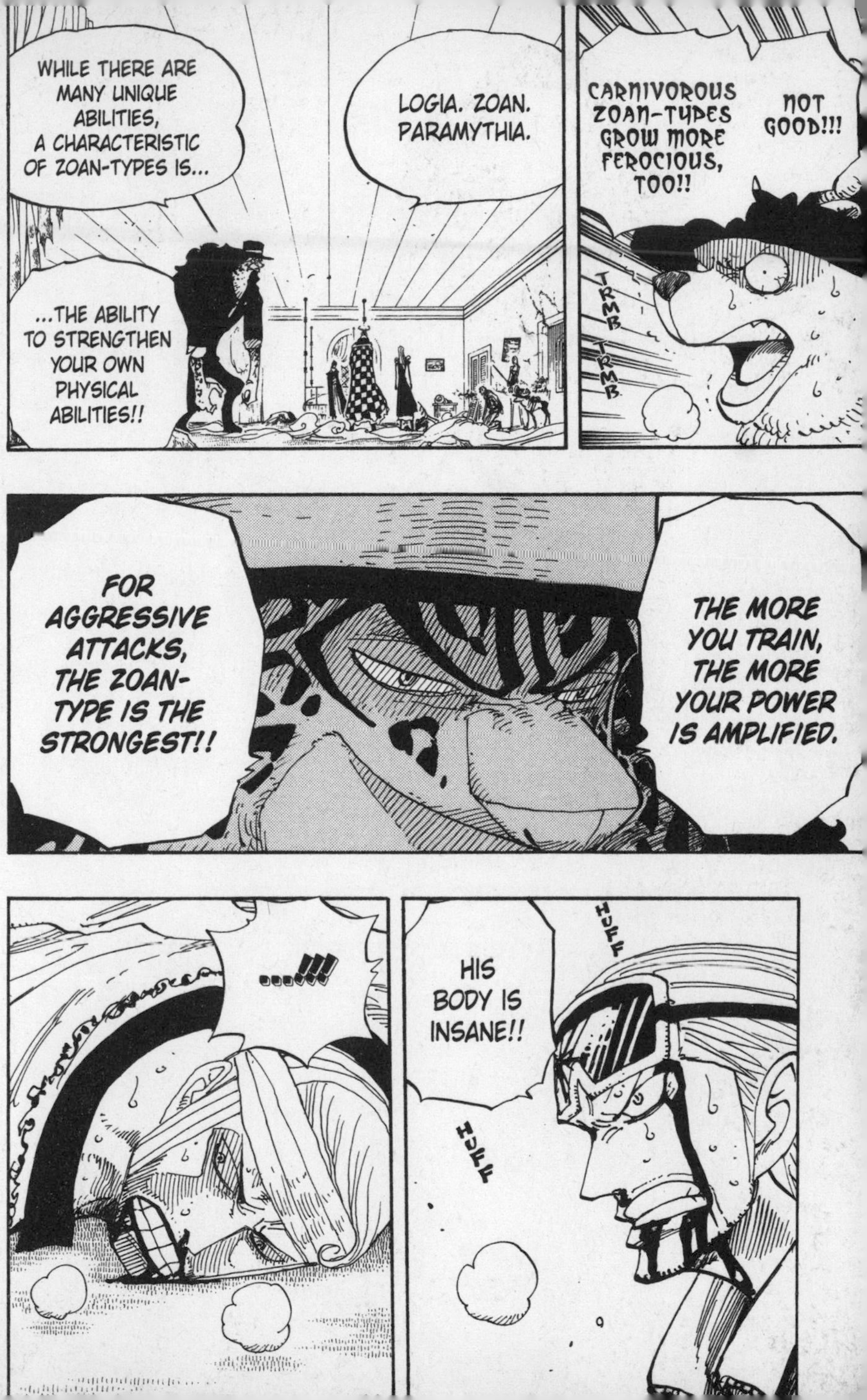
NOT GOOD!!!
CARNIVOROUS ZOAN-TYPES GROW MORE FEROCIOUS, TOO!!
TRMB TRMB
LOGIA. ZOAN. PARAMYTHIA.
WHILE THERE ARE MANY UNIQUE ABILITIES, A CHARACTERISTIC OF ZOAN-TYPES IS...
...THE ABILITY TO STRENGTHEN YOUR OWN PHYSICAL ABILITIES!!
THE MORE YOU TRAIN, THE MORE YOUR POWER IS AMPLIFIED.
FOR AGGRESSIVE ATTACKS, THE ZOAN-TYPE IS THE STRONGEST!!
HUFF
HIS BODY IS INSANE!!
HUFF
...!!!

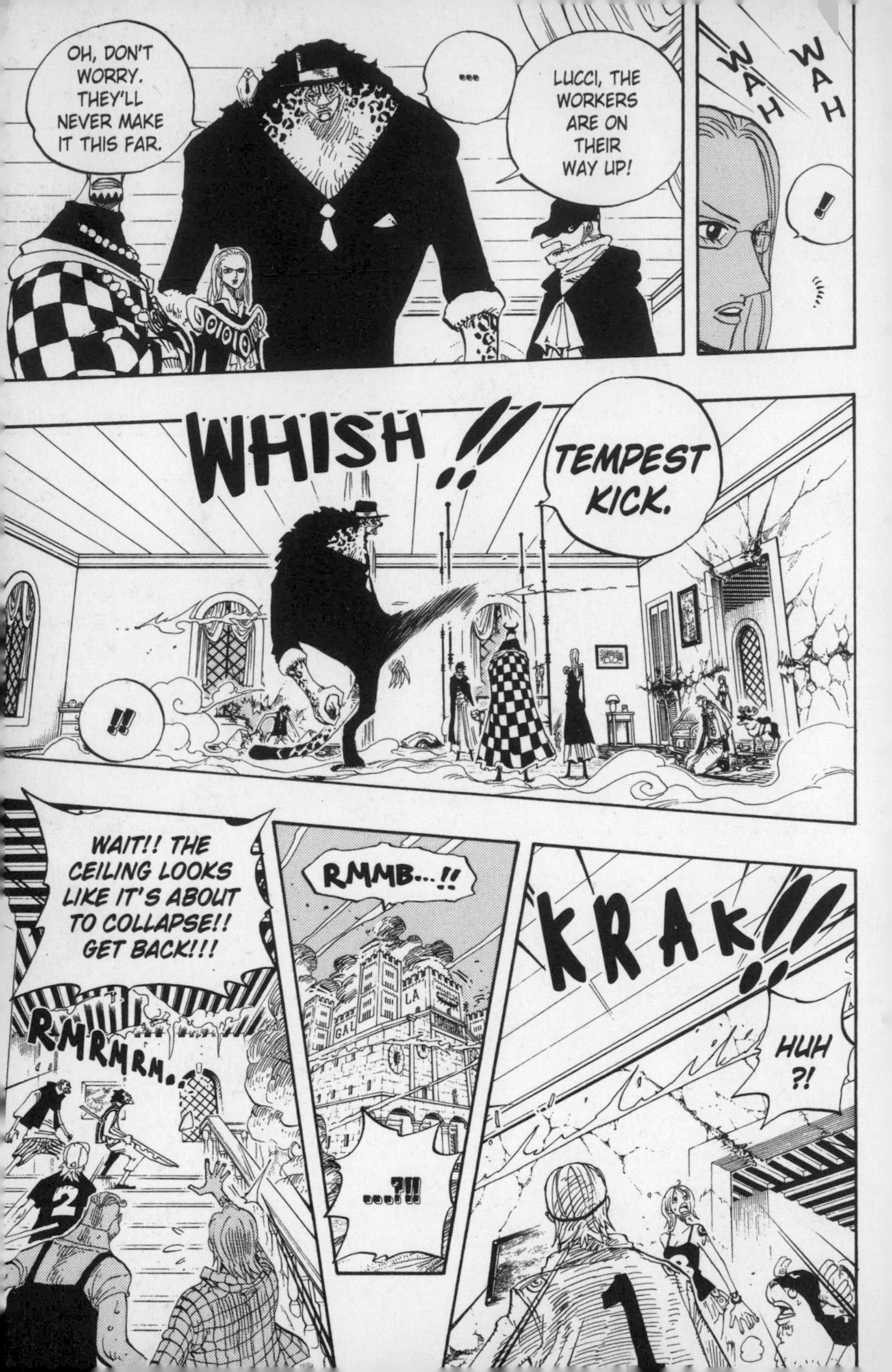
WAH WAH
!
LUCCI, THE WORKERS ARE ON THEIR WAY UP!
...
OH, DON'T WORRY. THEY'LL NEVER MAKE IT THIS FAR.
TEMPEST KICK.
WHISH!!
!!
KRAK!!
HUH?!
RMMB...!!
...?!!
WAIT!! THE CEILING LOOKS LIKE IT'S ABOUT TO COLLAPSE!! GET BACK!!!
RMRMRN.

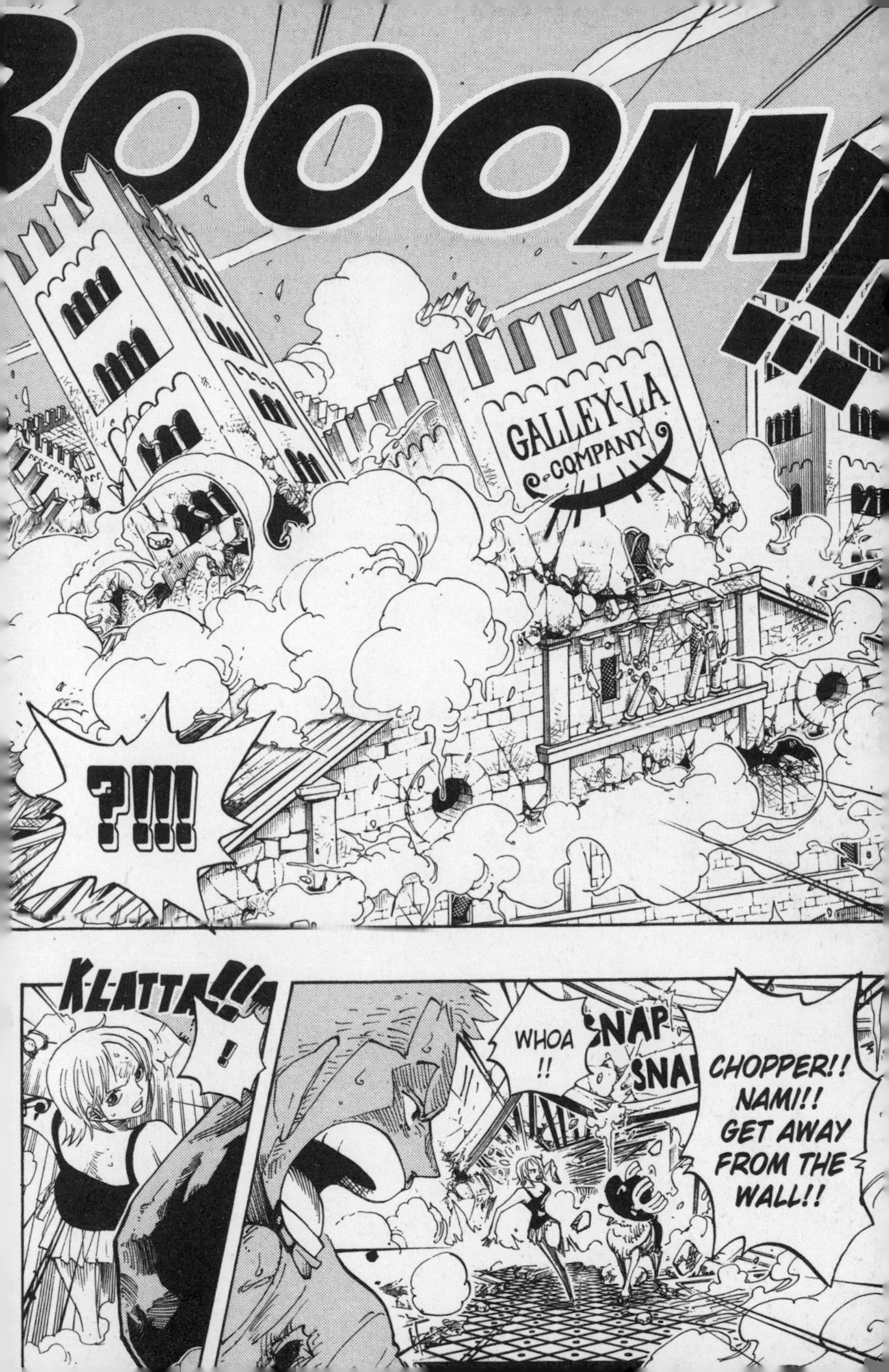
BOOOM!!
GALLEY-LA COMPANY
?!!!
CHOPPER!! NAMI!! GET AWAY FROM THE WALL!!
SNAP
SNA
WHOA !!
KLATTA!!
!

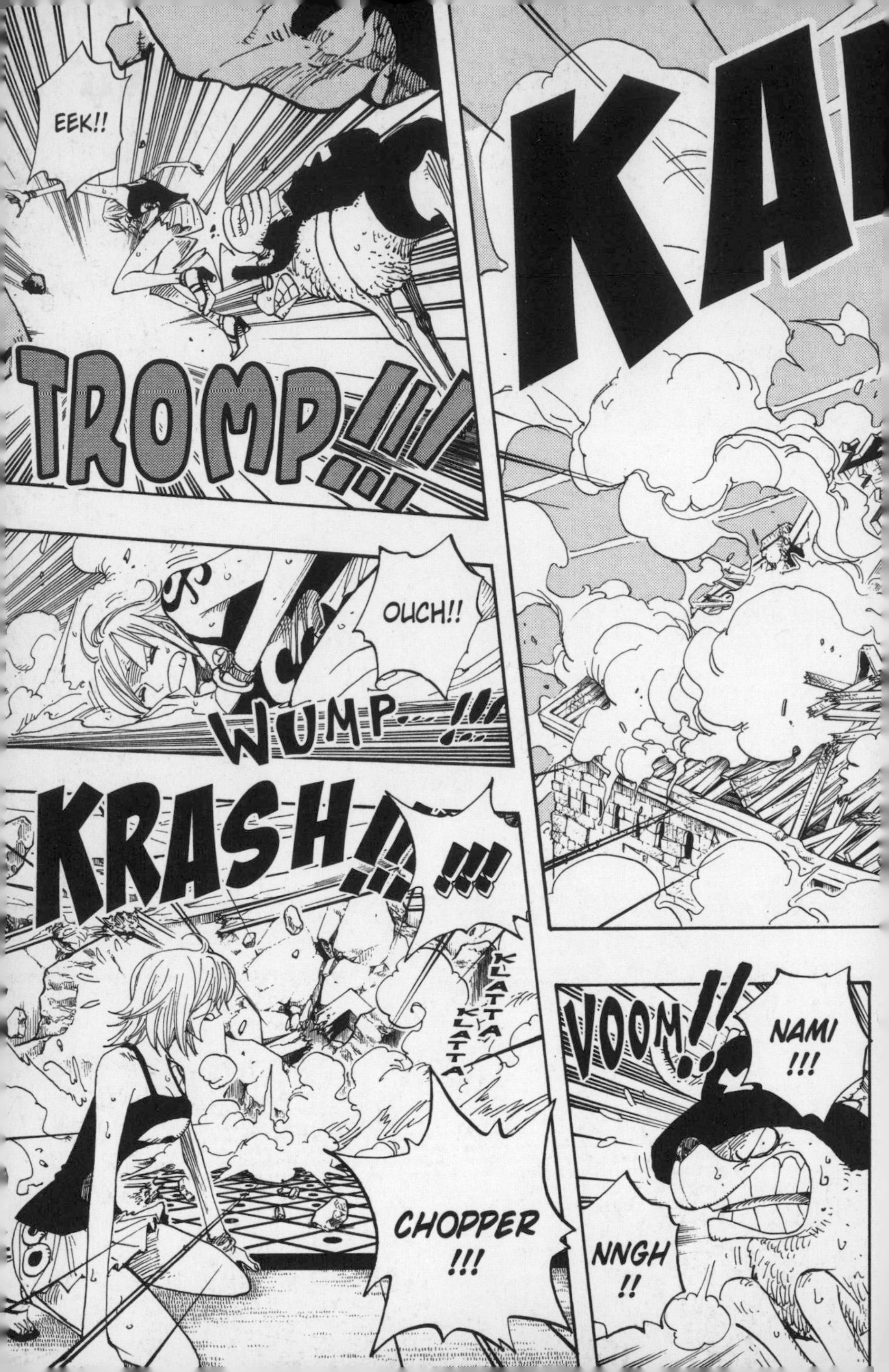
KA
EEK!!
TROMP!!!
OUCH!!
WUMP...!!
VOOM!!
NAMI !!!
NNGH !!
KRASH!!!
KLATTA KLATTA
CHOPPER !!!

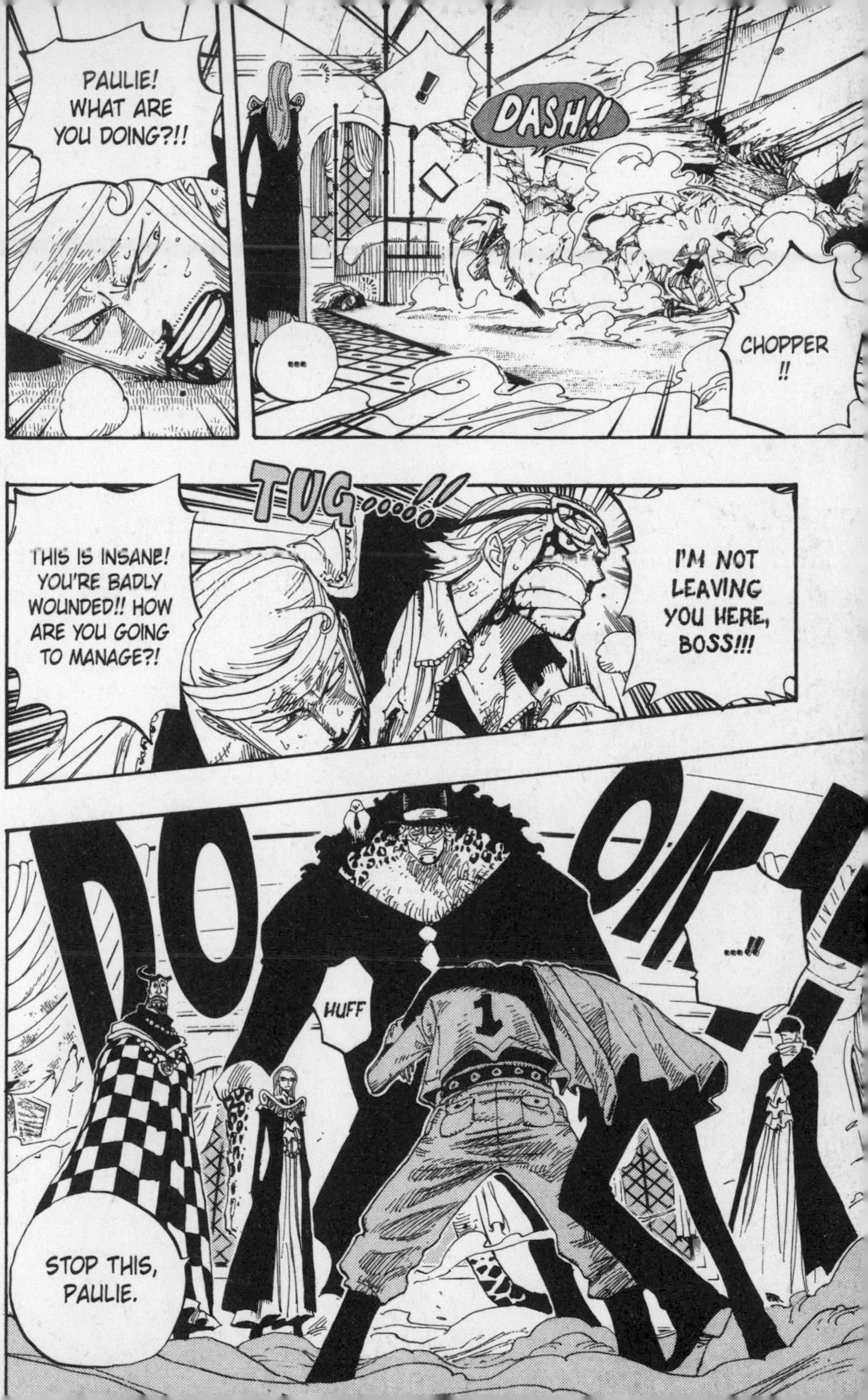
DASH!!
!
CHOPPER !!
...
PAULIE! WHAT ARE YOU DOING?!!
TUG...!!
I'M NOT LEAVING YOU HERE, BOSS!!!
THIS IS INSANE! YOU'RE BADLY WOUNDED!! HOW ARE YOU GOING TO MANAGE?!
DO—ON
...!!
HUFF
STOP THIS, PAULIE.

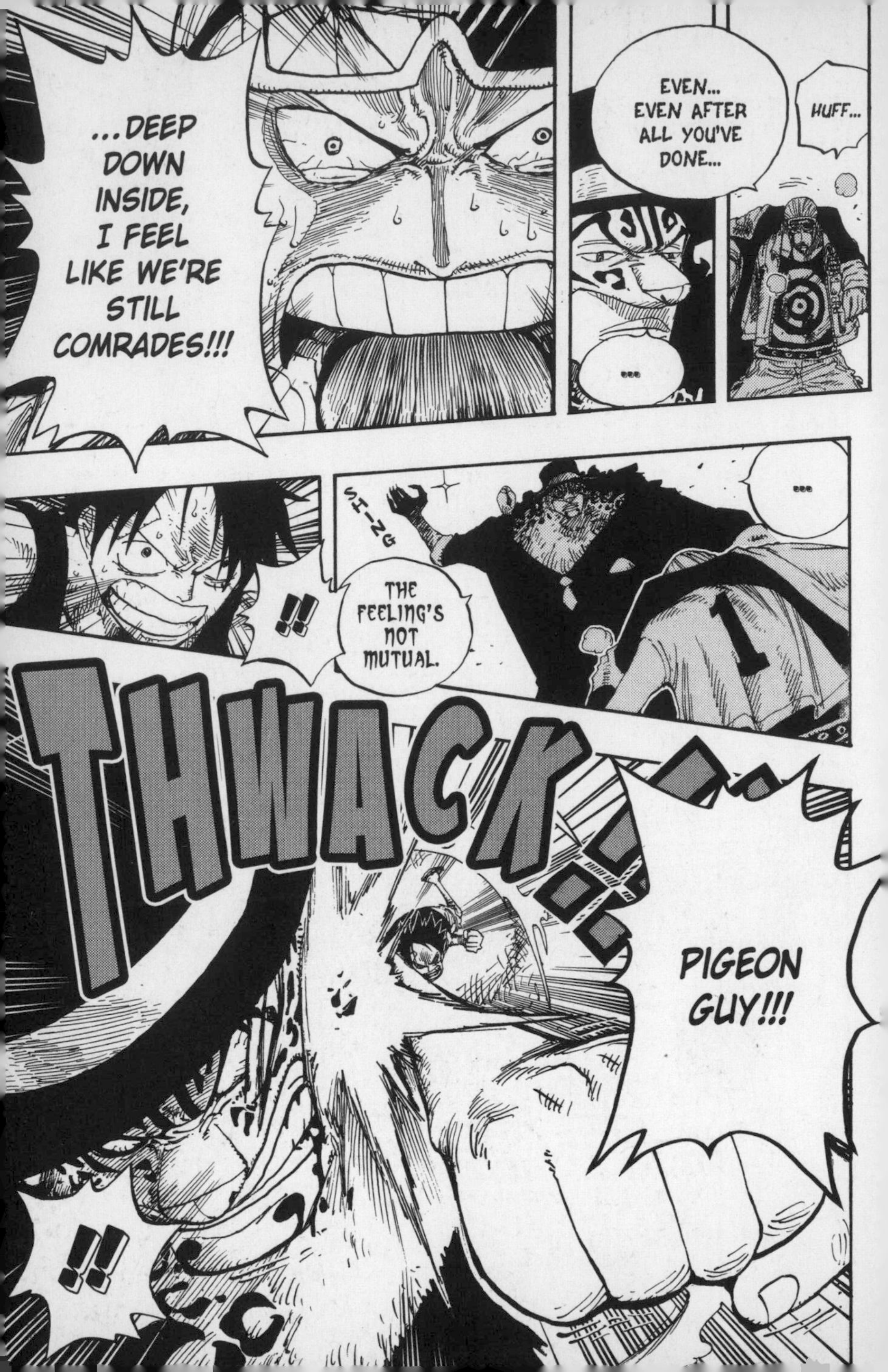
HUFF...
EVEN... EVEN AFTER ALL YOU'VE DONE...
...
...DEEP DOWN INSIDE, I FEEL LIKE WE'RE STILL COMRADES!!!
...
SHING
THE FEELING'S NOT MUTUAL.
!!
THWACK
PIGEON GUY!!!
!!

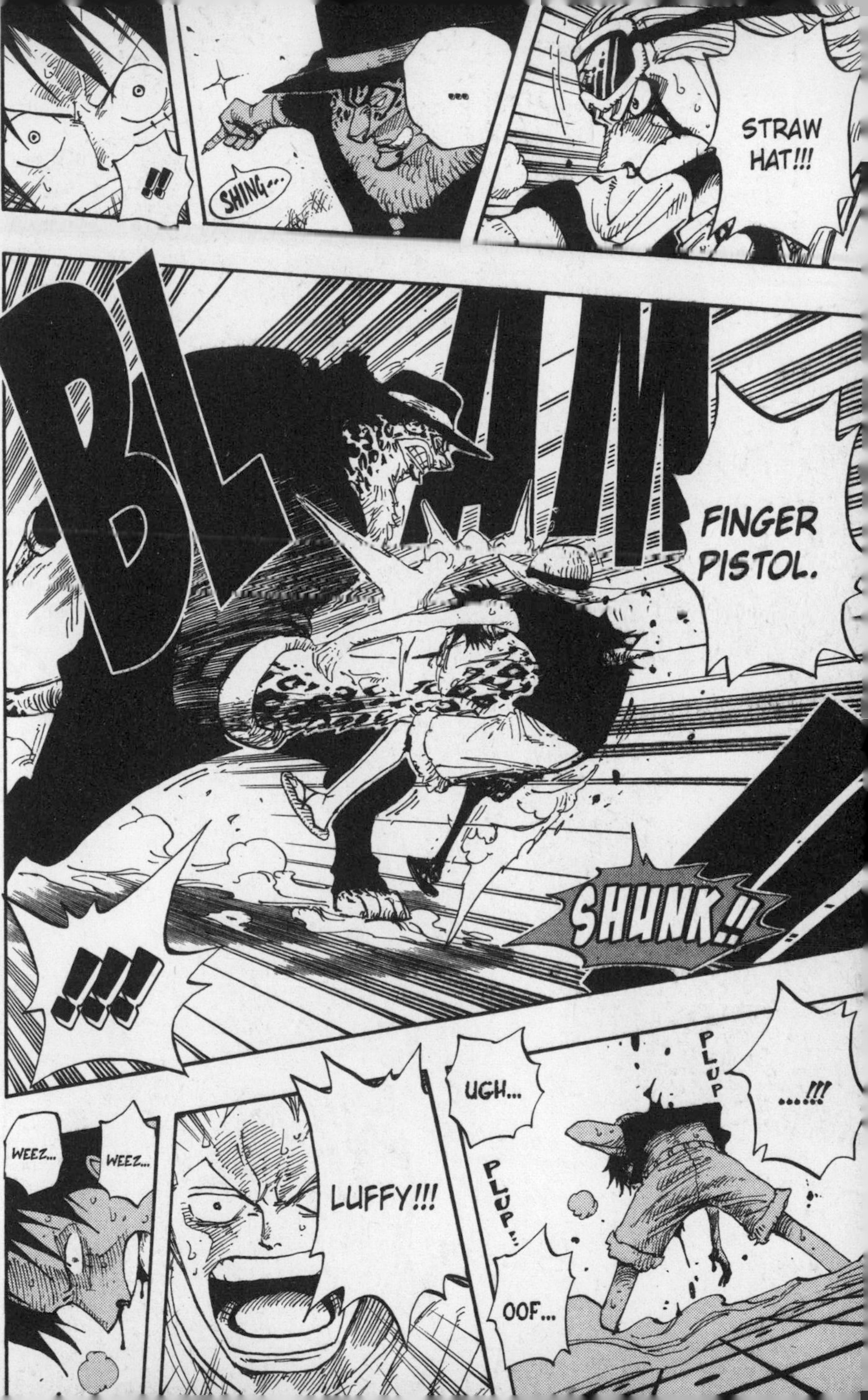
STRAW HAT!!!
...
SHING...
!!
FINGER PISTOL.
BLAM
SHUNK!!
!!!
...!!!
PLUP
UGH...
PLUP...
OOF...
LUFFY!!!
WEEZ...
WEEZ...

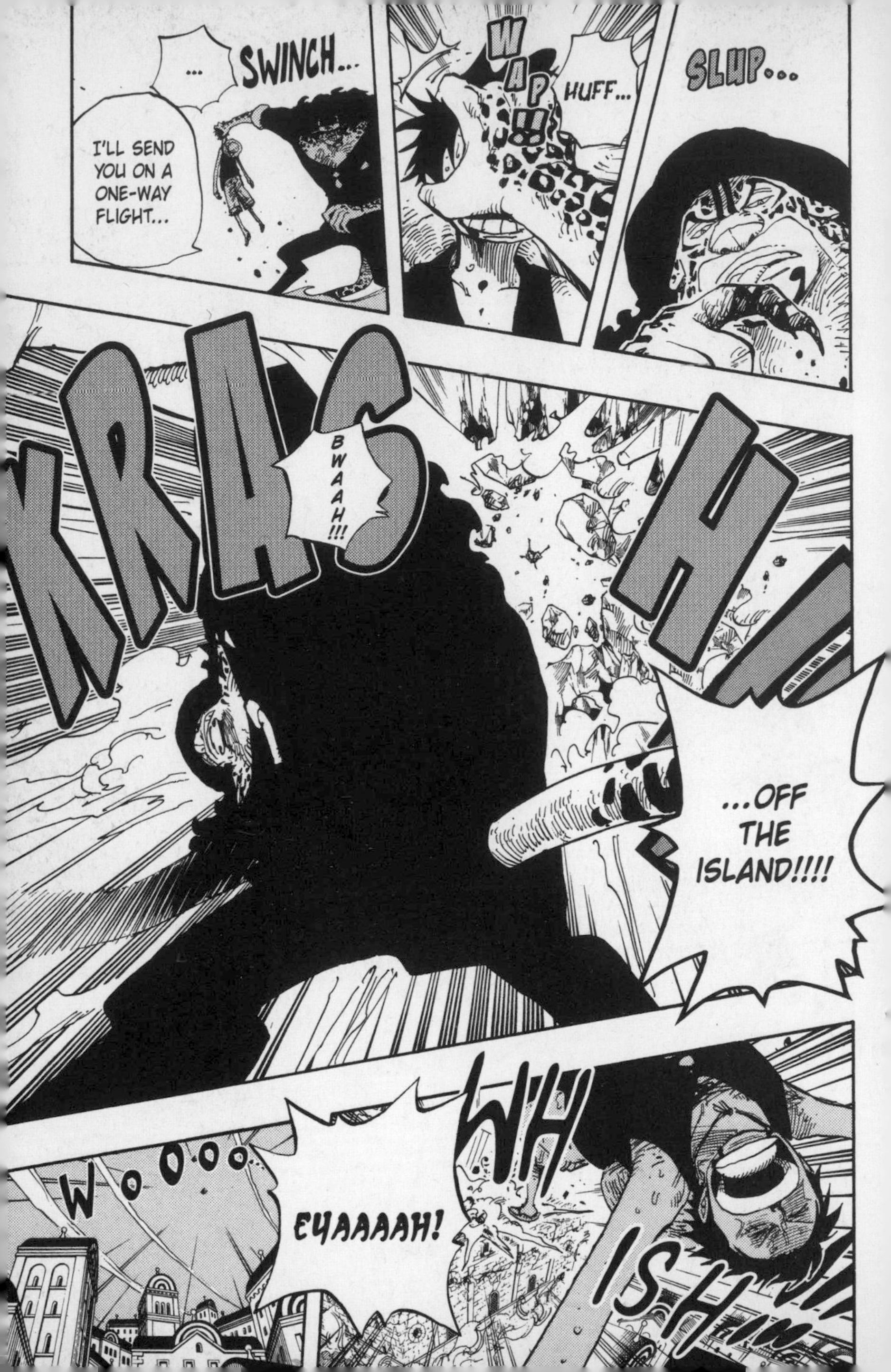
SLUP...
WAP!!
HUFF...
...
SWINCH...
I'LL SEND YOU ON A ONE-WAY FLIGHT...
KRASH
BWAAAH!!!
...OFF THE ISLAND!!!!
WHISH
EYAAAAH!
WOOOO...

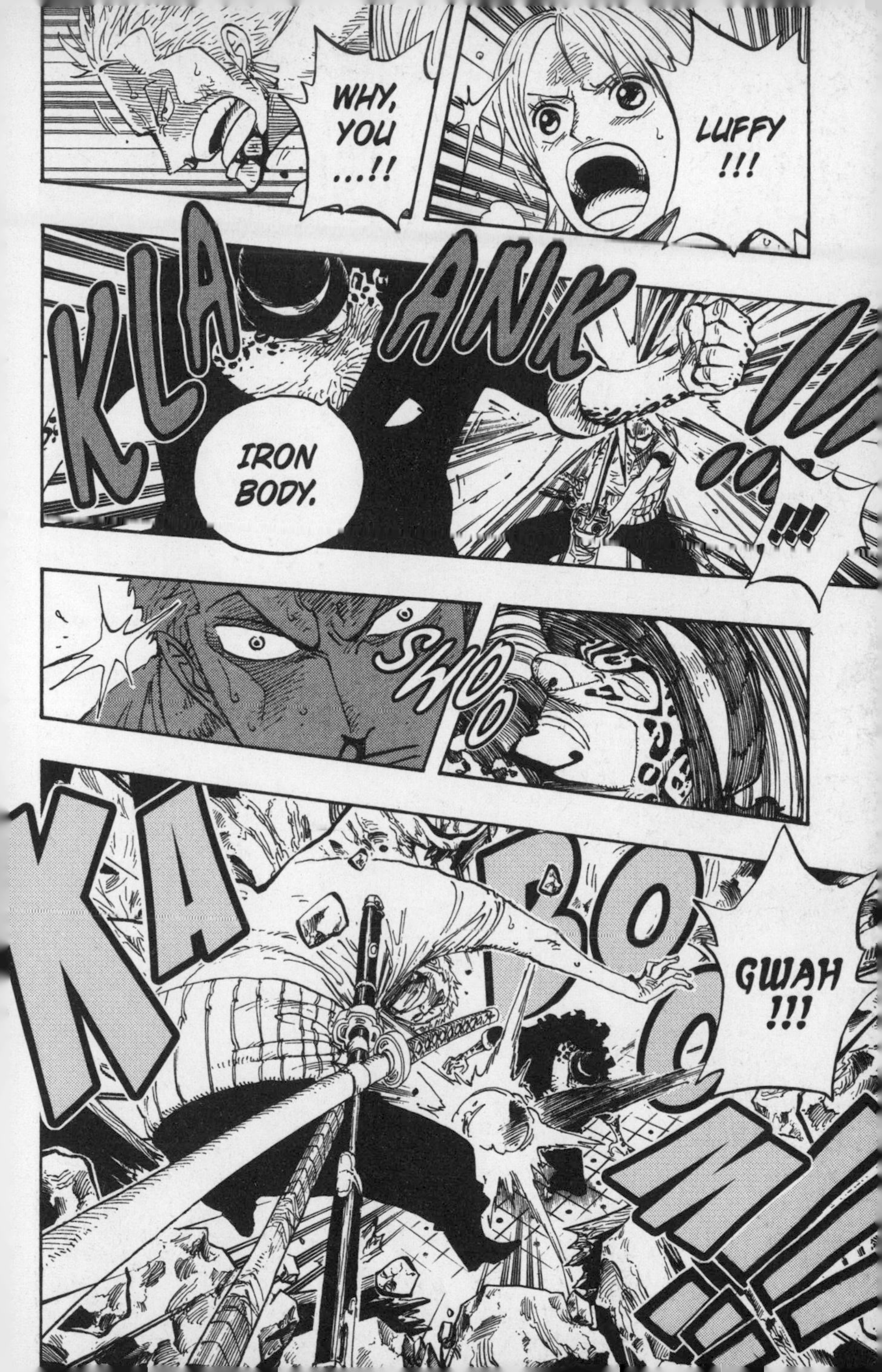
LUFFY !!!
WHY, YOU ...!!
KLA ANK
IRON BODY.
...!!!
SHOO
GWAH !!!
KA BO

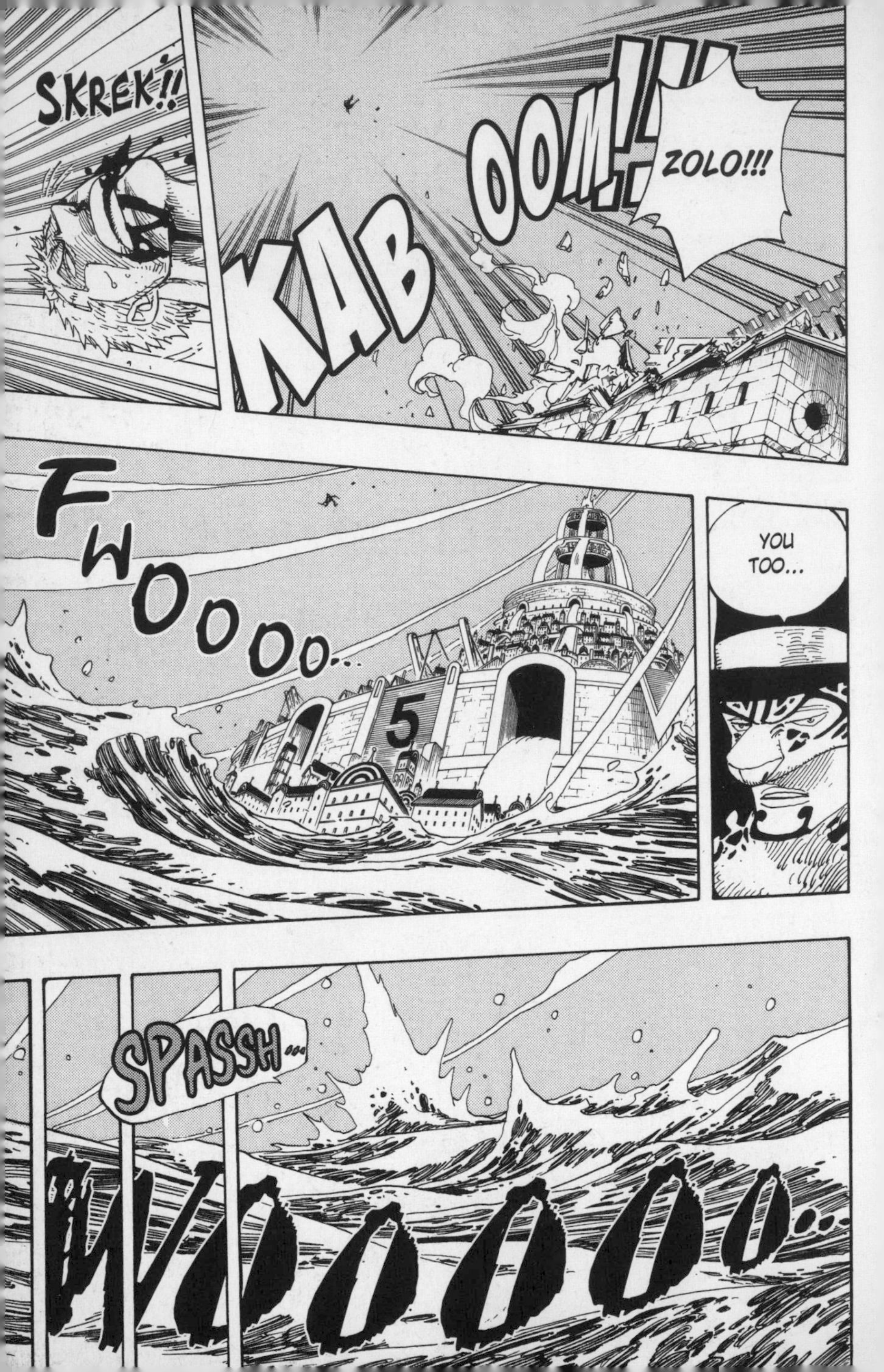
ZOLO!!!
KAB OOM!!!
SKREK!!
YOU TOO...
FWOOOO...
SPASSH...
WOOOOO...

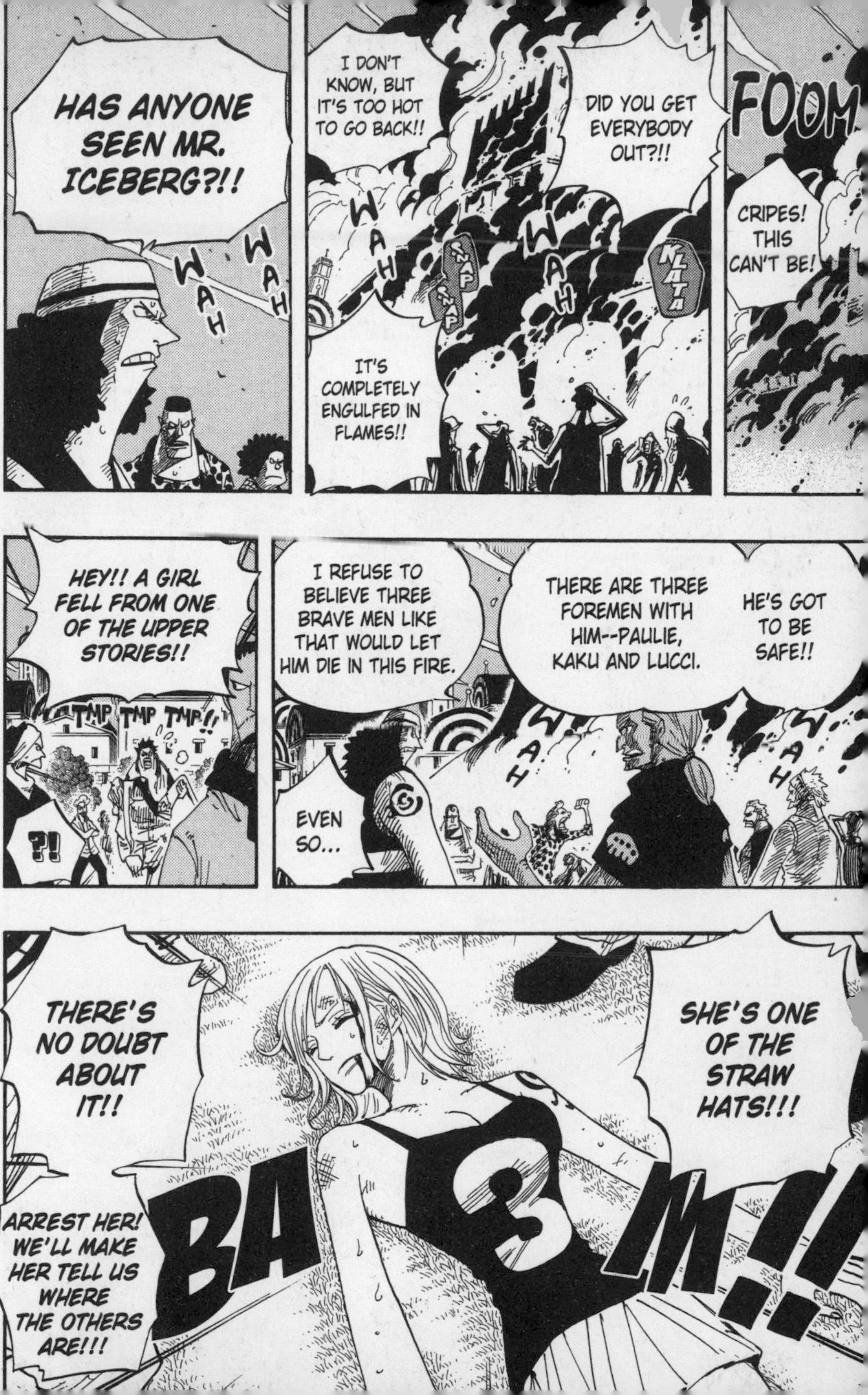
FOOM
CRIPES! THIS CAN'T BE!
DID YOU GET EVERYBODY OUT?!!
I DON'T KNOW, BUT IT'S TOO HOT TO GO BACK!!
WAH WAH
KLATA
SNAP SNAP
IT'S COMPLETELY ENGULFED IN FLAMES!!
HAS ANYONE SEEN MR. ICEBERG?!!
WAH WAH
THERE ARE THREE FOREMEN WITH HIM--PAULIE, KAKU AND LUCCI.
HE'S GOT TO BE SAFE!!
WAH
WAH
I REFUSE TO BELIEVE THREE BRAVE MEN LIKE THAT WOULD LET HIM DIE IN THIS FIRE.
EVEN SO...
HEY!! A GIRL FELL FROM ONE OF THE UPPER STORIES!!
TMP TMP TMP!!
?!
SHE'S ONE OF THE STRAW HATS!!!
BAM!!
THERE'S NO DOUBT ABOUT IT!!
ARREST HER! WE'LL MAKE HER TELL US WHERE THE OTHERS ARE!!!

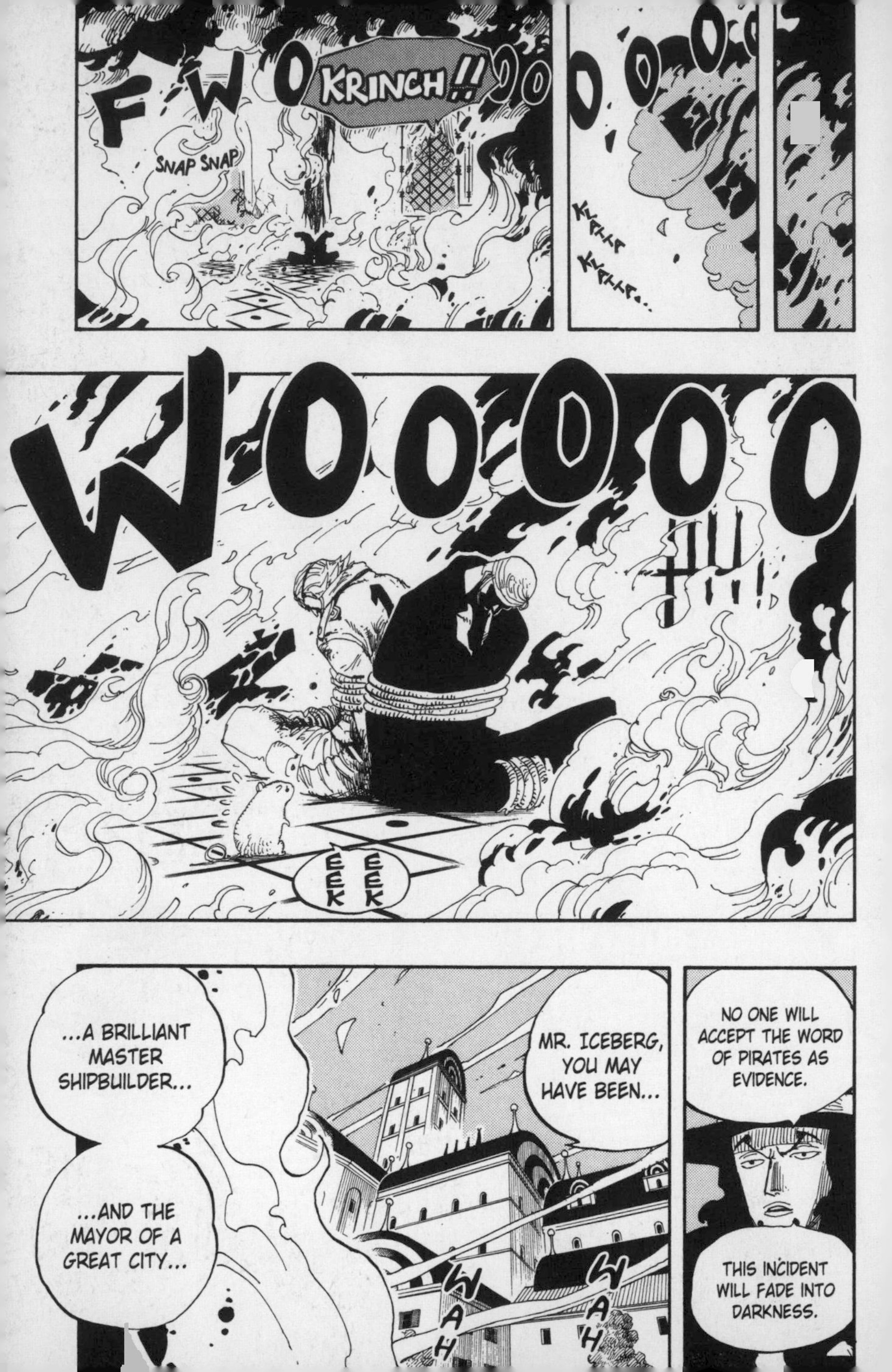
FWOOOO
KRINCH!!
SNAP SNAP
WOOOOO!!!
EEK EEK
NO ONE WILL ACCEPT THE WORD OF PIRATES AS EVIDENCE.
THIS INCIDENT WILL FADE INTO DARKNESS.
MR. ICEBERG, YOU MAY HAVE BEEN...
...A BRILLIANT MASTER SHIPBUILDER...
...AND THE MAYOR OF A GREAT CITY...
WAH
WAH

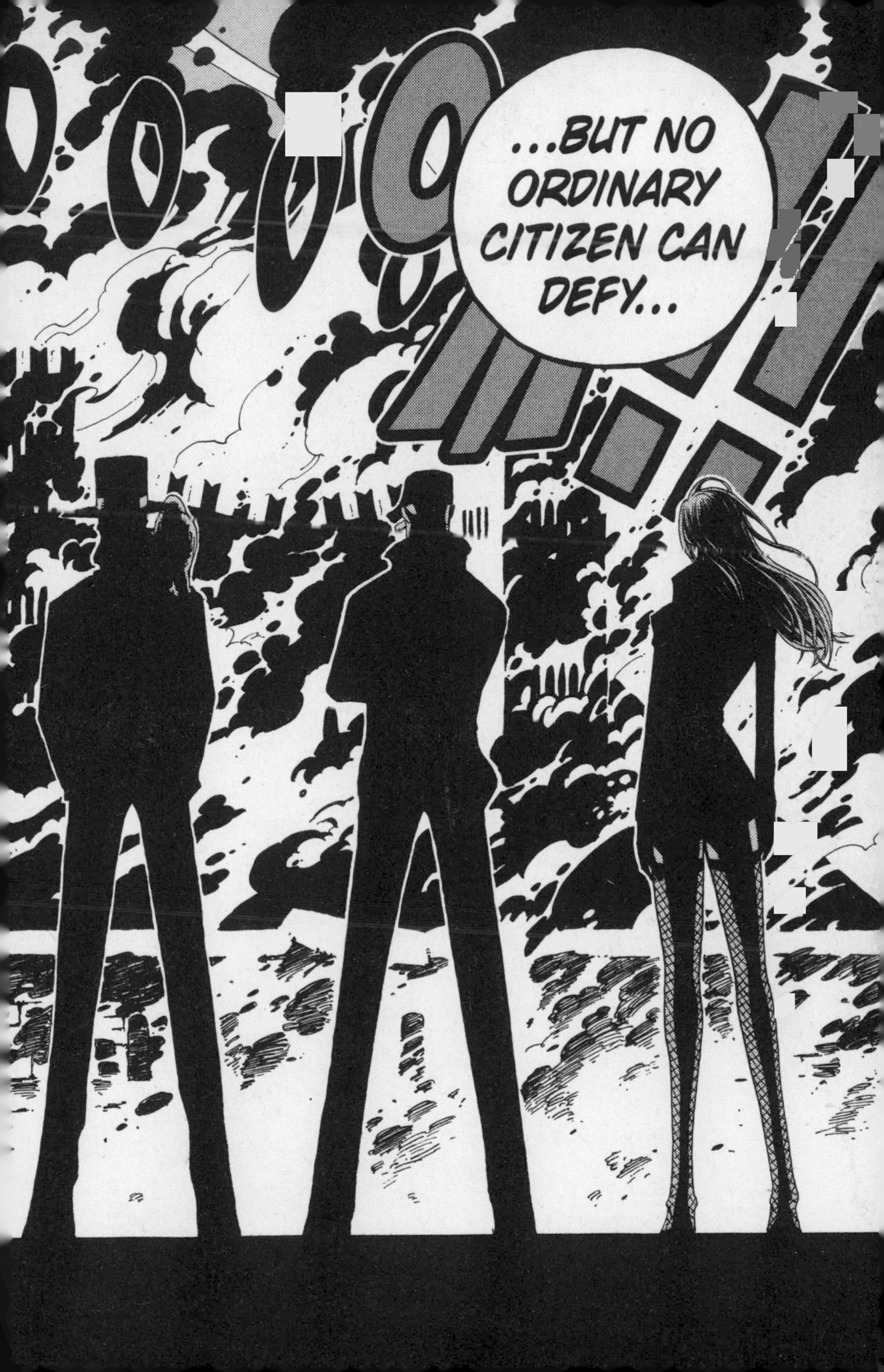
...BUT NO ORDINARY CITIZEN CAN DEFY...

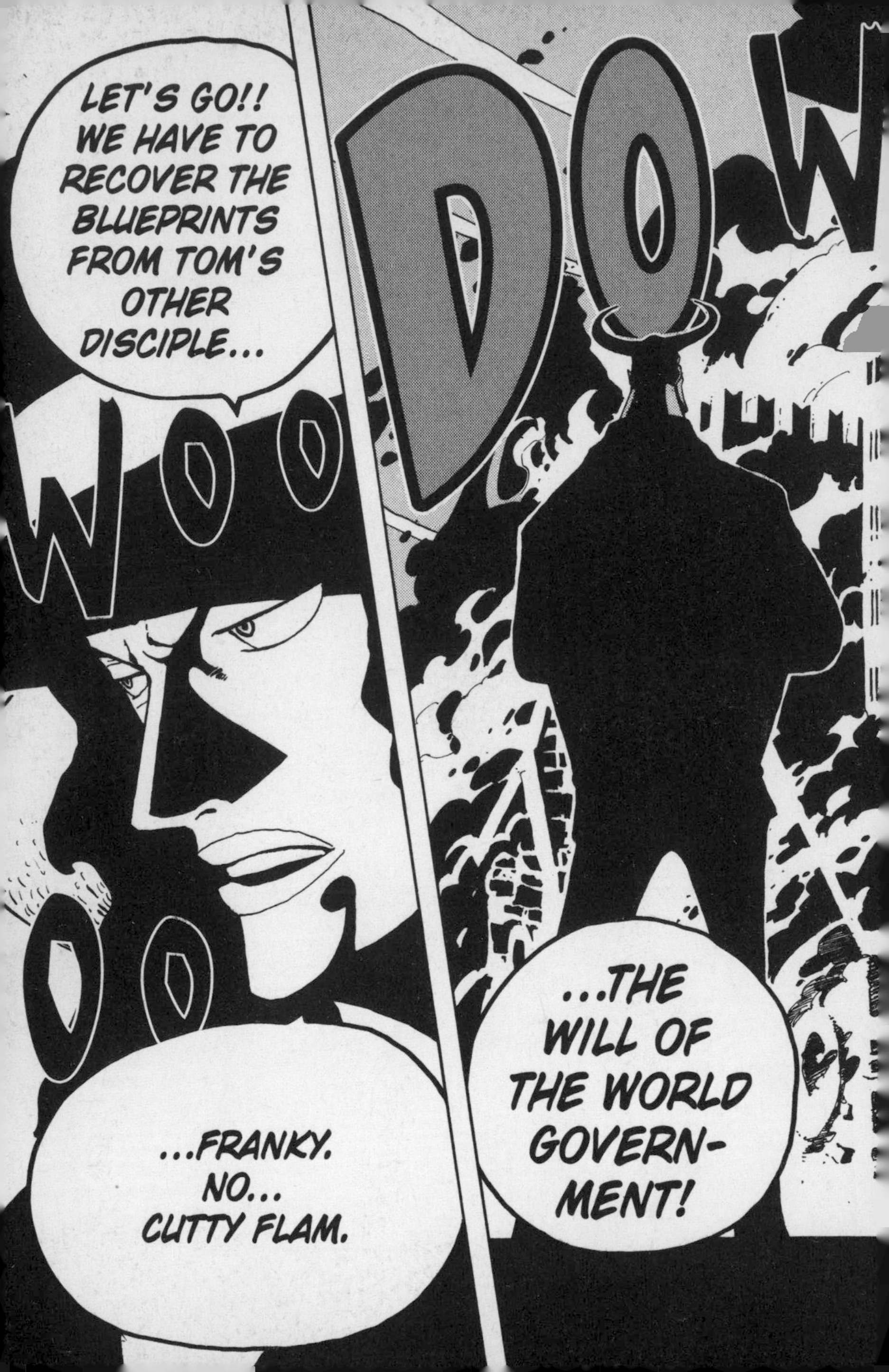
DOW
...THE WILL OF THE WORLD GOVERNMENT!
LET'S GO!! WE HAVE TO RECOVER THE BLUEPRINTS FROM TOM'S OTHER DISCIPLE...
WOOOO
...FRANKY. NO... CUTTY FLAM.

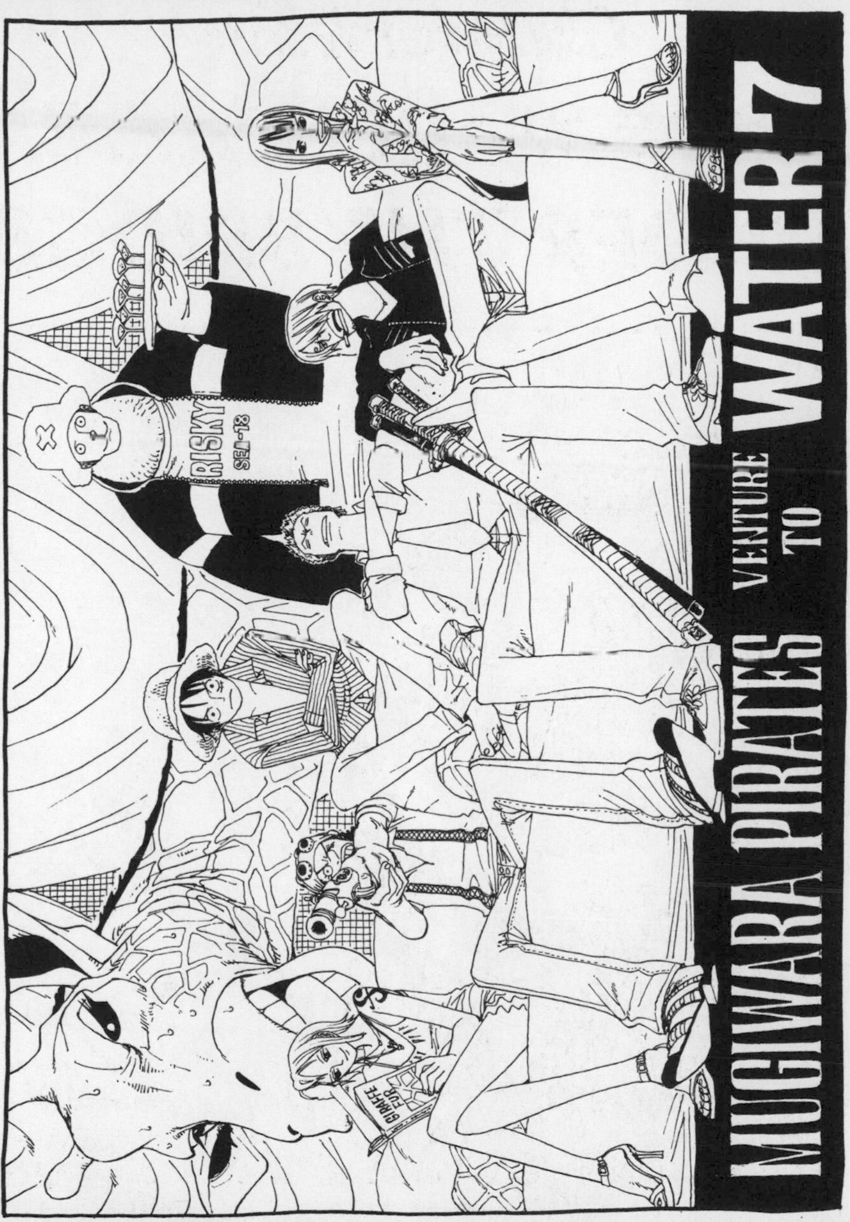
MUGIWARA PIRATES VENTURE TO WATER 7
RISKY
SEA-18
GIRAFFE FUR

Chapter 350: THE WAREHOUSE UNDER THE BRIDGE

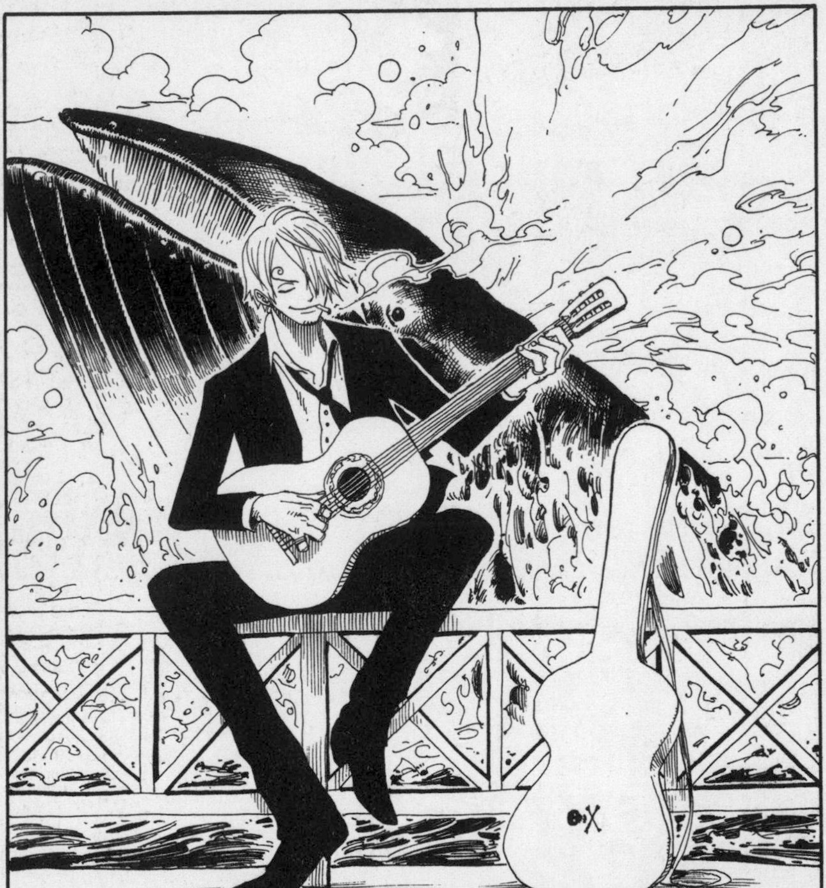

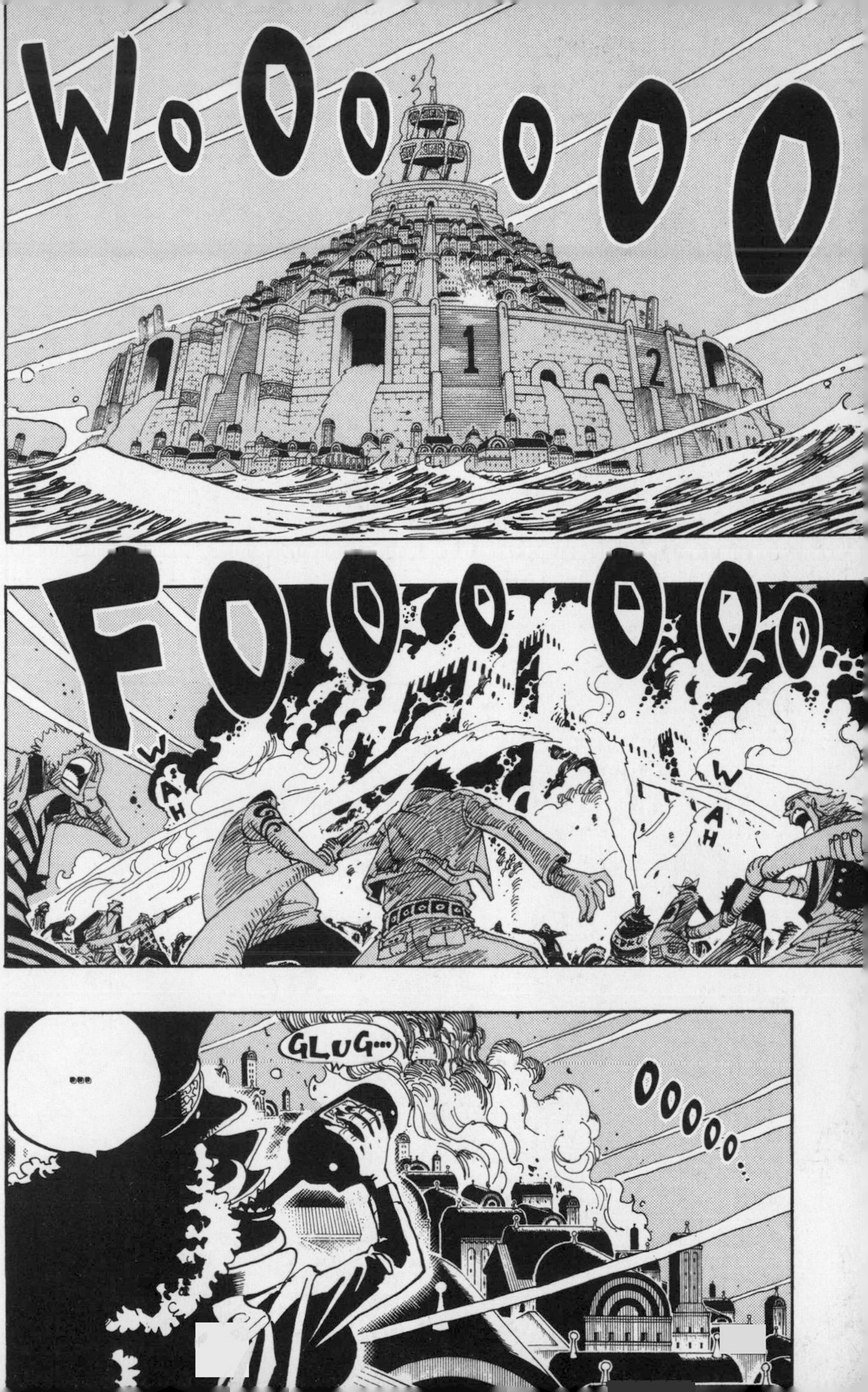
WOOOOOO
FOOOOOO...
WAAH
WAAH
OOOOO...
GLUG...
...

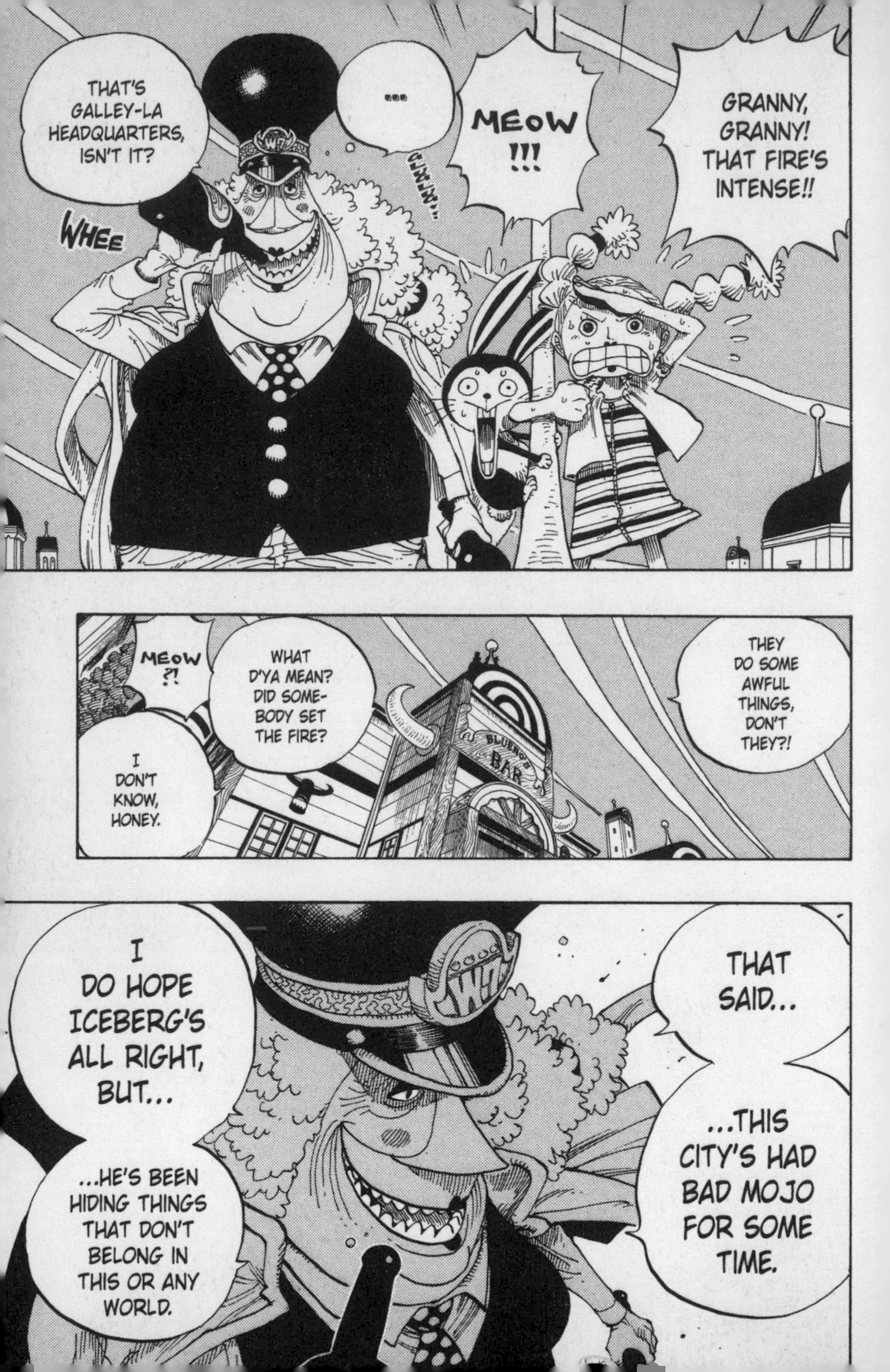
GRANNY, GRANNY! THAT FIRE'S INTENSE!!
MEOW !!!
...
THAT'S GALLEY-LA HEADQUARTERS, ISN'T IT?
WHEE
THEY DO SOME AWFUL THINGS, DON'T THEY?!
WHAT D'YA MEAN? DID SOMEBODY SET THE FIRE?
MEOW ?!
BAR
I DON'T KNOW, HONEY.
THAT SAID...
...THIS CITY'S HAD BAD MOJO FOR SOME TIME.
I DO HOPE ICEBERG'S ALL RIGHT, BUT...
...HE'S BEEN HIDING THINGS THAT DON'T BELONG IN THIS OR ANY WORLD.

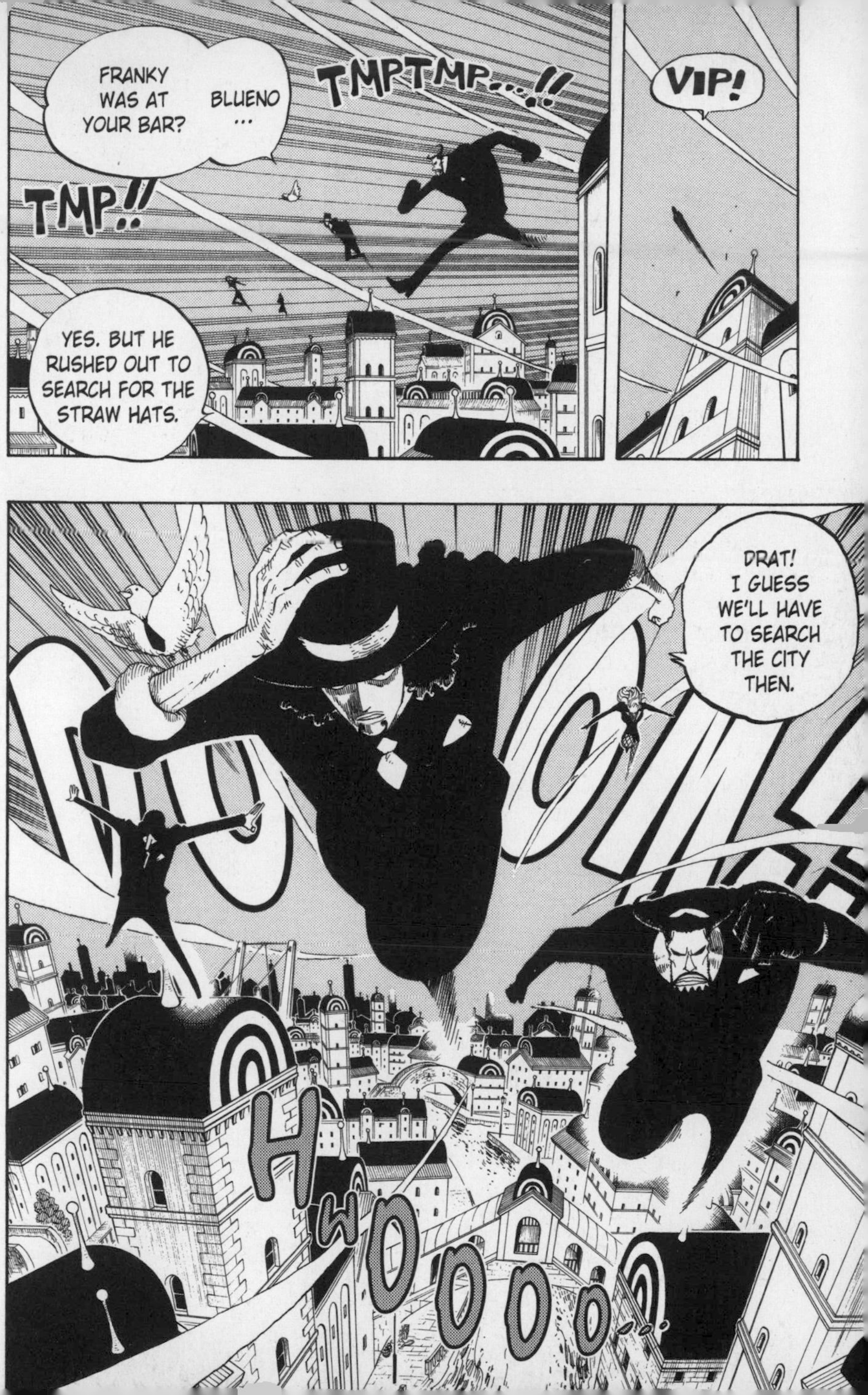
VIP!
TMPTMP...!!
BLUENO ...
FRANKY WAS AT YOUR BAR?
TMP!!
YES. BUT HE RUSHED OUT TO SEARCH FOR THE STRAW HATS.
DRAT! I GUESS WE'LL HAVE TO SEARCH THE CITY THEN.
HWOOOOO...

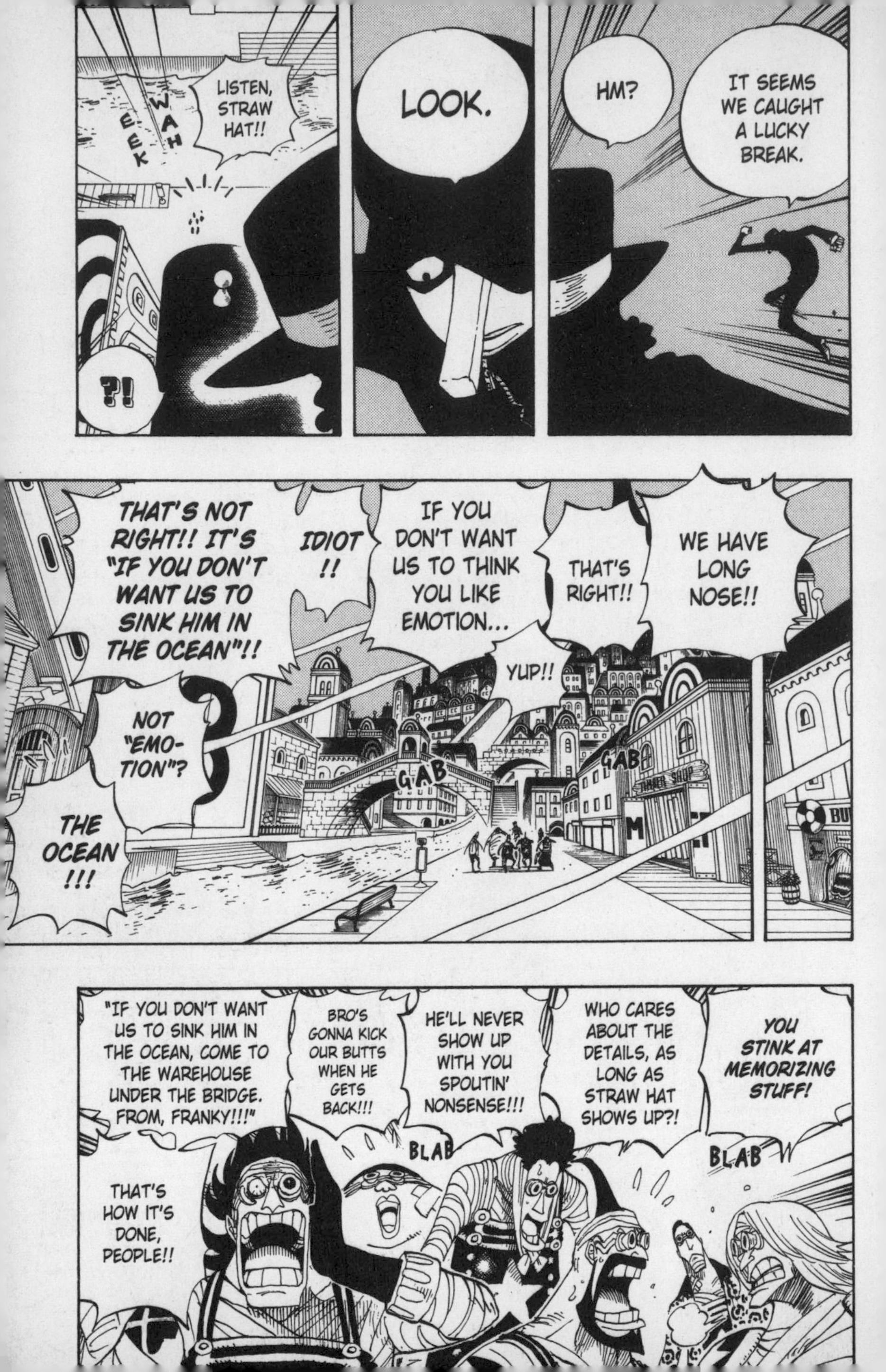
IT SEEMS WE CAUGHT A LUCKY BREAK.
HM?
LOOK.
LISTEN, STRAW HAT!!
WAH
EEEK
?!
WE HAVE LONG NOSE!!
THAT'S RIGHT!!
IF YOU DON'T WANT US TO THINK YOU LIKE EMOTION...
YUP!!
IDIOT!!
THAT'S NOT RIGHT!! IT'S "IF YOU DON'T WANT US TO SINK HIM IN THE OCEAN"!!
GAB
GAB
NOT "EMO-TION"?
THE OCEAN!!!
YOU STINK AT MEMORIZING STUFF!
WHO CARES ABOUT THE DETAILS, AS LONG AS STRAW HAT SHOWS UP?!
BLAB
HE'LL NEVER SHOW UP WITH YOU SPOUTIN' NONSENSE!!!
BRO'S GONNA KICK OUR BUTTS WHEN HE GETS BACK!!!
BLAB
"IF YOU DON'T WANT US TO SINK HIM IN THE OCEAN, COME TO THE WAREHOUSE UNDER THE BRIDGE. FROM, FRANKY!!!"
THAT'S HOW IT'S DONE, PEOPLE!!

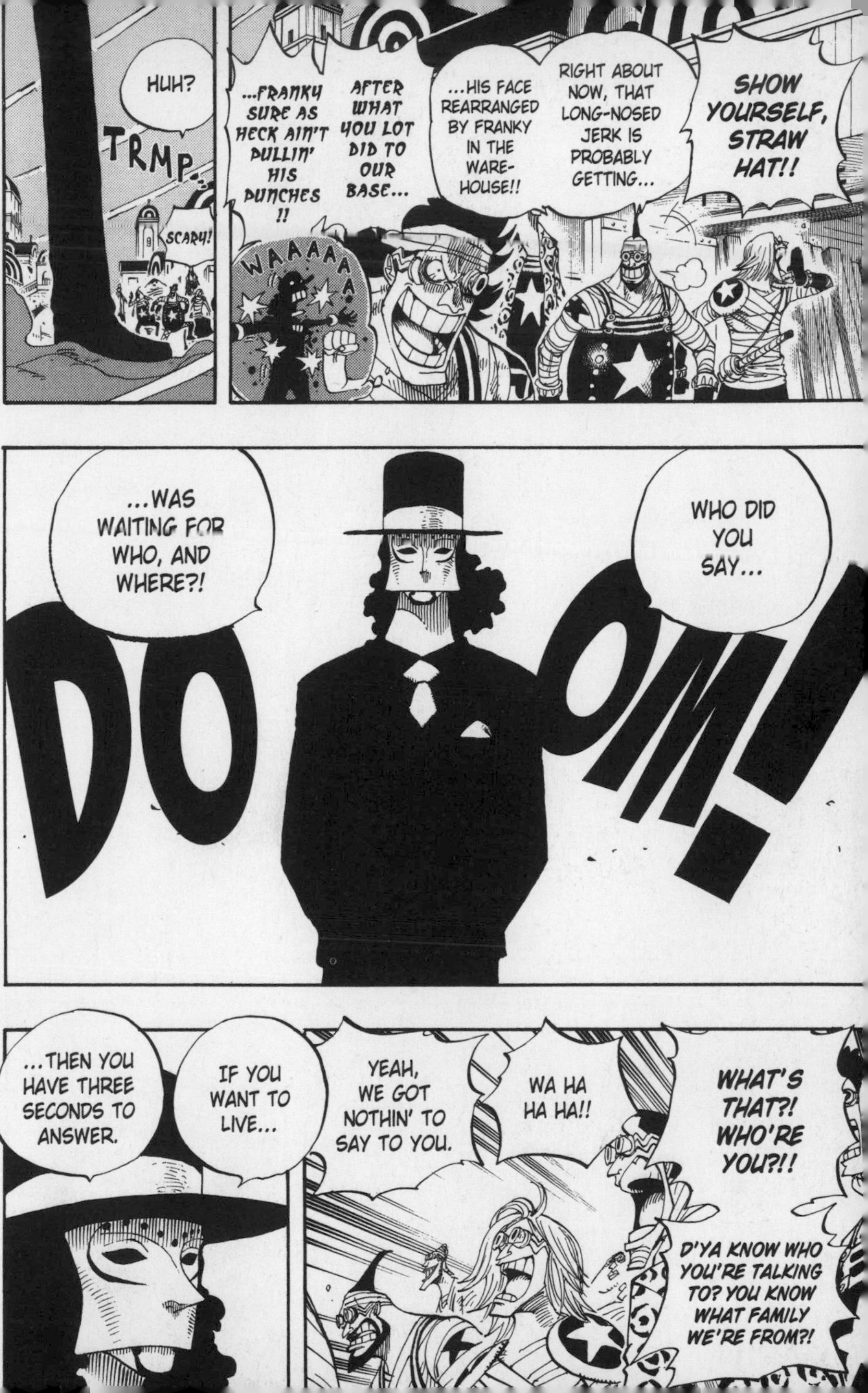
SHOW YOURSELF, STRAW HAT!!
RIGHT ABOUT NOW, THAT LONG-NOSED JERK IS PROBABLY GETTING...
...HIS FACE REARRANGED BY FRANKY IN THE WARE-HOUSE!!
AFTER WHAT YOU LOT DID TO OUR BASE...
...FRANKY SURE AS HECK AIN'T PULLIN' HIS PUNCHES !!
WAAAAAA
HUH?
TRMP
SCARY!
WHO DID YOU SAY...
...WAS WAITING FOR WHO, AND WHERE?!
DOOM!
WHAT'S THAT?! WHO'RE YOU?!!
WA HA HA HA!!
YEAH, WE GOT NOTHIN' TO SAY TO YOU.
D'YA KNOW WHO YOU'RE TALKING TO? YOU KNOW WHAT FAMILY WE'RE FROM?!
IF YOU WANT TO LIVE...
...THEN YOU HAVE THREE SECONDS TO ANSWER.

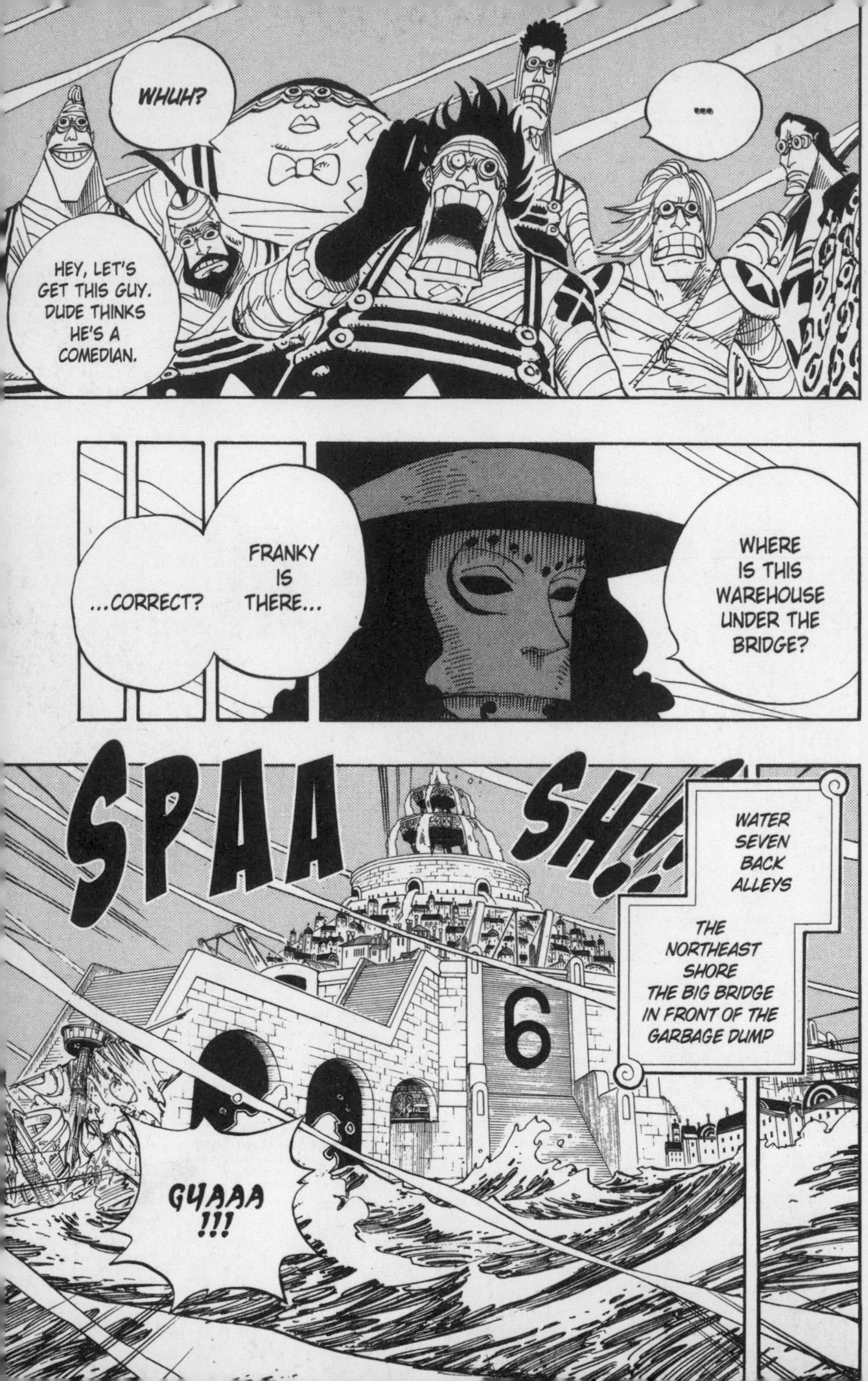
...
WHUH?
HEY, LET'S GET THIS GUY. DUDE THINKS HE'S A COMEDIAN.
WHERE IS THIS WAREHOUSE UNDER THE BRIDGE?
FRANKY IS THERE...
...CORRECT?
WATER SEVEN BACK ALLEYS
THE NORTHEAST SHORE THE BIG BRIDGE IN FRONT OF THE GARBAGE DUMP
SH
SPAA
6
GUAAA !!!

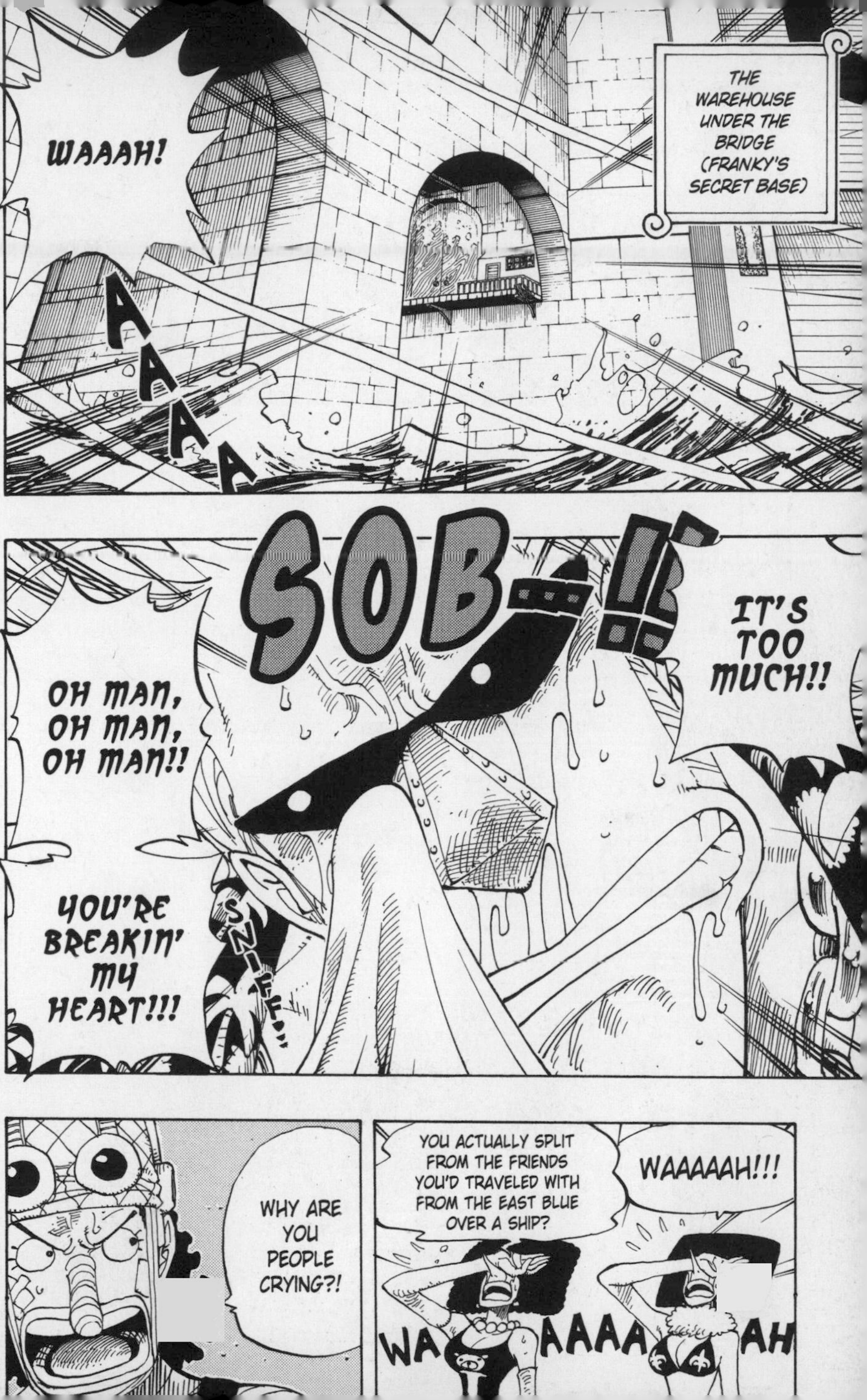
THE WAREHOUSE UNDER THE BRIDGE (FRANKY'S SECRET BASE)
WAAAH!
AAAA
IT'S TOO MUCH!!
SOB...!!
SNIFF..
OH MAN, OH MAN, OH MAN!!
YOU'RE BREAKIN' MY HEART!!!
WAAAAAH!!!
YOU ACTUALLY SPLIT FROM THE FRIENDS YOU'D TRAVELED WITH FROM THE EAST BLUE OVER A SHIP?
WA AAAA AH
WHY ARE YOU PEOPLE CRYING?!

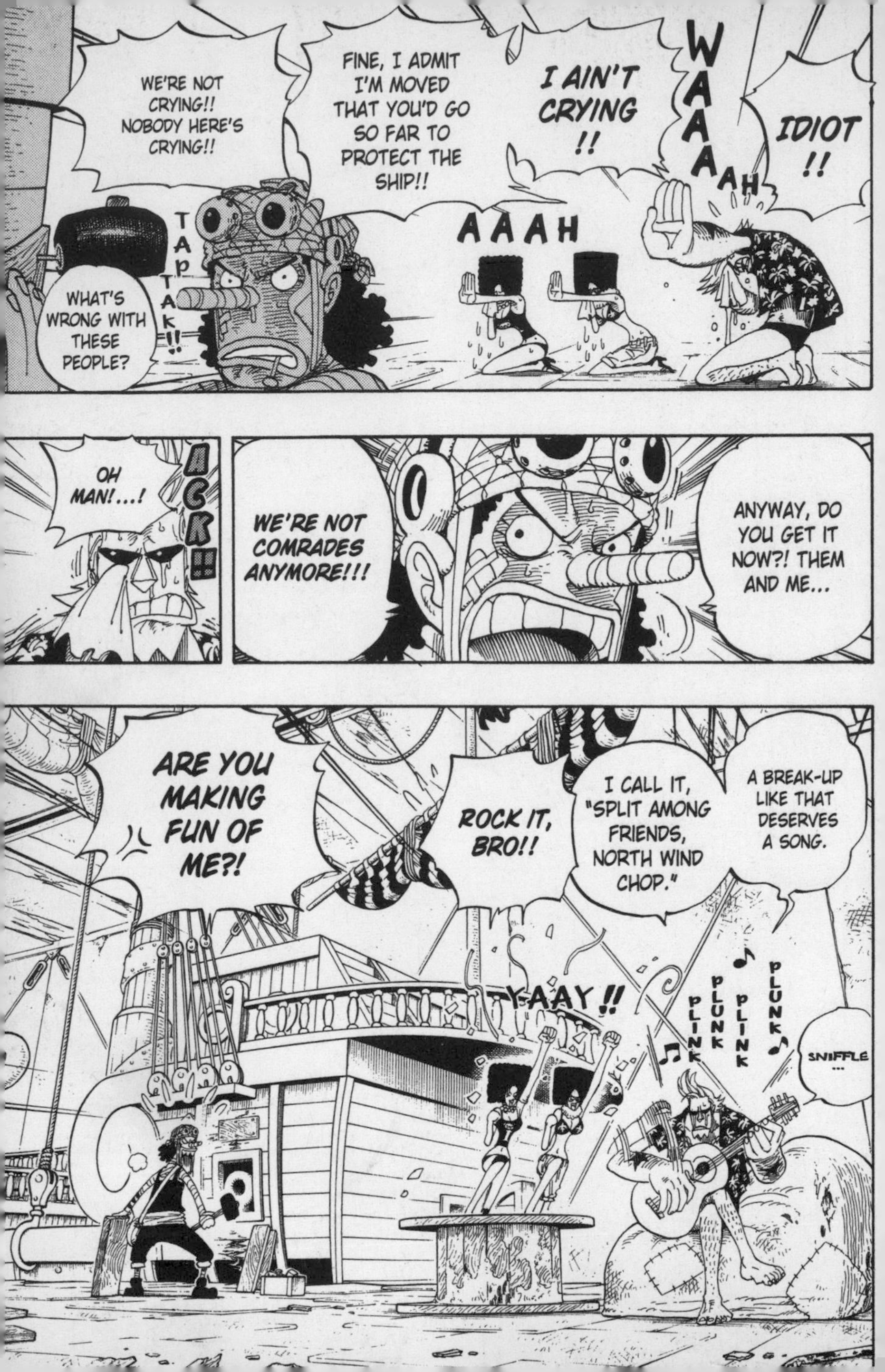
IDIOT!!
WAAAAAH
I AIN'T CRYING!!
AAAH
FINE, I ADMIT I'M MOVED THAT YOU'D GO SO FAR TO PROTECT THE SHIP!!
WE'RE NOT CRYING!! NOBODY HERE'S CRYING!!
TAP TAK!!
WHAT'S WRONG WITH THESE PEOPLE?
ANYWAY, DO YOU GET IT NOW?! THEM AND ME...
WE'RE NOT COMRADES ANYMORE!!!
ACK!!
OH MAN!...!
A BREAK-UP LIKE THAT DESERVES A SONG.
I CALL IT, "SPLIT AMONG FRIENDS, NORTH WIND CHOP."
ROCK IT, BRO!!
ARE YOU MAKING FUN OF ME?!
SNIFFLE...
PLUNK
PLINK
PLUNK
PLINK
YAAY!!

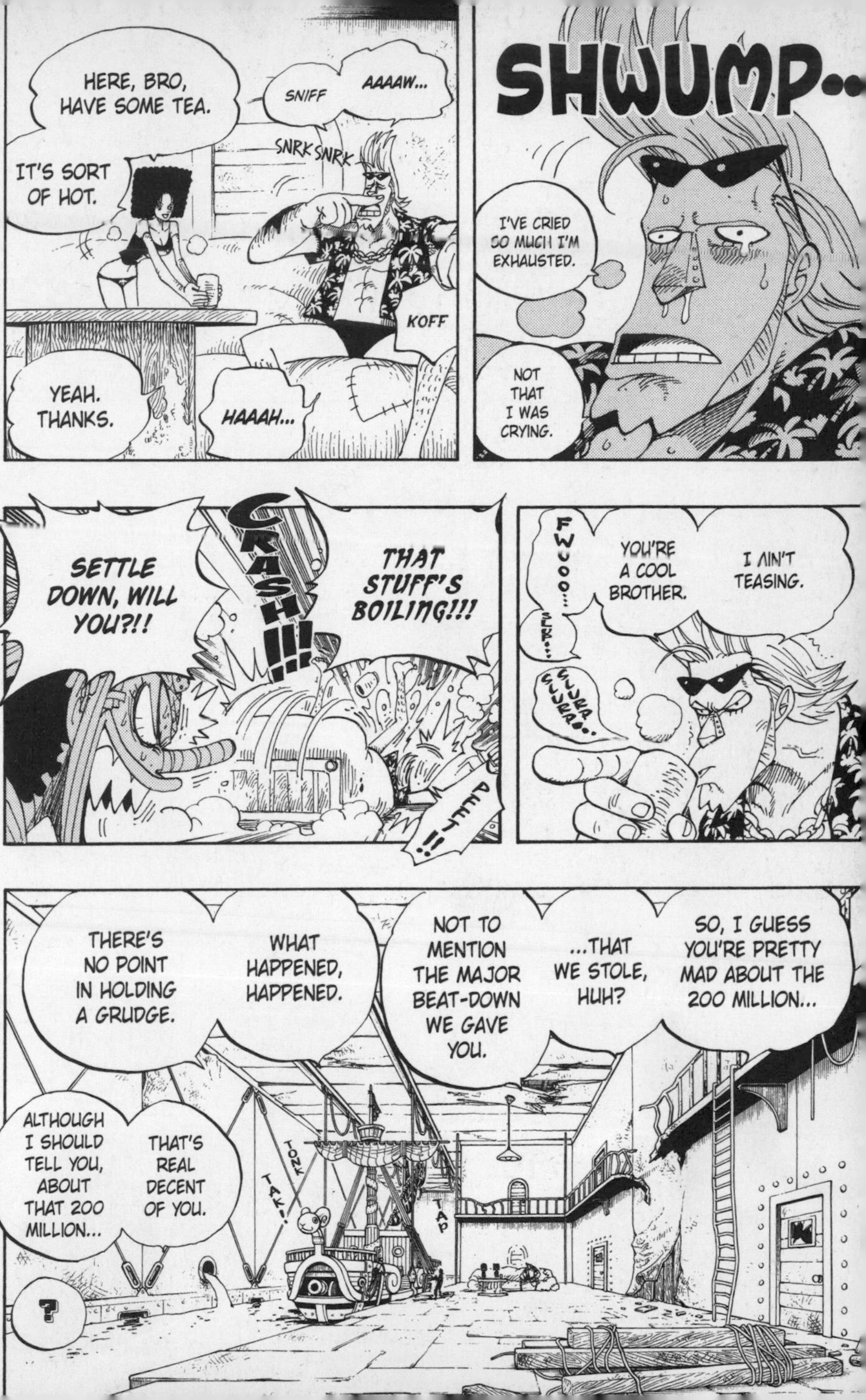
SHWUMP...
I'VE CRIED SO MUCH I'M EXHAUSTED.
NOT THAT I WAS CRYING.
AAAAW...
SNIFF
SNRK SNRK
HERE, BRO, HAVE SOME TEA.
IT'S SORT OF HOT.
KOFF
HAAAH...
YEAH. THANKS.
I AIN'T TEASING.
YOU'RE A COOL BROTHER.
FWUOO...
SLR...
SLURA SLURA...
THAT STUFF'S BOILING!!!
CRASH!!!
SETTLE DOWN, WILL YOU?!!
SO, I GUESS YOU'RE PRETTY MAD ABOUT THE 200 MILLION...
...THAT WE STOLE, HUH?
NOT TO MENTION THE MAJOR BEAT-DOWN WE GAVE YOU.
WHAT HAPPENED, HAPPENED.
THERE'S NO POINT IN HOLDING A GRUDGE.
THAT'S REAL DECENT OF YOU.
ALTHOUGH I SHOULD TELL YOU, ABOUT THAT 200 MILLION...
TONK
TAK!
TAP
?

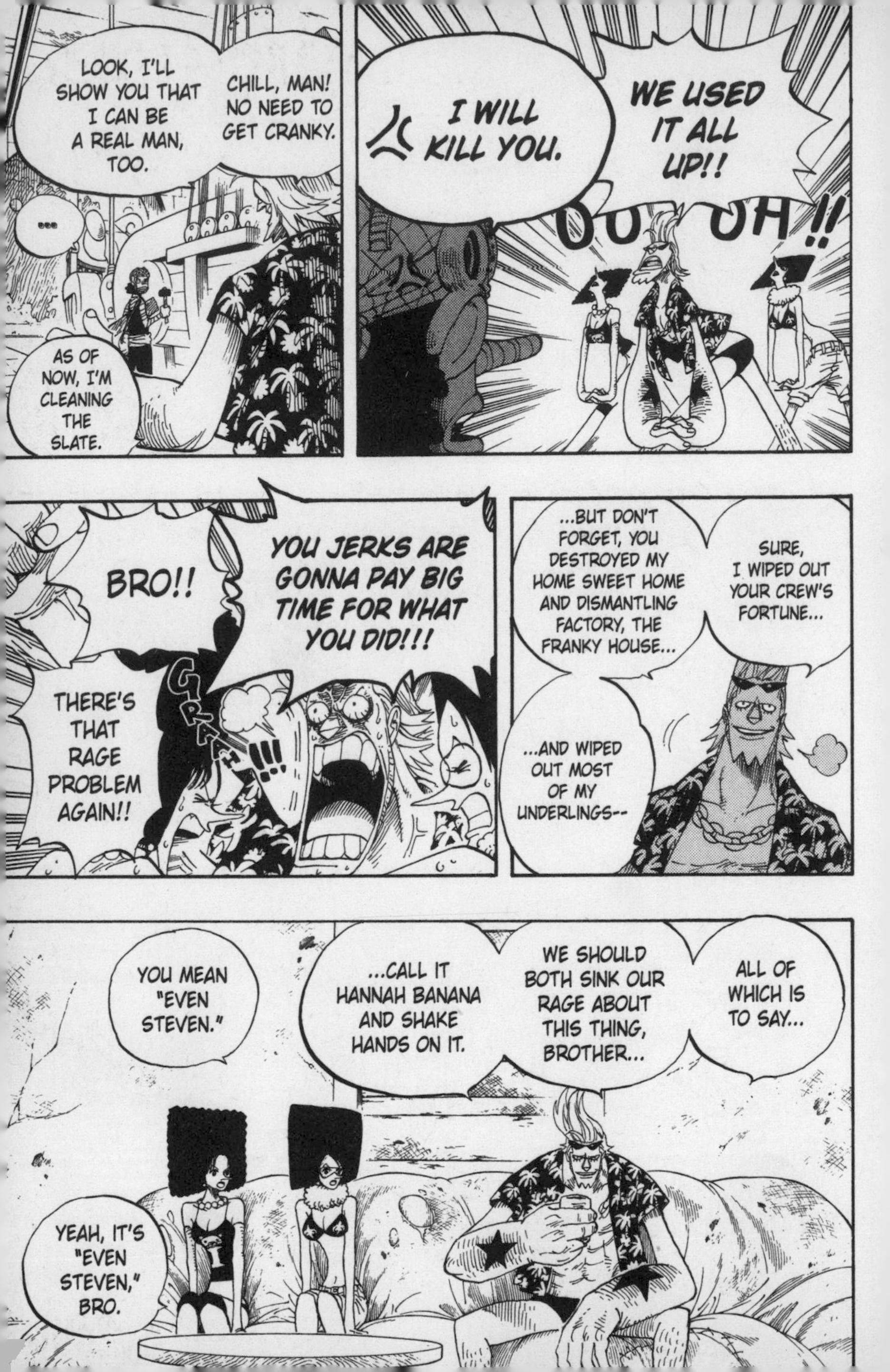
WE USED IT ALL UP!!
I WILL KILL YOU.
OO OH!!
CHILL, MAN! NO NEED TO GET CRANKY.
LOOK, I'LL SHOW YOU THAT I CAN BE A REAL MAN, TOO.
...
AS OF NOW, I'M CLEANING THE SLATE.
SURE, I WIPED OUT YOUR CREW'S FORTUNE...
...BUT DON'T FORGET, YOU DESTROYED MY HOME SWEET HOME AND DISMANTLING FACTORY, THE FRANKY HOUSE...
...AND WIPED OUT MOST OF MY UNDERLINGS--
YOU JERKS ARE GONNA PAY BIG TIME FOR WHAT YOU DID!!!
BRO!!
GRAAH!!!
THERE'S THAT RAGE PROBLEM AGAIN!!
ALL OF WHICH IS TO SAY...
WE SHOULD BOTH SINK OUR RAGE ABOUT THIS THING, BROTHER...
...CALL IT HANNAH BANANA AND SHAKE HANDS ON IT.
YOU MEAN "EVEN STEVEN."
YEAH, IT'S "EVEN STEVEN," BRO.

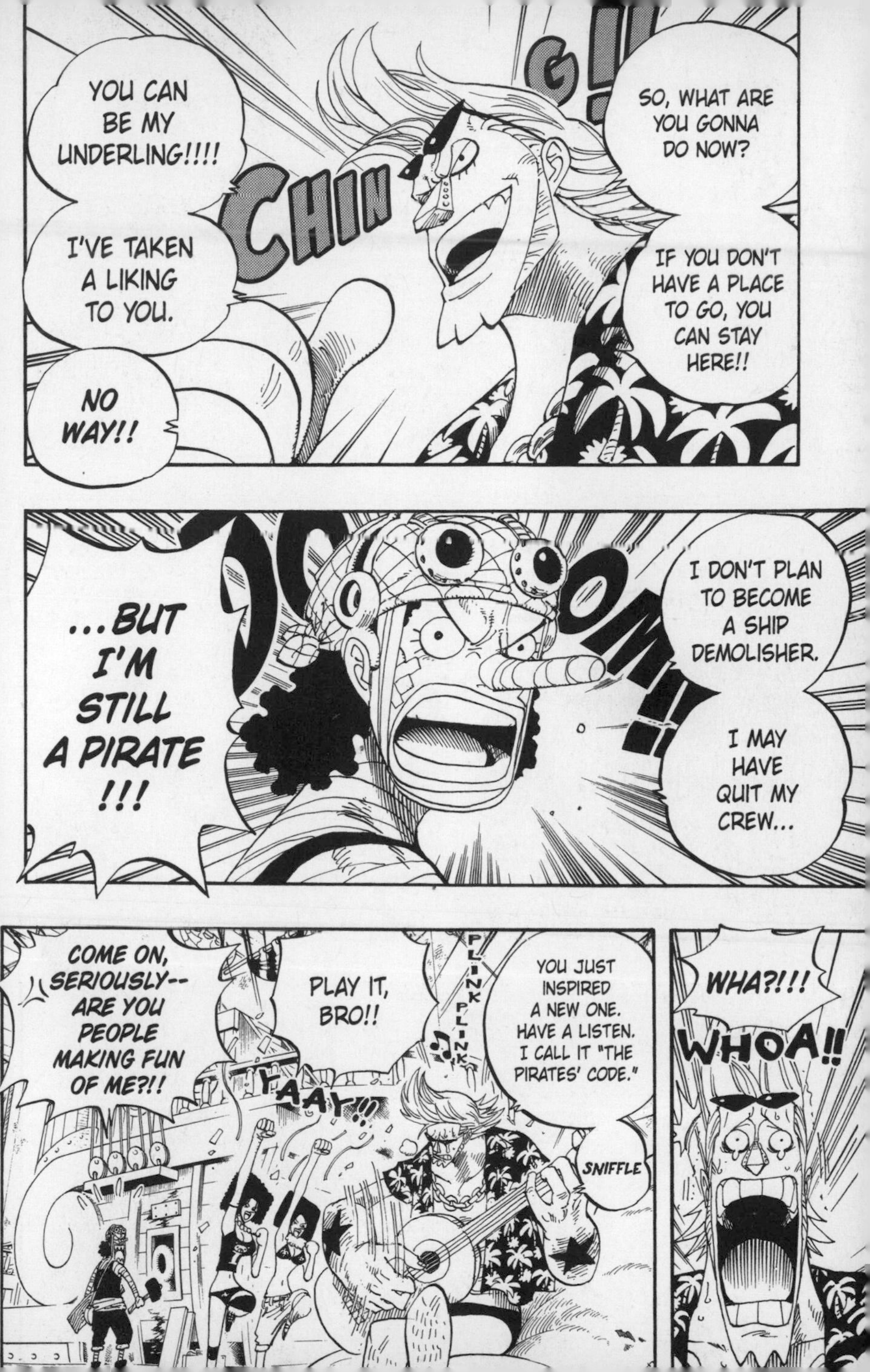
SO, WHAT ARE YOU GONNA DO NOW?
IF YOU DON'T HAVE A PLACE TO GO, YOU CAN STAY HERE!!
G!!
CHIN
YOU CAN BE MY UNDERLING!!!!
I'VE TAKEN A LIKING TO YOU.
NO WAY!!
I DON'T PLAN TO BECOME A SHIP DEMOLISHER.
I MAY HAVE QUIT MY CREW...
...BUT I'M STILL A PIRATE !!!
WHA?!!!
WHOA!!
YOU JUST INSPIRED A NEW ONE. HAVE A LISTEN. I CALL IT "THE PIRATES' CODE."
SNIFFLE
PLINK PLINK
PLAY IT, BRO!!
YAAY!!
COME ON, SERIOUSLY-- ARE YOU PEOPLE MAKING FUN OF ME?!!

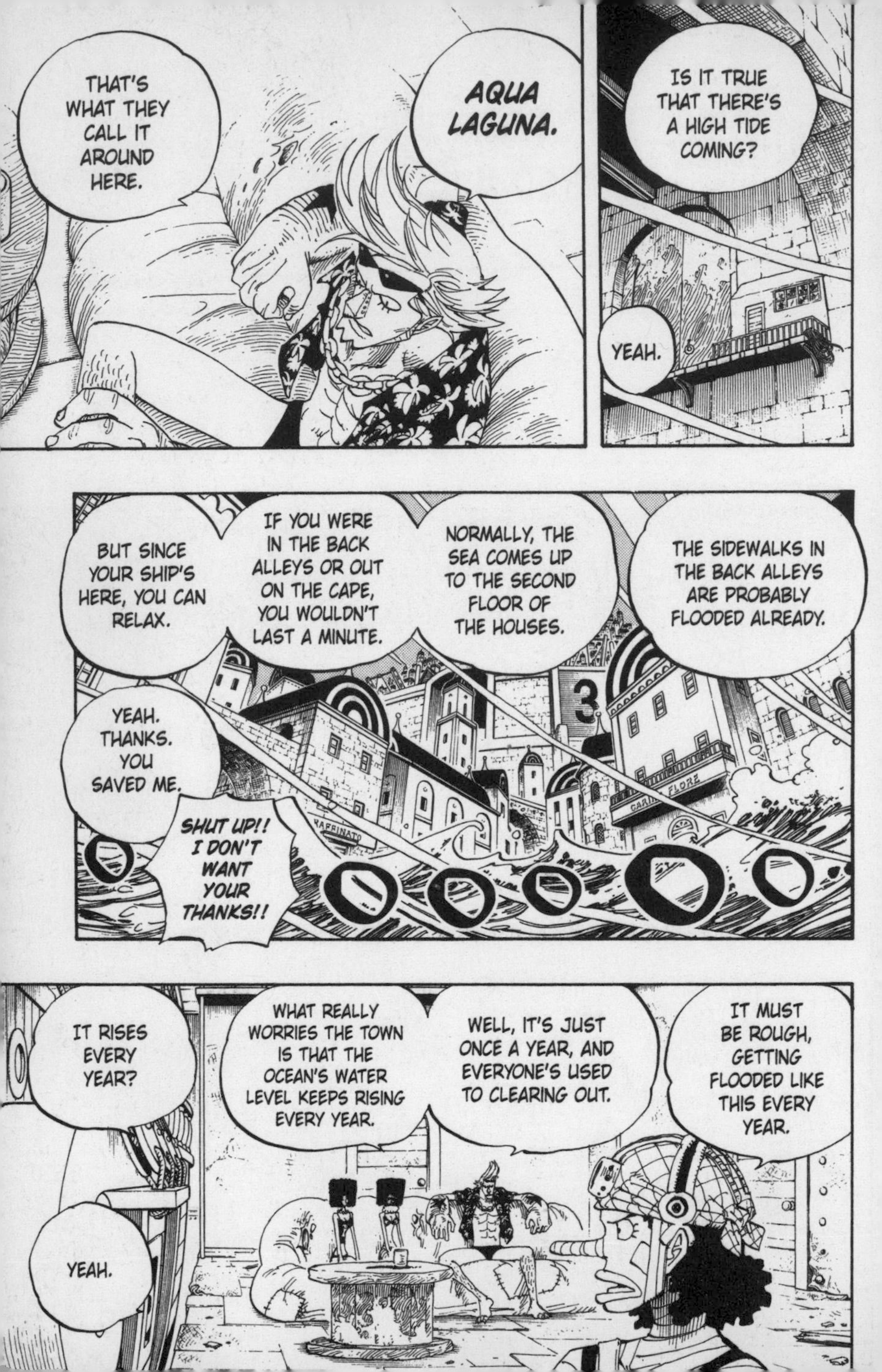
IS IT TRUE THAT THERE'S A HIGH TIDE COMING?
YEAH.
AQUA LAGUNA.
THAT'S WHAT THEY CALL IT AROUND HERE.
THE SIDEWALKS IN THE BACK ALLEYS ARE PROBABLY FLOODED ALREADY.
NORMALLY, THE SEA COMES UP TO THE SECOND FLOOR OF THE HOUSES.
IF YOU WERE IN THE BACK ALLEYS OR OUT ON THE CAPE, YOU WOULDN'T LAST A MINUTE.
BUT SINCE YOUR SHIP'S HERE, YOU CAN RELAX.
3
YEAH. THANKS. YOU SAVED ME.
SHUT UP!! I DON'T WANT YOUR THANKS!!
IT MUST BE ROUGH, GETTING FLOODED LIKE THIS EVERY YEAR.
WELL, IT'S JUST ONCE A YEAR, AND EVERYONE'S USED TO CLEARING OUT.
WHAT REALLY WORRIES THE TOWN IS THAT THE OCEAN'S WATER LEVEL KEEPS RISING EVERY YEAR.
IT RISES EVERY YEAR?
YEAH.

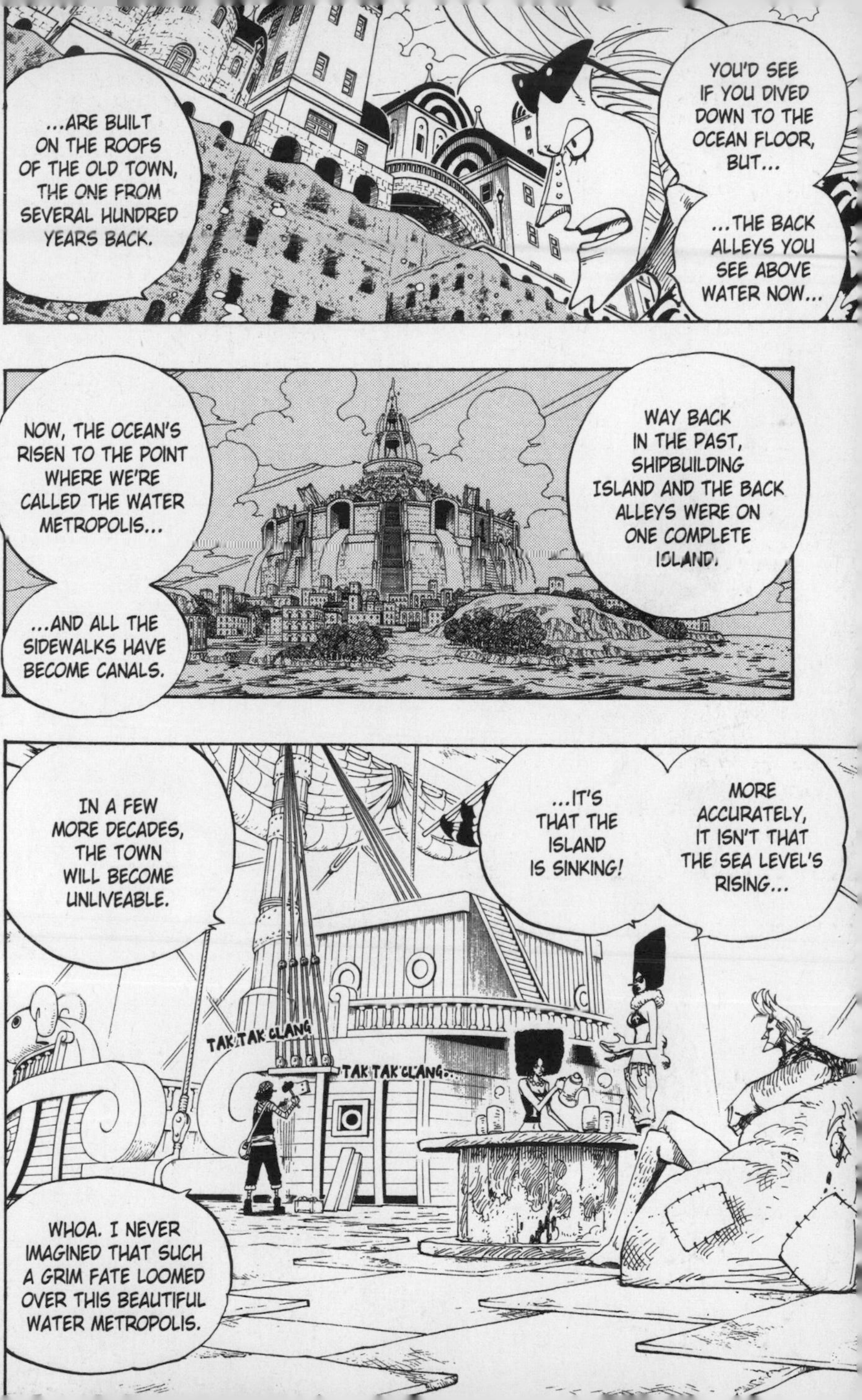
YOU'D SEE IF YOU DIVED DOWN TO THE OCEAN FLOOR, BUT...
...THE BACK ALLEYS YOU SEE ABOVE WATER NOW...
...ARE BUILT ON THE ROOFS OF THE OLD TOWN, THE ONE FROM SEVERAL HUNDRED YEARS BACK.
WAY BACK IN THE PAST, SHIPBUILDING ISLAND AND THE BACK ALLEYS WERE ON ONE COMPLETE ISLAND.
NOW, THE OCEAN'S RISEN TO THE POINT WHERE WE'RE CALLED THE WATER METROPOLIS...
...AND ALL THE SIDEWALKS HAVE BECOME CANALS.
MORE ACCURATELY, IT ISN'T THAT THE SEA LEVEL'S RISING...
...IT'S THAT THE ISLAND IS SINKING!
IN A FEW MORE DECADES, THE TOWN WILL BECOME UNLIVEABLE.
TAK TAK CLANG
TAK TAK CLANG...
WHOA. I NEVER IMAGINED THAT SUCH A GRIM FATE LOOMED OVER THIS BEAUTIFUL WATER METROPOLIS.

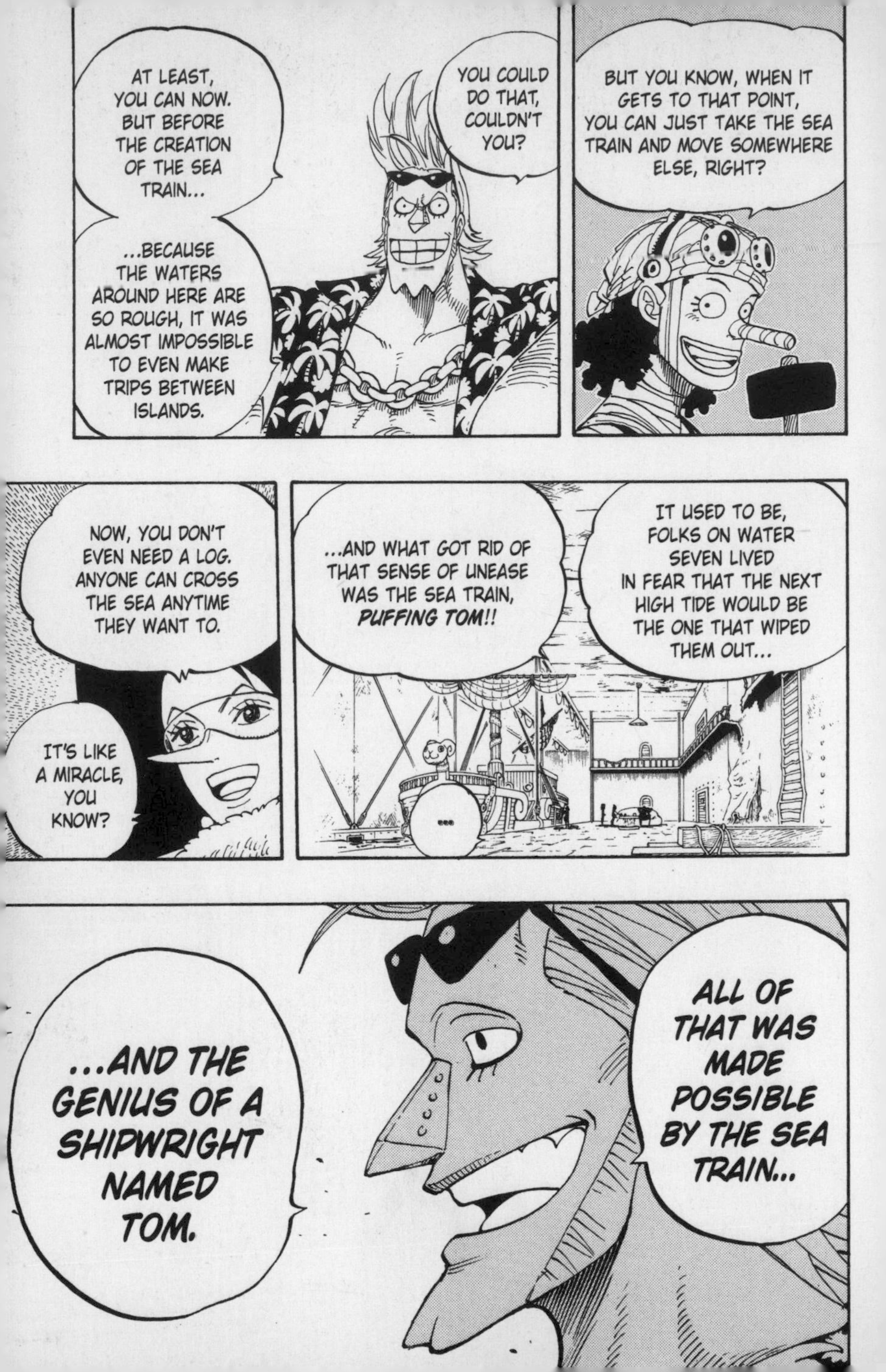
BUT YOU KNOW, WHEN IT GETS TO THAT POINT, YOU CAN JUST TAKE THE SEA TRAIN AND MOVE SOMEWHERE ELSE, RIGHT?
YOU COULD DO THAT, COULDN'T YOU?
AT LEAST, YOU CAN NOW. BUT BEFORE THE CREATION OF THE SEA TRAIN...
...BECAUSE THE WATERS AROUND HERE ARE SO ROUGH, IT WAS ALMOST IMPOSSIBLE TO EVEN MAKE TRIPS BETWEEN ISLANDS.
IT USED TO BE, FOLKS ON WATER SEVEN LIVED IN FEAR THAT THE NEXT HIGH TIDE WOULD BE THE ONE THAT WIPED THEM OUT...
...AND WHAT GOT RID OF THAT SENSE OF UNEASE WAS THE SEA TRAIN, PUFFING TOM!!
...
NOW, YOU DON'T EVEN NEED A LOG. ANYONE CAN CROSS THE SEA ANYTIME THEY WANT TO.
IT'S LIKE A MIRACLE, YOU KNOW?
ALL OF THAT WAS MADE POSSIBLE BY THE SEA TRAIN...
...AND THE GENIUS OF A SHIPWRIGHT NAMED TOM.

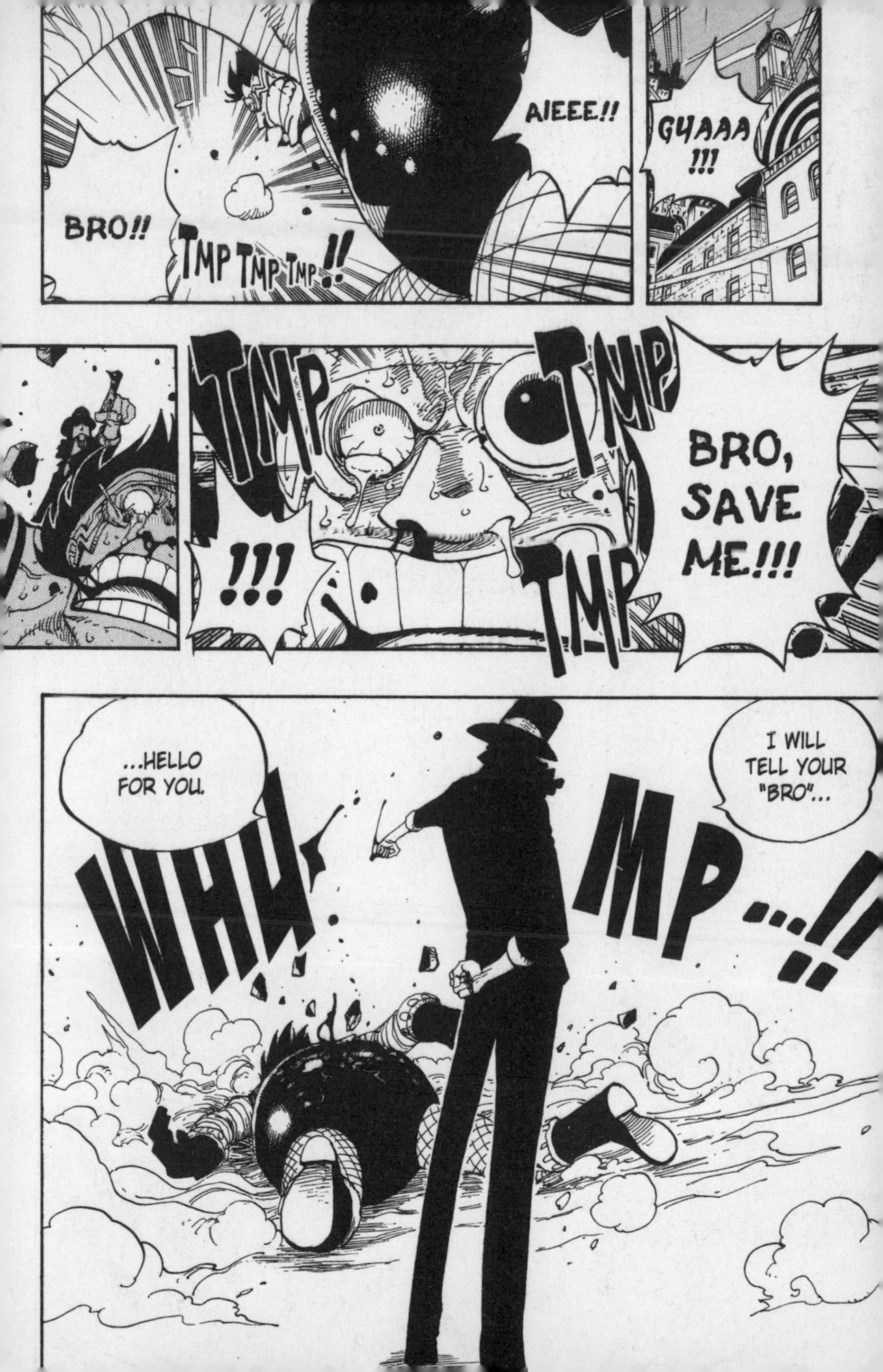
GYAAA!!!
AIEEE!!
BRO!!
TMP TMP TMP!!
BRO, SAVE ME!!!
TMP TMP TMP
!!!
I WILL TELL YOUR "BRO"...
...HELLO FOR YOU.
WHUMP...!!

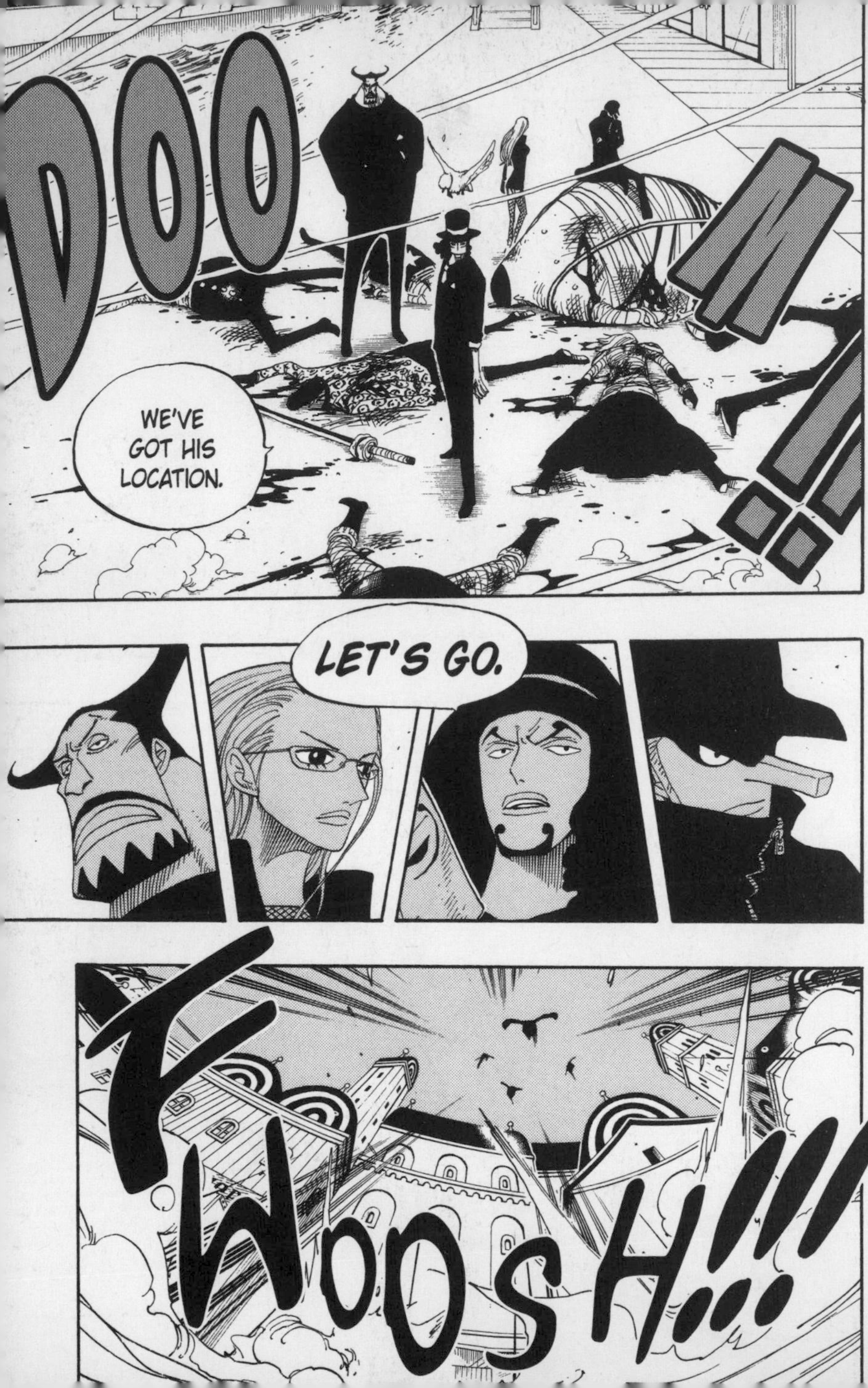
DOOM
WE'VE GOT HIS LOCATION.
LET'S GO.
WHOOSH!!!

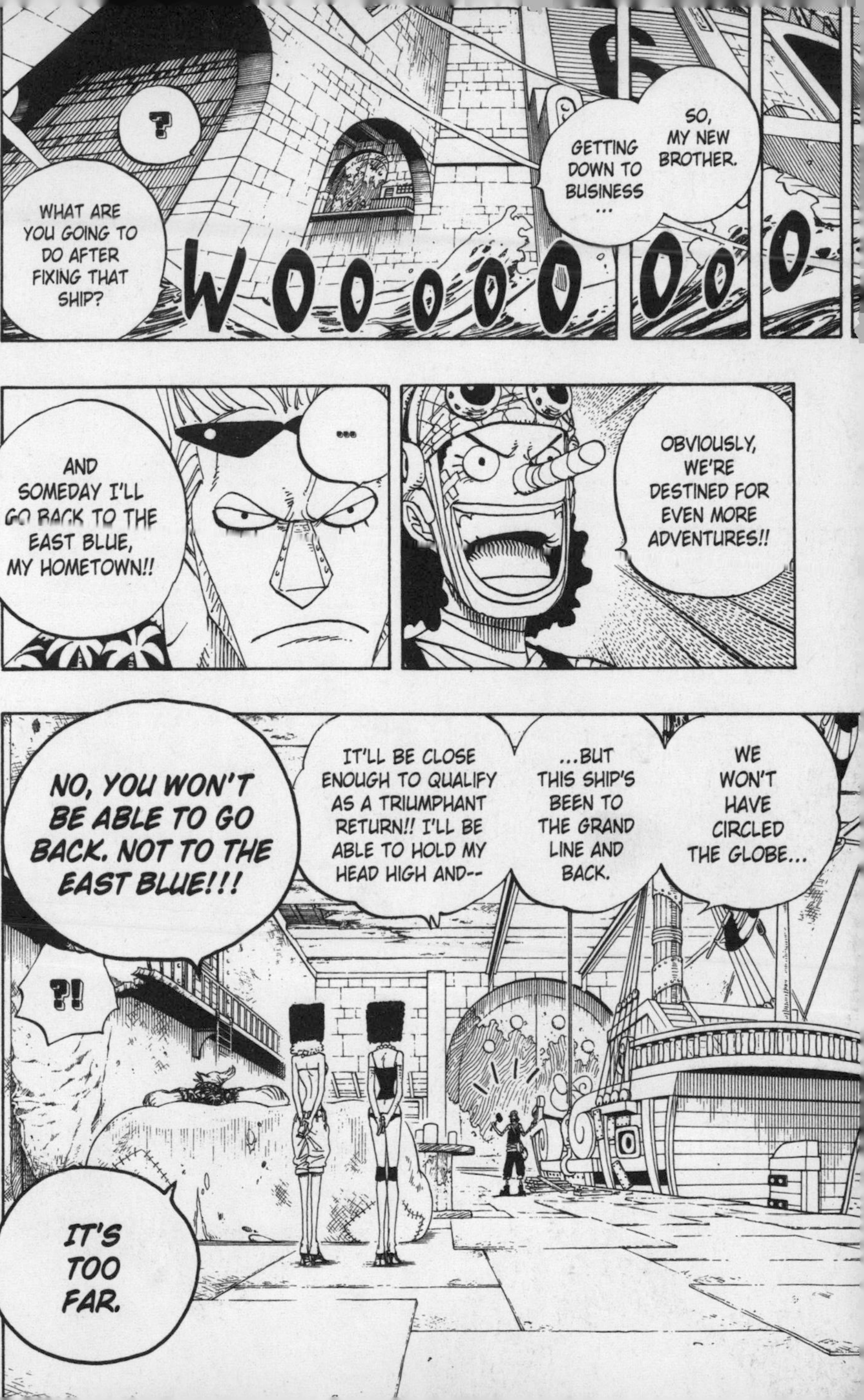
SO, MY NEW BROTHER.
GETTING DOWN TO BUSINESS...
WOOOOOOOOO
?
WHAT ARE YOU GOING TO DO AFTER FIXING THAT SHIP?
OBVIOUSLY, WE'RE DESTINED FOR EVEN MORE ADVENTURES!!
...
AND SOMEDAY I'LL GO BACK TO THE EAST BLUE, MY HOMETOWN!!
WE WON'T HAVE CIRCLED THE GLOBE...
...BUT THIS SHIP'S BEEN TO THE GRAND LINE AND BACK.
IT'LL BE CLOSE ENOUGH TO QUALIFY AS A TRIUMPHANT RETURN!! I'LL BE ABLE TO HOLD MY HEAD HIGH AND--
NO, YOU WON'T BE ABLE TO GO BACK. NOT TO THE EAST BLUE!!!
?!
IT'S TOO FAR.

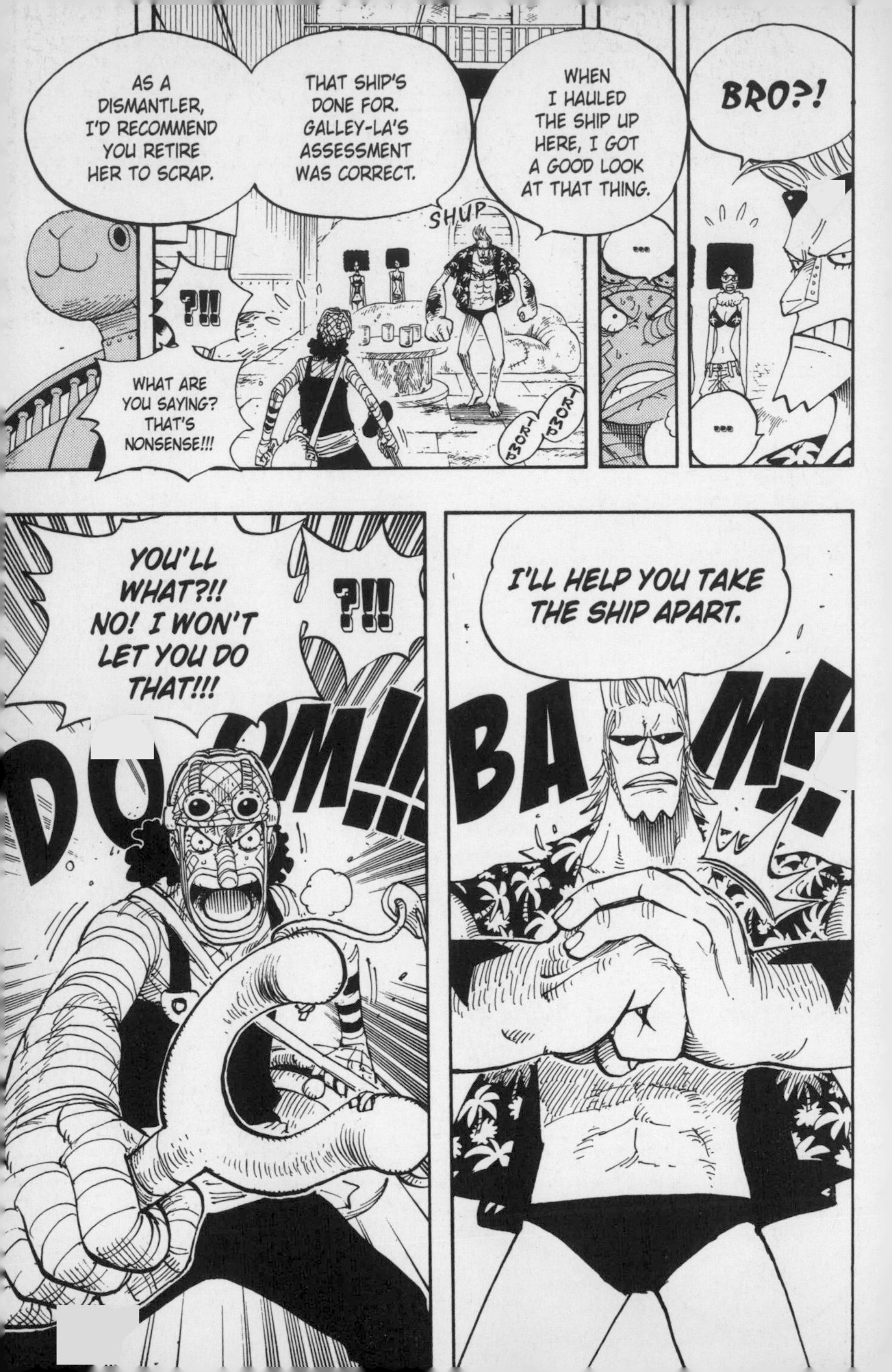
BRO?!
...
...
...
WHEN I HAULED THE SHIP UP HERE, I GOT A GOOD LOOK AT THAT THING.
THAT SHIP'S DONE FOR. GALLEY-LA'S ASSESSMENT WAS CORRECT.
AS A DISMANTLER, I'D RECOMMEND YOU RETIRE HER TO SCRAP.
SHUP
TROMP TROMP
?!!
WHAT ARE YOU SAYING? THAT'S NONSENSE!!!
I'LL HELP YOU TAKE THE SHIP APART.
BAM!!
?!!
YOU'LL WHAT?!! NO! I WON'T LET YOU DO THAT!!!
DOOM!!

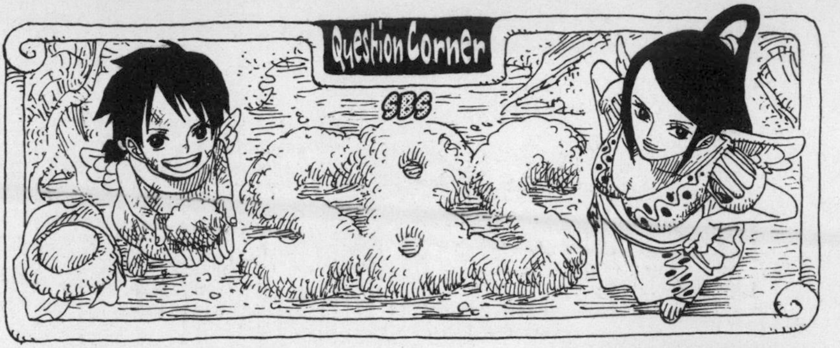
Question Corner
SBS

Reader: ***Did you call me? (Said as Eneru)***

--Oota-kun

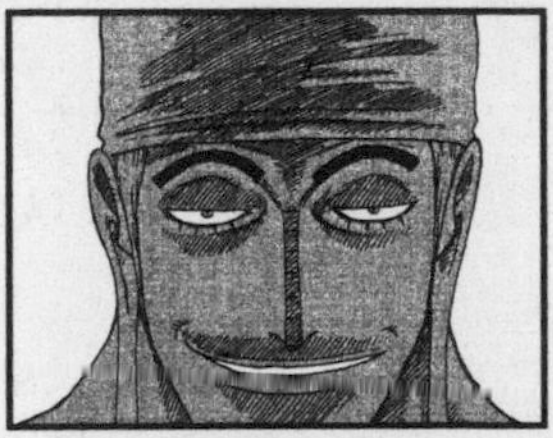

Oda: No, no... Huh? Wagh! Scary! It's Eneru! Ow-ow-ow-ow! I got zapped. Yeowch! Let's move on, okay?

Reader: Dear Oda Sensei, the scene where Kalifa prepared tea for Mr. Iceberg was absolutely gorgeous. What does it take to become a splendid secretary and woman like Kalifa?

--One Fan

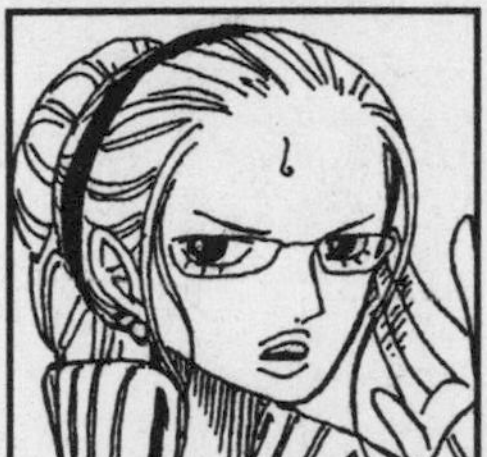

Oda: Glasses and documents. Yep. You should also say, "The insolence!"

Reader: How many marimos is your brain, Sensei? (Say Einstein's brain is "273 marimos.")

--Fish Cake

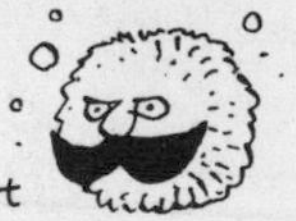

Oda: How many marimos, you ask? Well, when you're at my level, it's "Super Marimo"!! Hm. I sort of wish I hadn't said that now.

Reader: ***Yaaaay!!! *plonk* (putting on afro) Oh yeah! All right!!***

--Egg

Oda: Okay, next.

Reader: Shimabuu (Mitsutoshi Shimabukuro Sensei) said he went to a hot springs resort with about ten other manga artists near the end of last year. Did you go, Oda? Or did you not? Did you miss the bus?!

--MonTueWedThursFriSat

Oda: I went. There was snow at the hot spring, and it was pretty. It was an outdoor hot spring, so I ran around in the snow naked, and **I caught a cold!!** (Several others did too.)

Chapter 351:
KLABAUTERMANN

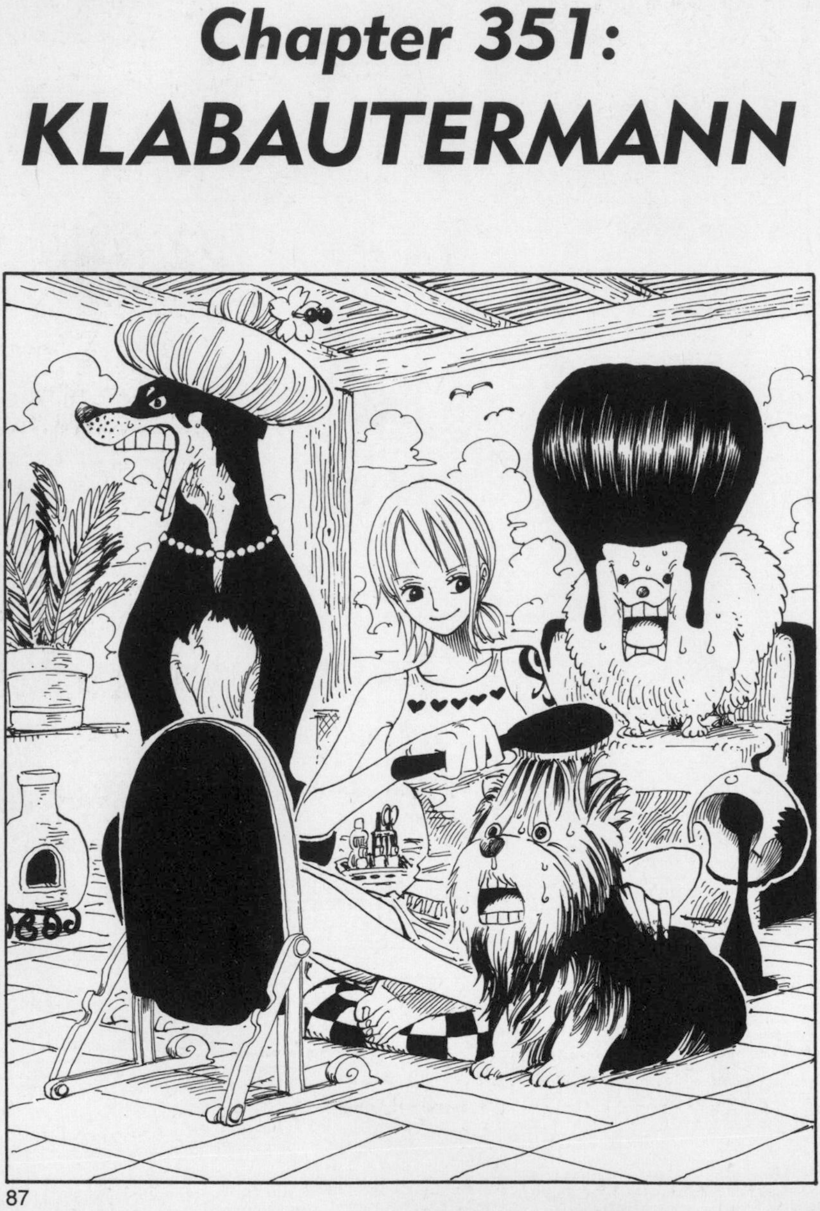

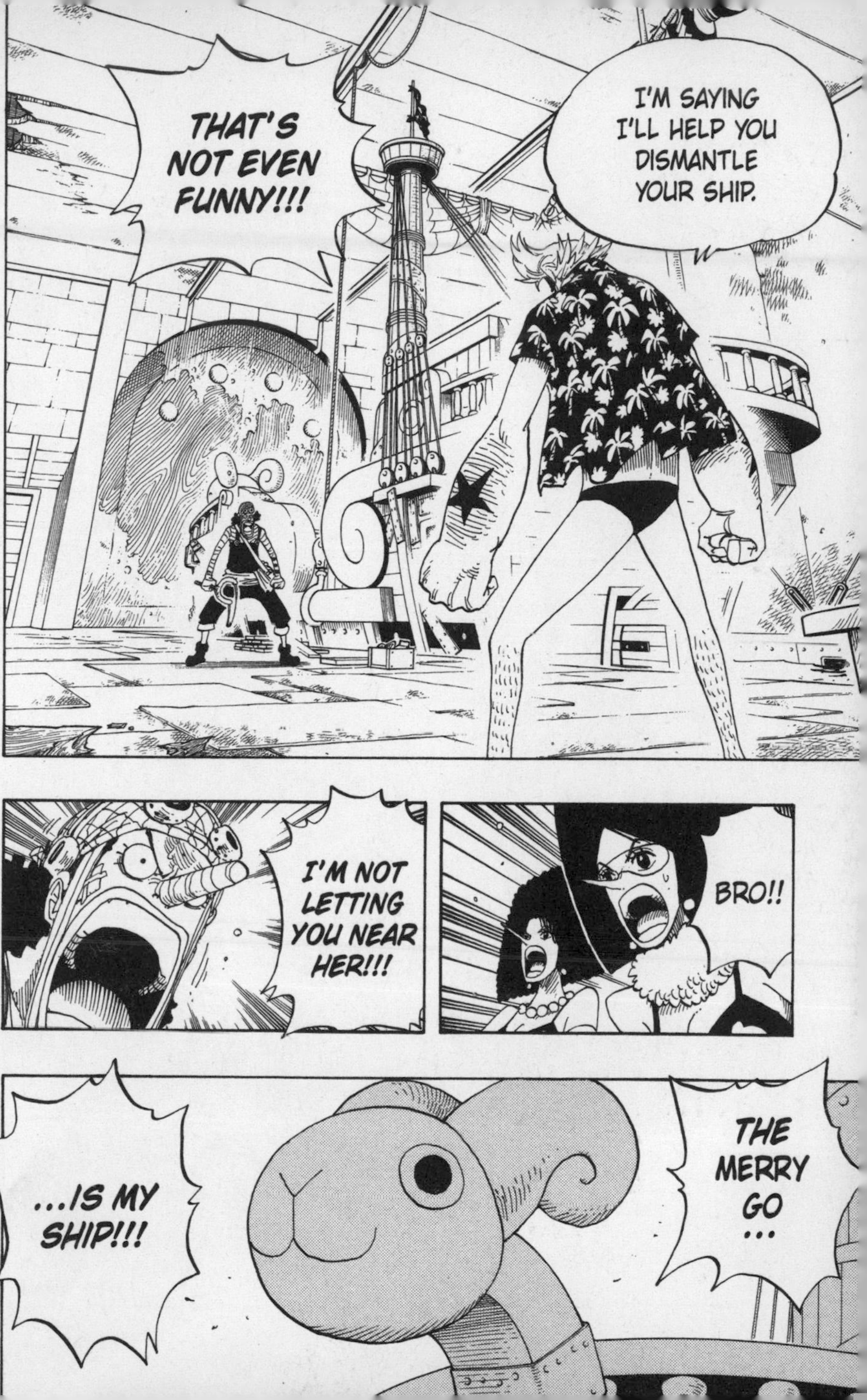
I'M SAYING I'LL HELP YOU DISMANTLE YOUR SHIP.
THAT'S NOT EVEN FUNNY!!!
BRO!!
I'M NOT LETTING YOU NEAR HER!!!
THE MERRY GO ...
...IS MY SHIP!!!

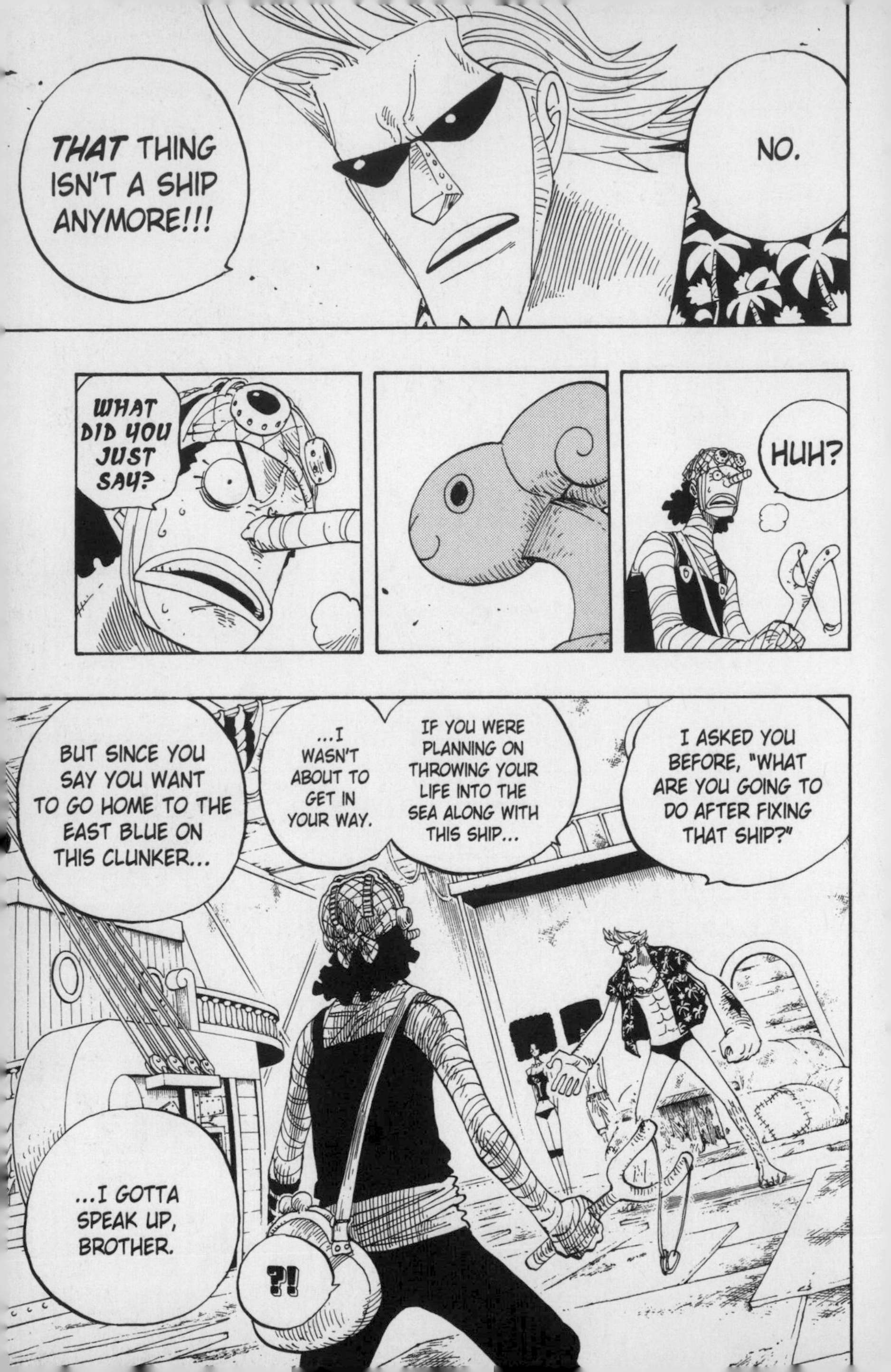
NO.
THAT THING ISN'T A SHIP ANYMORE!!!
HUH?
WHAT DID YOU JUST SAY?
I ASKED YOU BEFORE, "WHAT ARE YOU GOING TO DO AFTER FIXING THAT SHIP?"
IF YOU WERE PLANNING ON THROWING YOUR LIFE INTO THE SEA ALONG WITH THIS SHIP...
...I WASN'T ABOUT TO GET IN YOUR WAY.
BUT SINCE YOU SAY YOU WANT TO GO HOME TO THE EAST BLUE ON THIS CLUNKER...
...I GOTTA SPEAK UP, BROTHER.
?!

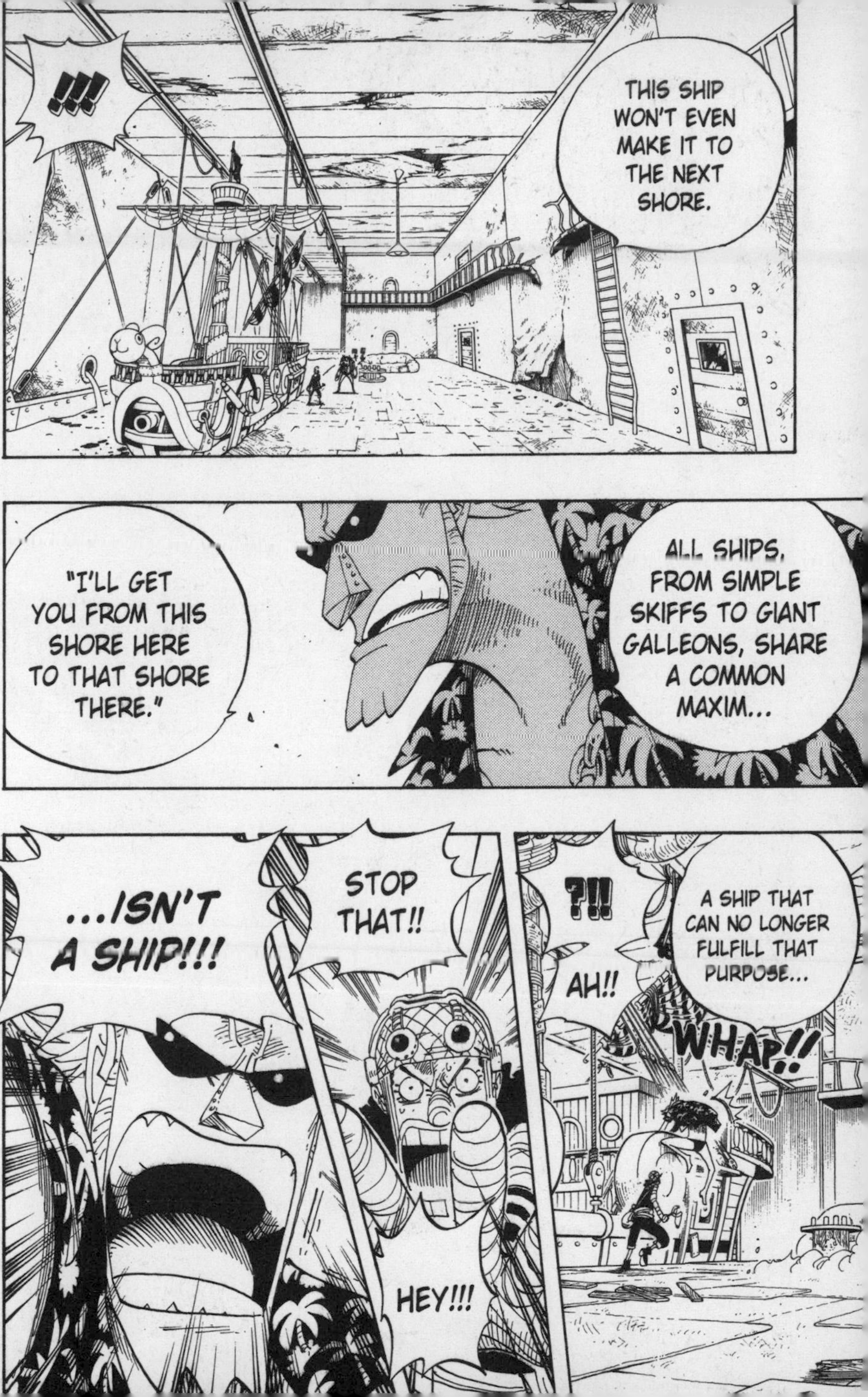
THIS SHIP WON'T EVEN MAKE IT TO THE NEXT SHORE.
!!!
ALL SHIPS, FROM SIMPLE SKIFFS TO GIANT GALLEONS, SHARE A COMMON MAXIM...
"I'LL GET YOU FROM THIS SHORE HERE TO THAT SHORE THERE."
A SHIP THAT CAN NO LONGER FULFILL THAT PURPOSE...
?!!
AH!!
WHAP!!
STOP THAT!!
HEY!!!
...ISN'T A SHIP!!!

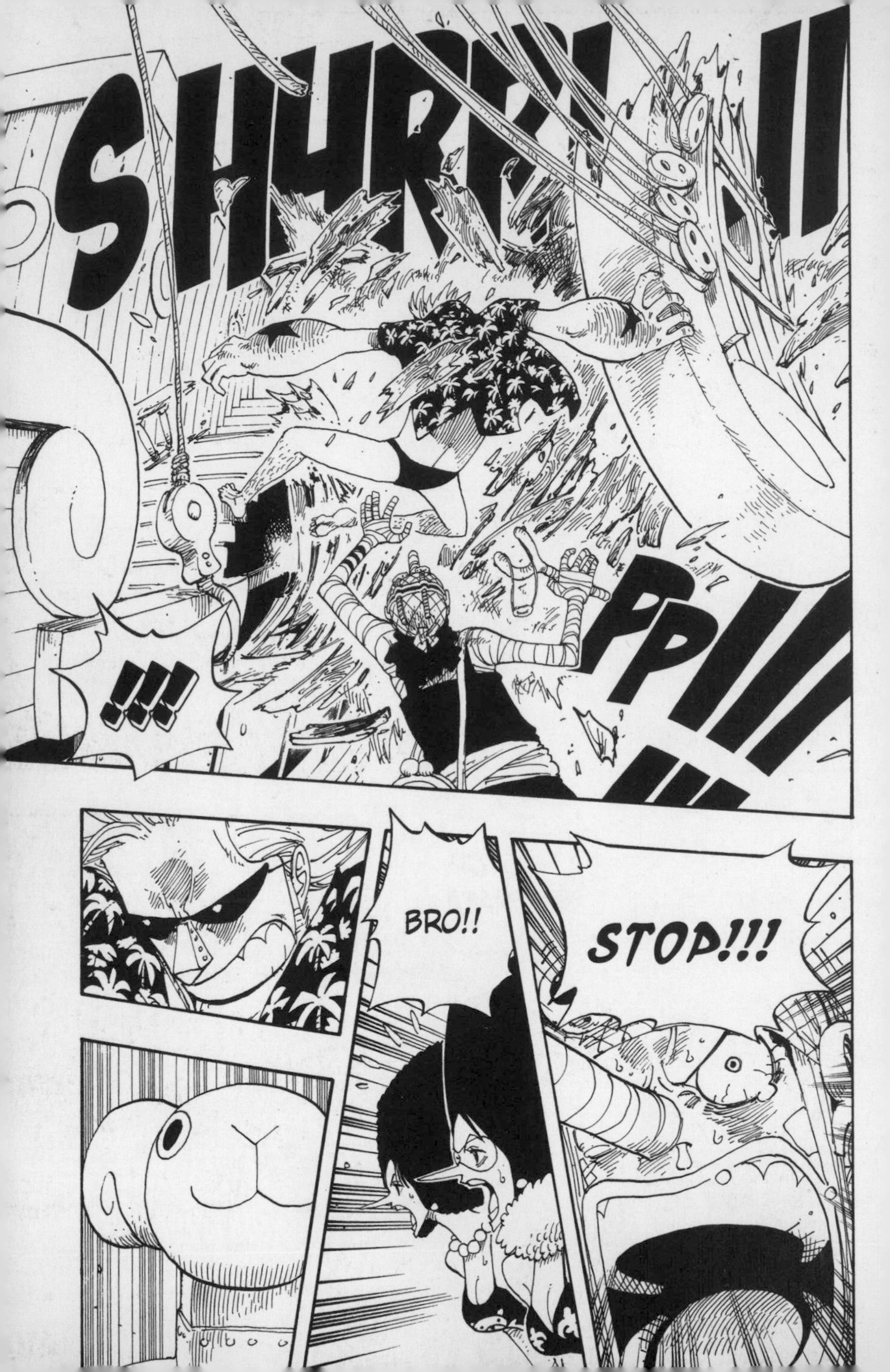
SHRAAK!!
PP!!!
!!!
STOP!!!
BRO!!

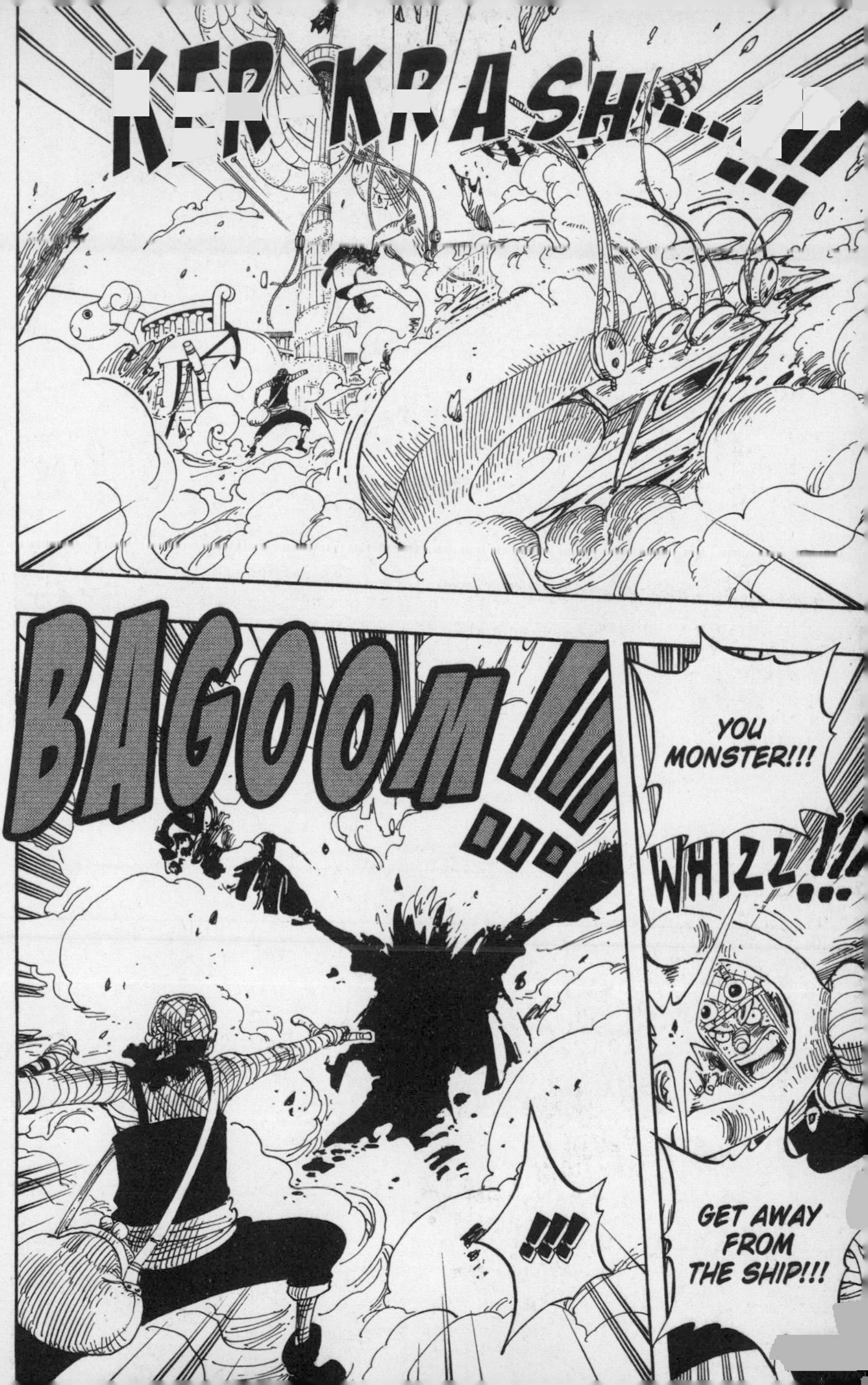
KER-KRASH...!!
YOU MONSTER!!!
WHIZZ!!...
GET AWAY FROM THE SHIP!!!
BAGOOM!!...
!!!

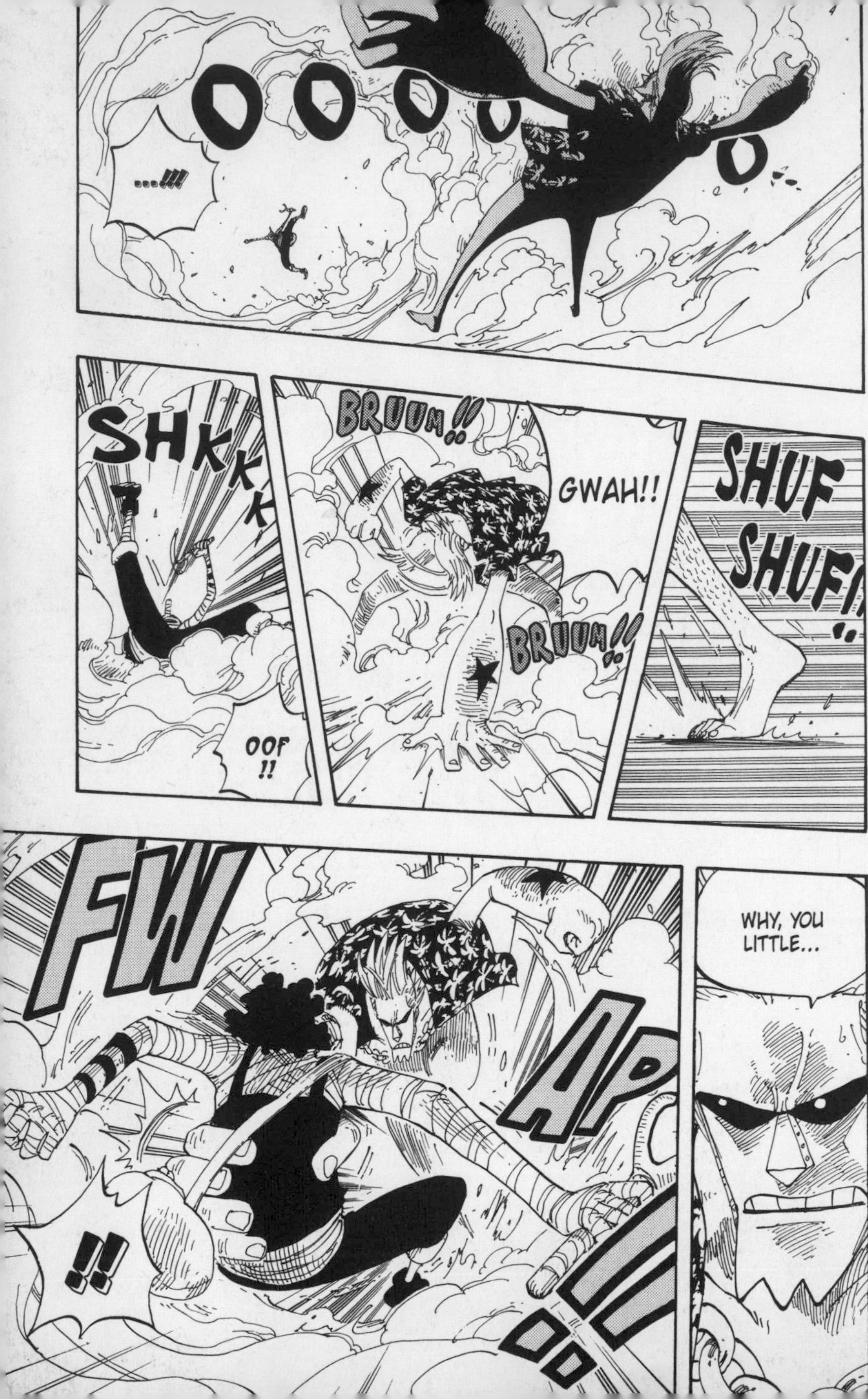
OOOOOO
...!!!
SHUF SHUF!!
BRUUM!!
GWAH!!
BRUUM!!
SHKKK
OOF !!
WHY, YOU LITTLE...
FWAP
!!

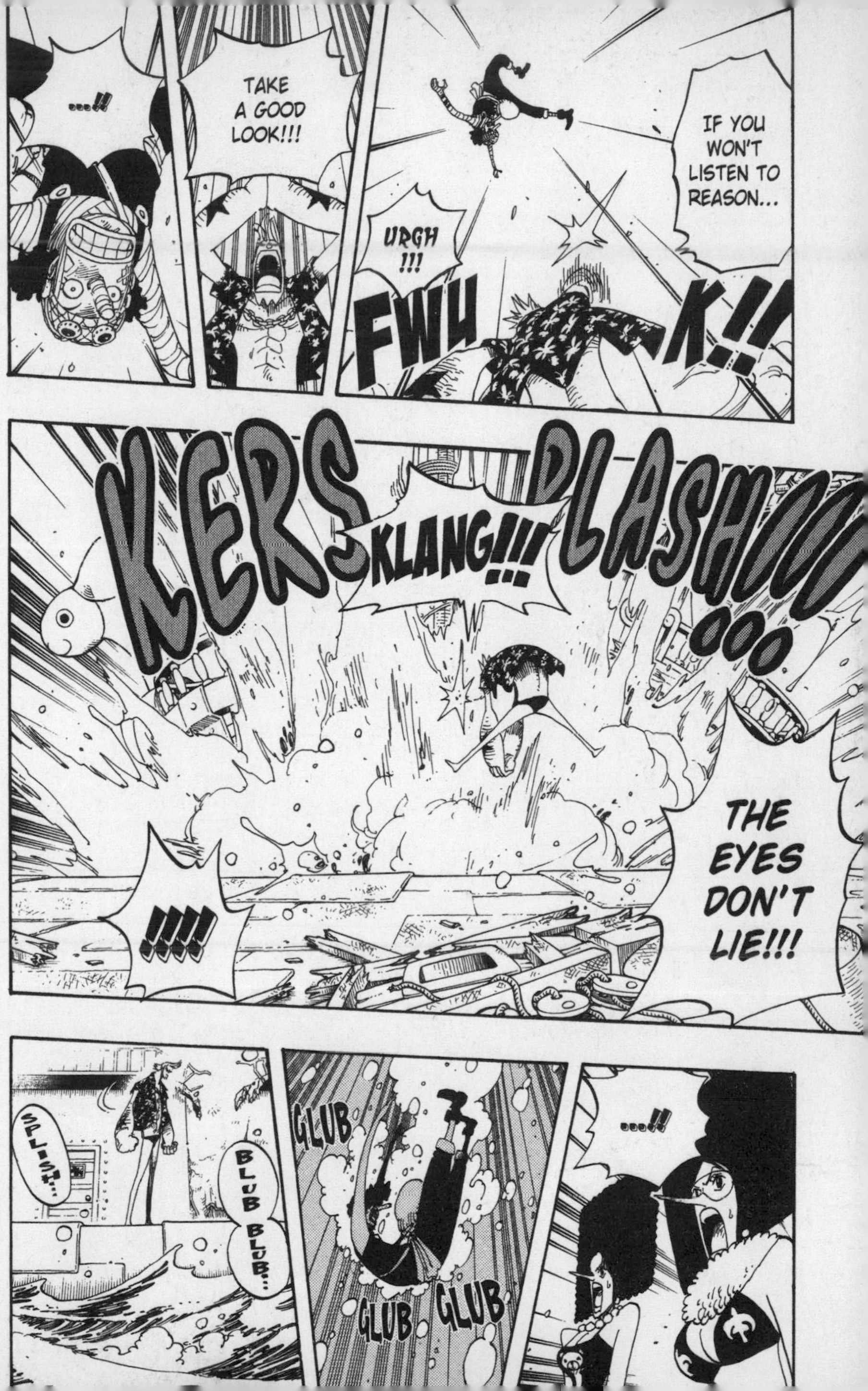

IF YOU WON'T LISTEN TO REASON...
URGH!!!
FWU K!!
TAKE A GOOD LOOK!!!
...!!
KERS PLASHOOO...
KLANG!!!
THE EYES DON'T LIE!!!
!!!!
...!!
GLUB
GLUB GLUB
SPLISH...
BLUB BLUB...

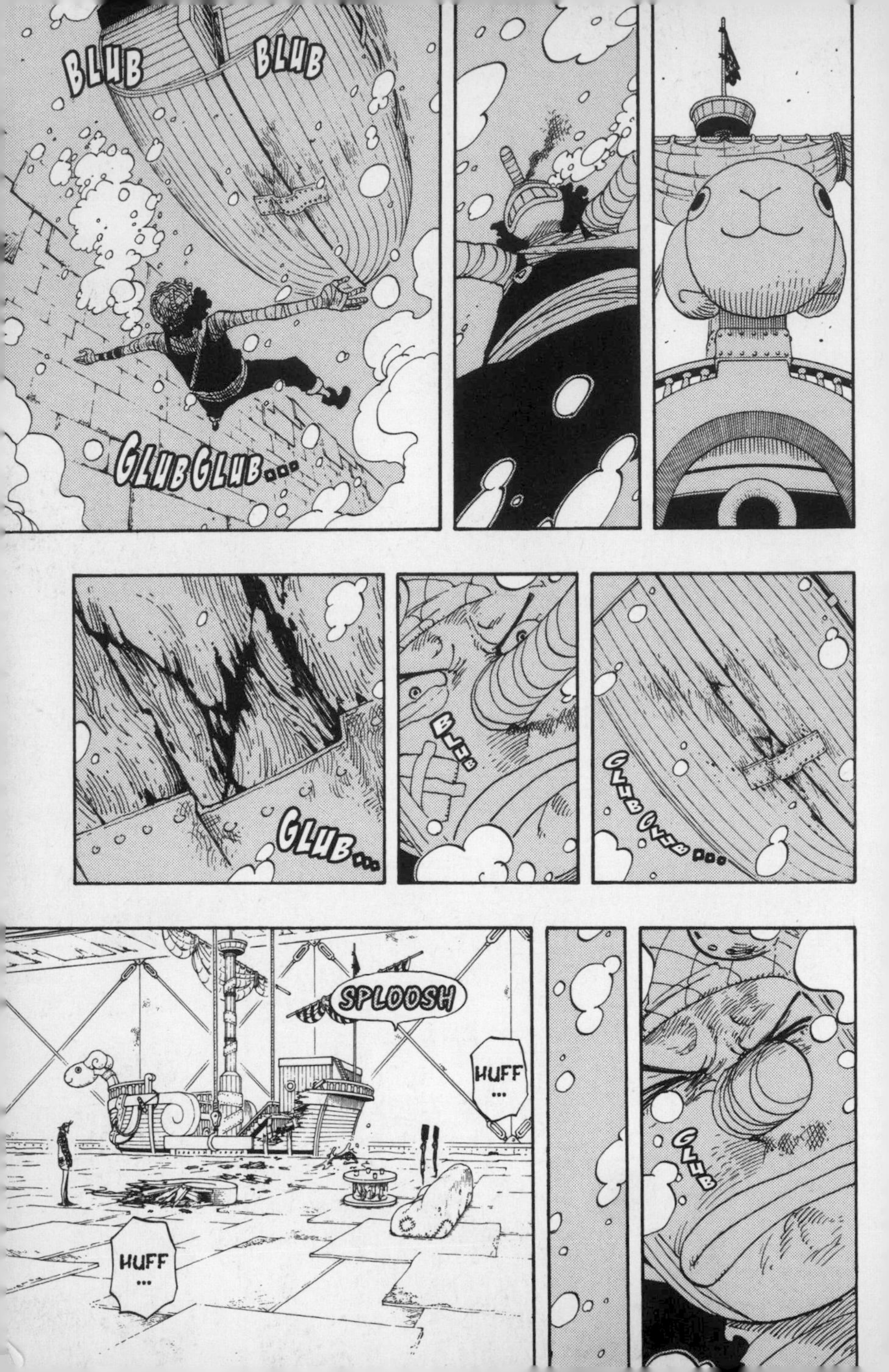
BLUB
BLUB
GLUB GLUB...
GLUB GLUB...
BLUB
GLUB...
SPLOOSH
HUFF...
HUFF...
GLUB

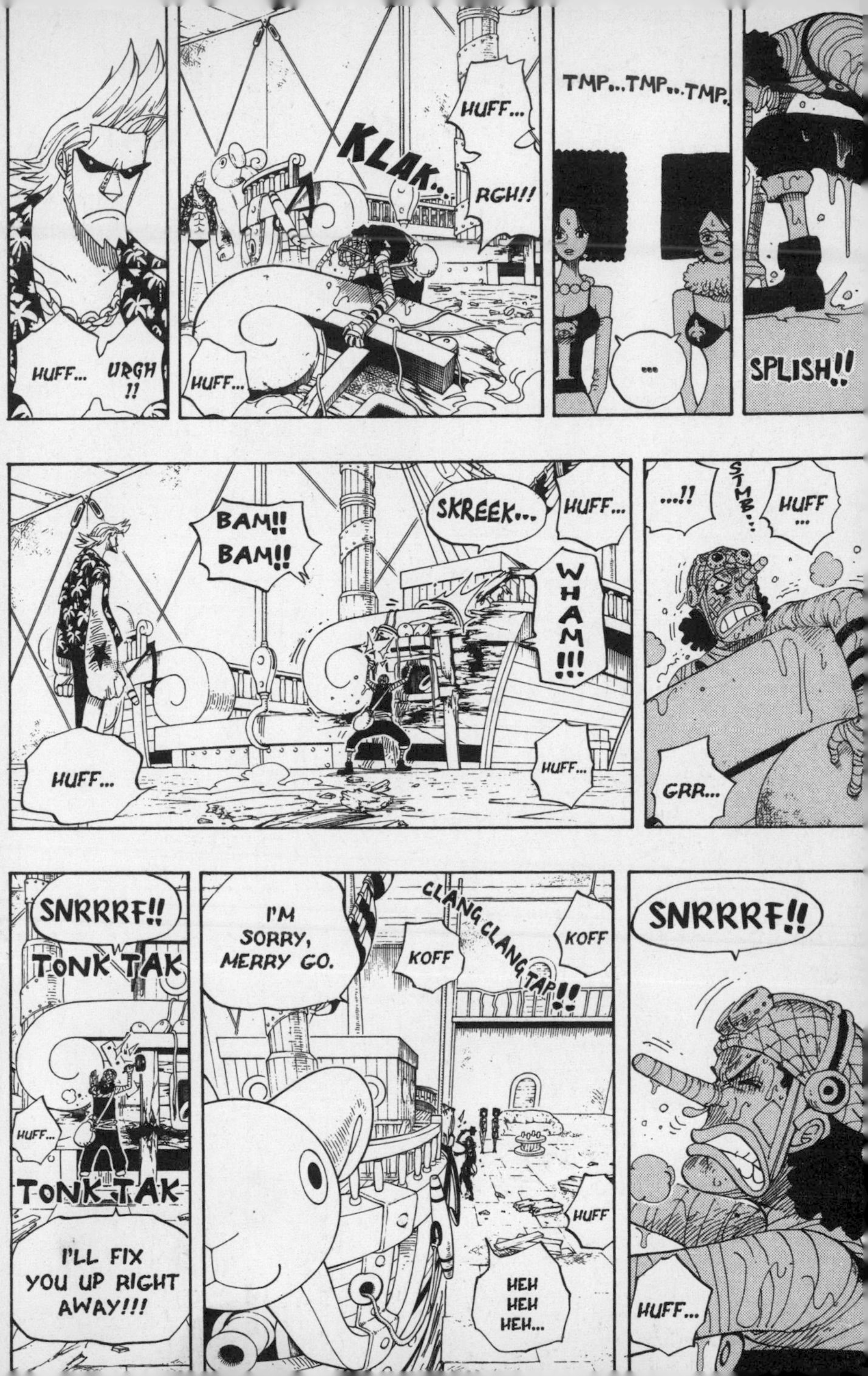
SPLISH!!
TMP...TMP...TMP...
...
HUFF...
KLAK...
RGH!!
HUFF...
HUFF... URGH!!
...!!
STMB...
HUFF...
GRR...
SKREEK...
HUFF...
BAM!! BAM!!
WHAM!!!
HUFF...
HUFF...
SNRRRF!!
HUFF...
CLANG CLANG TAP!!
KOFF
KOFF
I'M SORRY, MERRY GO.
HUFF
HEH HEH HEH...
SNRRRF!!
TONK TAK
HUFF...
TONK TAK
I'LL FIX YOU UP RIGHT AWAY!!!

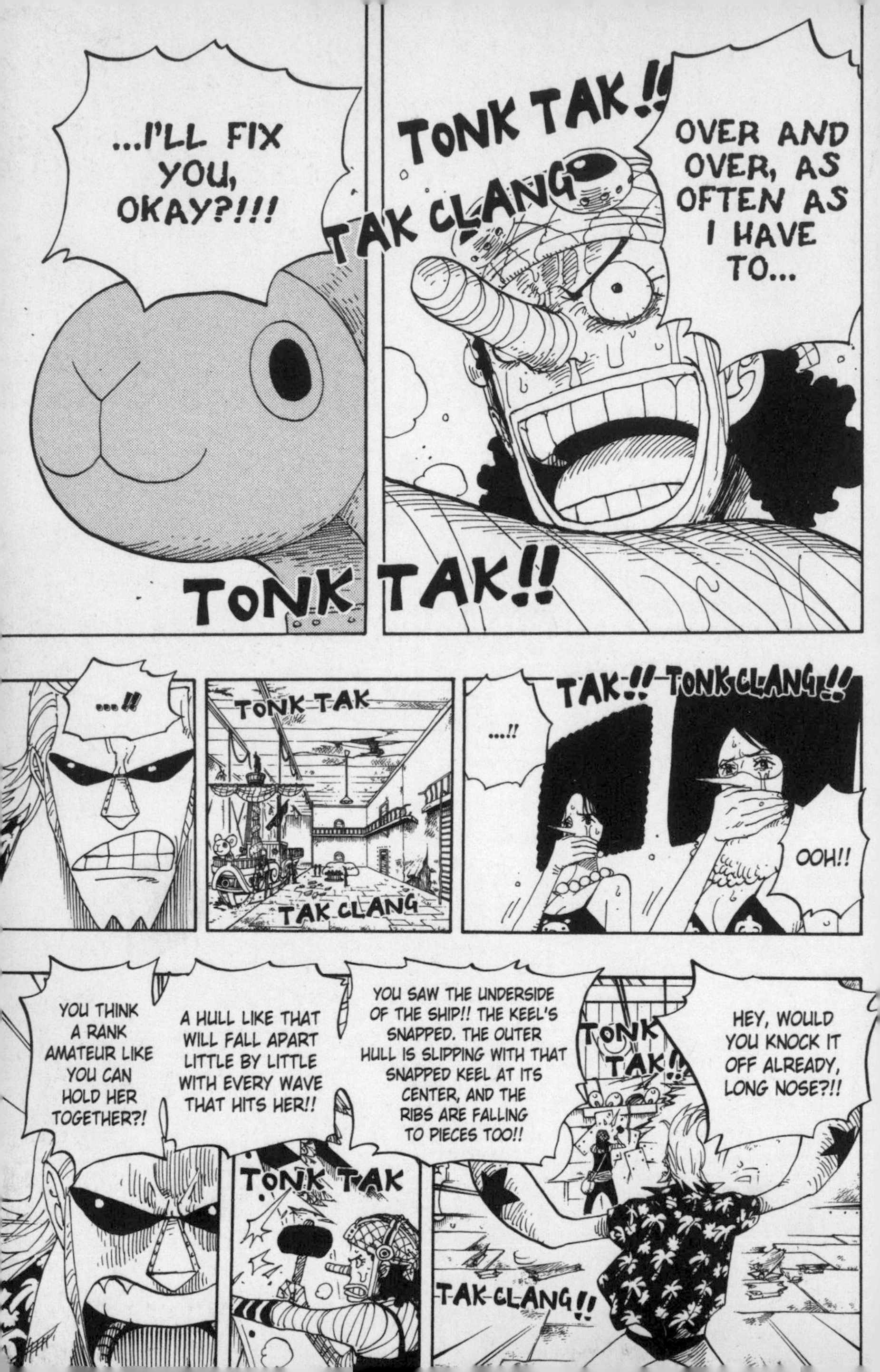
TONK TAK!!
OVER AND OVER, AS OFTEN AS I HAVE TO...
TAK CLANG
...I'LL FIX YOU, OKAY?!!!
TONK TAK!!
TAK!! TONK CLANG!!
...!!
OOH!!
TONK TAK
TAK CLANG
...!!
HEY, WOULD YOU KNOCK IT OFF ALREADY, LONG NOSE?!!
TONK TAK!!
TAK CLANG!!
YOU SAW THE UNDERSIDE OF THE SHIP!! THE KEEL'S SNAPPED. THE OUTER HULL IS SLIPPING WITH THAT SNAPPED KEEL AT ITS CENTER, AND THE RIBS ARE FALLING TO PIECES TOO!!
A HULL LIKE THAT WILL FALL APART LITTLE BY LITTLE WITH EVERY WAVE THAT HITS HER!!
TONK TAK
YOU THINK A RANK AMATEUR LIKE YOU CAN HOLD HER TOGETHER?!

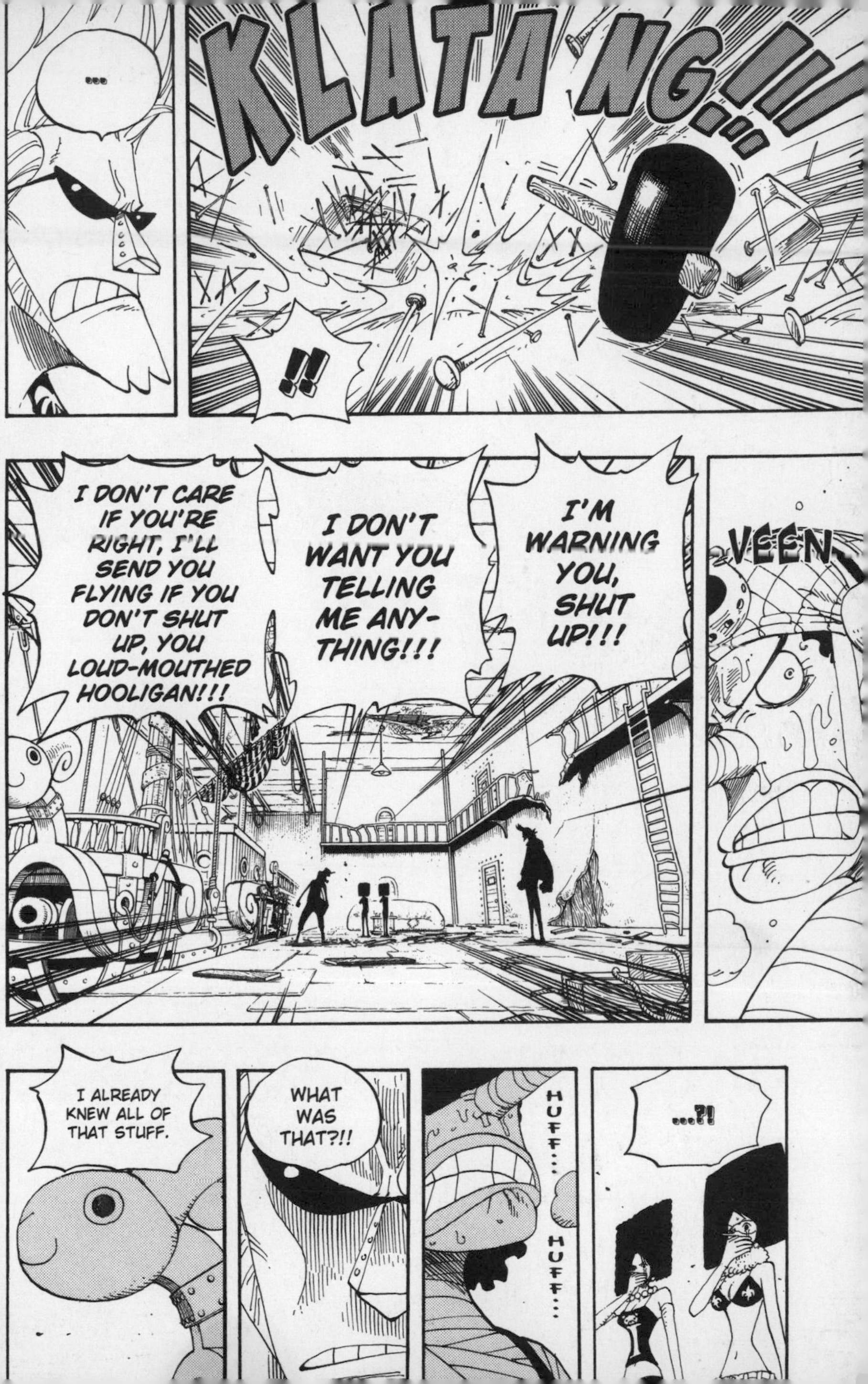
KLATANG!!!!
!!
...
VEEN...
I'M WARNING YOU, SHUT UP!!!
I DON'T WANT YOU TELLING ME ANY-THING!!!
I DON'T CARE IF YOU'RE RIGHT, I'LL SEND YOU FLYING IF YOU DON'T SHUT UP, YOU LOUD-MOUTHED HOOLIGAN!!!
...?!
HUFF...
HUFF...
WHAT WAS THAT?!!
I ALREADY KNEW ALL OF THAT STUFF.

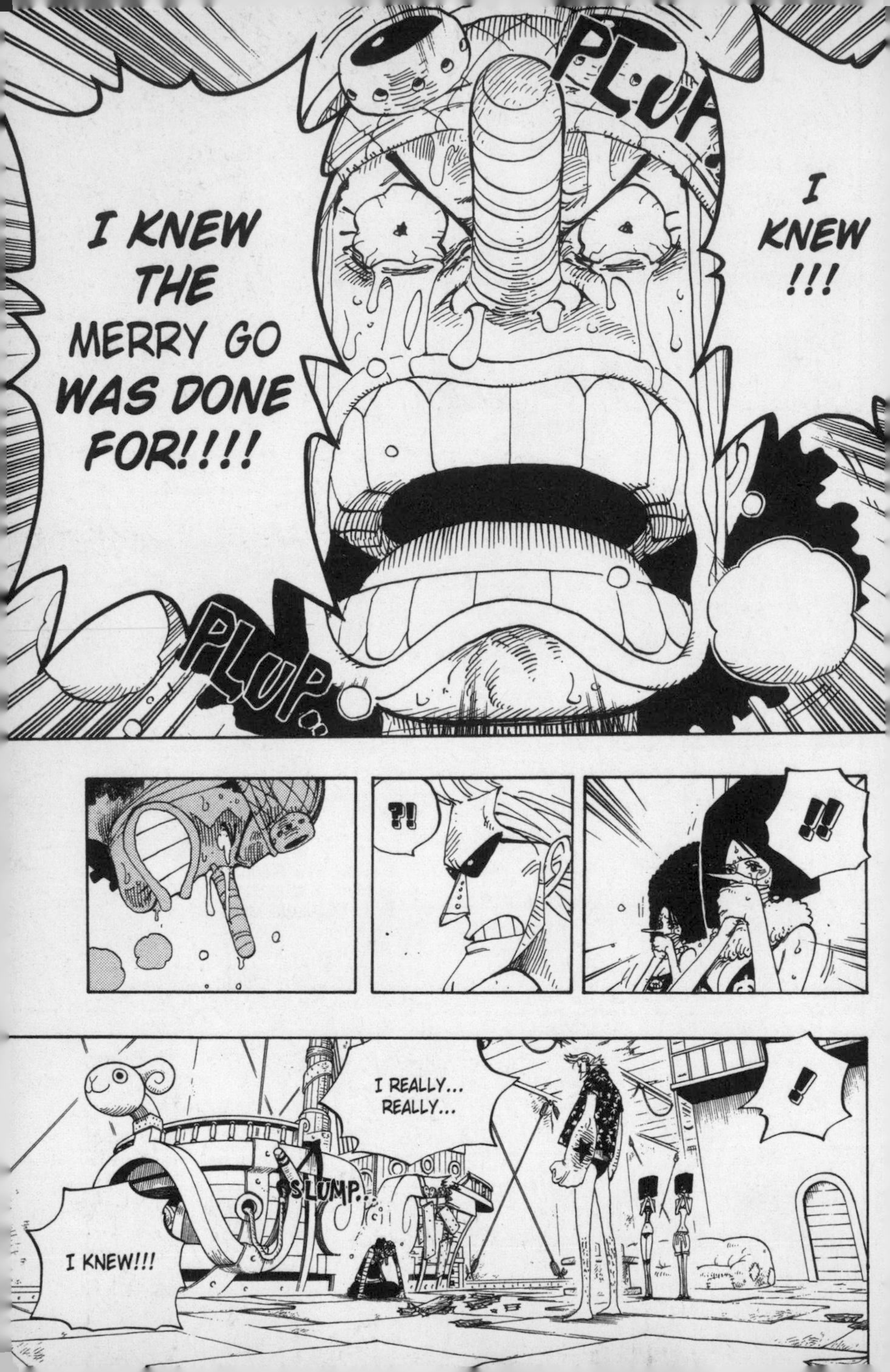

PLUP
I KNEW!!!
I KNEW THE MERRY GO WAS DONE FOR!!!!
PLUP
!!
?!
!
I REALLY... REALLY...
SLUMP...
I KNEW!!!

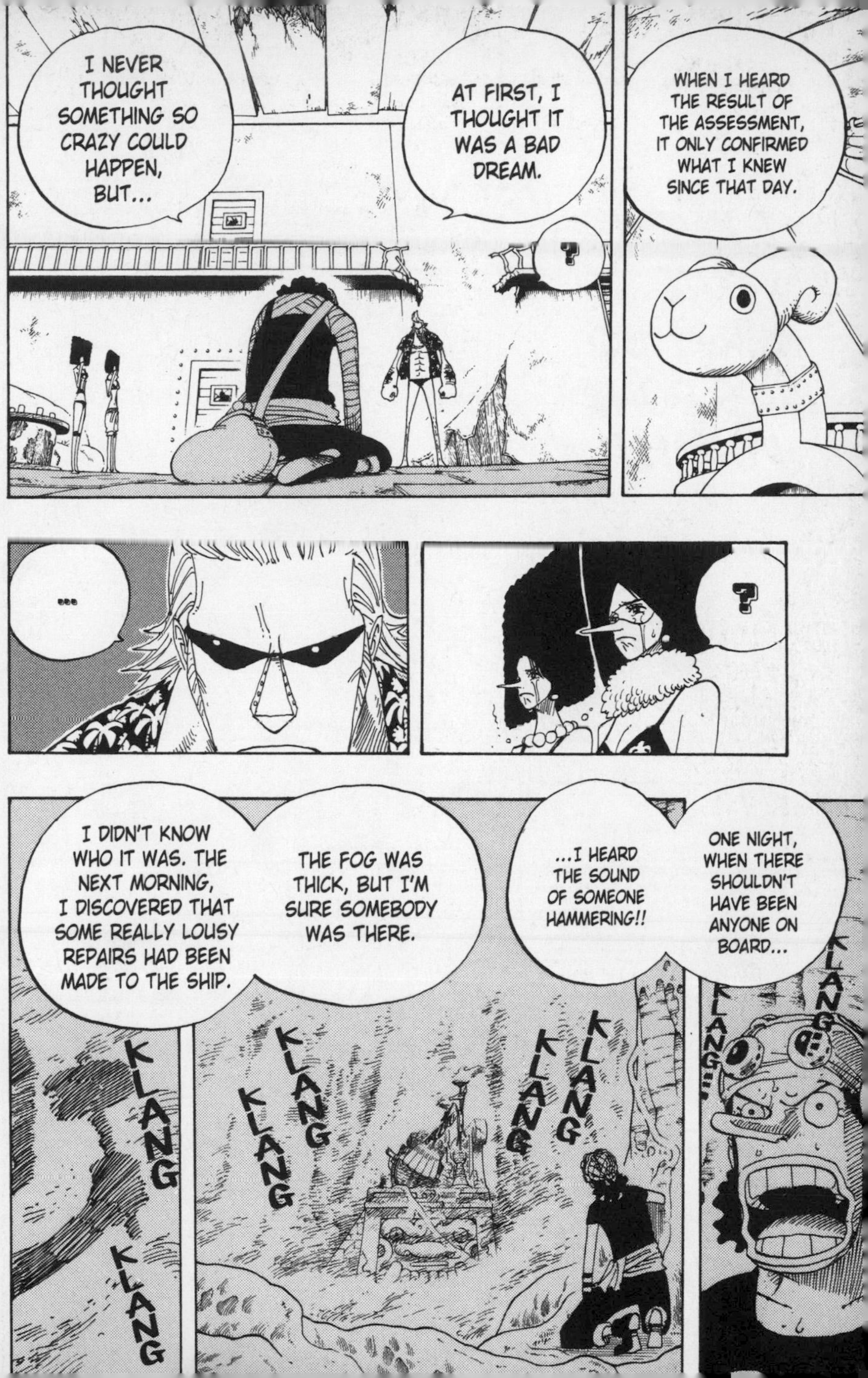
WHEN I HEARD THE RESULT OF THE ASSESSMENT, IT ONLY CONFIRMED WHAT I KNEW SINCE THAT DAY.
AT FIRST, I THOUGHT IT WAS A BAD DREAM.
?
I NEVER THOUGHT SOMETHING SO CRAZY COULD HAPPEN, BUT...
?
...
ONE NIGHT, WHEN THERE SHOULDN'T HAVE BEEN ANYONE ON BOARD...
...I HEARD THE SOUND OF SOMEONE HAMMERING!!
THE FOG WAS THICK, BUT I'M SURE SOMEBODY WAS THERE.
I DIDN'T KNOW WHO IT WAS. THE NEXT MORNING, I DISCOVERED THAT SOME REALLY LOUSY REPAIRS HAD BEEN MADE TO THE SHIP.
KLANG
KLANG!!
KLANG!!
KLANG
KLANG
KLANG
KLANG
KLANG
KLANG

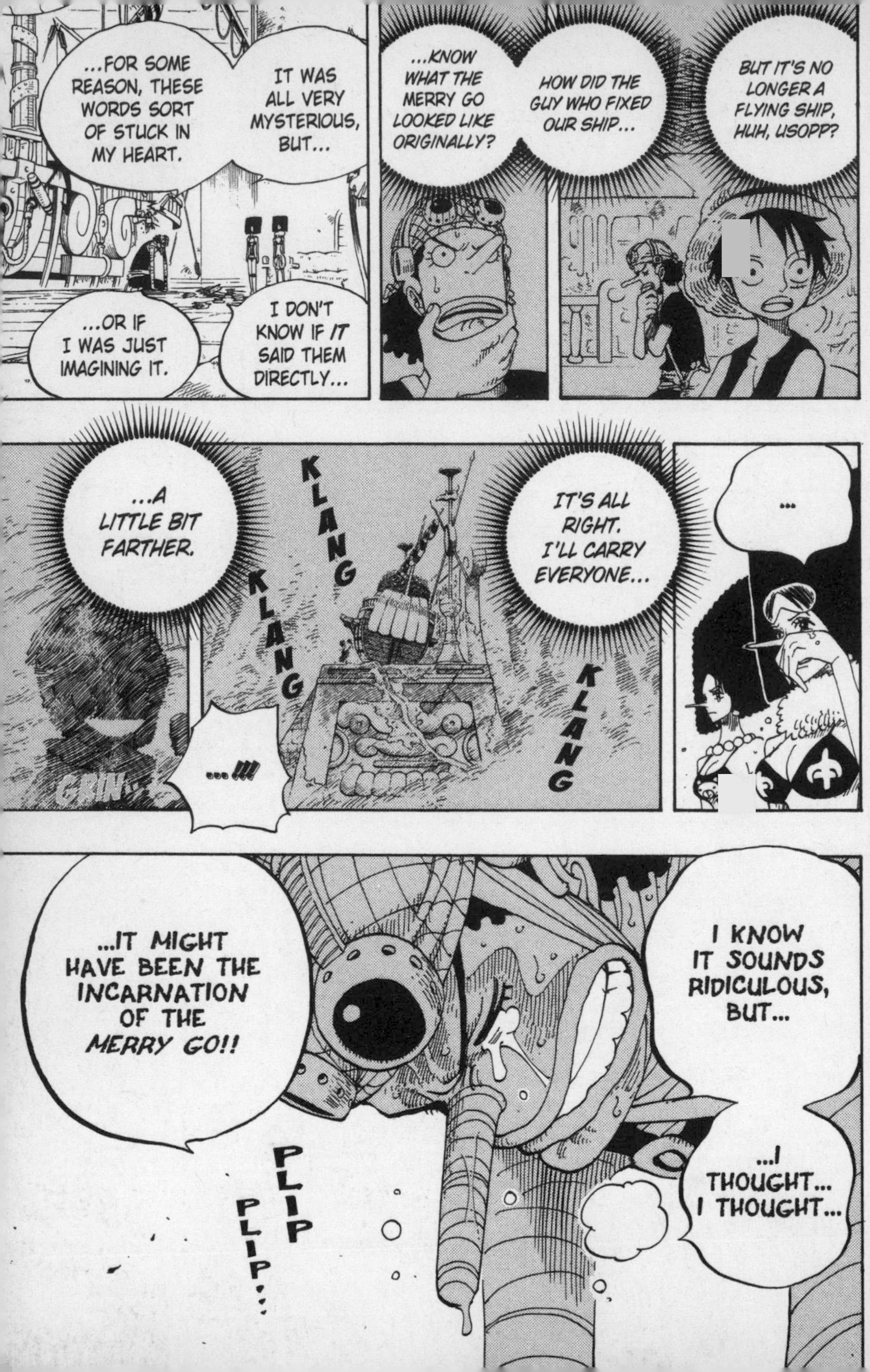
BUT IT'S NO LONGER A FLYING SHIP, HUH, USOPP?
HOW DID THE GUY WHO FIXED OUR SHIP...
...KNOW WHAT THE MERRY GO LOOKED LIKE ORIGINALLY?
IT WAS ALL VERY MYSTERIOUS, BUT...
...FOR SOME REASON, THESE WORDS SORT OF STUCK IN MY HEART.
I DON'T KNOW IF *IT* SAID THEM DIRECTLY...
...OR IF I WAS JUST IMAGINING IT.
...
IT'S ALL RIGHT. I'LL CARRY EVERYONE...
KLANG
KLANG
KLANG
...A LITTLE BIT FARTHER.
...!!!
GRIN
I KNOW IT SOUNDS RIDICULOUS, BUT...
...I THOUGHT... I THOUGHT...
...IT MIGHT HAVE BEEN THE INCARNATION OF THE *MERRY GO*!!
PLIP
PLIP
PLIP

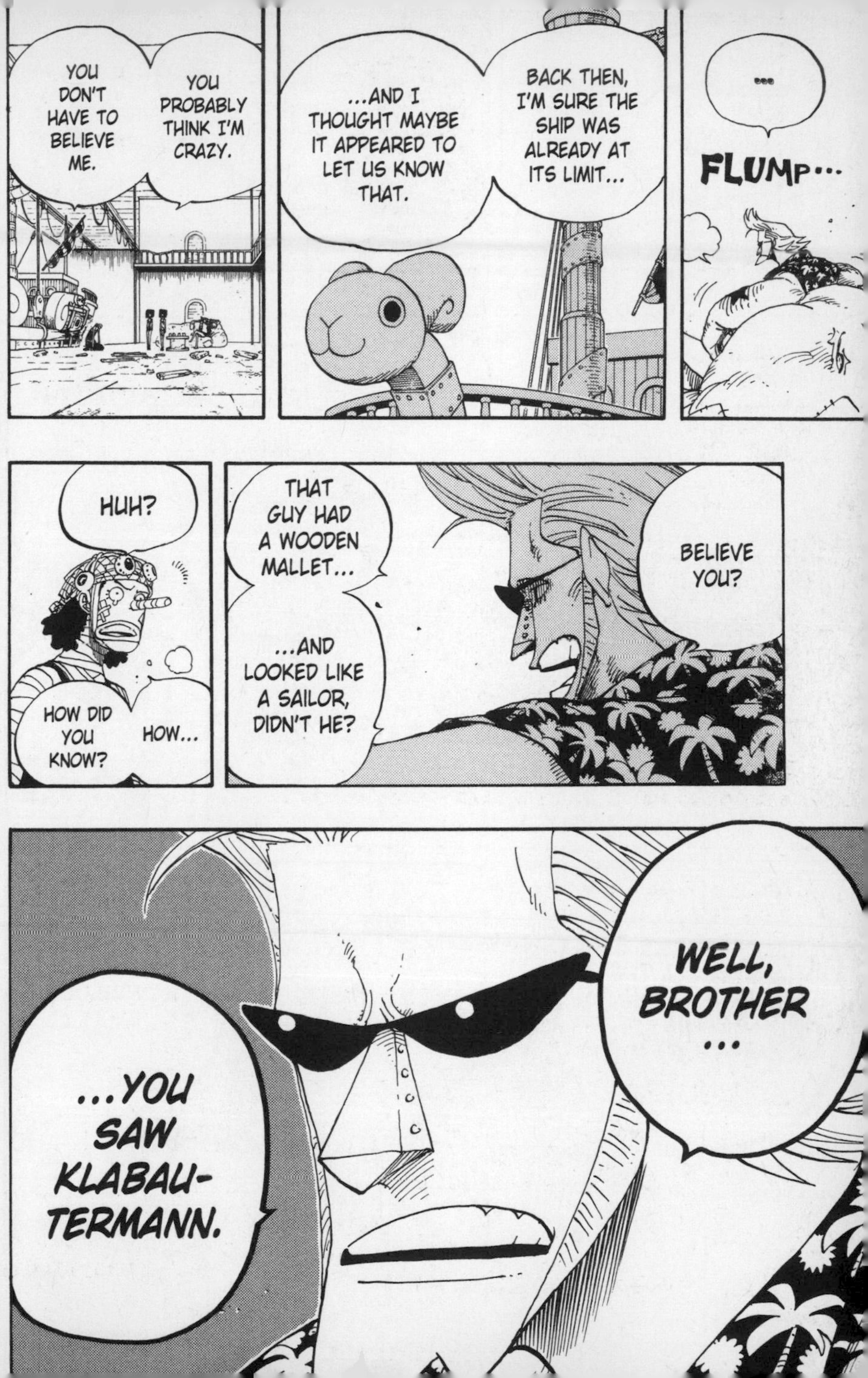
...
FLUMP...
BACK THEN, I'M SURE THE SHIP WAS ALREADY AT ITS LIMIT...
...AND I THOUGHT MAYBE IT APPEARED TO LET US KNOW THAT.
YOU PROBABLY THINK I'M CRAZY.
YOU DON'T HAVE TO BELIEVE ME.
BELIEVE YOU?
THAT GUY HAD A WOODEN MALLET...
...AND LOOKED LIKE A SAILOR, DIDN'T HE?
HUH?
HOW...
HOW DID YOU KNOW?
WELL, BROTHER...
...YOU SAW KLABAU-TERMANN.

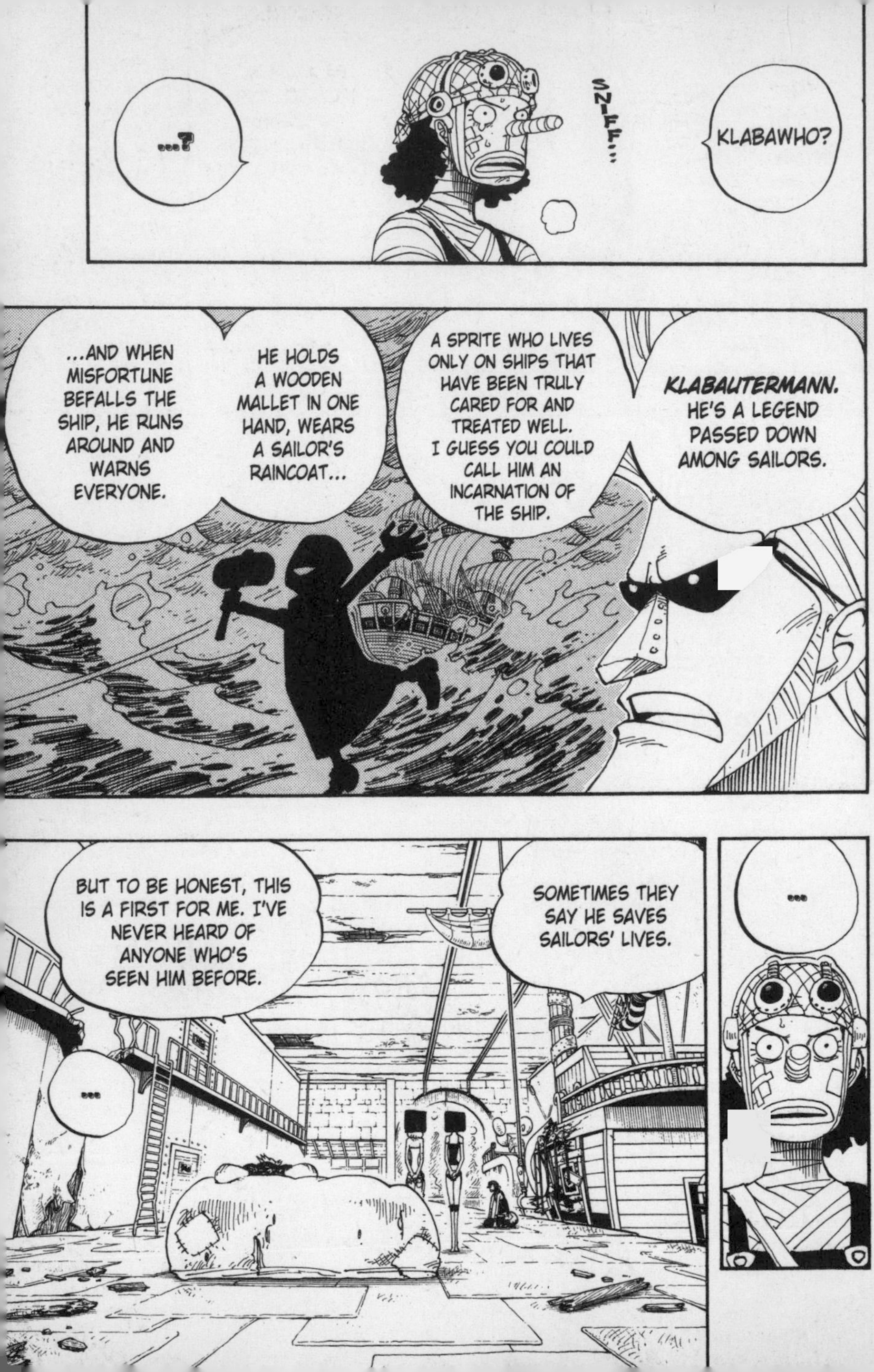
KLABAWHO?
SNIFF...
...?
KLABAUTERMANN. HE'S A LEGEND PASSED DOWN AMONG SAILORS.
A SPRITE WHO LIVES ONLY ON SHIPS THAT HAVE BEEN TRULY CARED FOR AND TREATED WELL. I GUESS YOU COULD CALL HIM AN INCARNATION OF THE SHIP.
HE HOLDS A WOODEN MALLET IN ONE HAND, WEARS A SAILOR'S RAINCOAT...
...AND WHEN MISFORTUNE BEFALLS THE SHIP, HE RUNS AROUND AND WARNS EVERYONE.
...
SOMETIMES THEY SAY HE SAVES SAILORS' LIVES.
BUT TO BE HONEST, THIS IS A FIRST FOR ME. I'VE NEVER HEARD OF ANYONE WHO'S SEEN HIM BEFORE.
...

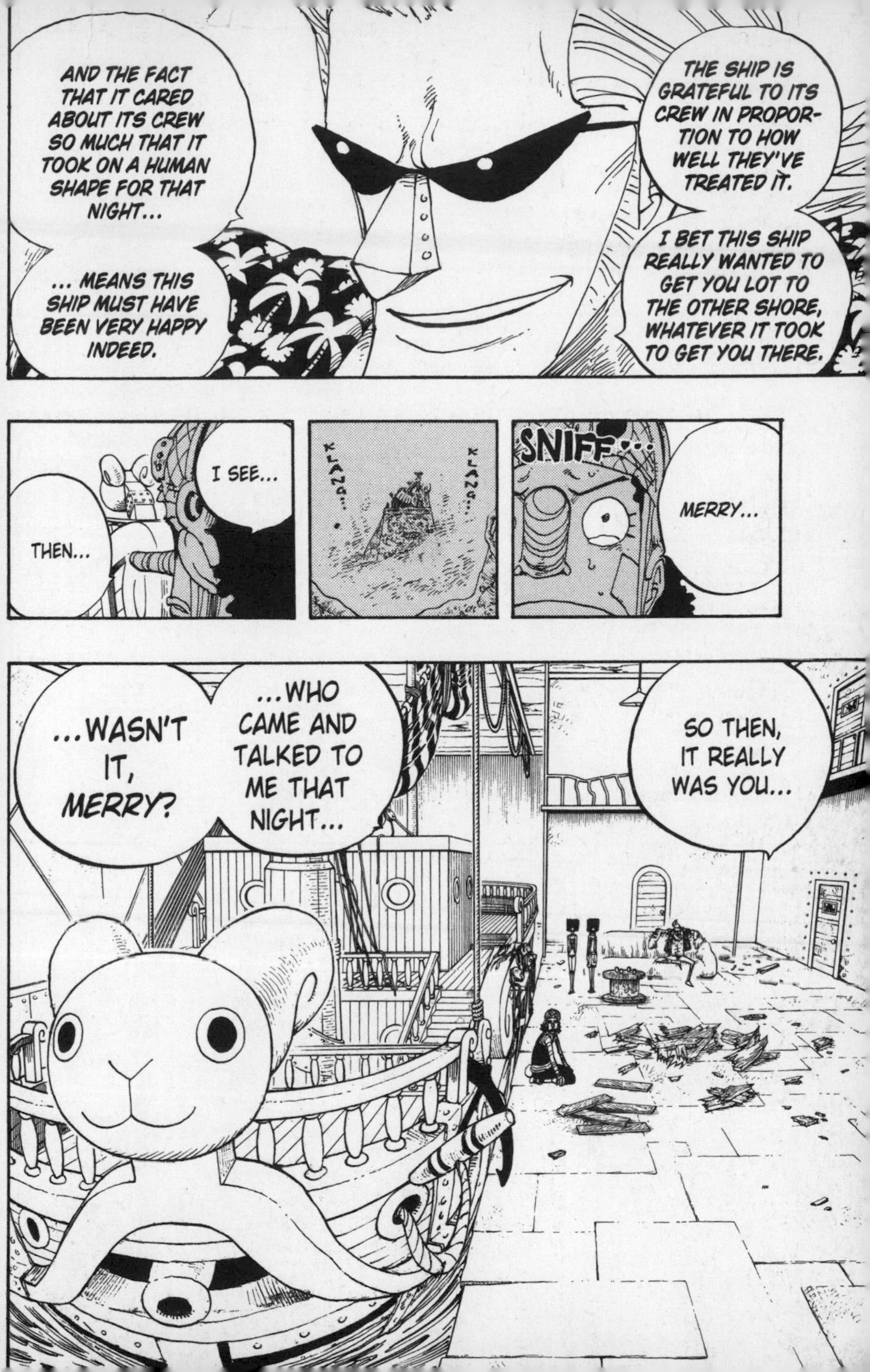
THE SHIP IS GRATEFUL TO ITS CREW IN PROPORTION TO HOW WELL THEY'VE TREATED IT.
I BET THIS SHIP REALLY WANTED TO GET YOU LOT TO THE OTHER SHORE, WHATEVER IT TOOK TO GET YOU THERE.
AND THE FACT THAT IT CARED ABOUT ITS CREW SO MUCH THAT IT TOOK ON A HUMAN SHAPE FOR THAT NIGHT...
... MEANS THIS SHIP MUST HAVE BEEN VERY HAPPY INDEED.
SNIFF...
MERRY...
KLANG...
KLANG...
I SEE...
THEN...
SO THEN, IT REALLY WAS YOU...
...WHO CAME AND TALKED TO ME THAT NIGHT...
...WASN'T IT, MERRY?

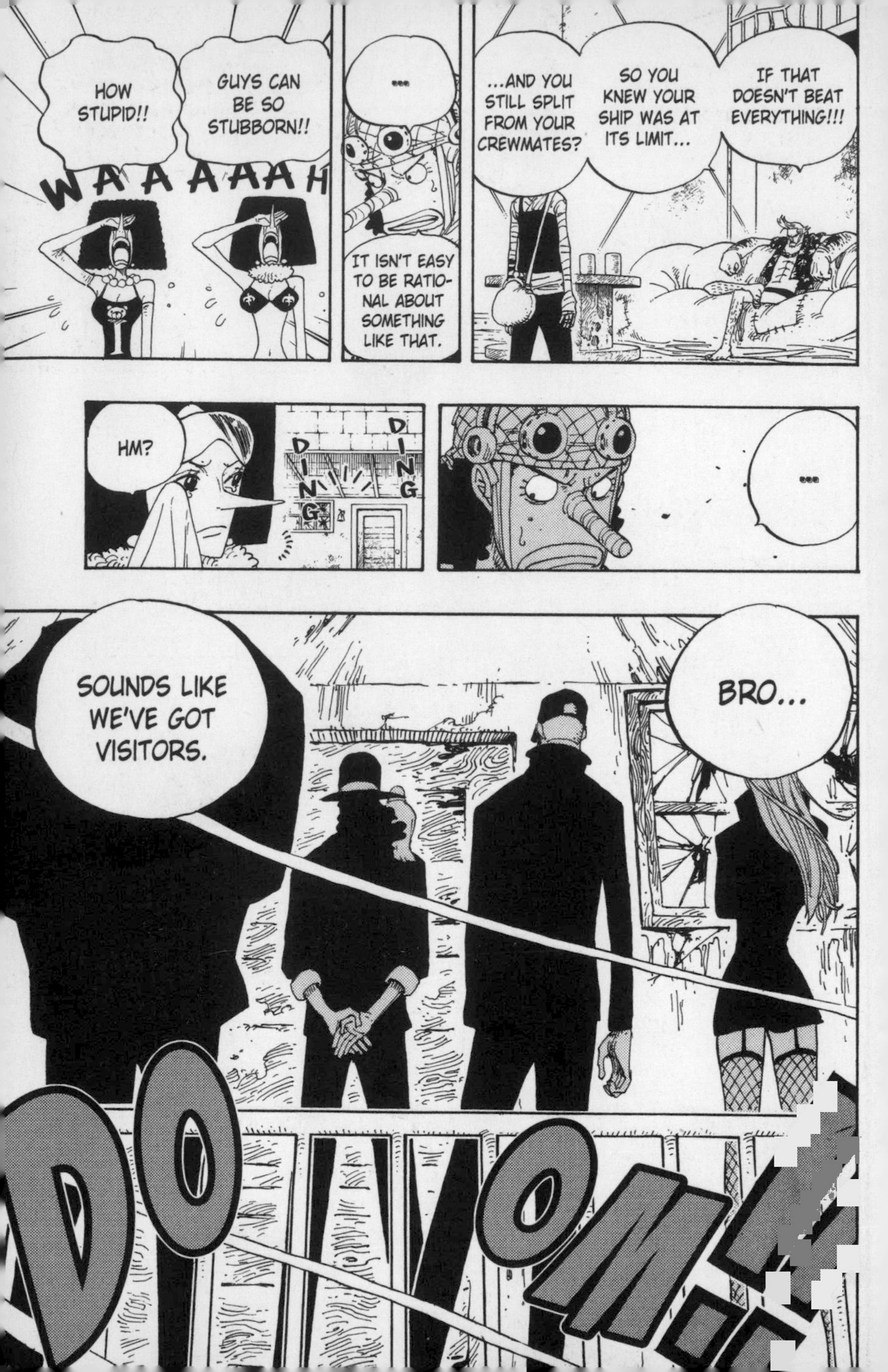
IF THAT DOESN'T BEAT EVERYTHING!!!
SO YOU KNEW YOUR SHIP WAS AT ITS LIMIT...
...AND YOU STILL SPLIT FROM YOUR CREWMATES?
...
IT ISN'T EASY TO BE RATIONAL ABOUT SOMETHING LIKE THAT.
GUYS CAN BE SO STUBBORN!!
HOW STUPID!!
WAAAAAH
...
DING
DING
HM?
BRO...
SOUNDS LIKE WE'VE GOT VISITORS.
DOOM!!

TOM'S WORKERS

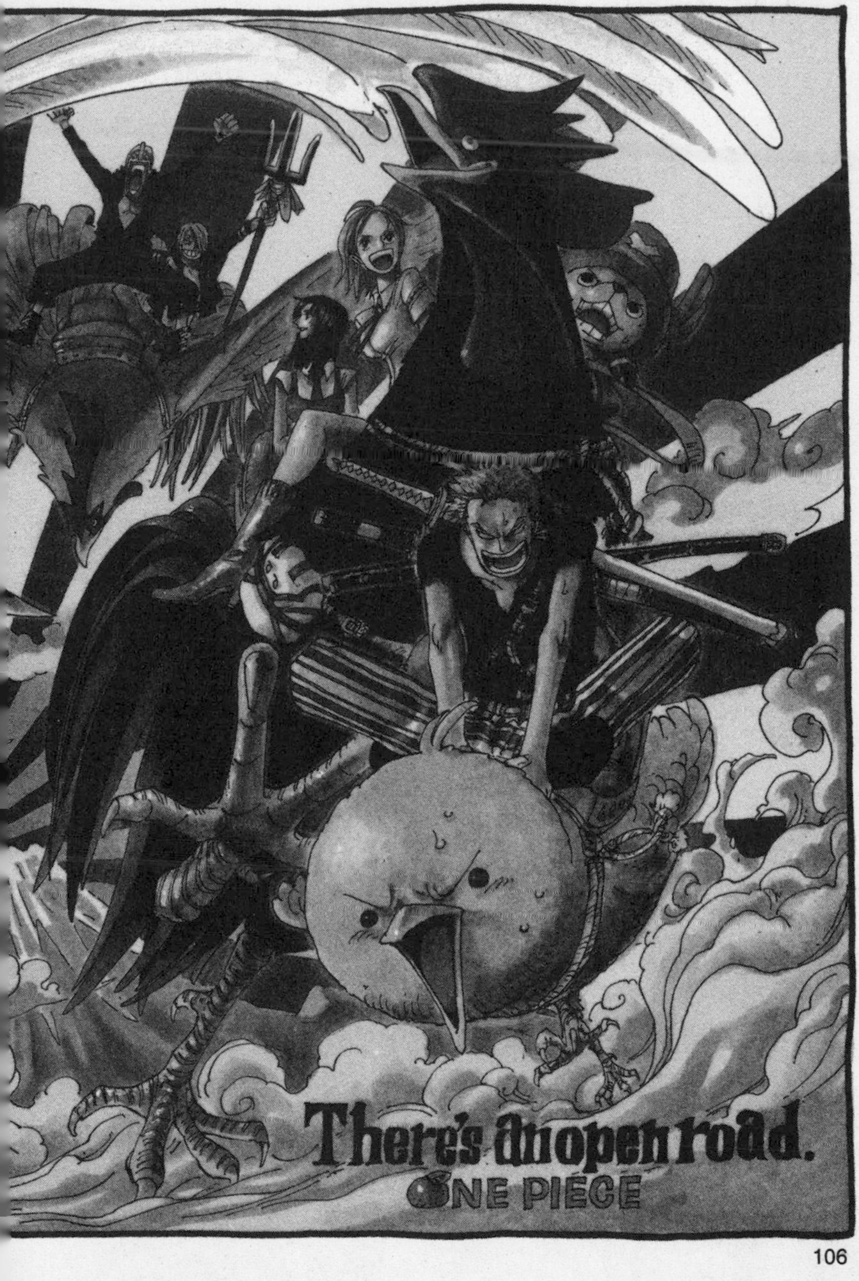
There's an open road.
ONE PIECE

Chapter 352:

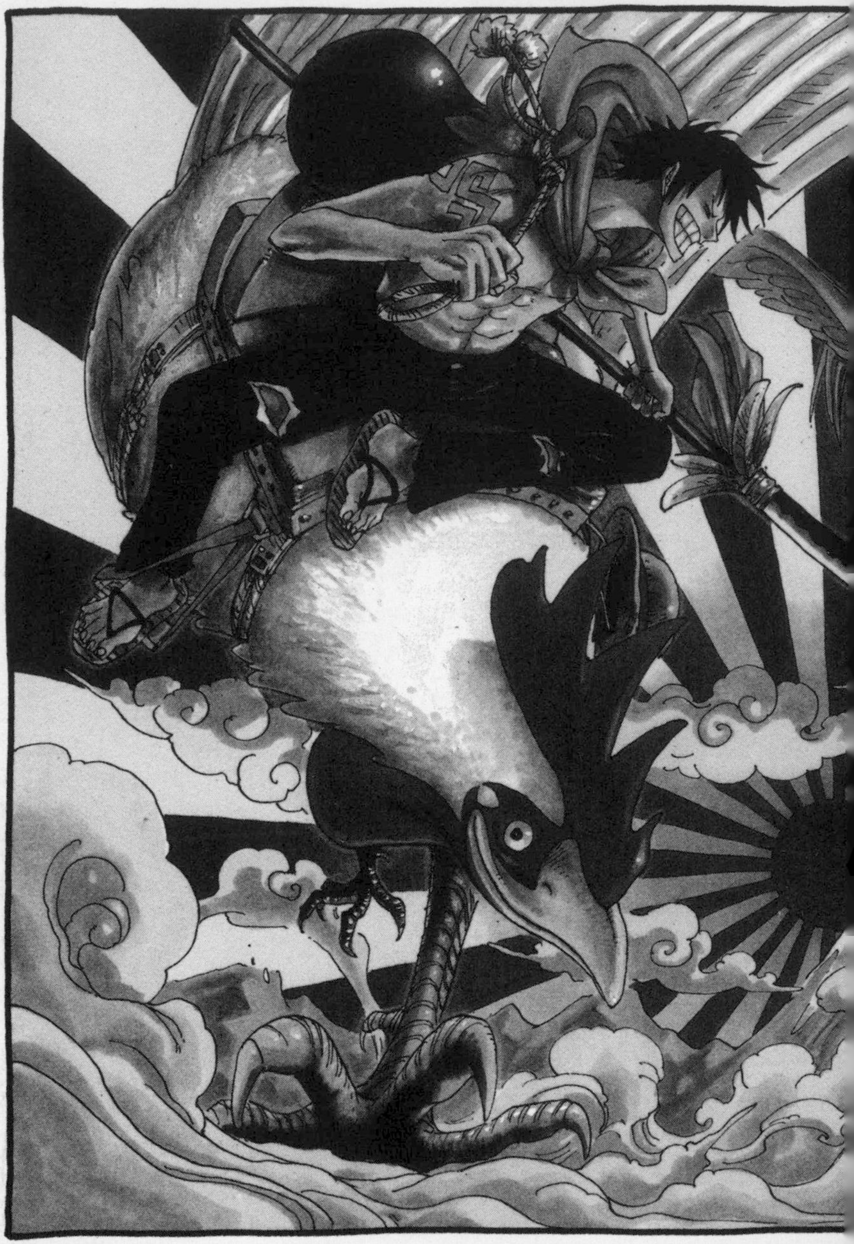

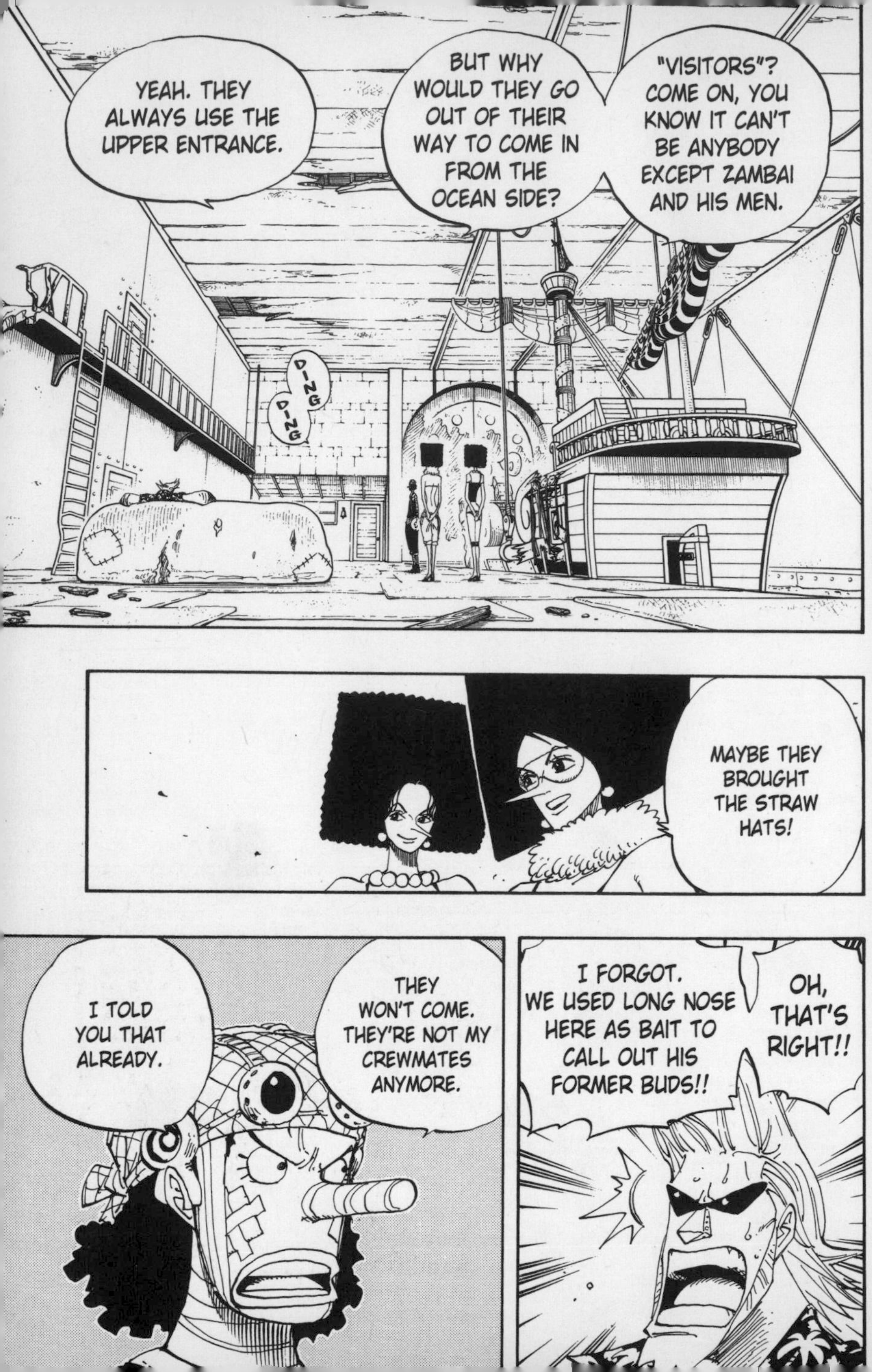
"VISITORS"? COME ON, YOU KNOW IT CAN'T BE ANYBODY EXCEPT ZAMBAI AND HIS MEN.
BUT WHY WOULD THEY GO OUT OF THEIR WAY TO COME IN FROM THE OCEAN SIDE?
YEAH. THEY ALWAYS USE THE UPPER ENTRANCE.
DING
DING
MAYBE THEY BROUGHT THE STRAW HATS!
OH, THAT'S RIGHT!!
I FORGOT. WE USED LONG NOSE HERE AS BAIT TO CALL OUT HIS FORMER BUDS!!
THEY WON'T COME. THEY'RE NOT MY CREWMATES ANYMORE.
I TOLD YOU THAT ALREADY.

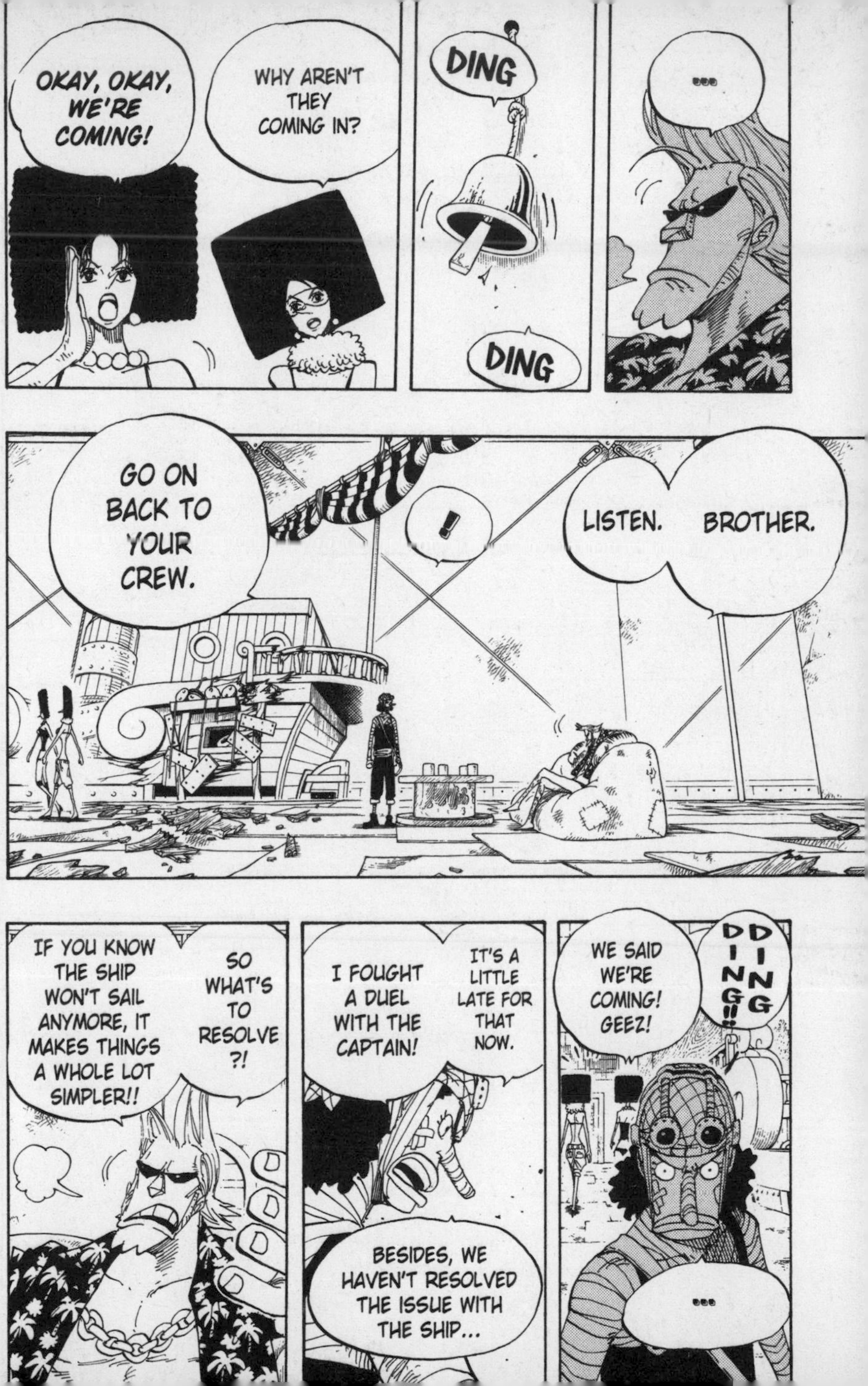
...
DING
DING
WHY AREN'T THEY COMING IN?
OKAY, OKAY, WE'RE COMING!
LISTEN. BROTHER.
!
GO ON BACK TO YOUR CREW.
DING DING!!
WE SAID WE'RE COMING! GEEZ!
...
IT'S A LITTLE LATE FOR THAT NOW.
I FOUGHT A DUEL WITH THE CAPTAIN!
BESIDES, WE HAVEN'T RESOLVED THE ISSUE WITH THE SHIP...
SO WHAT'S TO RESOLVE?!
IF YOU KNOW THE SHIP WON'T SAIL ANYMORE, IT MAKES THINGS A WHOLE LOT SIMPLER!!

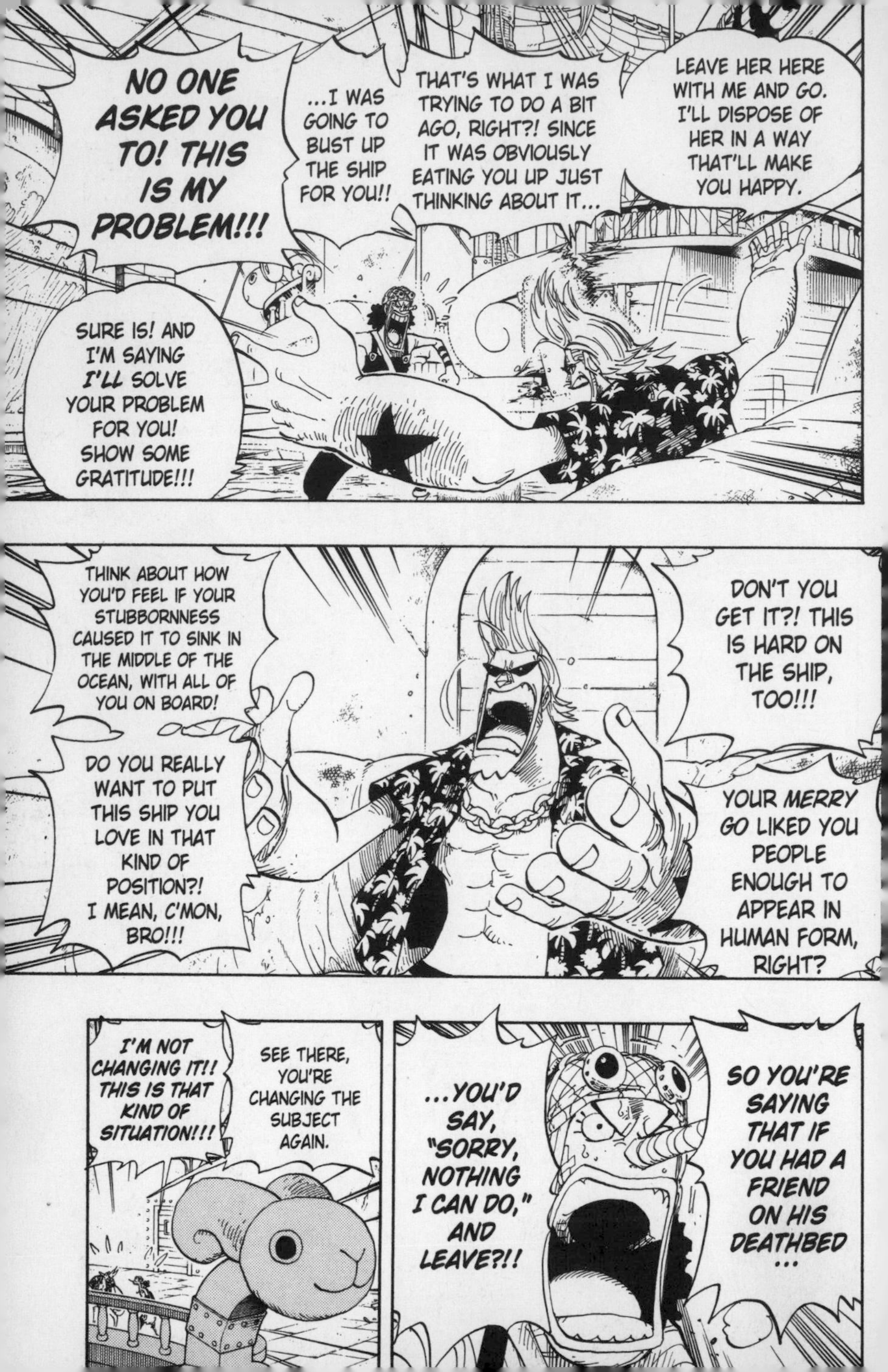
LEAVE HER HERE WITH ME AND GO. I'LL DISPOSE OF HER IN A WAY THAT'LL MAKE YOU HAPPY.
THAT'S WHAT I WAS TRYING TO DO A BIT AGO, RIGHT?! SINCE IT WAS OBVIOUSLY EATING YOU UP JUST THINKING ABOUT IT...
...I WAS GOING TO BUST UP THE SHIP FOR YOU!!
NO ONE ASKED YOU TO! THIS IS MY PROBLEM!!!
SURE IS! AND I'M SAYING *I'LL* SOLVE YOUR PROBLEM FOR YOU! SHOW SOME GRATITUDE!!!
DON'T YOU GET IT?! THIS IS HARD ON THE SHIP, TOO!!!
YOUR MERRY GO LIKED YOU PEOPLE ENOUGH TO APPEAR IN HUMAN FORM, RIGHT?
THINK ABOUT HOW YOU'D FEEL IF YOUR STUBBORNNESS CAUSED IT TO SINK IN THE MIDDLE OF THE OCEAN, WITH ALL OF YOU ON BOARD!
DO YOU REALLY WANT TO PUT THIS SHIP YOU LOVE IN THAT KIND OF POSITION?! I MEAN, C'MON, BRO!!!
SO YOU'RE SAYING THAT IF YOU HAD A FRIEND ON HIS DEATHBED ...
...YOU'D SAY, "SORRY, NOTHING I CAN DO," AND LEAVE?!!
SEE THERE, YOU'RE CHANGING THE SUBJECT AGAIN.
I'M NOT CHANGING IT!! THIS IS THAT KIND OF SITUATION!!!

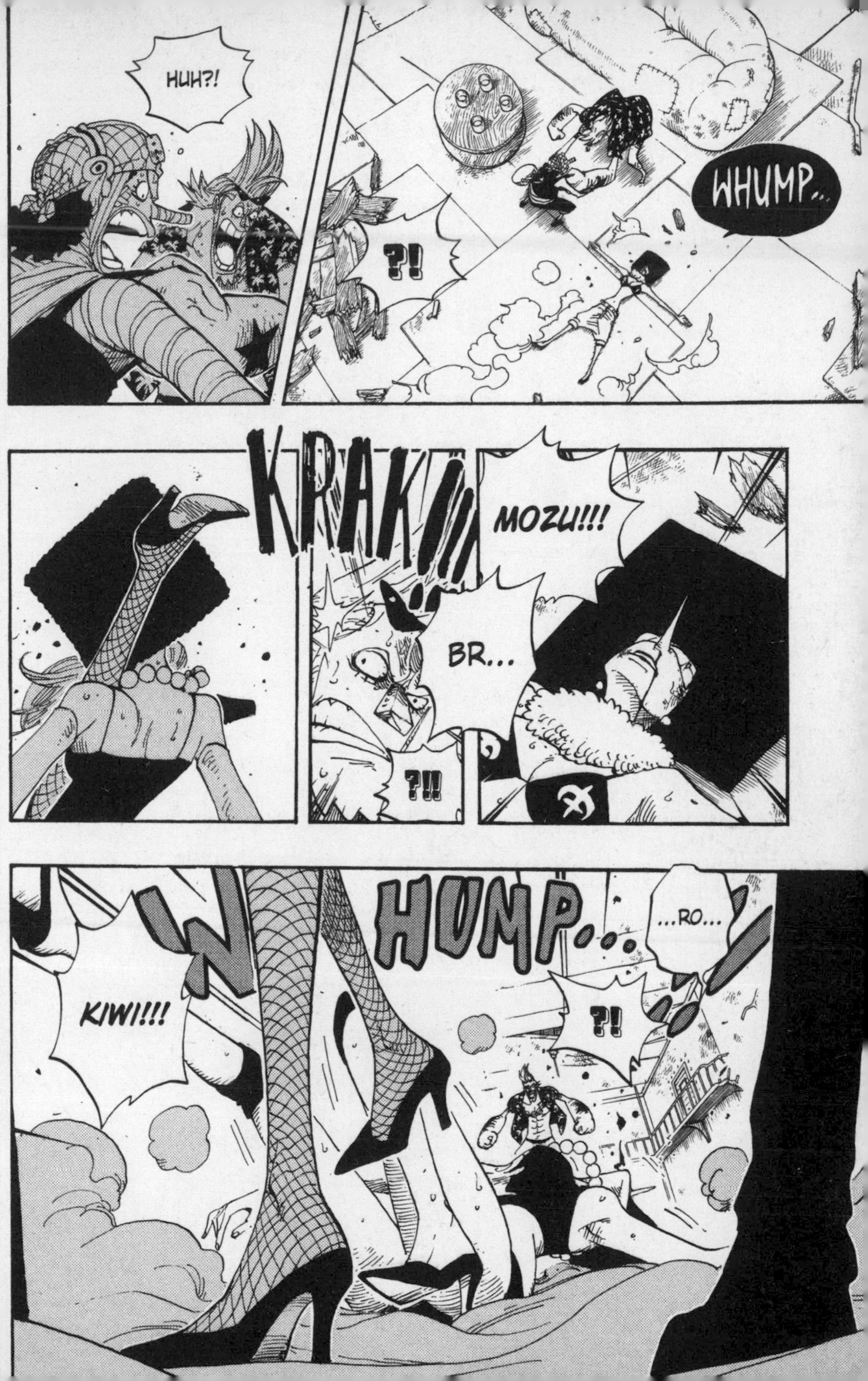

WHUMP...
?!
HUH?!
MOZU!!!
KRAK
BR...
?!!
...RO...
W HUMP...
?!
KIWI!!!

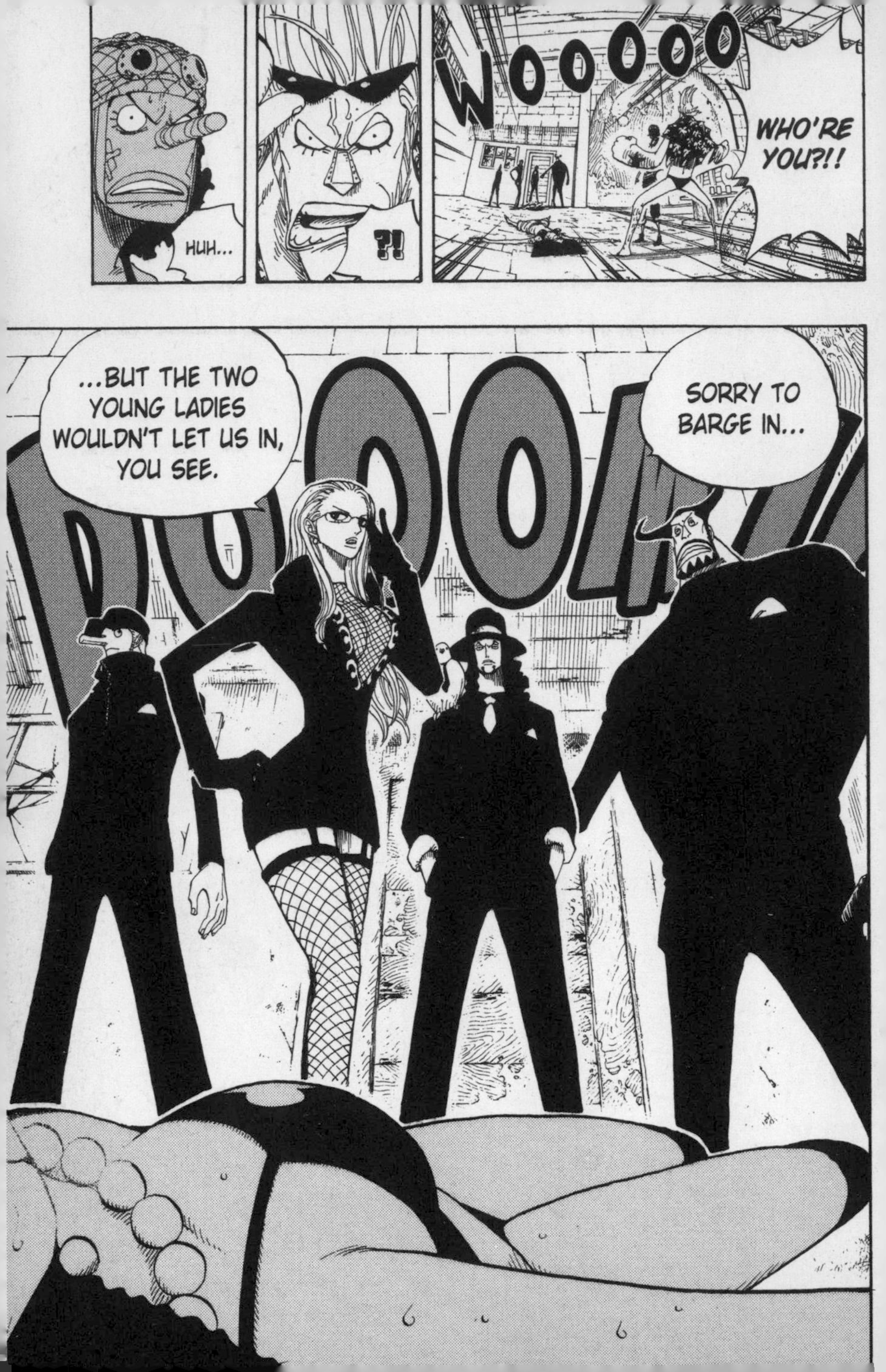
WOOOOO
WHO'RE YOU?!!
?!
HUH...
SORRY TO BARGE IN...
...BUT THE TWO YOUNG LADIES WOULDN'T LET US IN, YOU SEE.

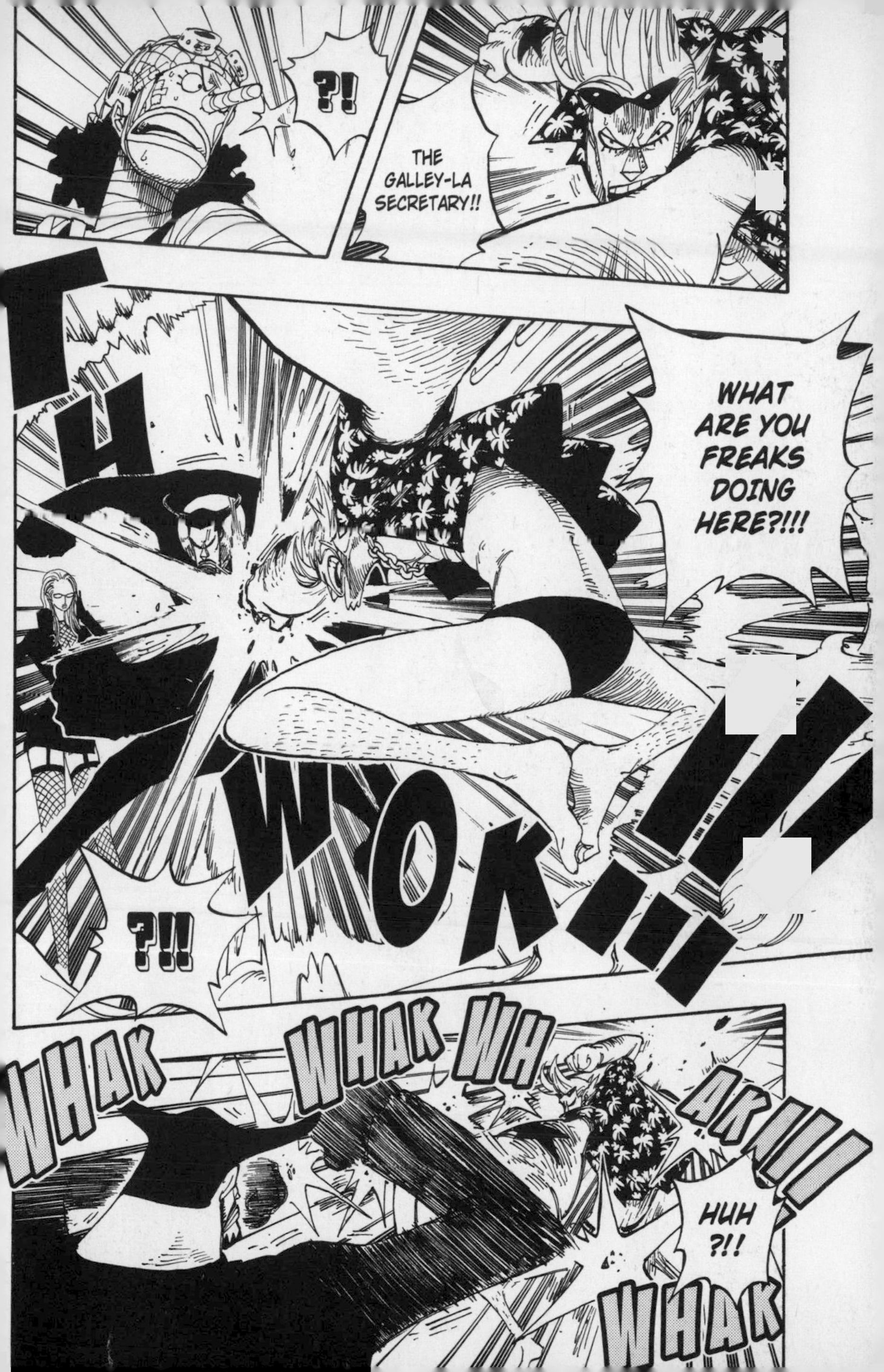
THE GALLEY-LA SECRETARY!!
?!
WHAT ARE YOU FREAKS DOING HERE?!!!
THWOK!!!
?!!
WHAK WHAK WH AK!!!
HUH ?!!
WHAK

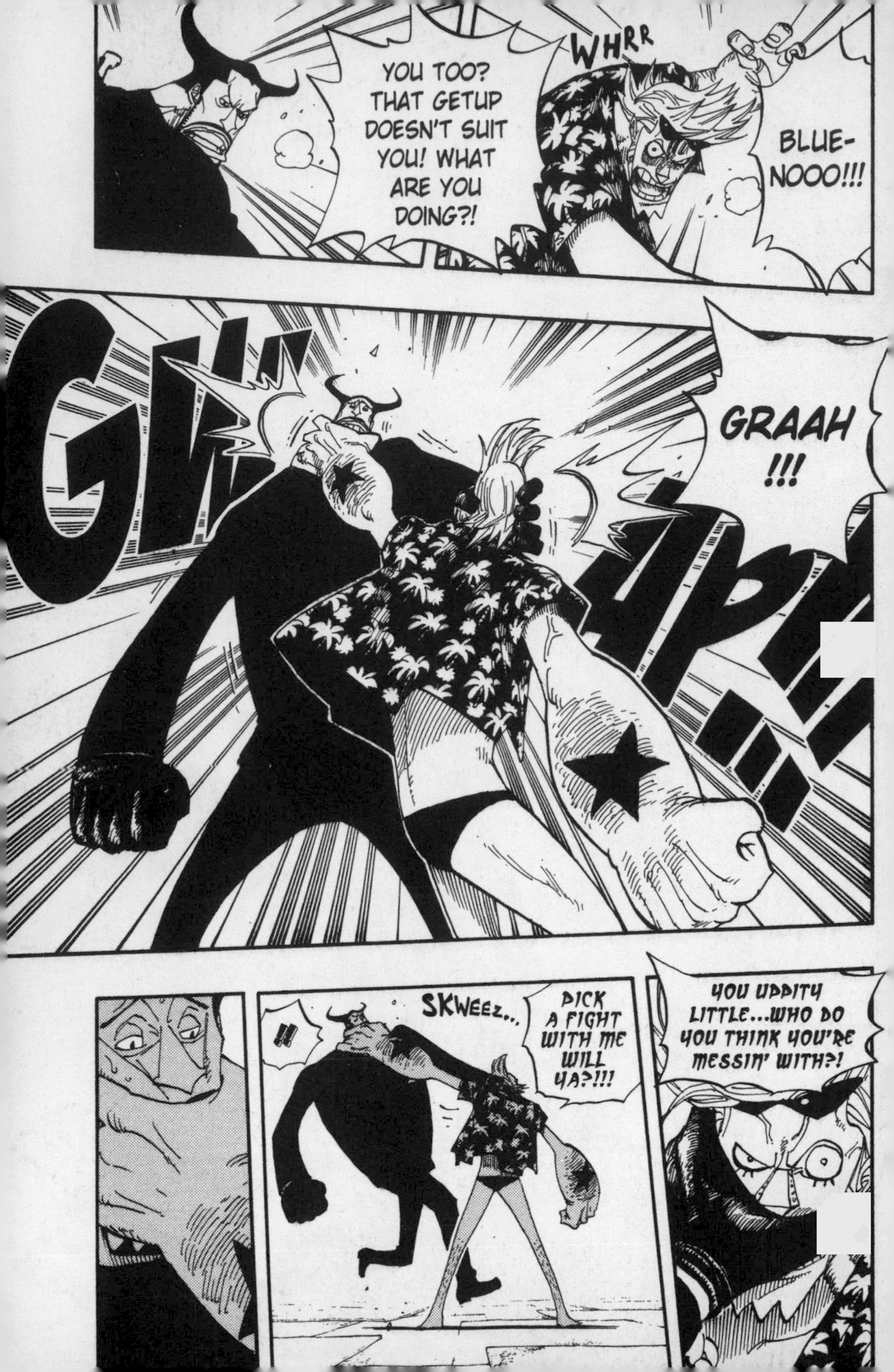
WHRR
BLUE-NOOO!!!
YOU TOO? THAT GETUP DOESN'T SUIT YOU! WHAT ARE YOU DOING?!
GRAAH!!!
YOU UPPITY LITTLE...WHO DO YOU THINK YOU'RE MESSIN' WITH?!
PICK A FIGHT WITH ME WILL YA?!!!
SKWEEZ...
!!

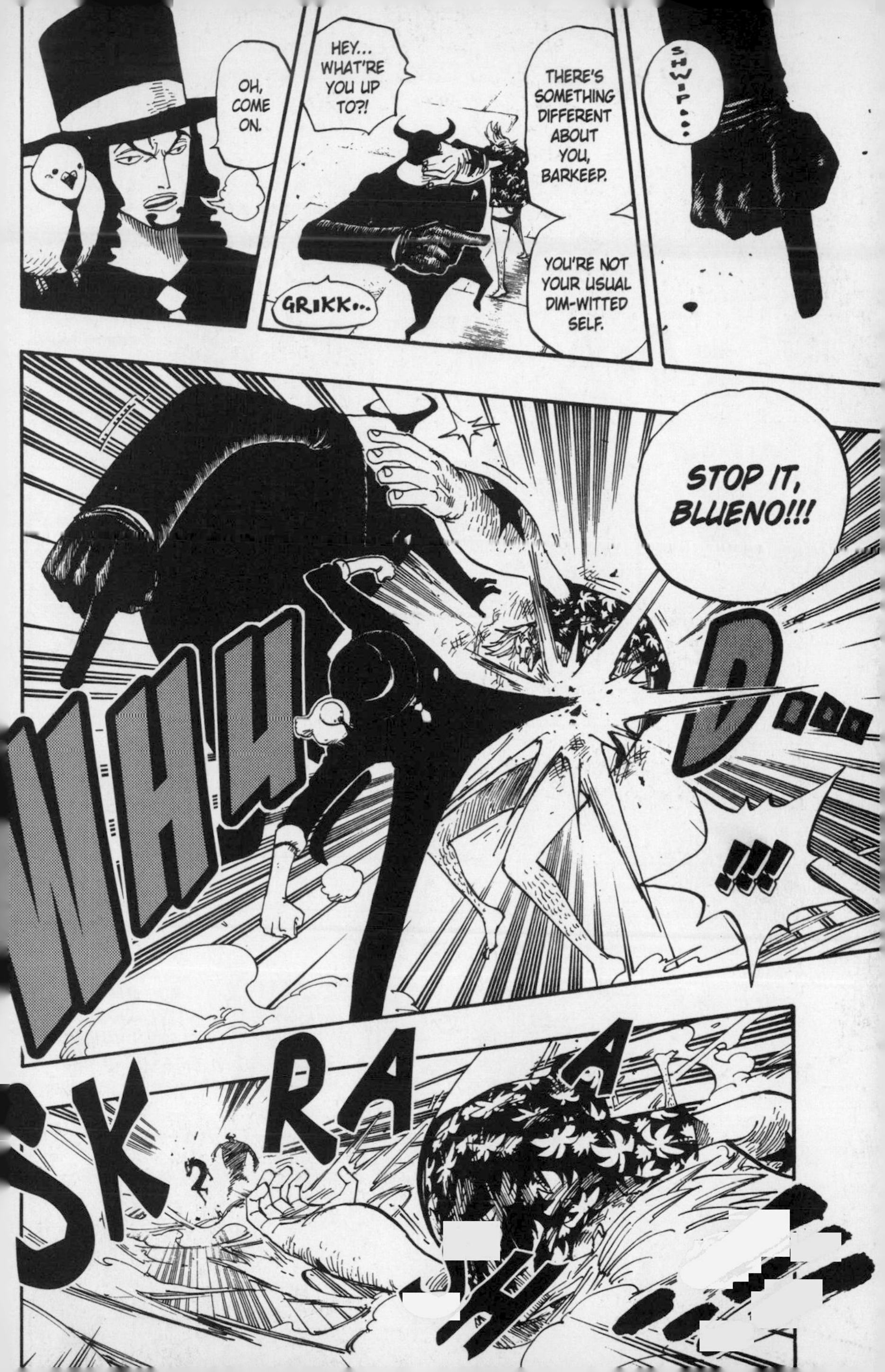
SHWIP...
THERE'S SOMETHING DIFFERENT ABOUT YOU, BARKEEP.
YOU'RE NOT YOUR USUAL DIM-WITTED SELF.
HEY... WHAT'RE YOU UP TO?!
GRIKK...
OH, COME ON.
STOP IT, BLUENO!!!
D...
!!!
WHU

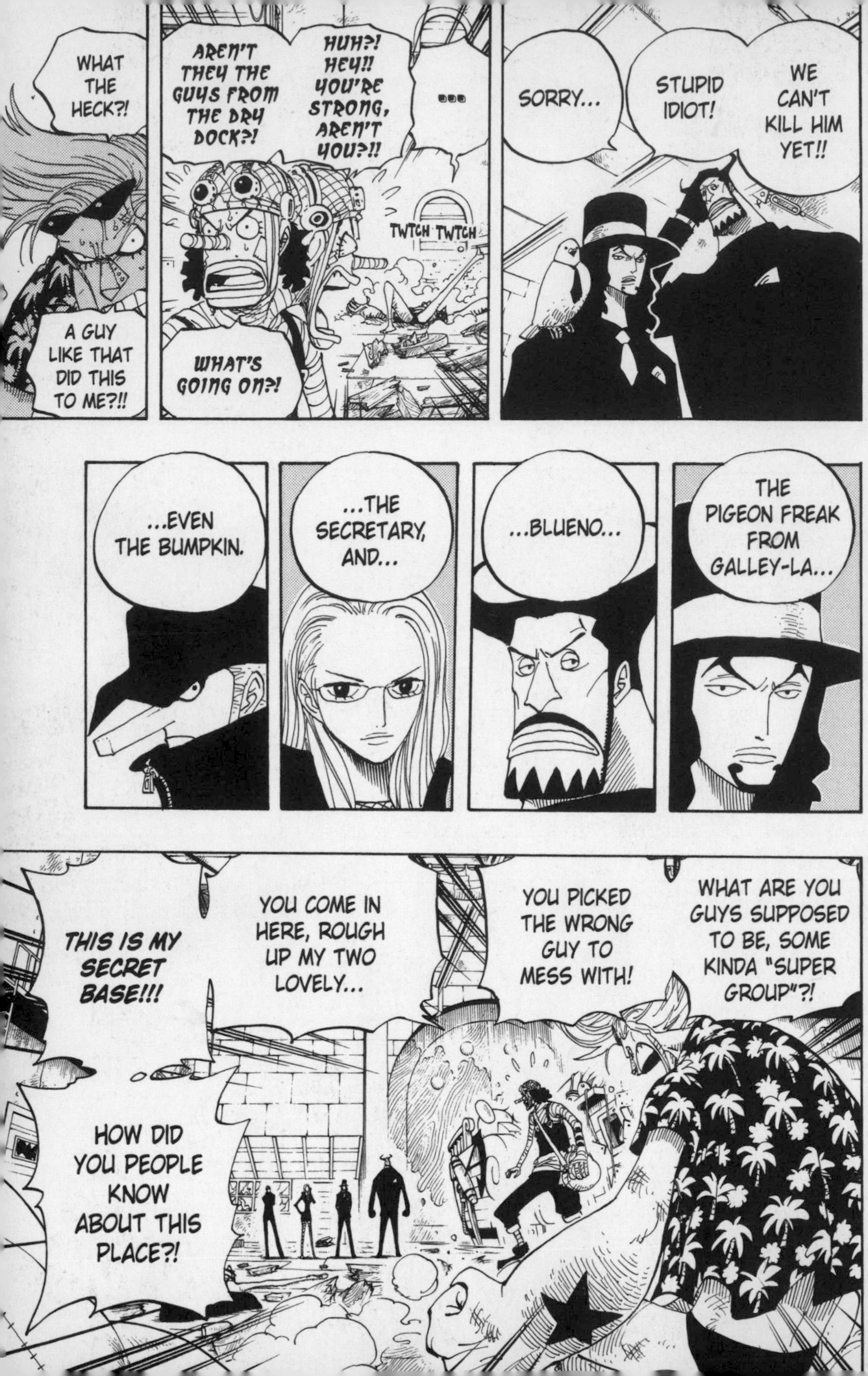
WE CAN'T KILL HIM YET!!
STUPID IDIOT!
SORRY...
...
HUH?! HEY!! YOU'RE STRONG, AREN'T YOU?!!
AREN'T THEY THE GUYS FROM THE DRY DOCK?!
TWTCH TWTCH
WHAT'S GOING ON?!
WHAT THE HECK?!
A GUY LIKE THAT DID THIS TO ME?!!
THE PIGEON FREAK FROM GALLEY-LA...
...BLUENO...
...THE SECRETARY, AND...
...EVEN THE BUMPKIN.
WHAT ARE YOU GUYS SUPPOSED TO BE, SOME KINDA "SUPER GROUP"?!
YOU PICKED THE WRONG GUY TO MESS WITH!
YOU COME IN HERE, ROUGH UP MY TWO LOVELY...
THIS IS MY SECRET BASE!!!
HOW DID YOU PEOPLE KNOW ABOUT THIS PLACE?!

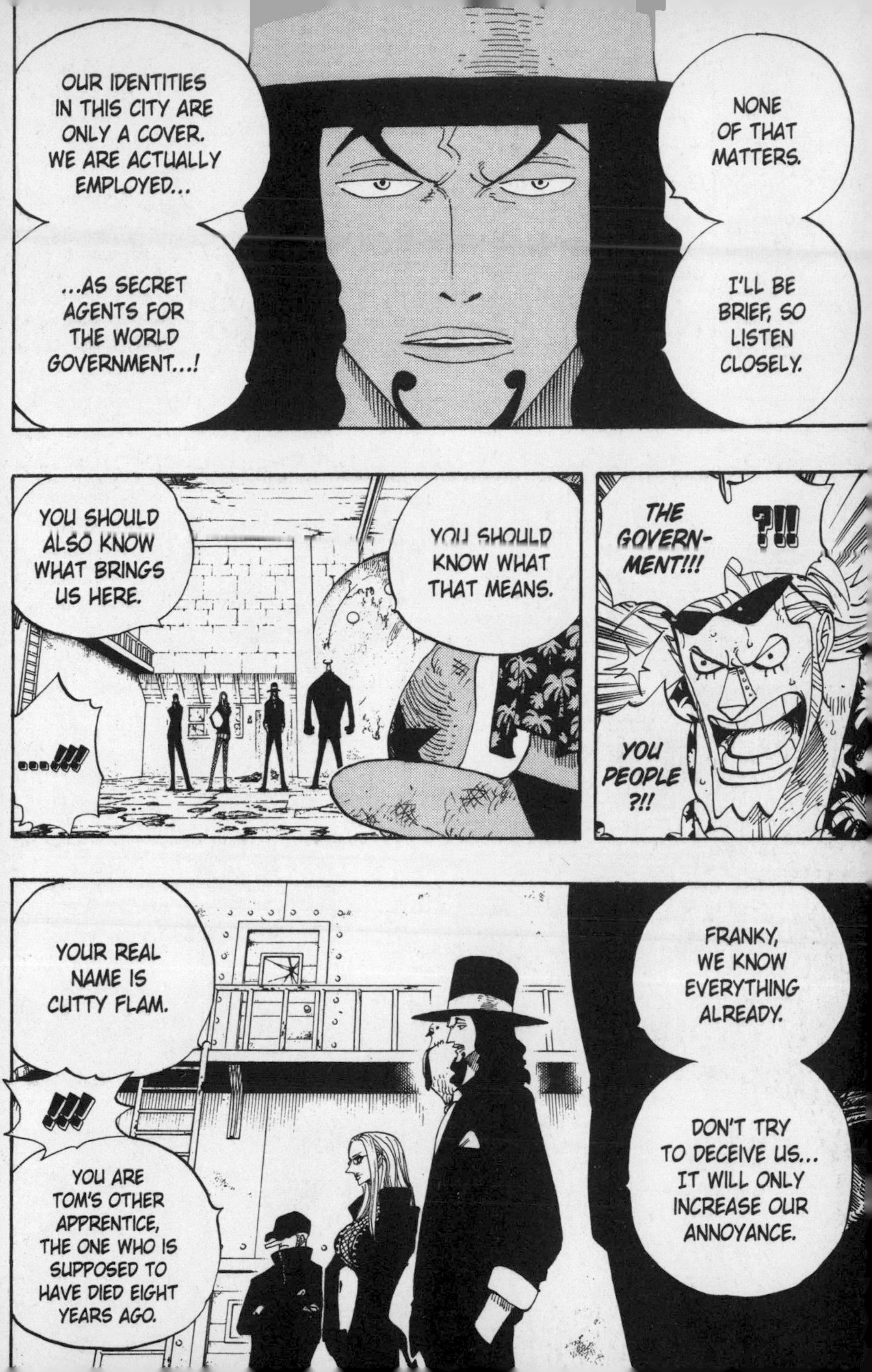
NONE OF THAT MATTERS.
I'LL BE BRIEF, SO LISTEN CLOSELY.
OUR IDENTITIES IN THIS CITY ARE ONLY A COVER. WE ARE ACTUALLY EMPLOYED...
...AS SECRET AGENTS FOR THE WORLD GOVERNMENT...!
?!!
THE GOVERNMENT!!!
YOU PEOPLE ?!!
YOU SHOULD KNOW WHAT THAT MEANS.
YOU SHOULD ALSO KNOW WHAT BRINGS US HERE.
...!!!
FRANKY, WE KNOW EVERYTHING ALREADY.
DON'T TRY TO DECEIVE US... IT WILL ONLY INCREASE OUR ANNOYANCE.
YOUR REAL NAME IS CUTTY FLAM.
!!!
YOU ARE TOM'S OTHER APPRENTICE, THE ONE WHO IS SUPPOSED TO HAVE DIED EIGHT YEARS AGO.

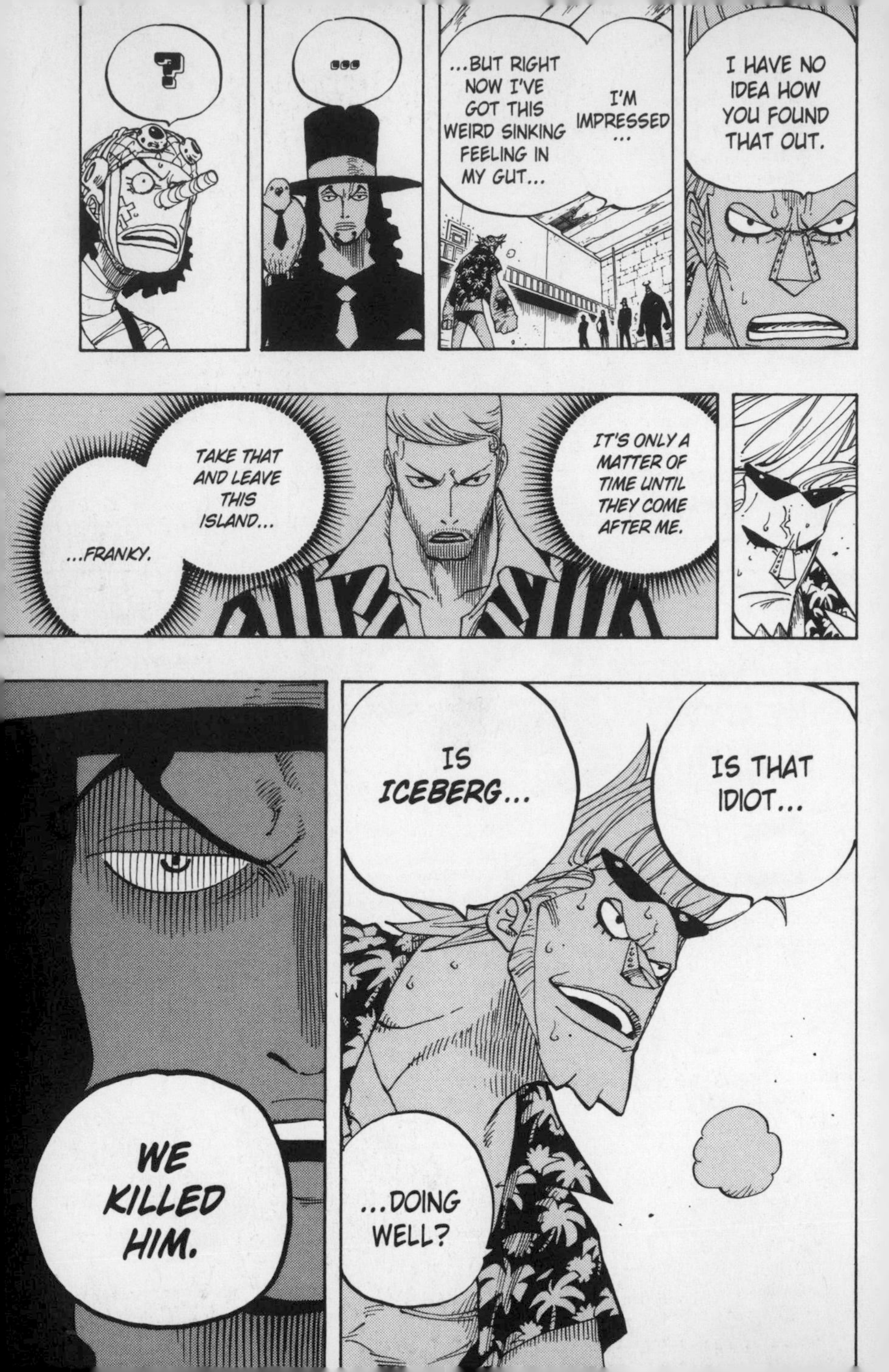
I HAVE NO IDEA HOW YOU FOUND THAT OUT.
I'M IMPRESSED...
...BUT RIGHT NOW I'VE GOT THIS WEIRD SINKING FEELING IN MY GUT...
...
?
IT'S ONLY A MATTER OF TIME UNTIL THEY COME AFTER ME.
TAKE THAT AND LEAVE THIS ISLAND...
...FRANKY.
IS THAT IDIOT...
IS ICEBERG...
...DOING WELL?
WE KILLED HIM.

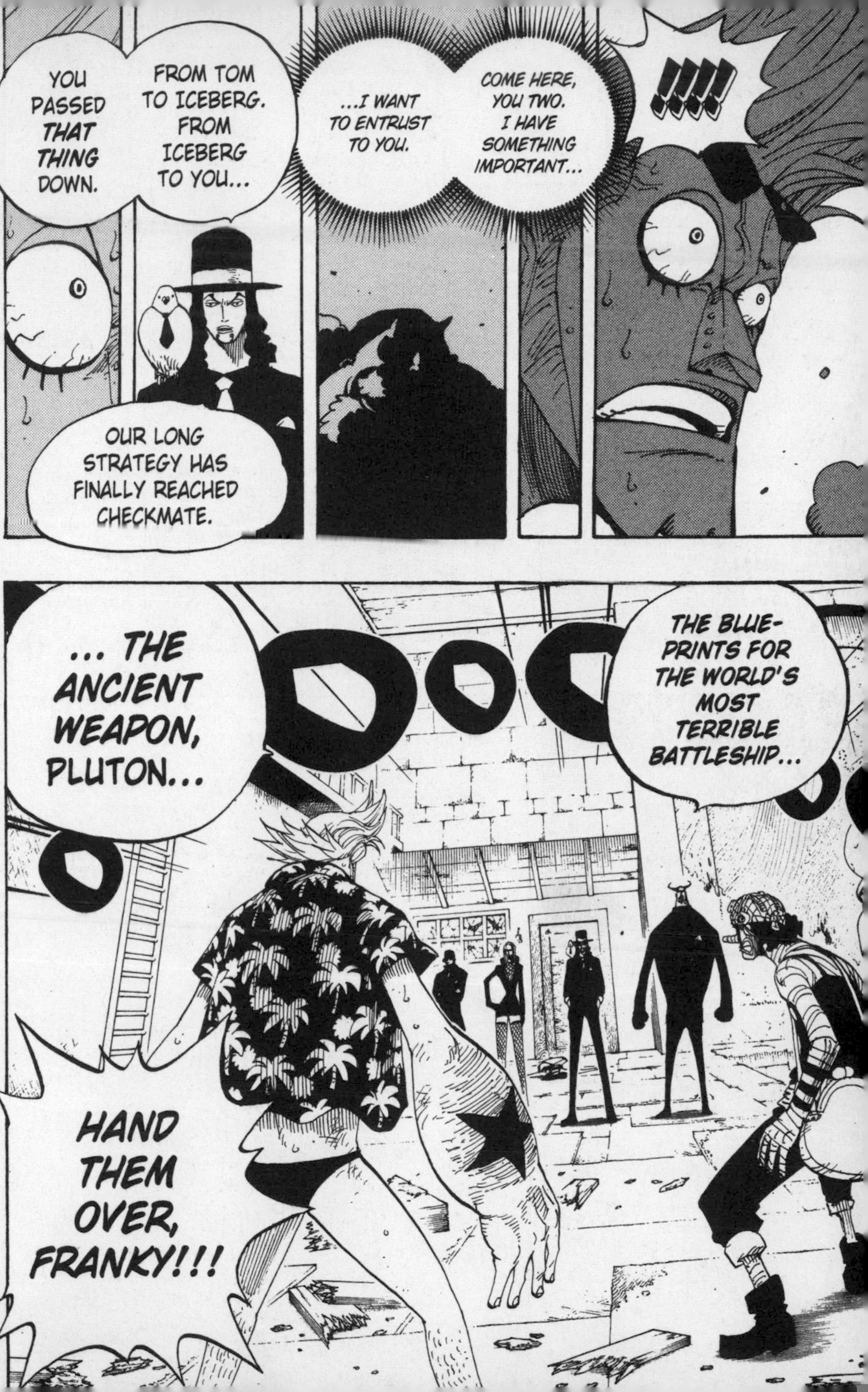
!!!!
COME HERE, YOU TWO. I HAVE SOMETHING IMPORTANT...
...I WANT TO ENTRUST TO YOU.
FROM TOM TO ICEBERG. FROM ICEBERG TO YOU...
YOU PASSED THAT THING DOWN.
OUR LONG STRATEGY HAS FINALLY REACHED CHECKMATE.
THE BLUE-PRINTS FOR THE WORLD'S MOST TERRIBLE BATTLESHIP...
... THE ANCIENT WEAPON, PLUTON...
HAND THEM OVER, FRANKY!!!

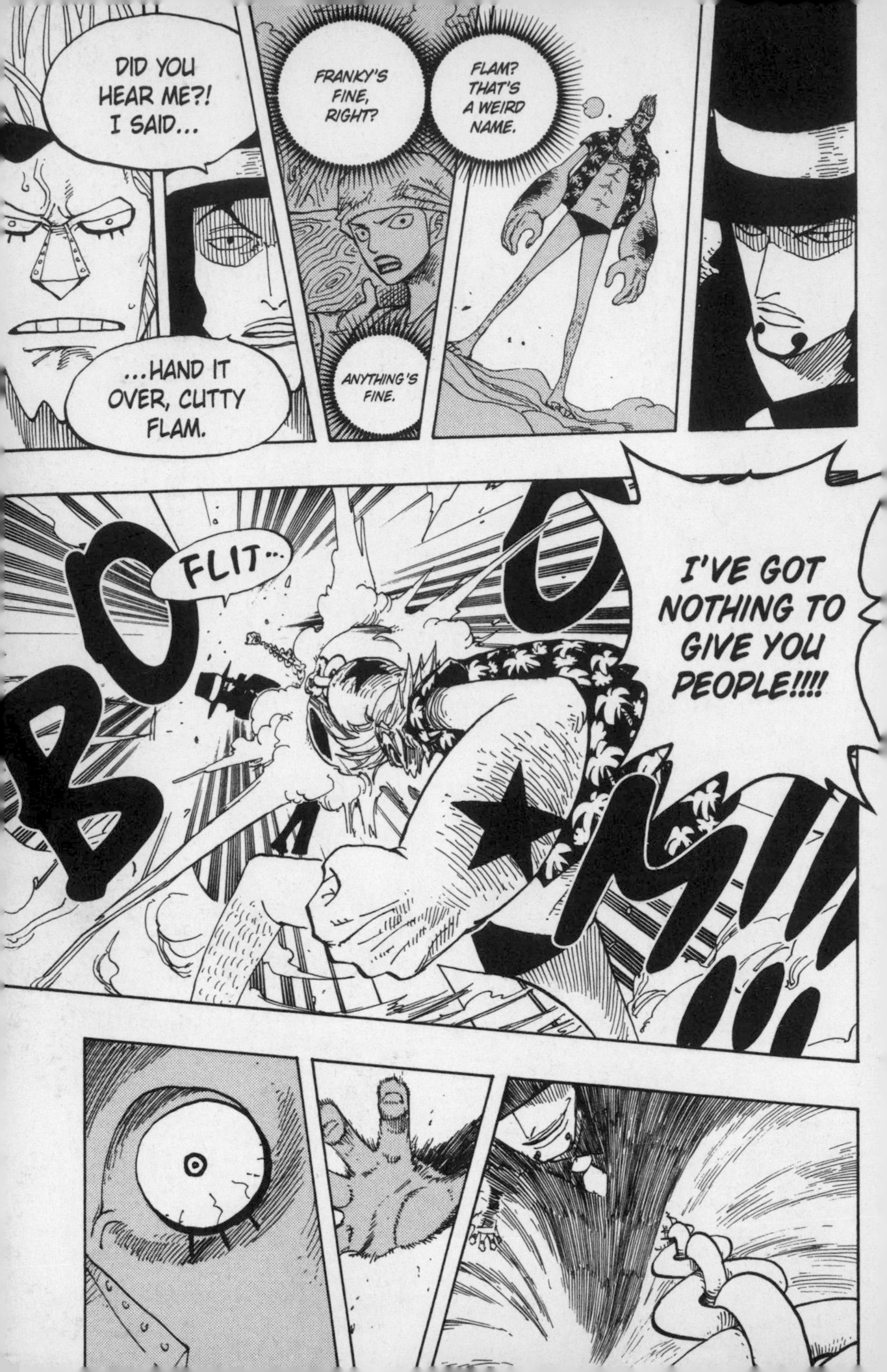
FLAM? THAT'S A WEIRD NAME.
FRANKY'S FINE, RIGHT?
ANYTHING'S FINE.
DID YOU HEAR ME?! I SAID...
...HAND IT OVER, CUTTY FLAM.
I'VE GOT NOTHING TO GIVE YOU PEOPLE!!!!
FLIT...
BOOM!!

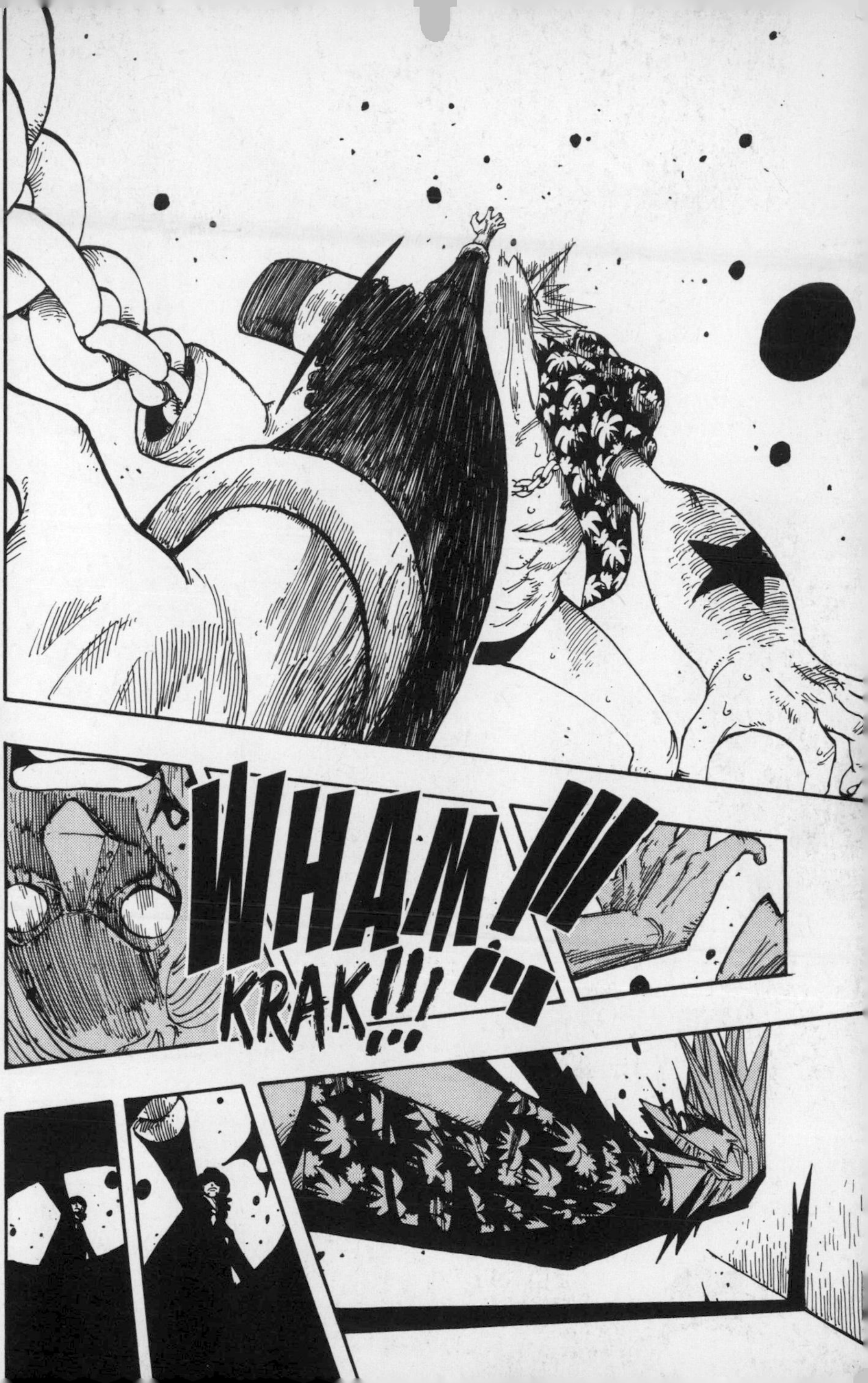
WHAM!!!
KRAK!!!

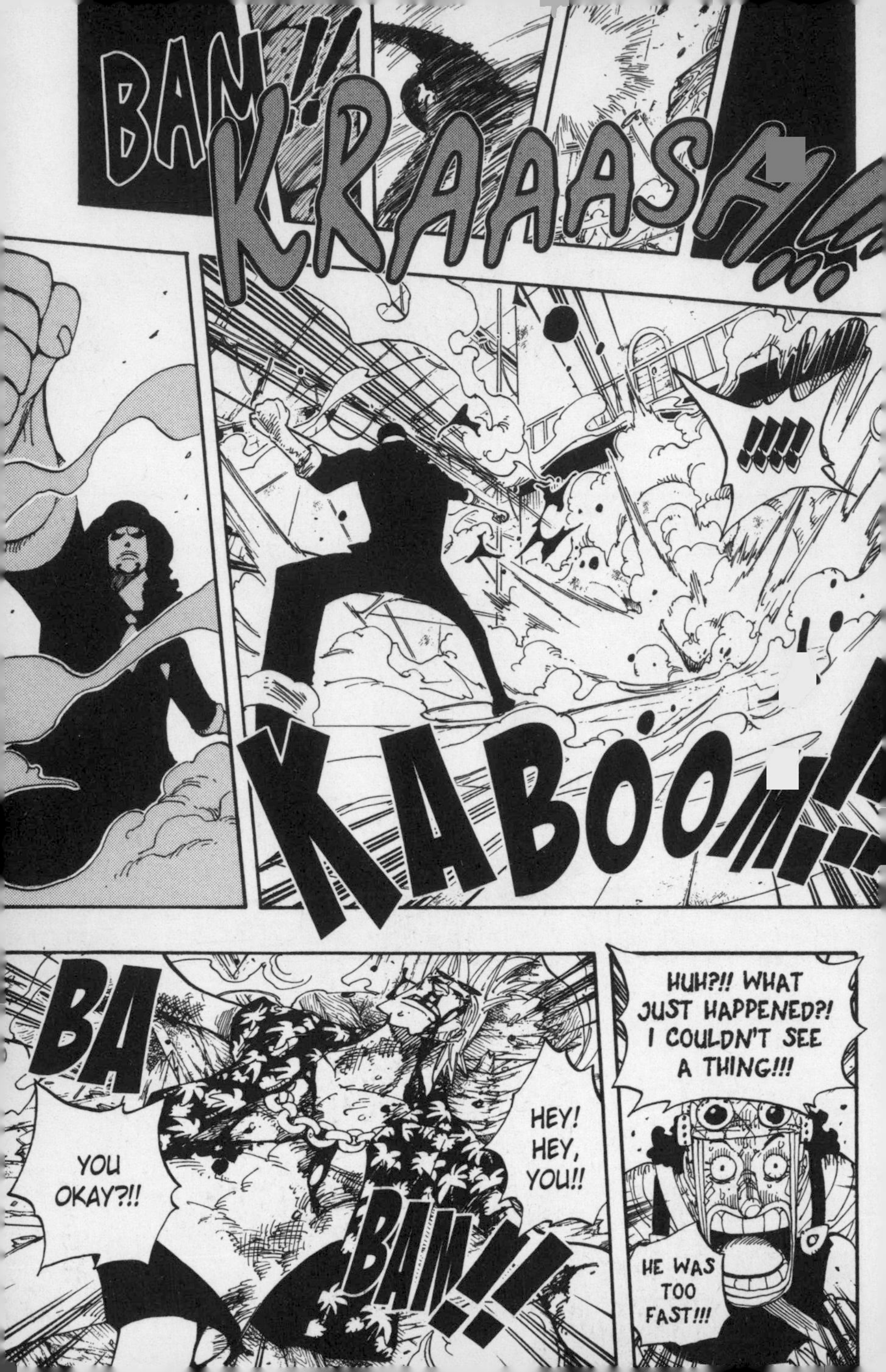
BAM!!
KRAAASH!!
!!!!
KABOOM!!
HUH?!! WHAT JUST HAPPENED?! I COULDN'T SEE A THING!!!
HE WAS TOO FAST!!!
HEY! HEY, YOU!!
YOU OKAY?!!
BA
BAM!!

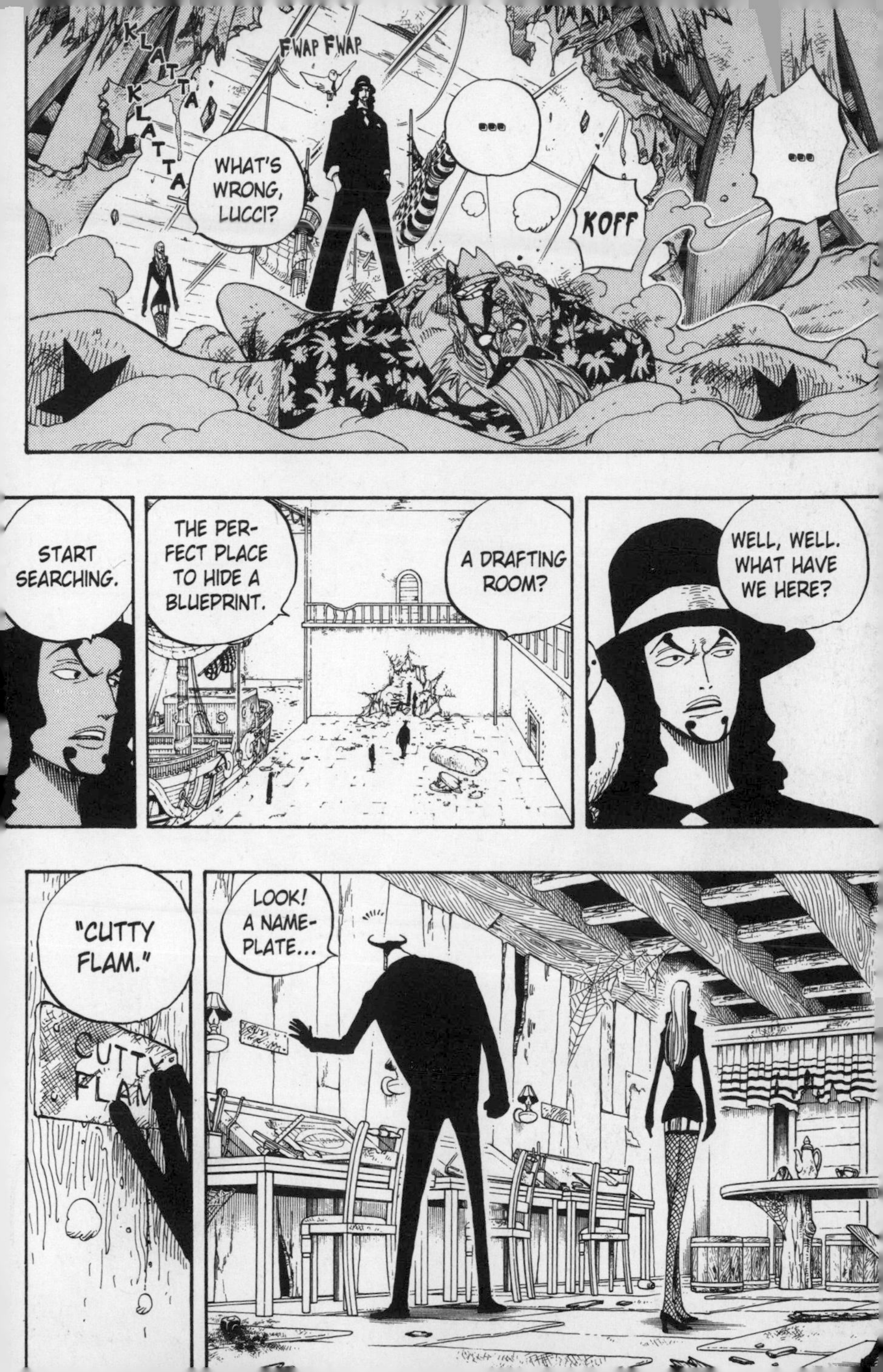
...
...
FWAP FWAP
KOFF
WHAT'S WRONG, LUCCI?
KLATTA KLATTA
WELL, WELL. WHAT HAVE WE HERE?
A DRAFTING ROOM?
THE PERFECT PLACE TO HIDE A BLUEPRINT.
START SEARCHING.
LOOK! A NAME-PLATE...
"CUTTY FLAM."
CUTTY FLAM

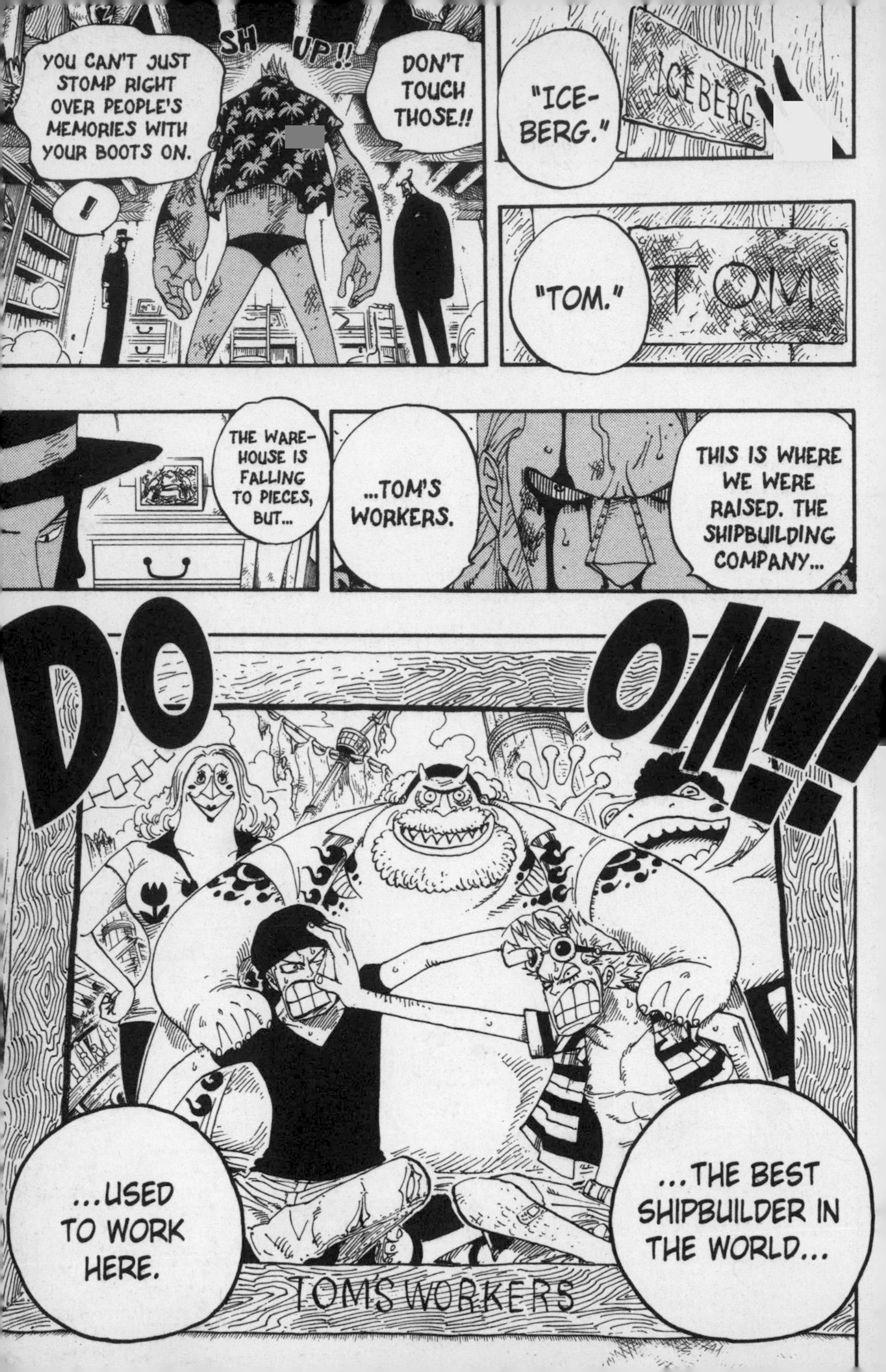
"ICE-BERG."
ICEBERG
"TOM."
TOM
SH UP!!
DON'T TOUCH THOSE!!
YOU CAN'T JUST STOMP RIGHT OVER PEOPLE'S MEMORIES WITH YOUR BOOTS ON.
!
THIS IS WHERE WE WERE RAISED. THE SHIPBUILDING COMPANY...
...TOM'S WORKERS.
THE WARE-HOUSE IS FALLING TO PIECES, BUT...
DO
OM!!
...THE BEST SHIPBUILDER IN THE WORLD...
...USED TO WORK HERE.
TOM'S WORKERS

Chapter 353:
THE LEGENDARY SHIPWRIGHT

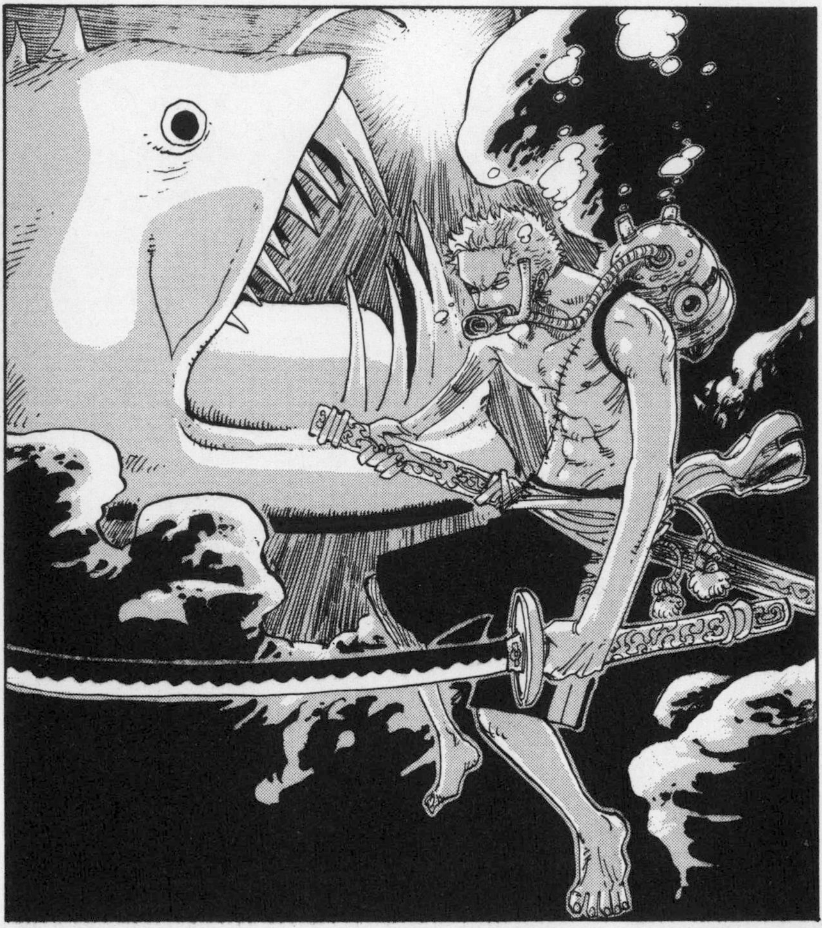

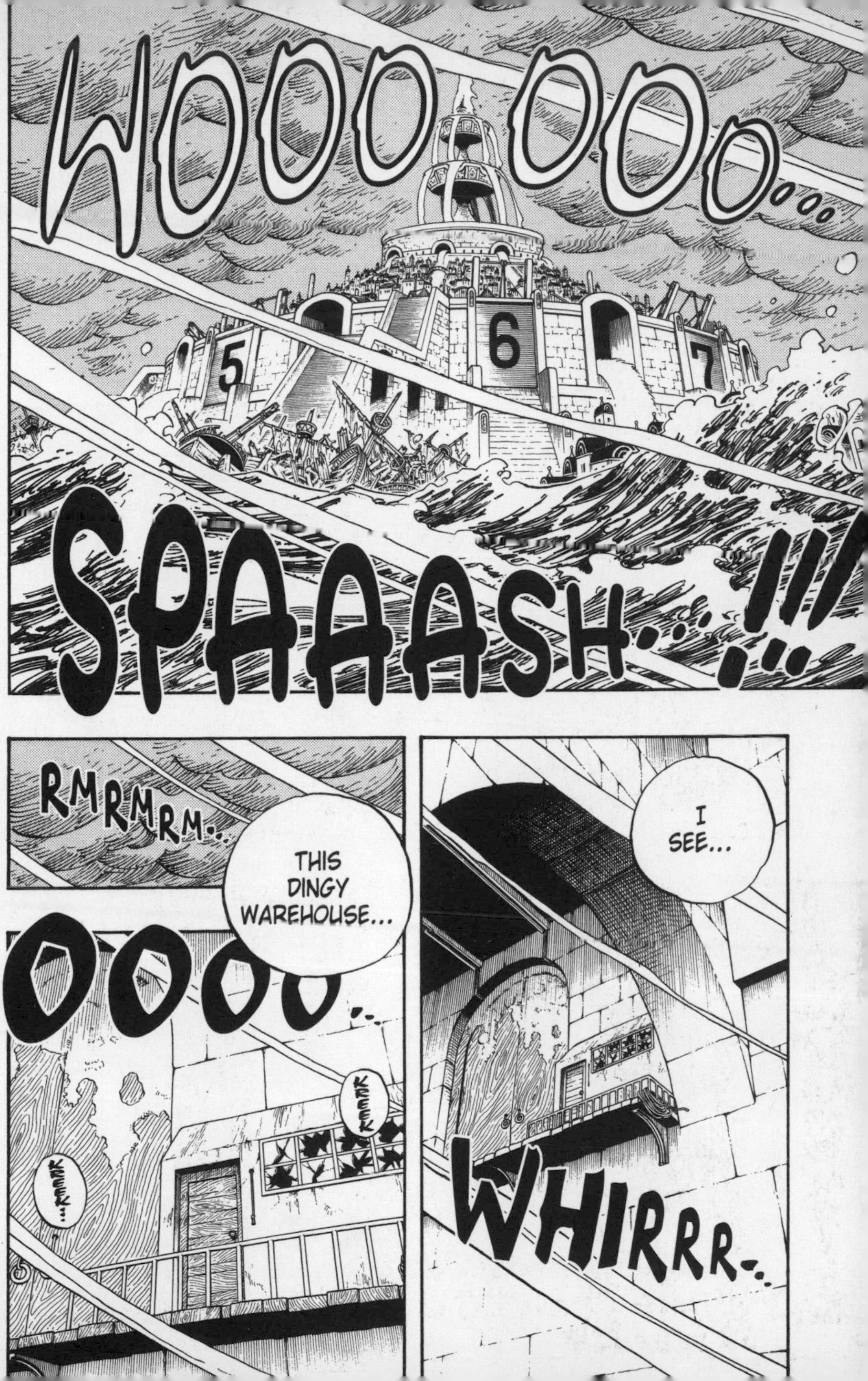
WOOO OOOo...
SPAAASH...!!!
I SEE...
WHIRRR...
RMRMRM..
THIS DINGY WAREHOUSE...
OOOO..
KREEK
KREEK...

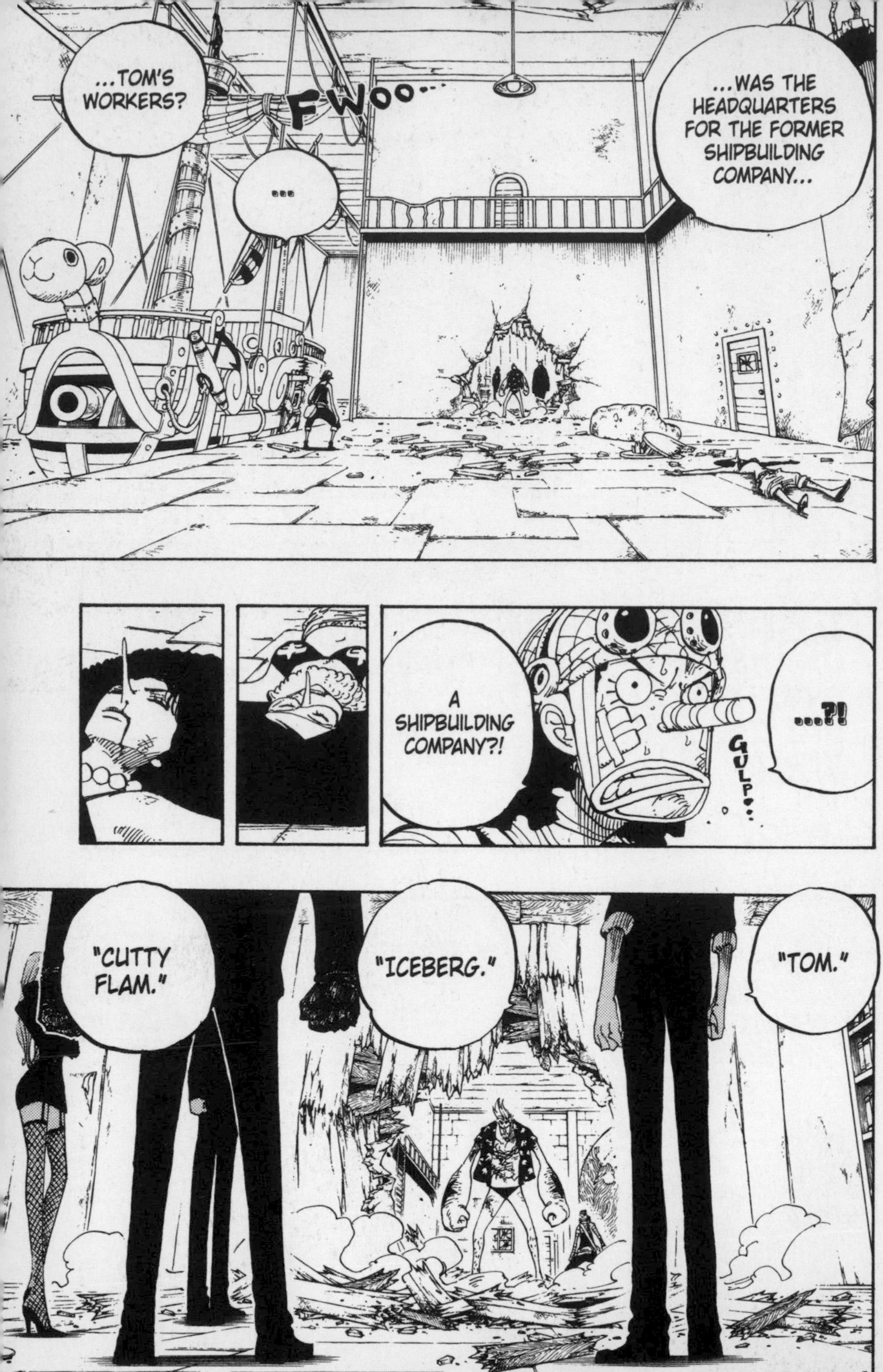
...WAS THE HEADQUARTERS FOR THE FORMER SHIPBUILDING COMPANY...
FWOO...
...TOM'S WORKERS?
...
...?!
GULP...
A SHIPBUILDING COMPANY?!
"TOM."
"ICEBERG."
"CUTTY FLAM."

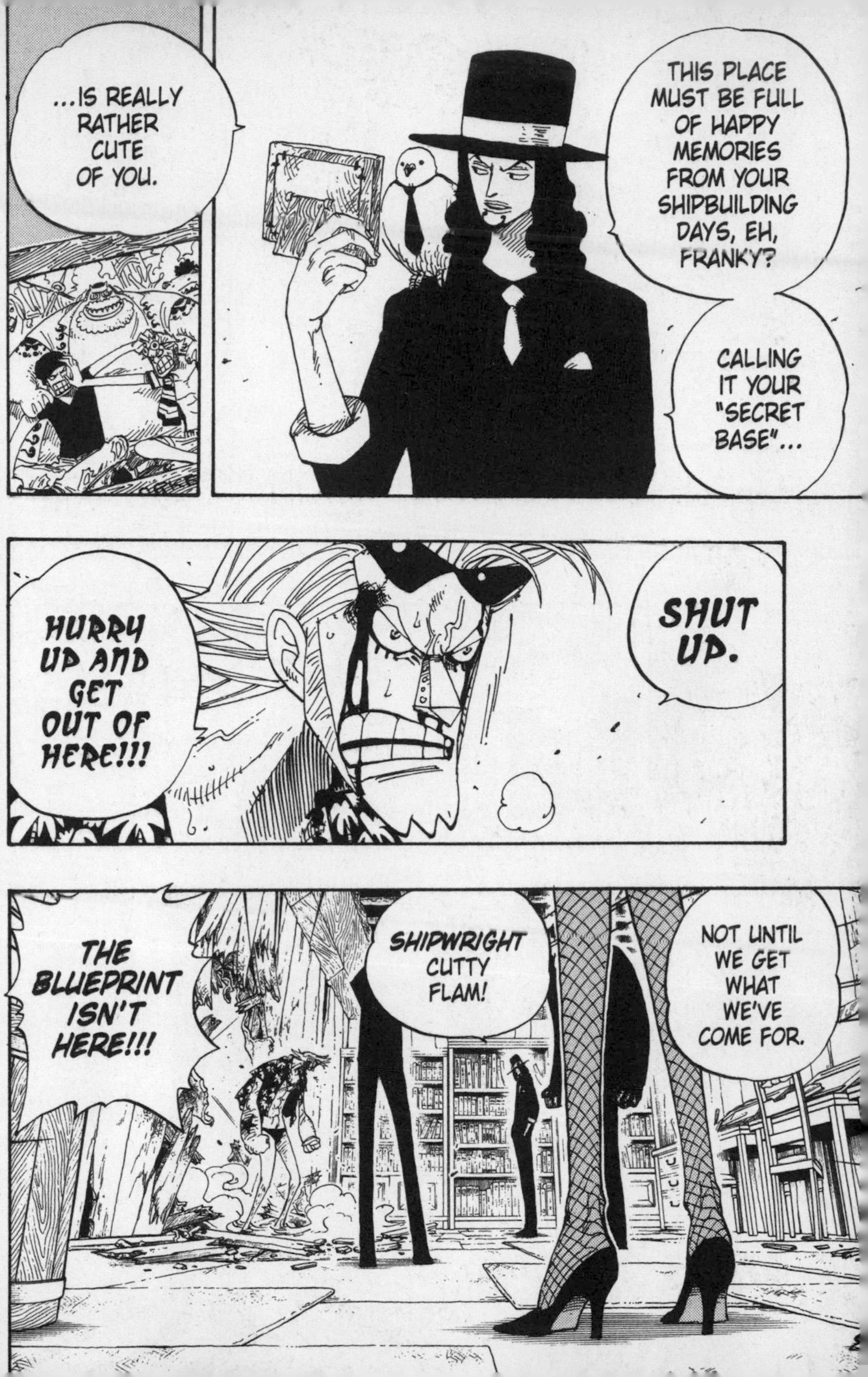
THIS PLACE MUST BE FULL OF HAPPY MEMORIES FROM YOUR SHIPBUILDING DAYS, EH, FRANKY?
CALLING IT YOUR "SECRET BASE"...
...IS REALLY RATHER CUTE OF YOU.
SHUT UP.
HURRY UP AND GET OUT OF HERE!!!
NOT UNTIL WE GET WHAT WE'VE COME FOR.
SHIPWRIGHT CUTTY FLAM!
THE BLUEPRINT ISN'T HERE!!!

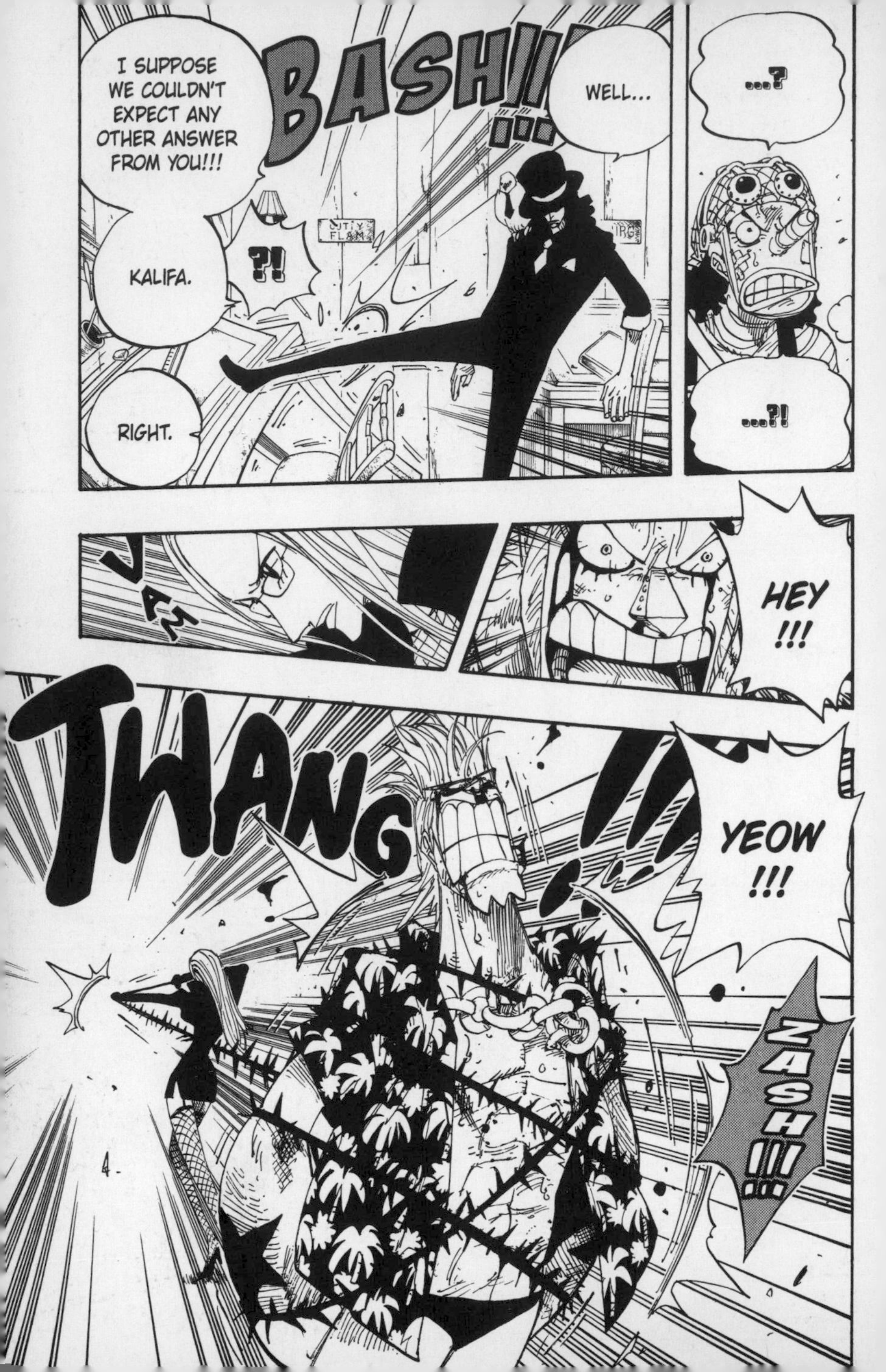
...?
...?!
WELL...
BASH!!
!!!
I SUPPOSE WE COULDN'T EXPECT ANY OTHER ANSWER FROM YOU!!!
?!
KALIFA.
RIGHT.
HEY !!!
YEOW !!!
THANG!!
ZASH!!!

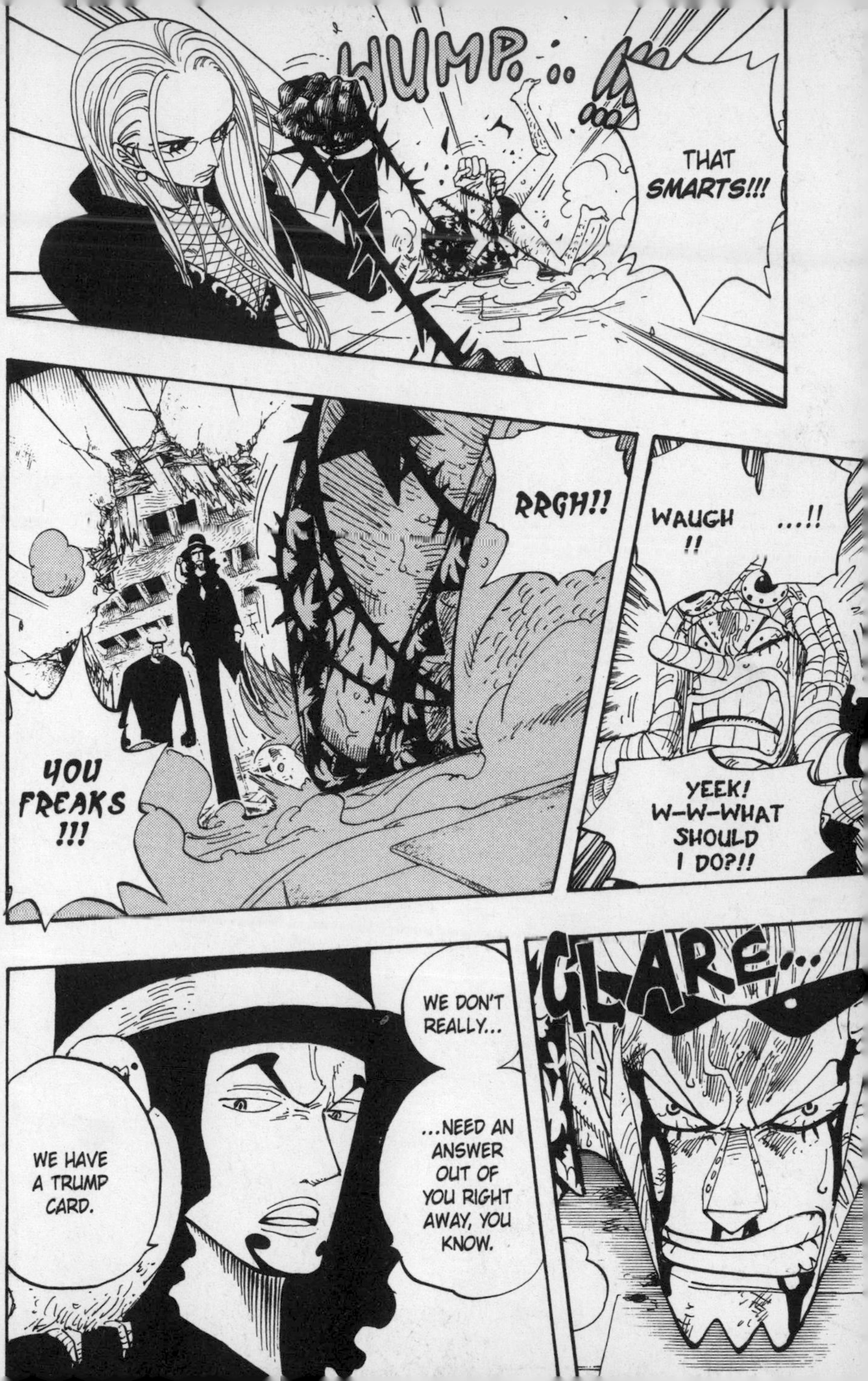
HUMP...
THAT SMARTS!!!
WAUGH!!
...!!
YEEK! W-W-WHAT SHOULD I DO?!!
RRGH!!
YOU FREAKS!!!
GLARE...
WE DON'T REALLY...
...NEED AN ANSWER OUT OF YOU RIGHT AWAY, YOU KNOW.
WE HAVE A TRUMP CARD.

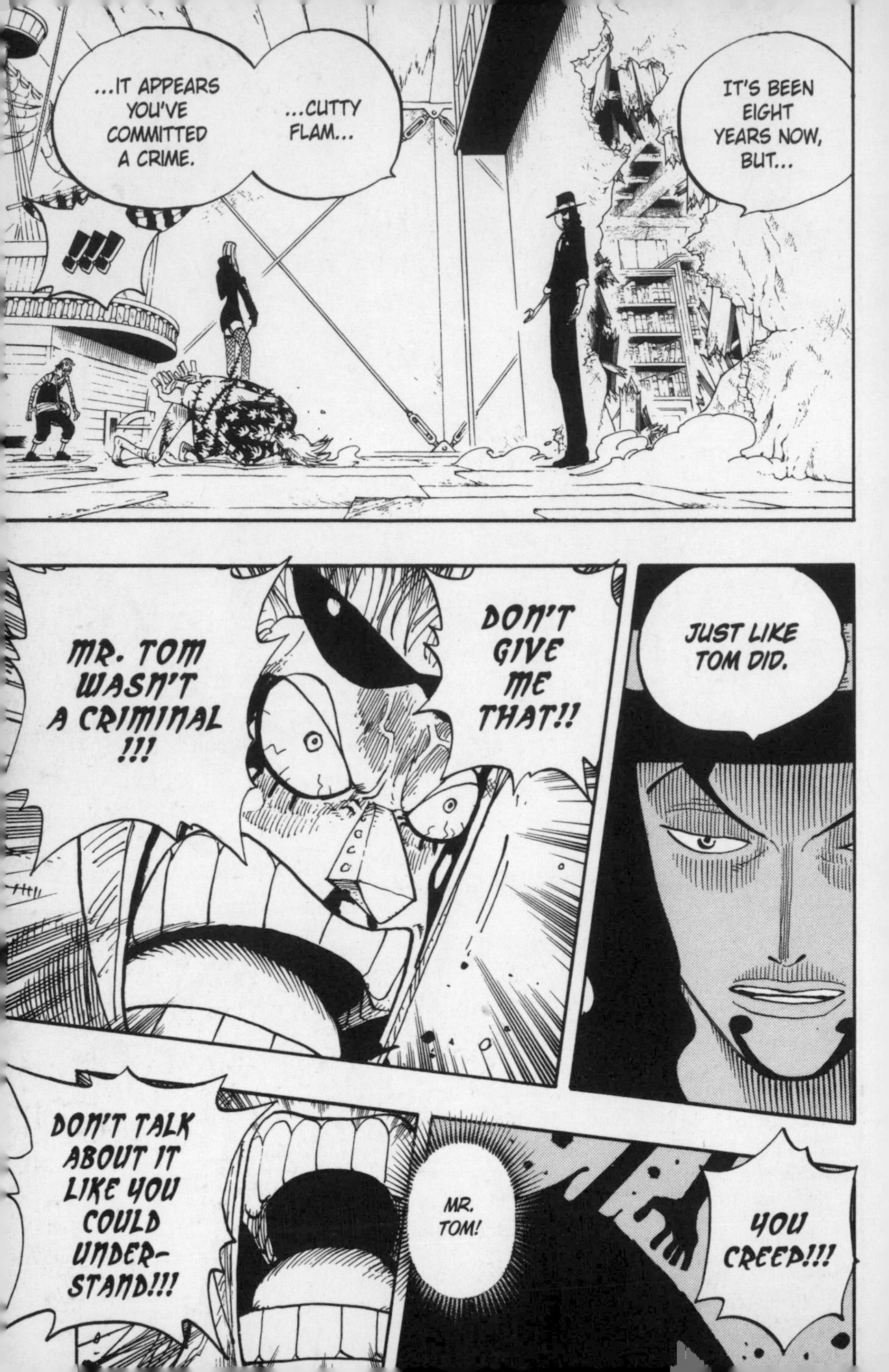
IT'S BEEN EIGHT YEARS NOW, BUT...
...CUTTY FLAM...
...IT APPEARS YOU'VE COMMITTED A CRIME.
!!!!
JUST LIKE TOM DID.
DON'T GIVE ME THAT!!
MR. TOM WASN'T A CRIMINAL !!!
YOU CREEP!!!
MR. TOM!
DON'T TALK ABOUT IT LIKE YOU COULD UNDER-STAND!!!

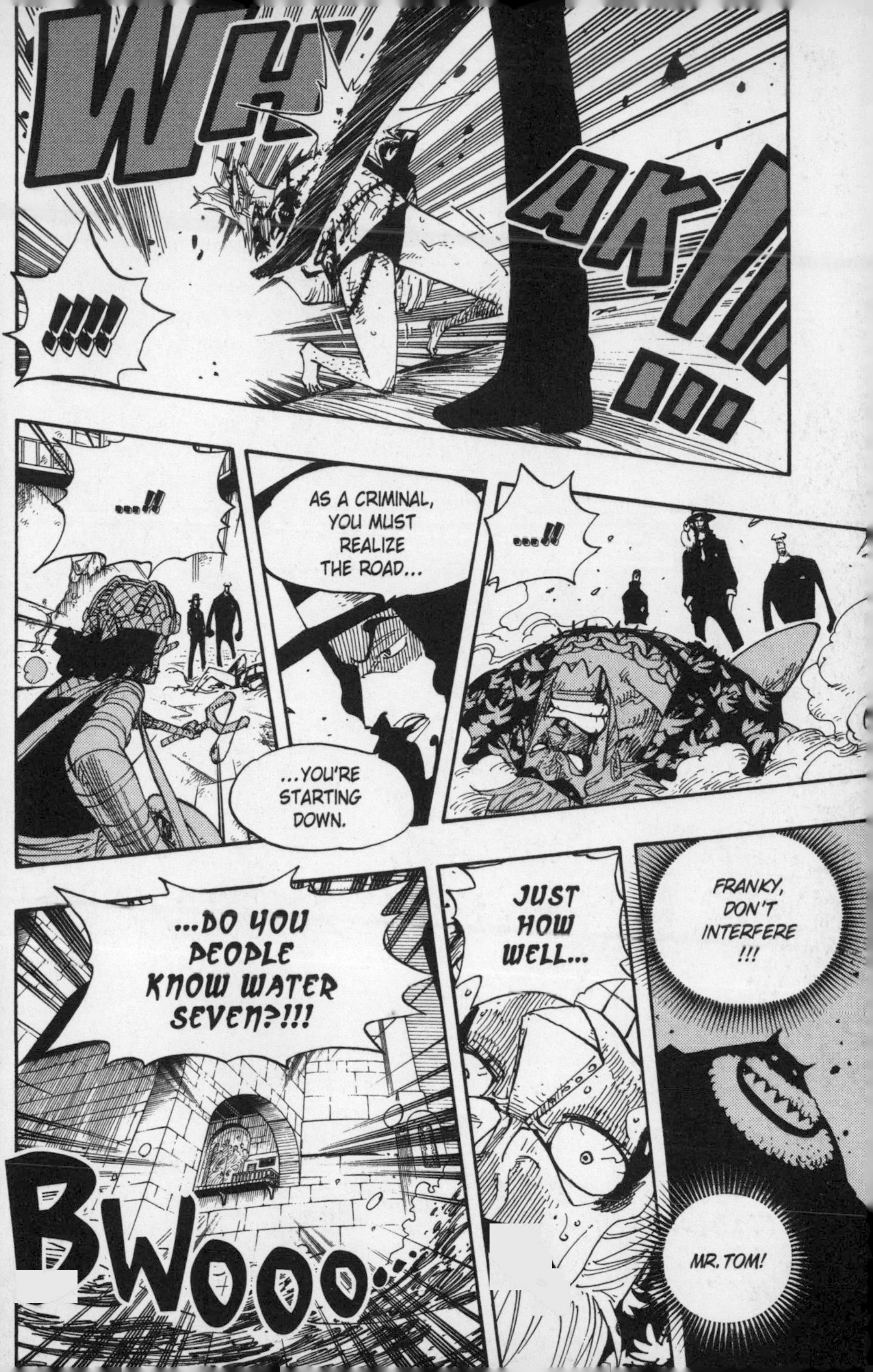
WHAK!!!
!!!!
...!!
AS A CRIMINAL, YOU MUST REALIZE THE ROAD...
...YOU'RE STARTING DOWN.
...!!
FRANKY, DON'T INTERFERE !!!
MR.TOM!
JUST HOW WELL...
...DO YOU PEOPLE KNOW WATER SEVEN?!!!
BWOOO...

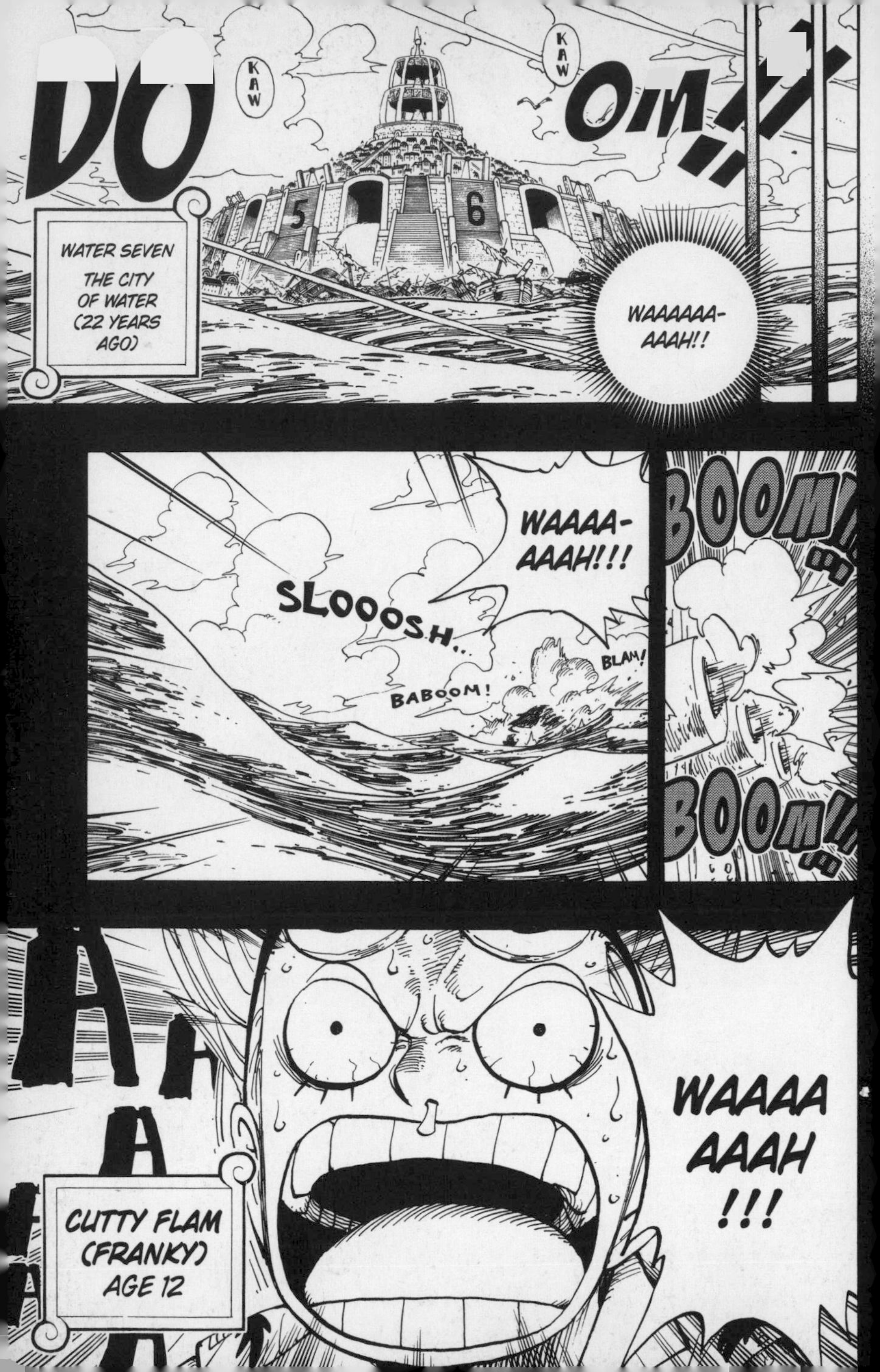

DOOM!!
KAW KAW
KAW KAW
WAAAAAA-AAAH!!
WATER SEVEN THE CITY OF WATER (22 YEARS AGO)
BOOM!!
BOOM!!
WAAAA-AAAH!!!
SLOOOSH..
BLAM!
BABOOM!
WAAAA AAAH !!!
CUTTY FLAM (FRANKY) AGE 12

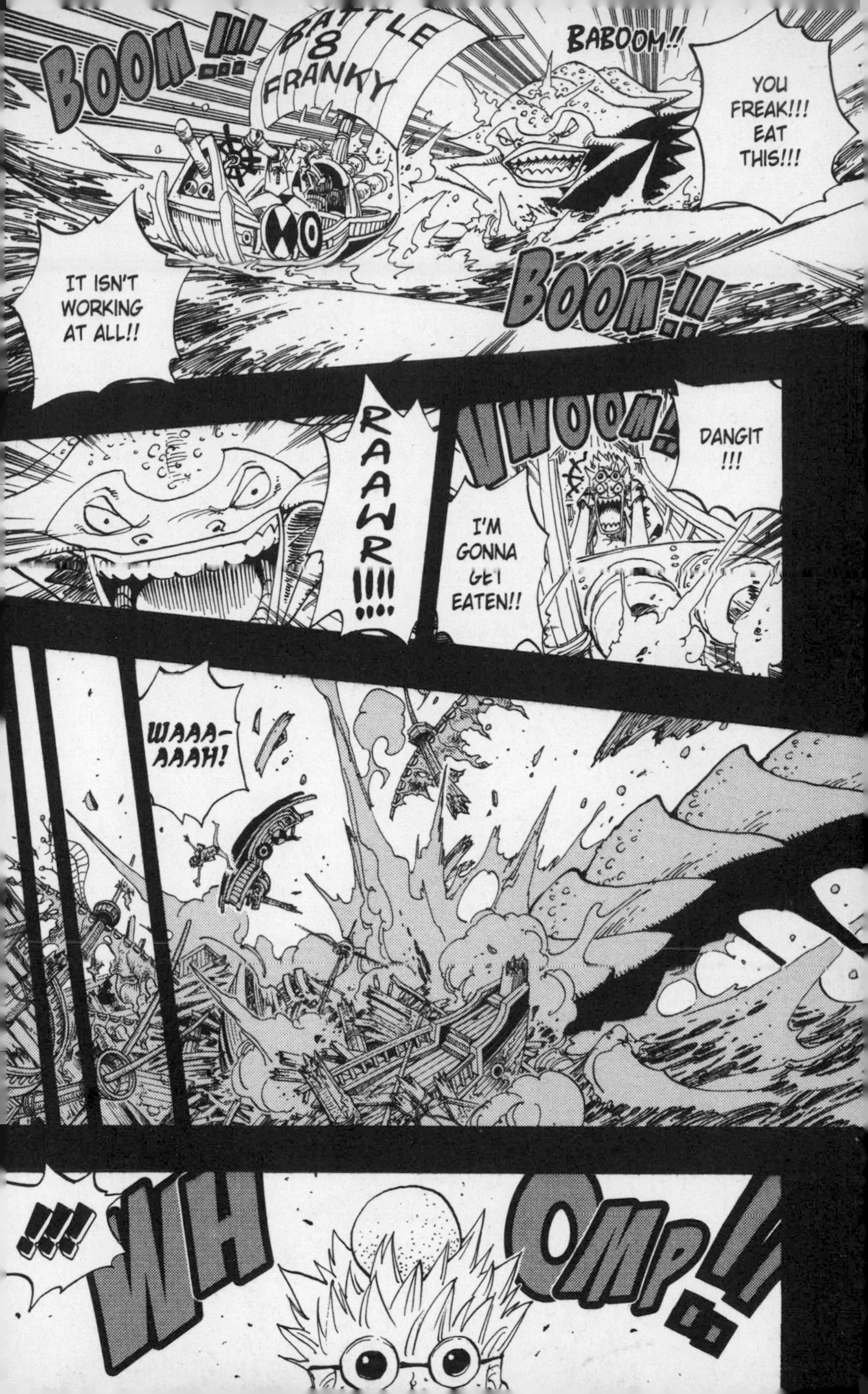
YOU FREAK!!! EAT THIS!!!
BABOOM!!
BATTLE 8 FRANKY
BOOM!!!...
BOOM!!
IT ISN'T WORKING AT ALL!!
DANGIT!!!
VWOOM!!
I'M GONNA GET EATEN!!
RAAAWR!!!!
WAAA-AAAH!
WHOMP!!..
!!!

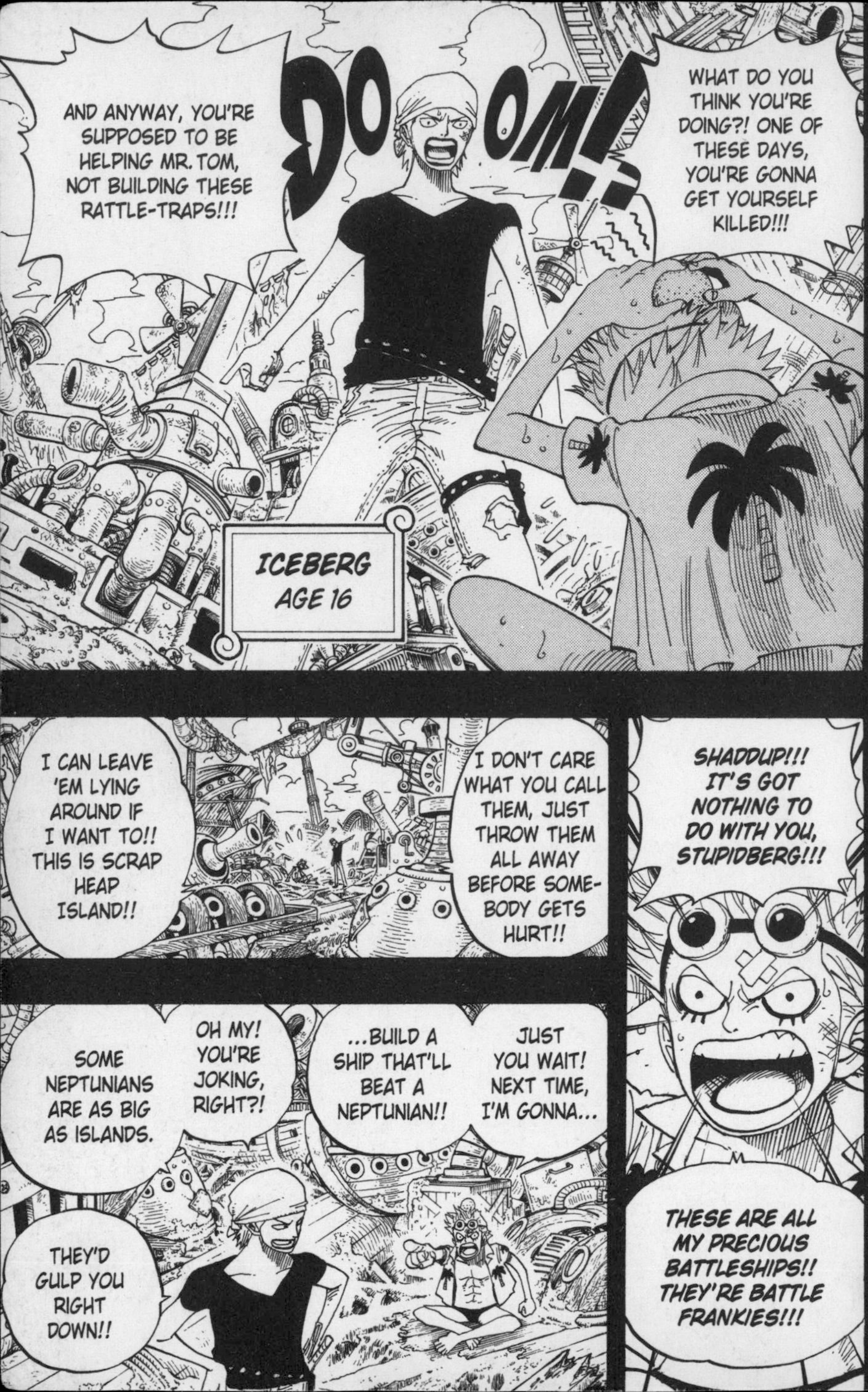
WHAT DO YOU THINK YOU'RE DOING?! ONE OF THESE DAYS, YOU'RE GONNA GET YOURSELF KILLED!!!
DOOM!?
AND ANYWAY, YOU'RE SUPPOSED TO BE HELPING MR. TOM, NOT BUILDING THESE RATTLE-TRAPS!!!
ICEBERG AGE 16
SHADDUP!!! IT'S GOT NOTHING TO DO WITH YOU, STUPIDBERG!!!
THESE ARE ALL MY PRECIOUS BATTLESHIPS!! THEY'RE BATTLE FRANKIES!!!
I DON'T CARE WHAT YOU CALL THEM, JUST THROW THEM ALL AWAY BEFORE SOMEBODY GETS HURT!!
I CAN LEAVE 'EM LYING AROUND IF I WANT TO!! THIS IS SCRAP HEAP ISLAND!!
JUST YOU WAIT! NEXT TIME, I'M GONNA...
...BUILD A SHIP THAT'LL BEAT A NEPTUNIAN!!
OH MY! YOU'RE JOKING, RIGHT?!
SOME NEPTUNIANS ARE AS BIG AS ISLANDS.
THEY'D GULP YOU RIGHT DOWN!!

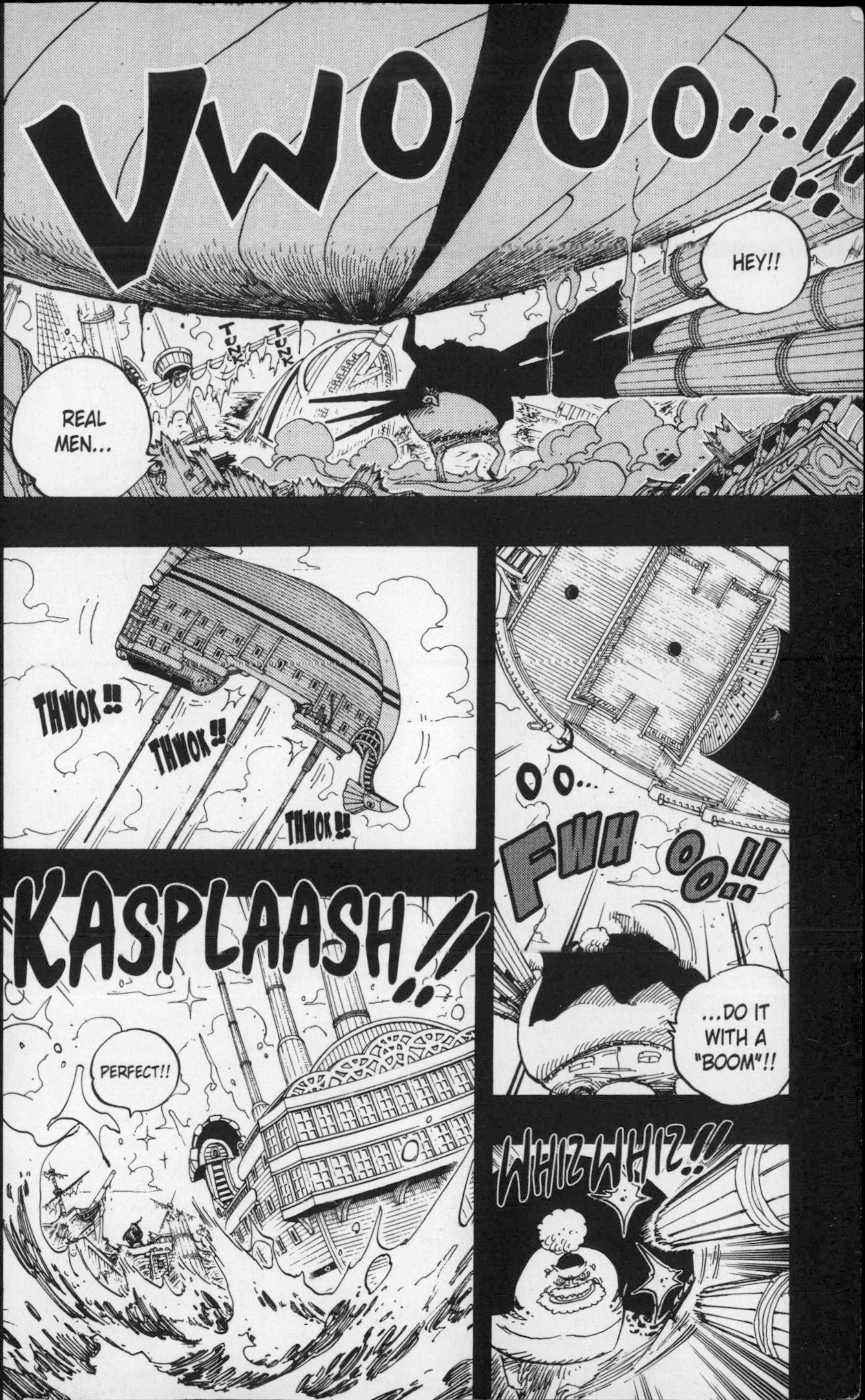
VWOOOO..!!
HEY!!
TUNK
TUNK
REAL MEN...
O O...
FWH OO..!!
...DO IT WITH A "BOOM"!!
WHIZWHIZ!!
THWOK!!
THWOK!!
THWOK!!
KASPLAASH!!
PERFECT!!

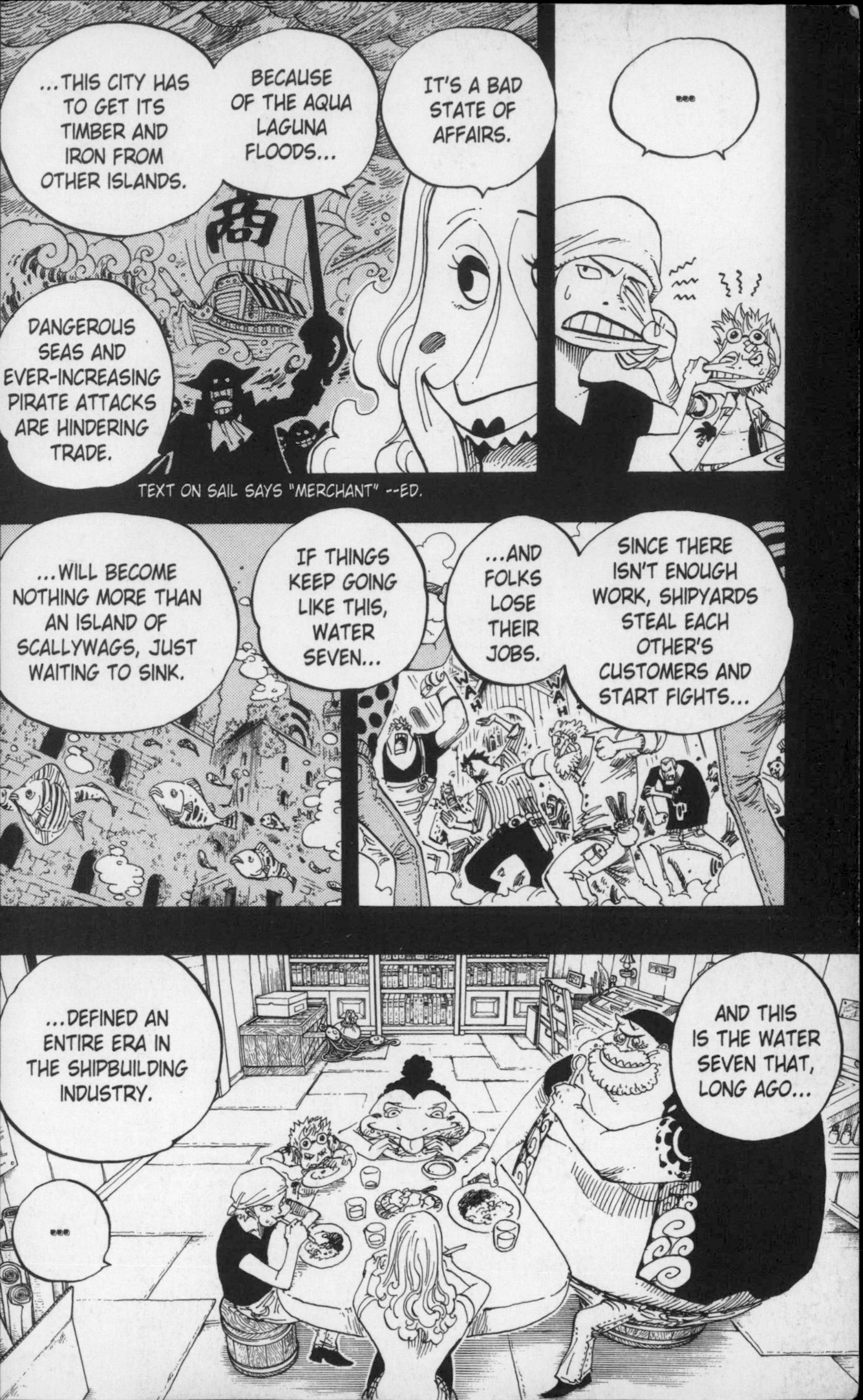
...
IT'S A BAD STATE OF AFFAIRS.
BECAUSE OF THE AQUA LAGUNA FLOODS...
...THIS CITY HAS TO GET ITS TIMBER AND IRON FROM OTHER ISLANDS.
DANGEROUS SEAS AND EVER-INCREASING PIRATE ATTACKS ARE HINDERING TRADE.
TEXT ON SAIL SAYS "MERCHANT" --ED.
SINCE THERE ISN'T ENOUGH WORK, SHIPYARDS STEAL EACH OTHER'S CUSTOMERS AND START FIGHTS...
...AND FOLKS LOSE THEIR JOBS.
WAH
WAH
IF THINGS KEEP GOING LIKE THIS, WATER SEVEN...
...WILL BECOME NOTHING MORE THAN AN ISLAND OF SCALLYWAGS, JUST WAITING TO SINK.
AND THIS IS THE WATER SEVEN THAT, LONG AGO...
...DEFINED AN ENTIRE ERA IN THE SHIPBUILDING INDUSTRY.
...

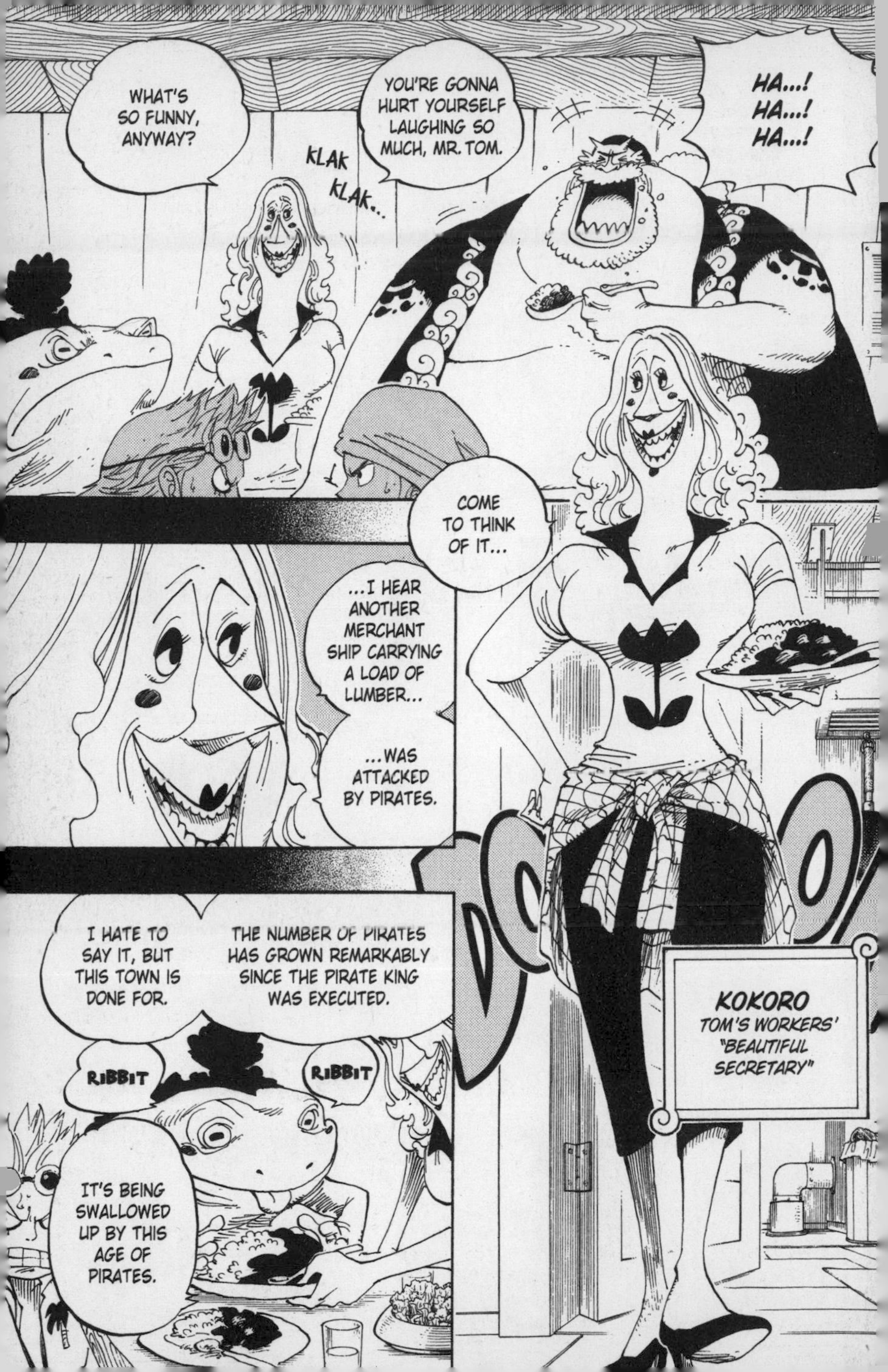
HA...! HA...! HA...!
YOU'RE GONNA HURT YOURSELF LAUGHING SO MUCH, MR. TOM.
KLAK KLAK...
WHAT'S SO FUNNY, ANYWAY?
COME TO THINK OF IT...
KOKORO
TOM'S WORKERS' "BEAUTIFUL SECRETARY"
...I HEAR ANOTHER MERCHANT SHIP CARRYING A LOAD OF LUMBER...
...WAS ATTACKED BY PIRATES.
THE NUMBER OF PIRATES HAS GROWN REMARKABLY SINCE THE PIRATE KING WAS EXECUTED.
I HATE TO SAY IT, BUT THIS TOWN IS DONE FOR.
RIBBIT
RIBBIT
IT'S BEING SWALLOWED UP BY THIS AGE OF PIRATES.

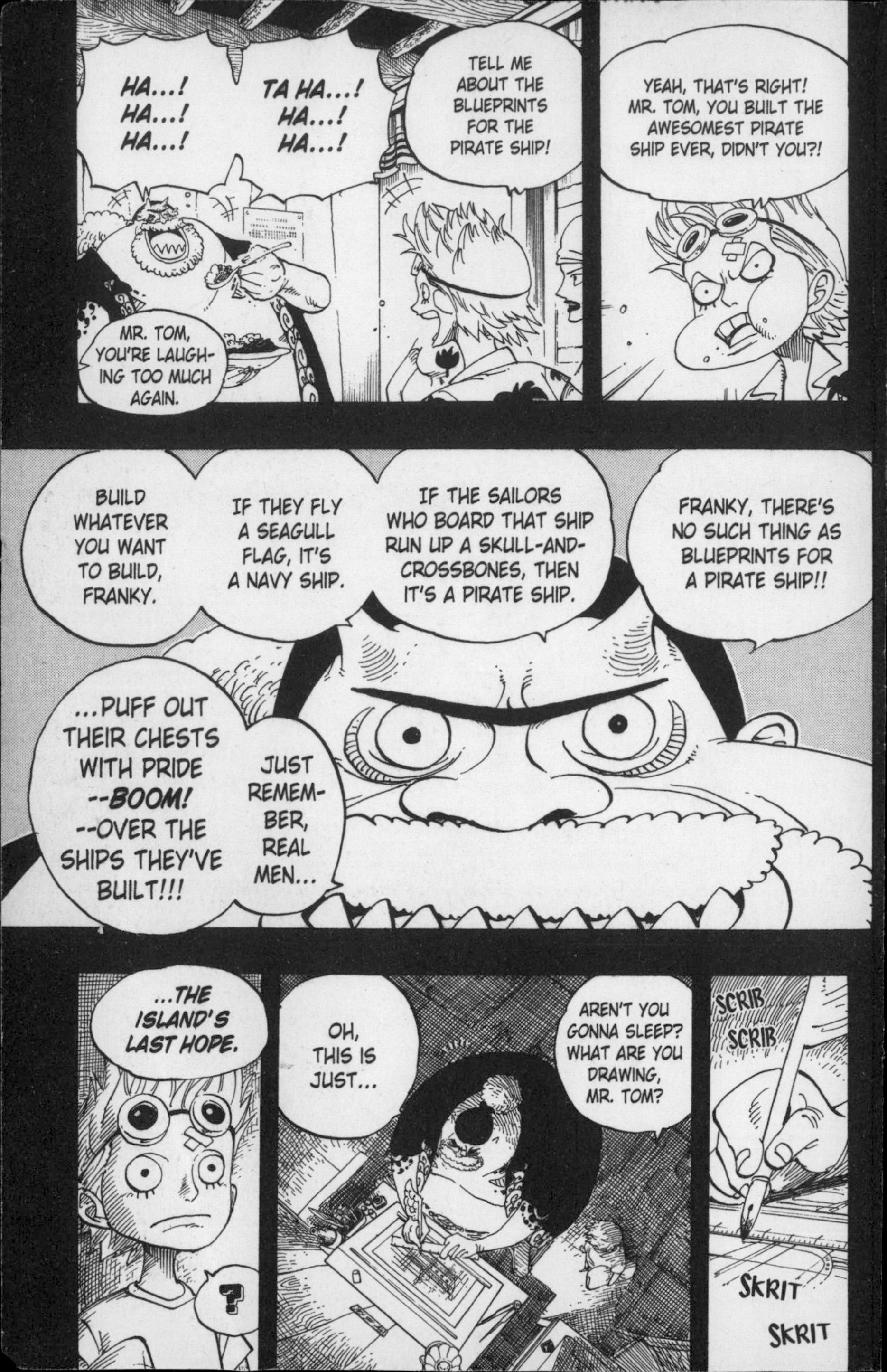
YEAH, THAT'S RIGHT! MR. TOM, YOU BUILT THE AWESOMEST PIRATE SHIP EVER, DIDN'T YOU?!
TELL ME ABOUT THE BLUEPRINTS FOR THE PIRATE SHIP!
TA HA...! HA...! HA...!
HA...! HA...! HA...!
MR. TOM, YOU'RE LAUGHING TOO MUCH AGAIN.
FRANKY, THERE'S NO SUCH THING AS BLUEPRINTS FOR A PIRATE SHIP!!
IF THE SAILORS WHO BOARD THAT SHIP RUN UP A SKULL-AND-CROSSBONES, THEN IT'S A PIRATE SHIP.
IF THEY FLY A SEAGULL FLAG, IT'S A NAVY SHIP.
BUILD WHATEVER YOU WANT TO BUILD, FRANKY.
JUST REMEMBER, REAL MEN...
...PUFF OUT THEIR CHESTS WITH PRIDE --BOOM! --OVER THE SHIPS THEY'VE BUILT!!!
SCRIB
SCRIB
SKRIT
SKRIT
AREN'T YOU GONNA SLEEP? WHAT ARE YOU DRAWING, MR. TOM?
OH, THIS IS JUST...
...THE ISLAND'S LAST HOPE.
?

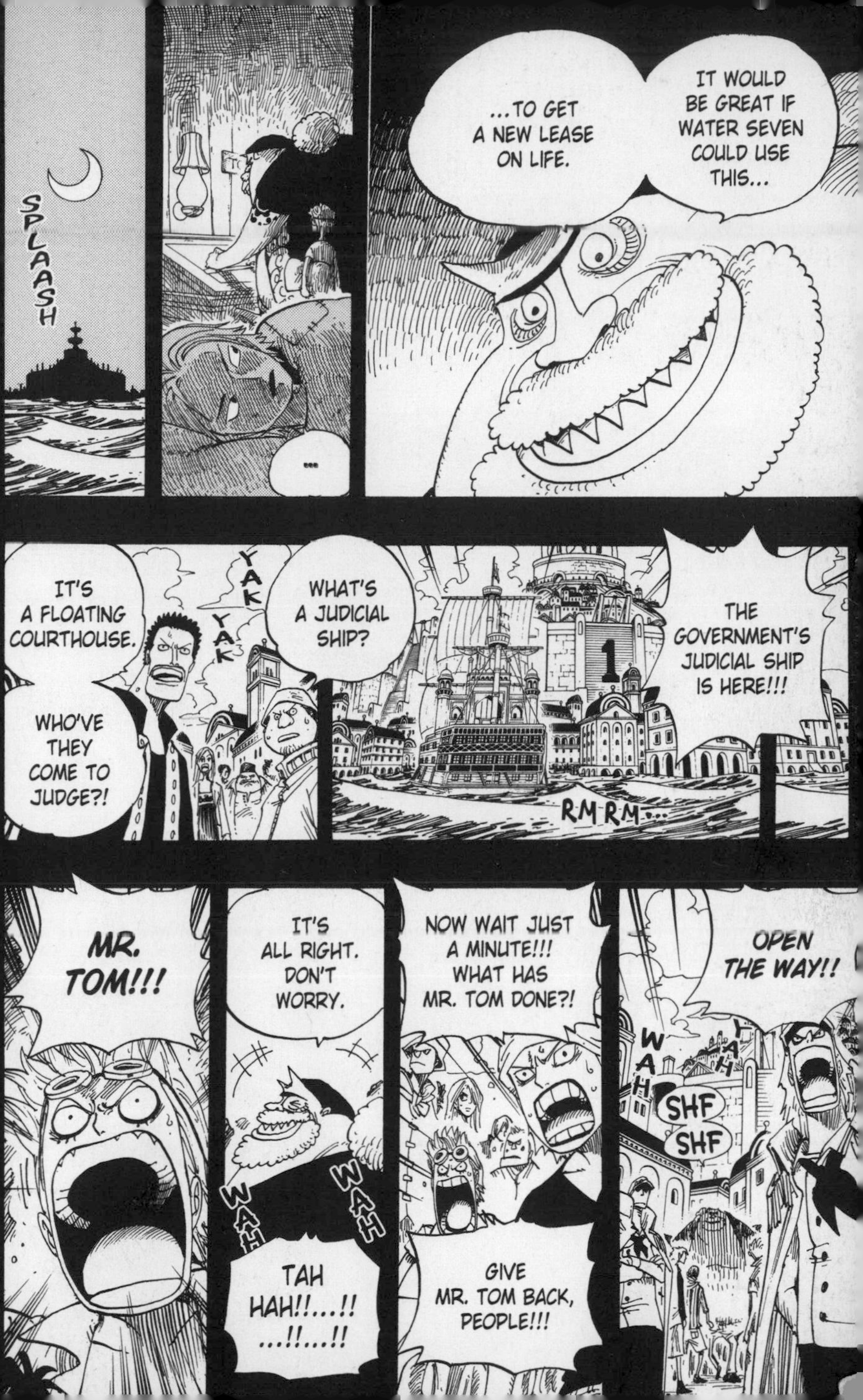
IT WOULD BE GREAT IF WATER SEVEN COULD USE THIS...
...TO GET A NEW LEASE ON LIFE.
...
SPLAASH
THE GOVERNMENT'S JUDICIAL SHIP IS HERE!!!
RM RM...
WHAT'S A JUDICIAL SHIP?
YAK YAK
IT'S A FLOATING COURTHOUSE.
WHO'VE THEY COME TO JUDGE?!
OPEN THE WAY!!
WAH WAH
SHF SHF
NOW WAIT JUST A MINUTE!!! WHAT HAS MR. TOM DONE?!
GIVE MR. TOM BACK, PEOPLE!!!
IT'S ALL RIGHT. DON'T WORRY.
WAH WAH
TAH HAH!!...!! ...!!...!!
MR. TOM!!!

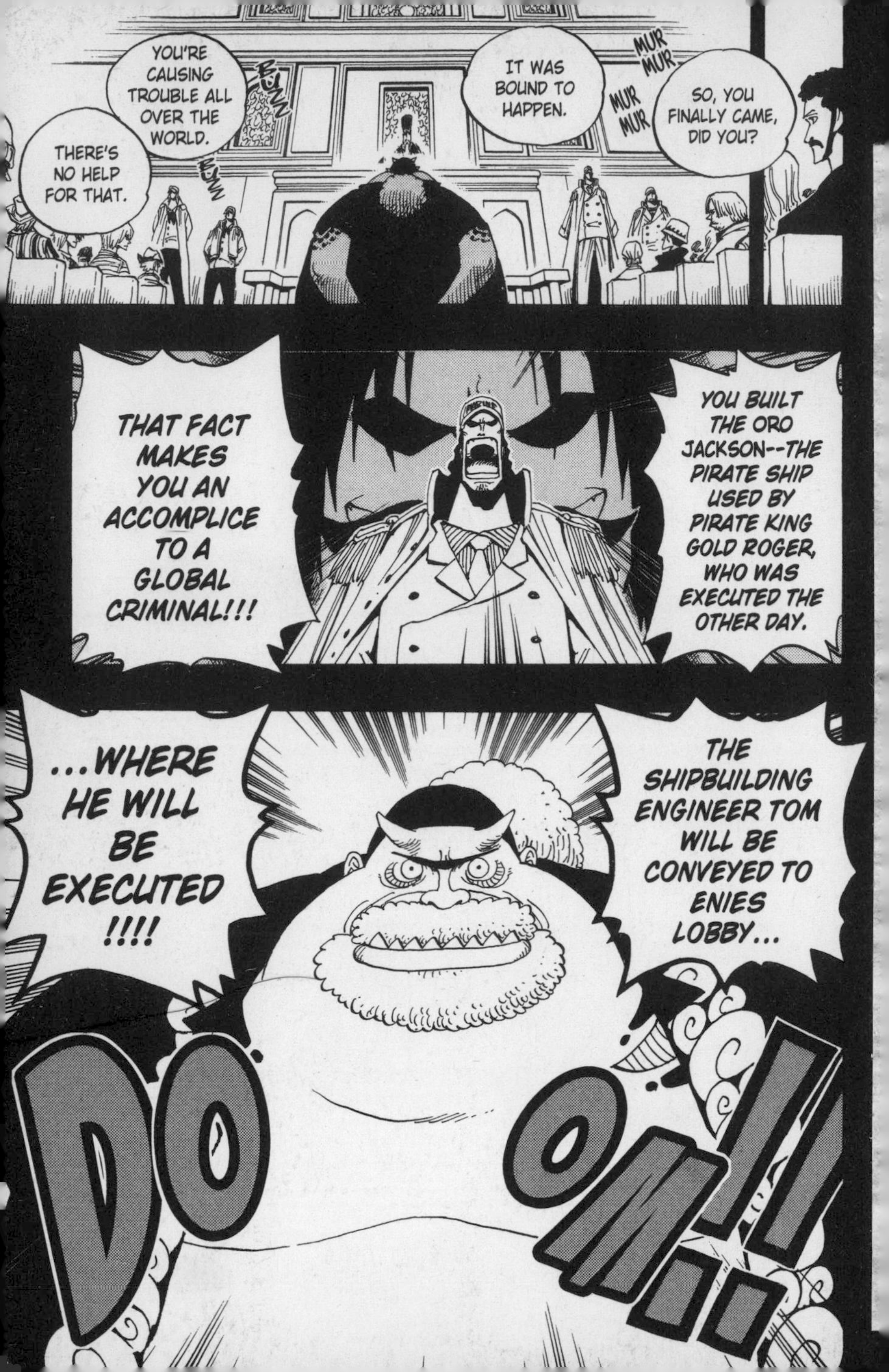
SO, YOU FINALLY CAME, DID YOU?
MUR MUR
IT WAS BOUND TO HAPPEN.
MUR MUR
YOU'RE CAUSING TROUBLE ALL OVER THE WORLD.
THERE'S NO HELP FOR THAT.
YOU BUILT THE ORO JACKSON--THE PIRATE SHIP USED BY PIRATE KING GOLD ROGER, WHO WAS EXECUTED THE OTHER DAY.
THAT FACT MAKES YOU AN ACCOMPLICE TO A GLOBAL CRIMINAL!!!
THE SHIPBUILDING ENGINEER TOM WILL BE CONVEYED TO ENIES LOBBY...
...WHERE HE WILL BE EXECUTED!!!!
DOON!!

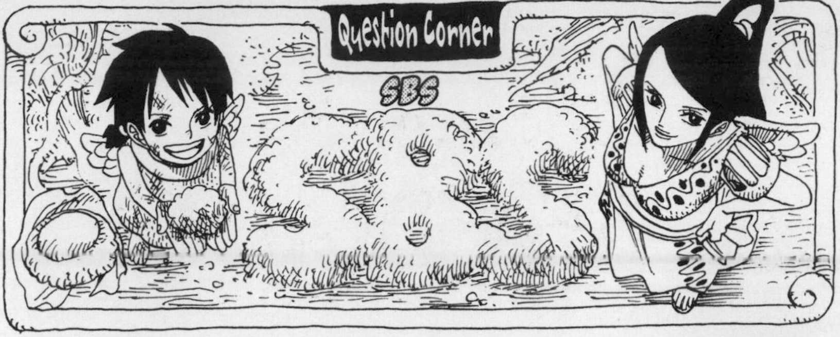

Question Corner
SBS

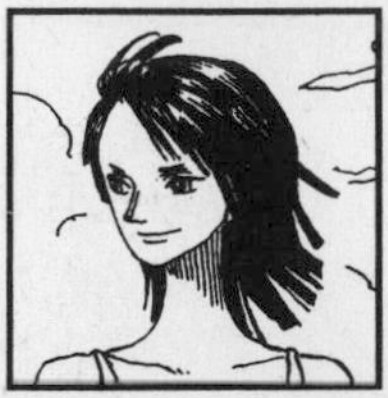

Reader: Hello, Oda Sensei. I am the president of the Japanese Association of Healthy Boys (present membership: one), Richie Usapon. I have something I would like to ask you, Oda Sensei, or rather, to ask Sanji.

"Please tell me Robin's measurements!"

I'm really, truly, desperately serious.

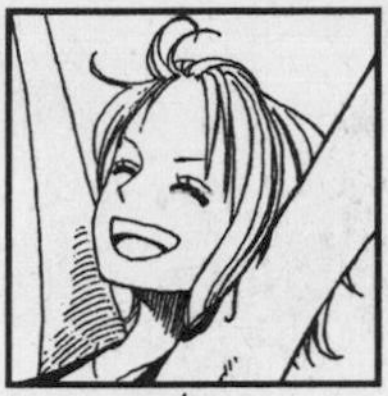

Reader: Hello, Oda sensei! In volume 36, you said Nami's gotten curvier than she was before. In that case, what are Nami's measurements now? I'm very sure all the guys in the country are dying to know this, so please give us a straight answer!

--Saru no Puutaro

Oda: Honestly, what are you people?! Are you all measurement explorers or something?! Honestly, I get a lot of these questions! There's no end to 'em, so fine, I'll just settle the whole thing here! Firmly! C'mon out, Mr. Cook!

Sanji: Don't tease me like that! Well, I do understand the situation. Leave it to me! According to my scope, their measurements are as follows!

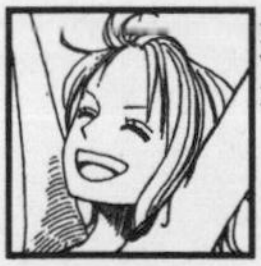

Bust 37.4"
Waist 21.7"
Hips 33.5"
(Height 5'5")

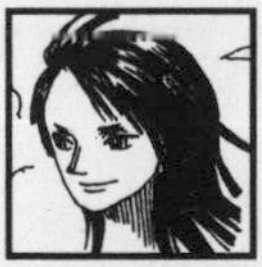

Bust 39"
Waist 23"
Hips 35"
(Height 6'2")

Yowza! Awesome! Fascinating, huh!

Oda: Agh! It's Nami! Run away! *kapwing* (Escaping)

Sanji: Ooh, Namiii! ♡

Nami: You don't have to publish ***everything*****!** ***WHACK!***

Sanji: AAAAaaaa...

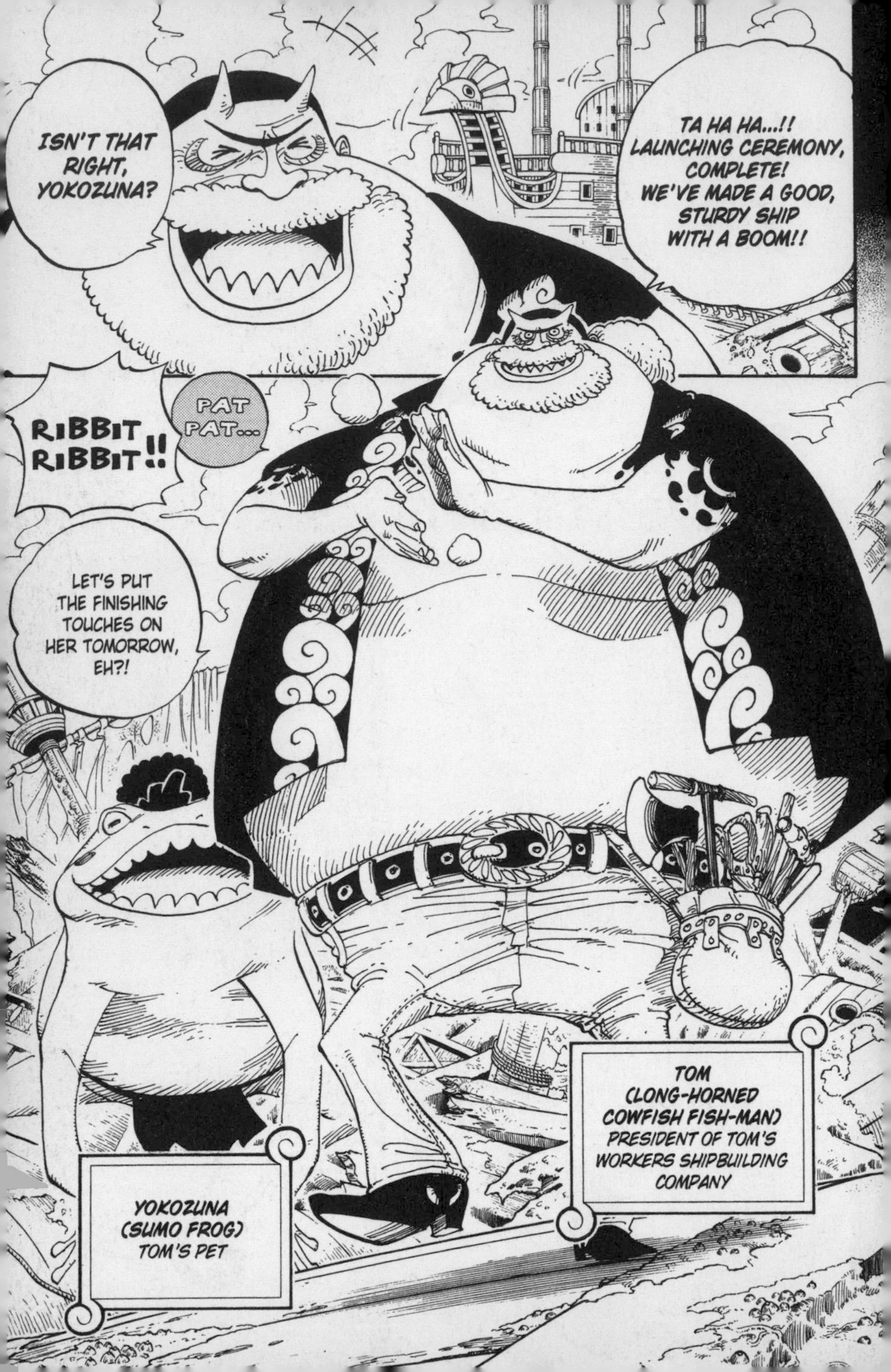

TA HA HA...!! LAUNCHING CEREMONY, COMPLETE! WE'VE MADE A GOOD, STURDY SHIP WITH A BOOM!!
ISN'T THAT RIGHT, YOKOZUNA?
PAT PAT...
RIBBIT RIBBIT!!
LET'S PUT THE FINISHING TOUCHES ON HER TOMORROW, EH?!
TOM (LONG-HORNED COWFISH FISH-MAN) PRESIDENT OF TOM'S WORKERS SHIPBUILDING COMPANY
YOKOZUNA (SUMO FROG) TOM'S PET

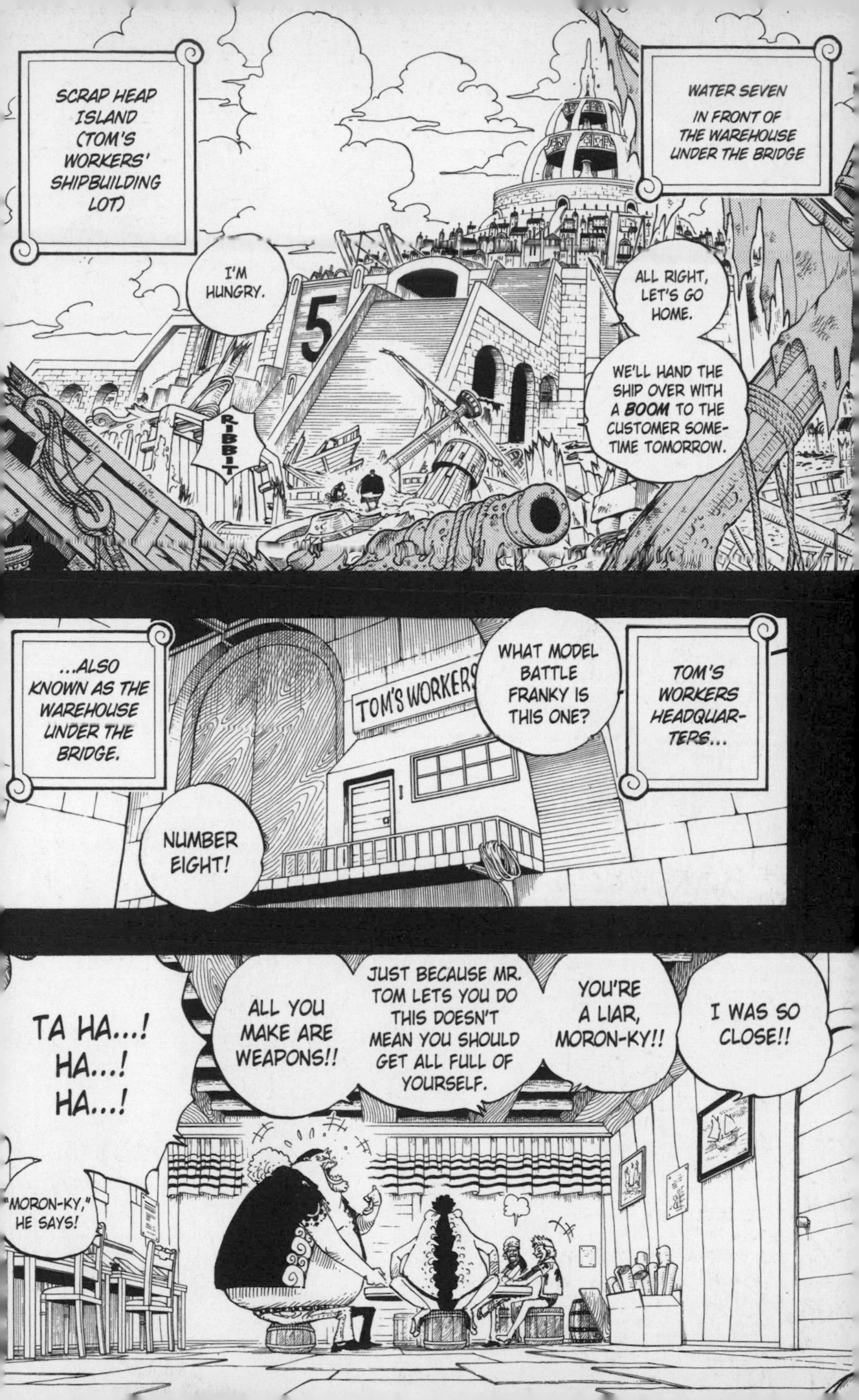
WATER SEVEN IN FRONT OF THE WAREHOUSE UNDER THE BRIDGE
SCRAP HEAP ISLAND (TOM'S WORKERS' SHIPBUILDING LOT)
ALL RIGHT, LET'S GO HOME.
WE'LL HAND THE SHIP OVER WITH A **BOOM** TO THE CUSTOMER SOMETIME TOMORROW.
I'M HUNGRY.
RIBBIT
5
TOM'S WORKERS HEADQUARTERS...
WHAT MODEL BATTLE FRANKY IS THIS ONE?
...ALSO KNOWN AS THE WAREHOUSE UNDER THE BRIDGE.
TOM'S WORKERS
NUMBER EIGHT!
I WAS SO CLOSE!!
YOU'RE A LIAR, MORON-KY!!
JUST BECAUSE MR. TOM LETS YOU DO THIS DOESN'T MEAN YOU SHOULD GET ALL FULL OF YOURSELF.
ALL YOU MAKE ARE WEAPONS!!
TA HA...! HA...! HA...!
"MORON-KY," HE SAYS!

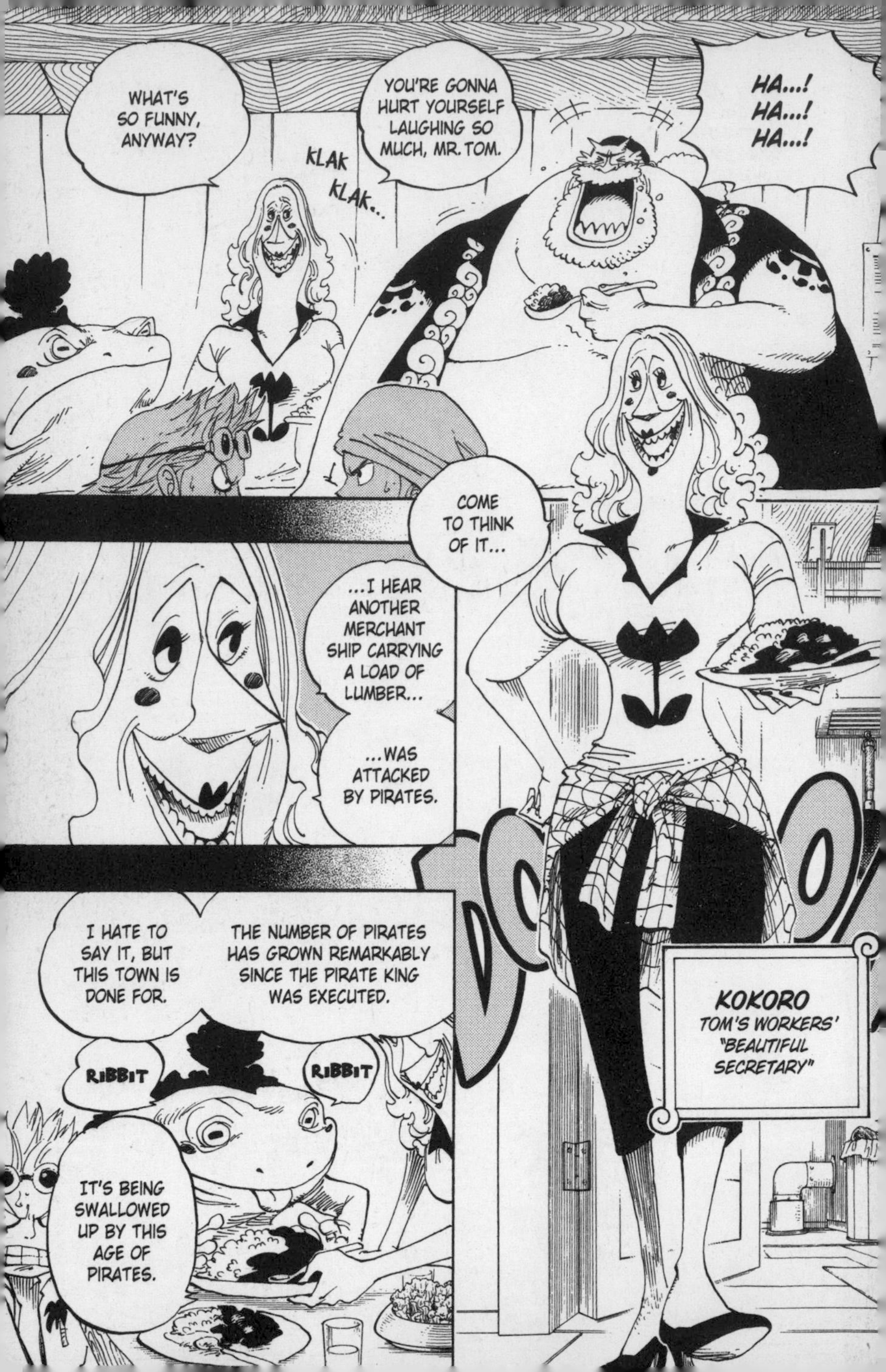
HA...! HA...! HA...!
YOU'RE GONNA HURT YOURSELF LAUGHING SO MUCH, MR. TOM.
KLAK KLAK...
WHAT'S SO FUNNY, ANYWAY?
COME TO THINK OF IT...
KOKORO
TOM'S WORKERS' "BEAUTIFUL SECRETARY"
...I HEAR ANOTHER MERCHANT SHIP CARRYING A LOAD OF LUMBER...
...WAS ATTACKED BY PIRATES.
THE NUMBER OF PIRATES HAS GROWN REMARKABLY SINCE THE PIRATE KING WAS EXECUTED.
I HATE TO SAY IT, BUT THIS TOWN IS DONE FOR.
RIBBIT
RIBBIT
IT'S BEING SWALLOWED UP BY THIS AGE OF PIRATES.

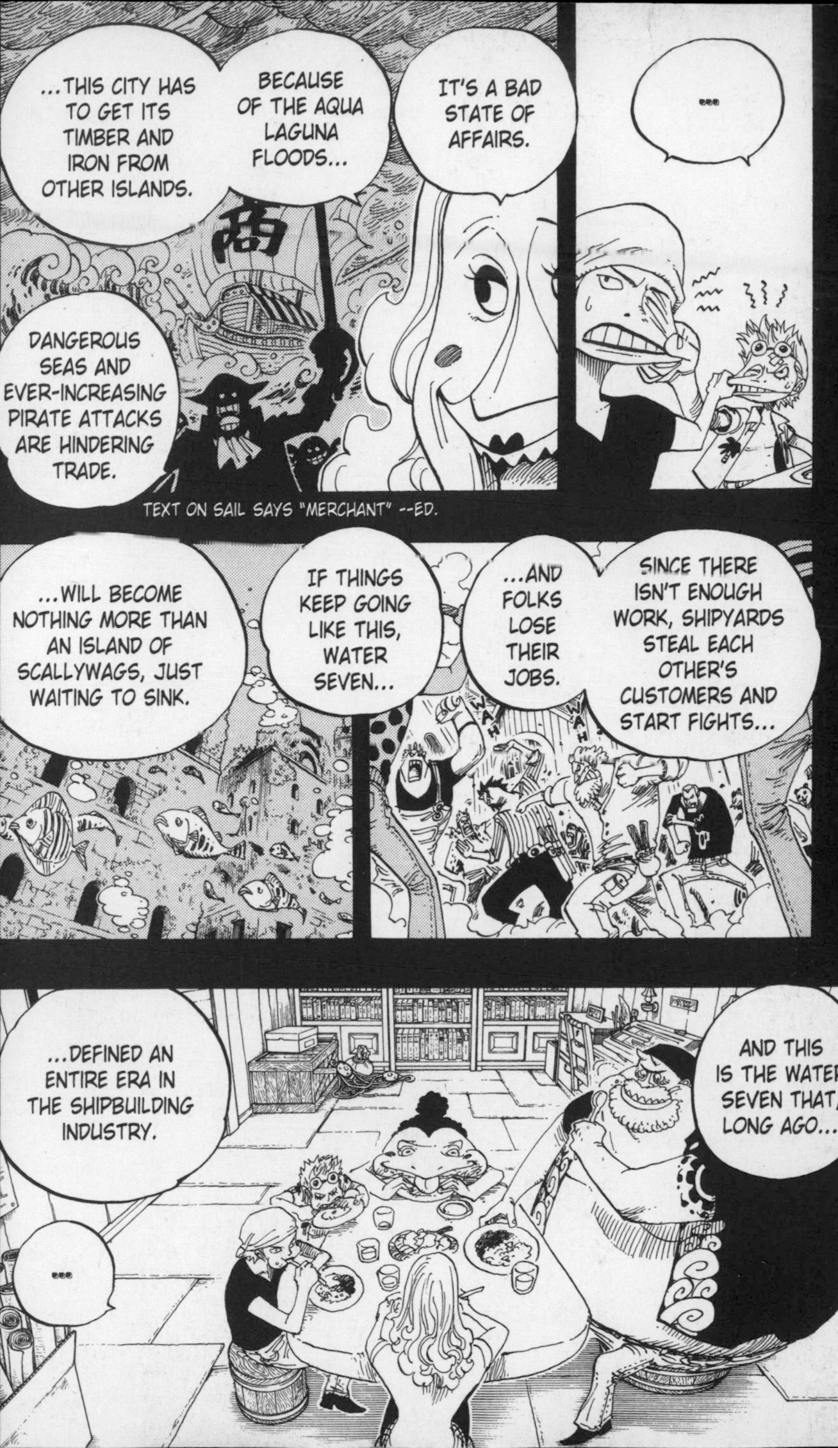
...
IT'S A BAD STATE OF AFFAIRS.
BECAUSE OF THE AQUA LAGUNA FLOODS...
...THIS CITY HAS TO GET ITS TIMBER AND IRON FROM OTHER ISLANDS.
DANGEROUS SEAS AND EVER-INCREASING PIRATE ATTACKS ARE HINDERING TRADE.
TEXT ON SAIL SAYS "MERCHANT" --ED.
SINCE THERE ISN'T ENOUGH WORK, SHIPYARDS STEAL EACH OTHER'S CUSTOMERS AND START FIGHTS...
...AND FOLKS LOSE THEIR JOBS.
WAH
WAH
IF THINGS KEEP GOING LIKE THIS, WATER SEVEN...
...WILL BECOME NOTHING MORE THAN AN ISLAND OF SCALLYWAGS, JUST WAITING TO SINK.
AND THIS IS THE WATER SEVEN THAT, LONG AGO...
...DEFINED AN ENTIRE ERA IN THE SHIPBUILDING INDUSTRY.
...

Chapter 354:
SEA TRAIN

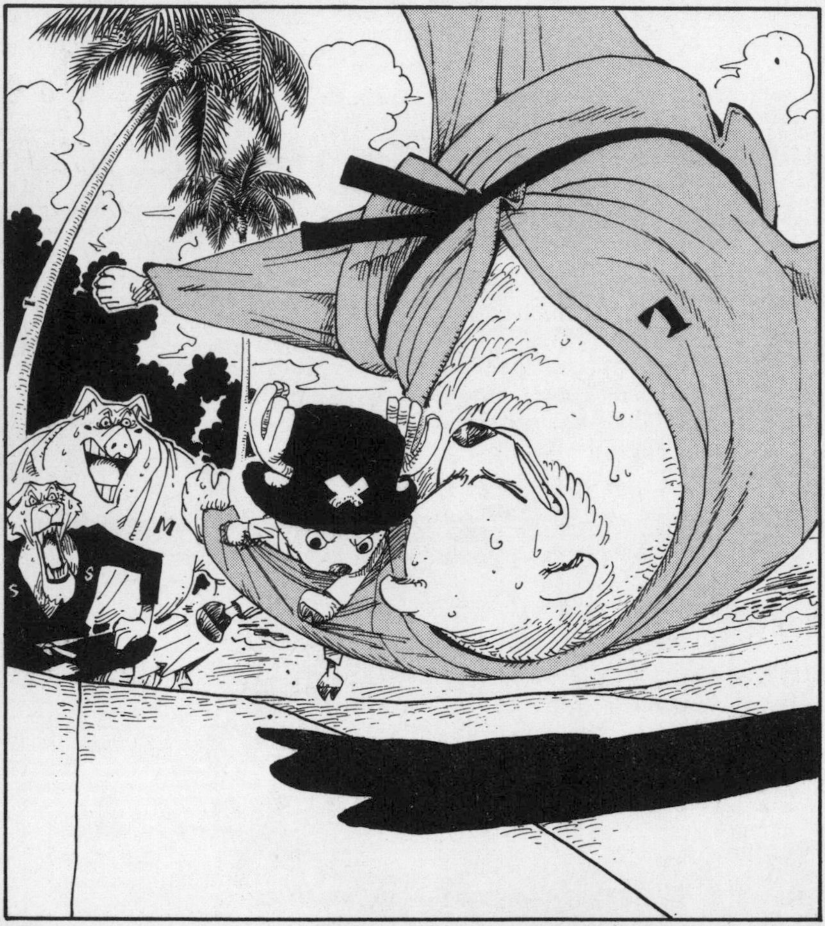

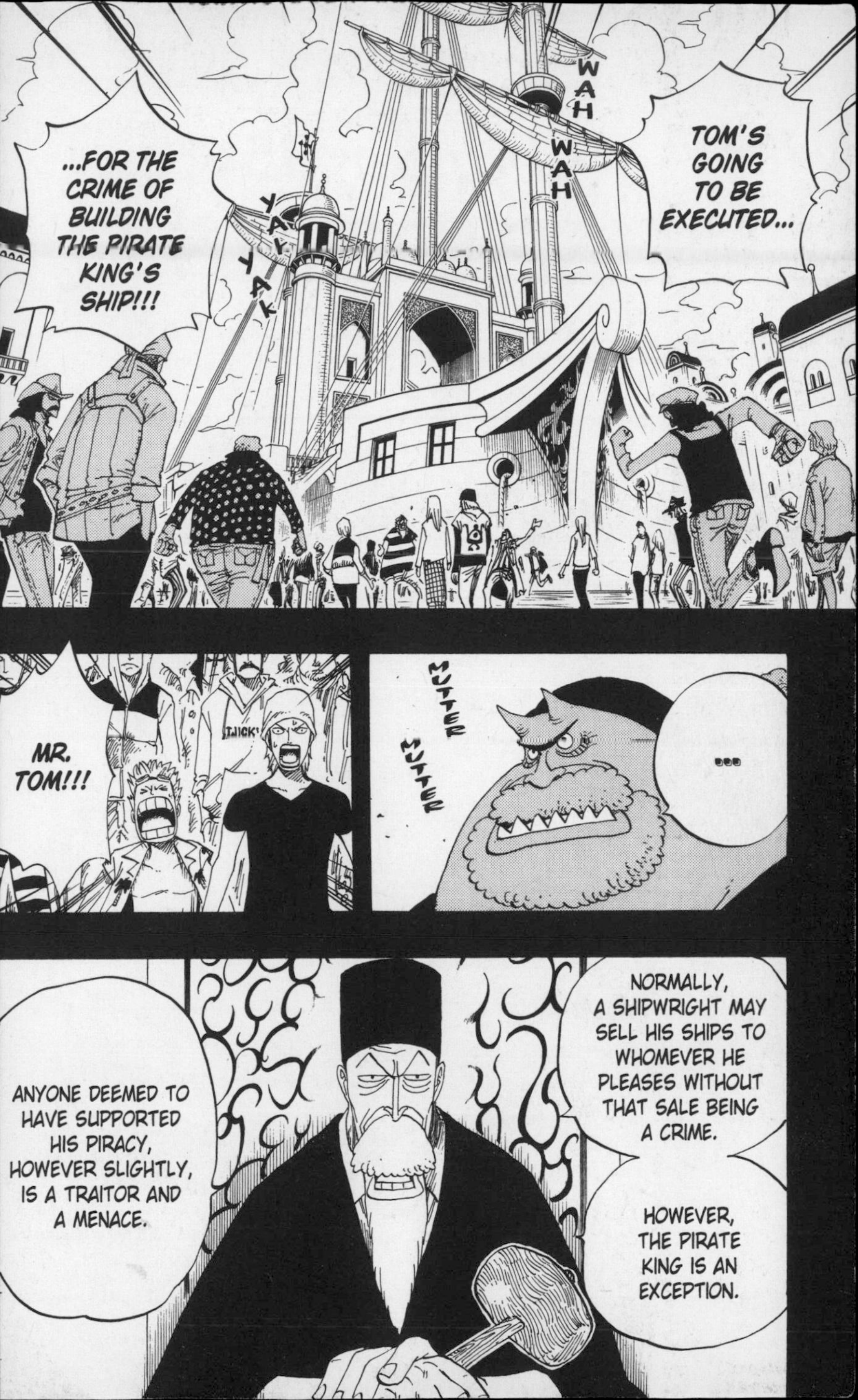
WAH WAH
TOM'S GOING TO BE EXECUTED...
YAK YAK
...FOR THE CRIME OF BUILDING THE PIRATE KING'S SHIP!!!
MUTTER MUTTER
...
MR. TOM!!!
NORMALLY, A SHIPWRIGHT MAY SELL HIS SHIPS TO WHOMEVER HE PLEASES WITHOUT THAT SALE BEING A CRIME.
HOWEVER, THE PIRATE KING IS AN EXCEPTION.
ANYONE DEEMED TO HAVE SUPPORTED HIS PIRACY, HOWEVER SLIGHTLY, IS A TRAITOR AND A MENACE.

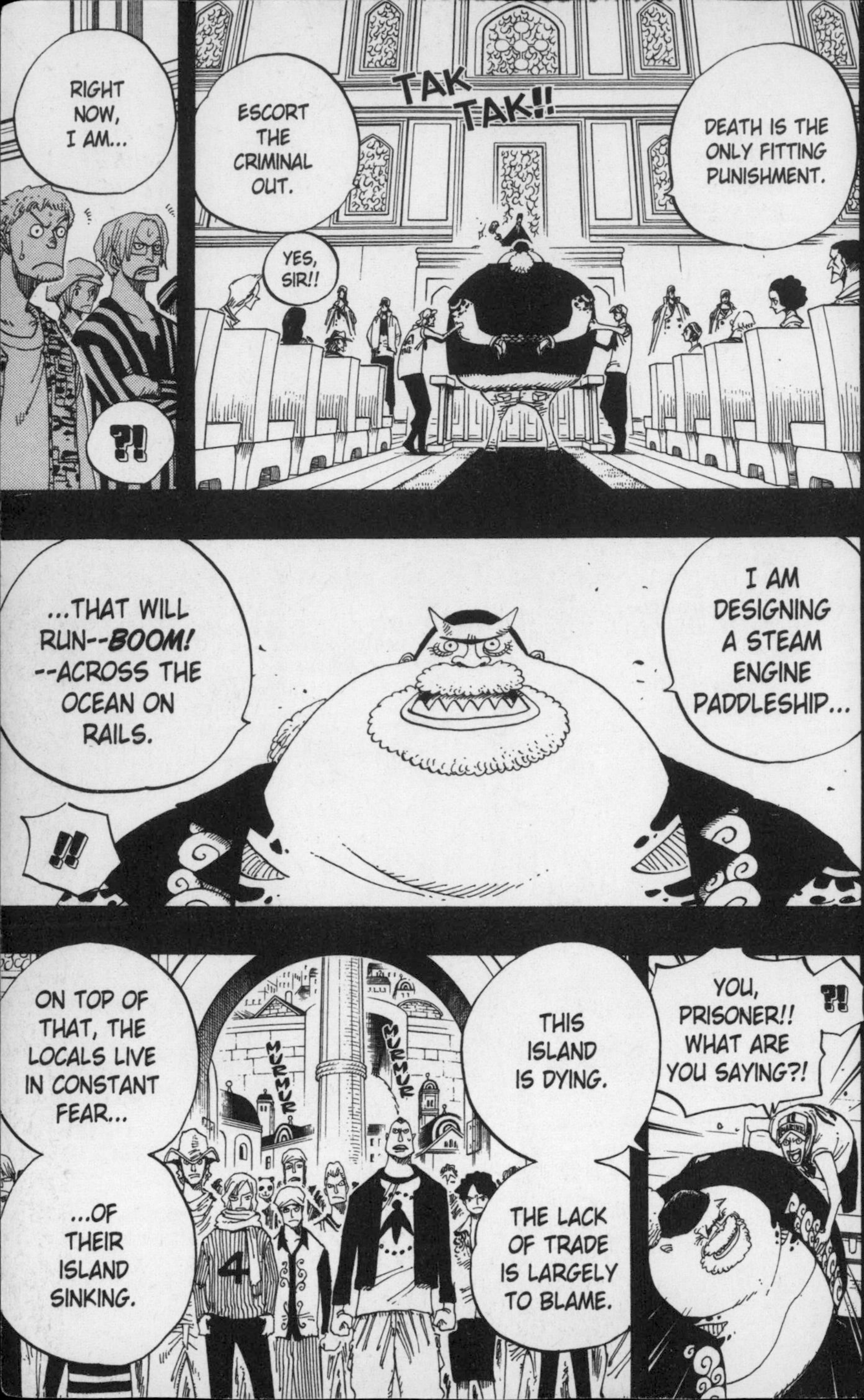
DEATH IS THE ONLY FITTING PUNISHMENT.
TAK TAK!!
ESCORT THE CRIMINAL OUT.
YES, SIR!!
RIGHT NOW, I AM...
?!
I AM DESIGNING A STEAM ENGINE PADDLESHIP...
...THAT WILL RUN--*BOOM!* --ACROSS THE OCEAN ON RAILS.
!!
?!
YOU, PRISONER!! WHAT ARE YOU SAYING?!
THIS ISLAND IS DYING.
THE LACK OF TRADE IS LARGELY TO BLAME.
MURMUR
MURMUR
ON TOP OF THAT, THE LOCALS LIVE IN CONSTANT FEAR...
...OF THEIR ISLAND SINKING.

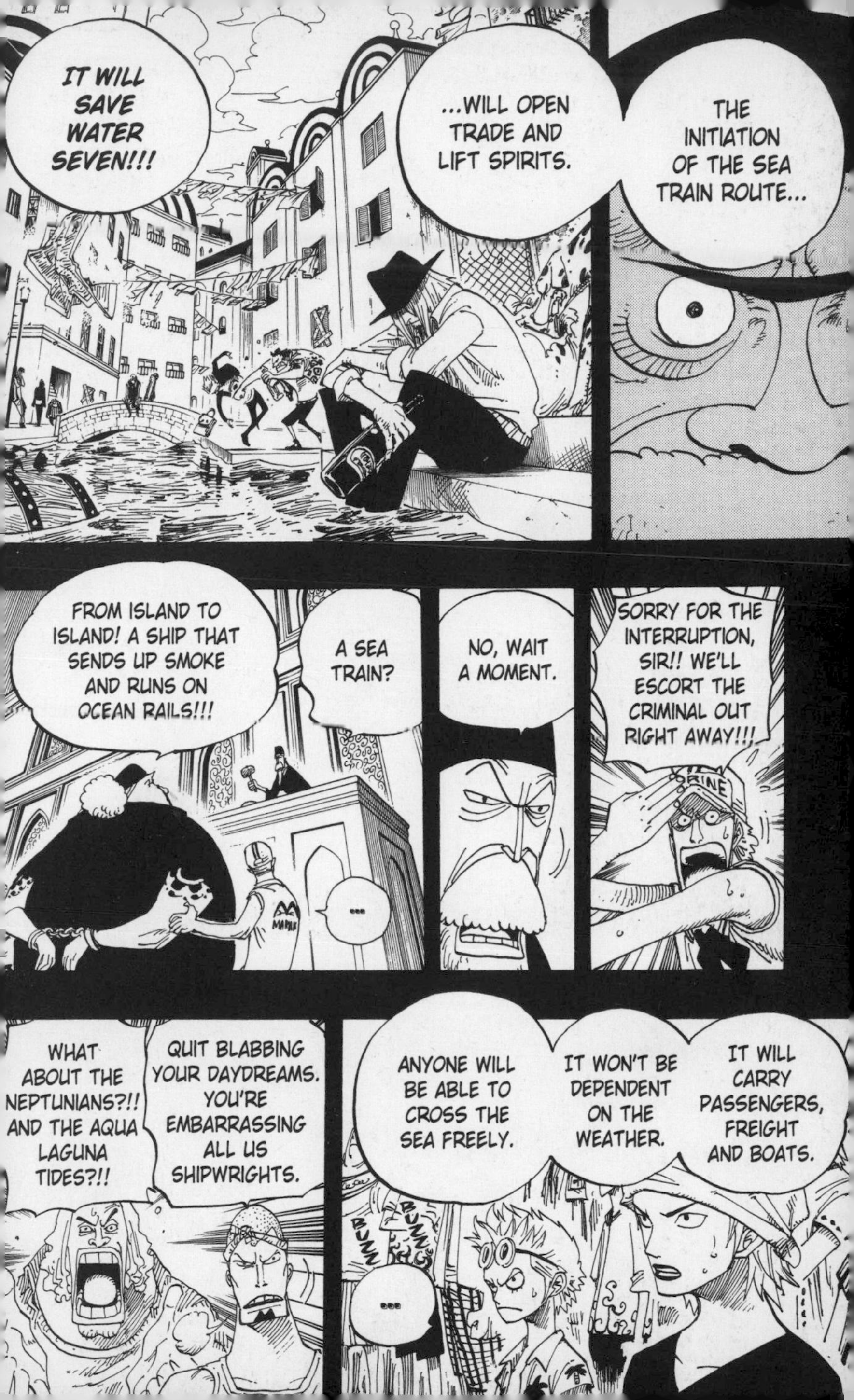
THE INITIATION OF THE SEA TRAIN ROUTE...
...WILL OPEN TRADE AND LIFT SPIRITS.
IT WILL SAVE WATER SEVEN!!!
SORRY FOR THE INTERRUPTION, SIR!! WE'LL ESCORT THE CRIMINAL OUT RIGHT AWAY!!!
NO, WAIT A MOMENT.
A SEA TRAIN?
FROM ISLAND TO ISLAND! A SHIP THAT SENDS UP SMOKE AND RUNS ON OCEAN RAILS!!!
...
IT WILL CARRY PASSENGERS, FREIGHT AND BOATS.
IT WON'T BE DEPENDENT ON THE WEATHER.
ANYONE WILL BE ABLE TO CROSS THE SEA FREELY.
BUZZ
BUZZ
BUZZ
...
QUIT BLABBING YOUR DAYDREAMS. YOU'RE EMBARRASSING ALL US SHIPWRIGHTS.
WHAT ABOUT THE NEPTUNIANS?!! AND THE AQUA LAGUNA TIDES?!!

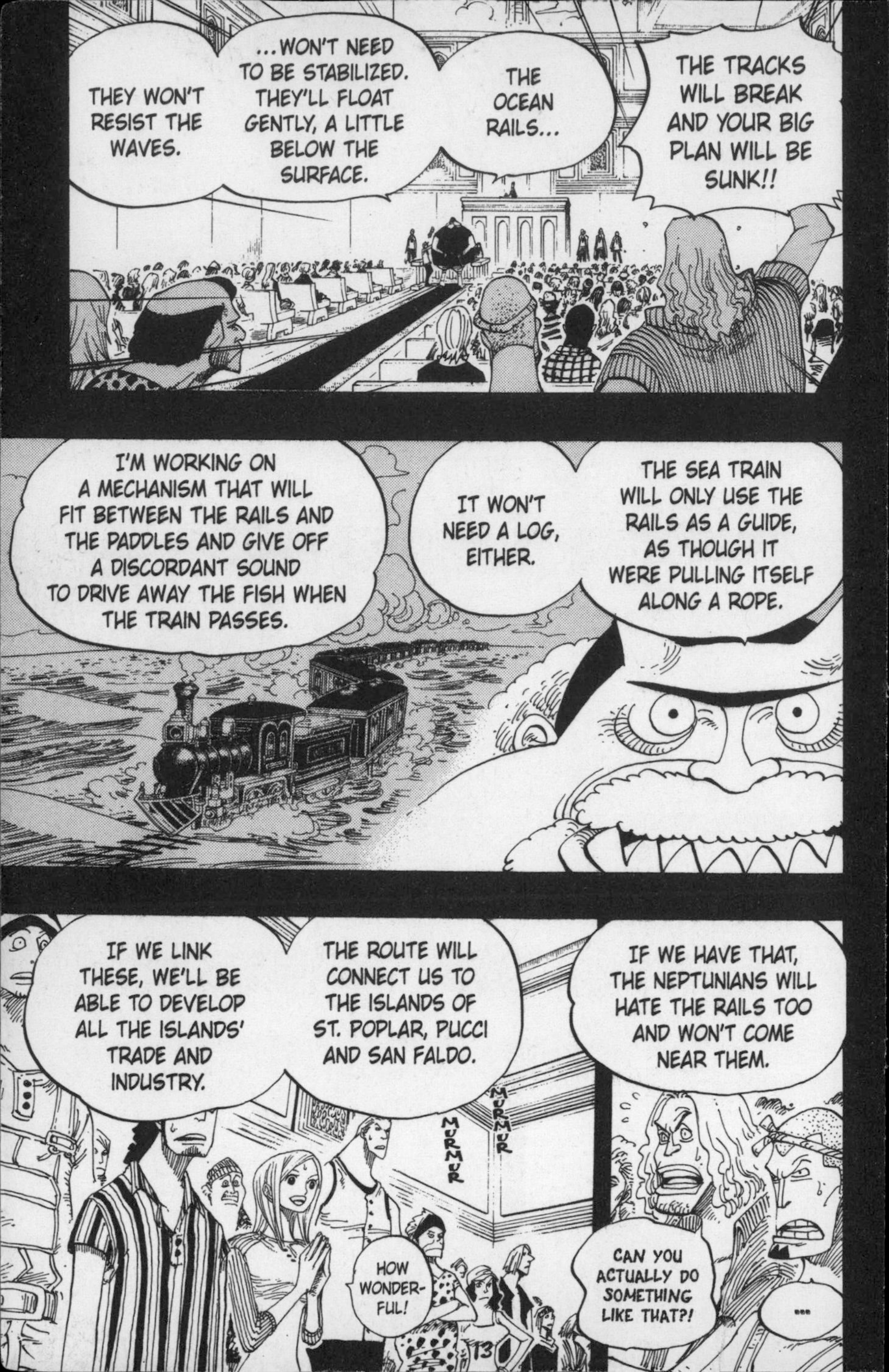
THE TRACKS WILL BREAK AND YOUR BIG PLAN WILL BE SUNK!!
THE OCEAN RAILS...
...WON'T NEED TO BE STABILIZED. THEY'LL FLOAT GENTLY, A LITTLE BELOW THE SURFACE.
THEY WON'T RESIST THE WAVES.
THE SEA TRAIN WILL ONLY USE THE RAILS AS A GUIDE, AS THOUGH IT WERE PULLING ITSELF ALONG A ROPE.
IT WON'T NEED A LOG, EITHER.
I'M WORKING ON A MECHANISM THAT WILL FIT BETWEEN THE RAILS AND THE PADDLES AND GIVE OFF A DISCORDANT SOUND TO DRIVE AWAY THE FISH WHEN THE TRAIN PASSES.
IF WE HAVE THAT, THE NEPTUNIANS WILL HATE THE RAILS TOO AND WON'T COME NEAR THEM.
CAN YOU ACTUALLY DO SOMETHING LIKE THAT?!
...
THE ROUTE WILL CONNECT US TO THE ISLANDS OF ST. POPLAR, PUCCI AND SAN FALDO.
IF WE LINK THESE, WE'LL BE ABLE TO DEVELOP ALL THE ISLANDS' TRADE AND INDUSTRY.
MURMUR
MURMUR
HOW WONDERFUL!

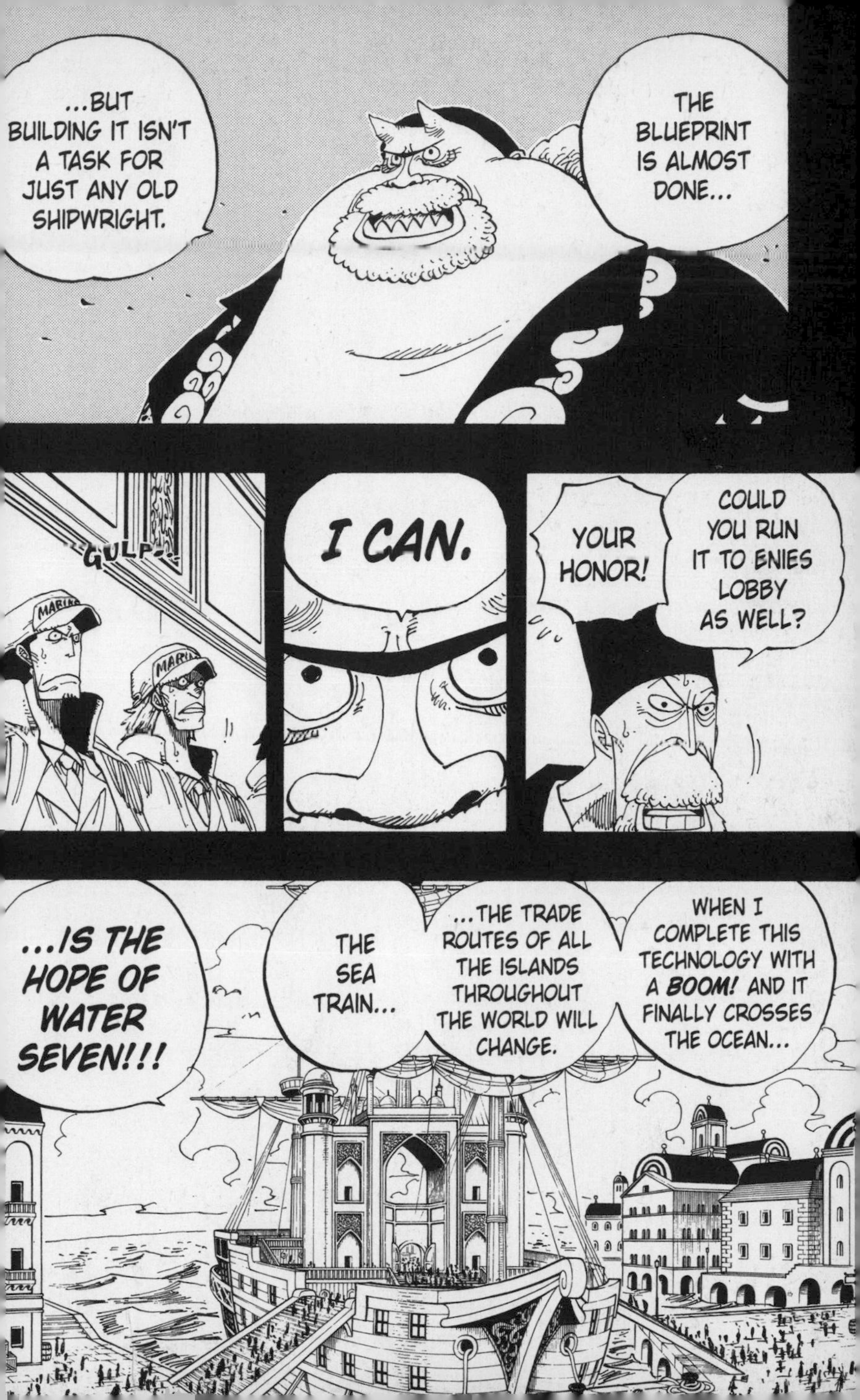
THE BLUEPRINT IS ALMOST DONE...
...BUT BUILDING IT ISN'T A TASK FOR JUST ANY OLD SHIPWRIGHT.
COULD YOU RUN IT TO ENIES LOBBY AS WELL?
YOUR HONOR!
I CAN.
GULP...
WHEN I COMPLETE THIS TECHNOLOGY WITH A **BOOM!** AND IT FINALLY CROSSES THE OCEAN...
...THE TRADE ROUTES OF ALL THE ISLANDS THROUGHOUT THE WORLD WILL CHANGE.
THE SEA TRAIN...
...IS THE HOPE OF WATER SEVEN!!!

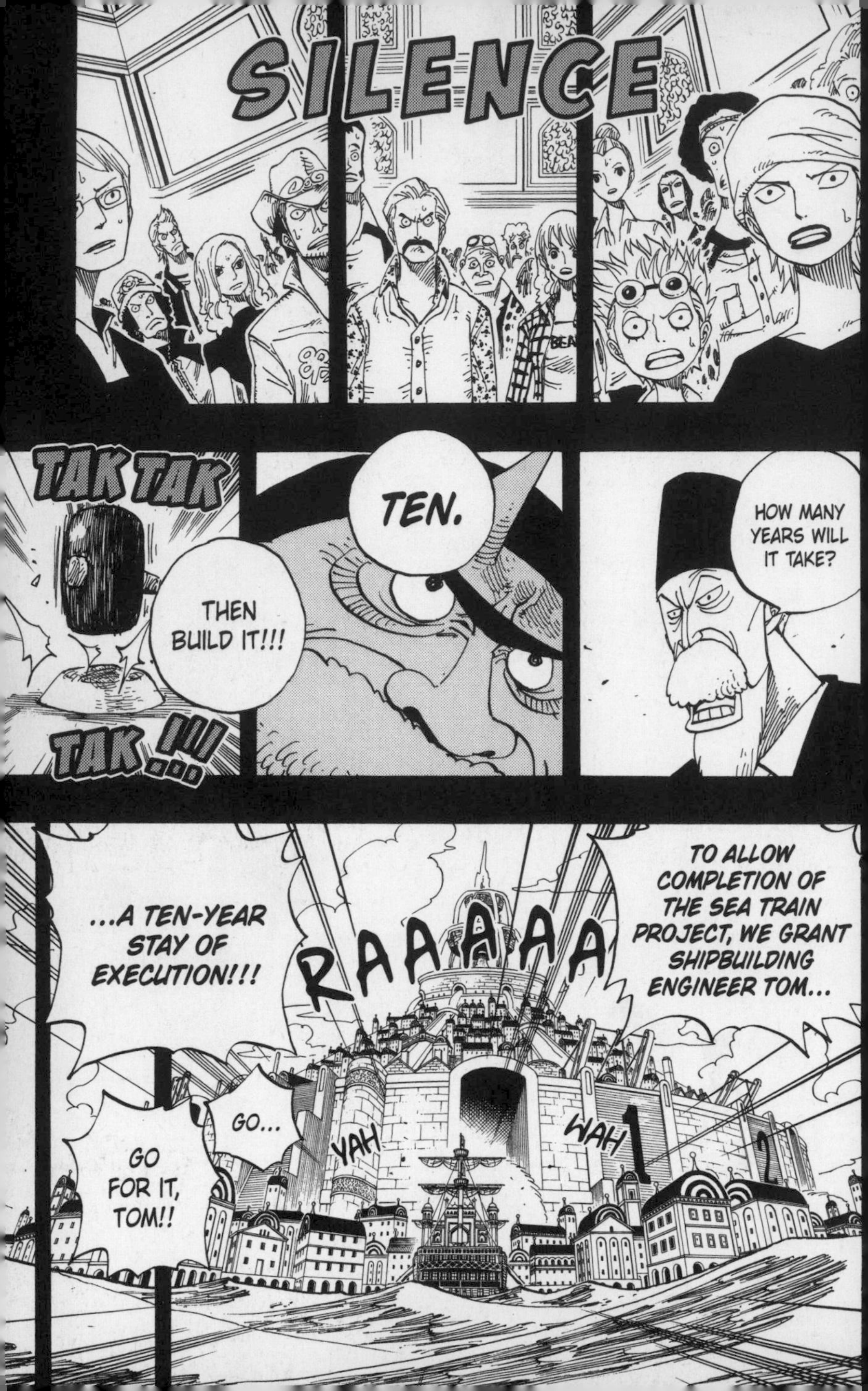
SILENCE
HOW MANY YEARS WILL IT TAKE?
TEN.
THEN BUILD IT!!!
TAK TAK
TAK...!!!
TO ALLOW COMPLETION OF THE SEA TRAIN PROJECT, WE GRANT SHIPBUILDING ENGINEER TOM...
RAAAAAA
...A TEN-YEAR STAY OF EXECUTION!!!
WAH
YAH
GO...
GO FOR IT, TOM!!

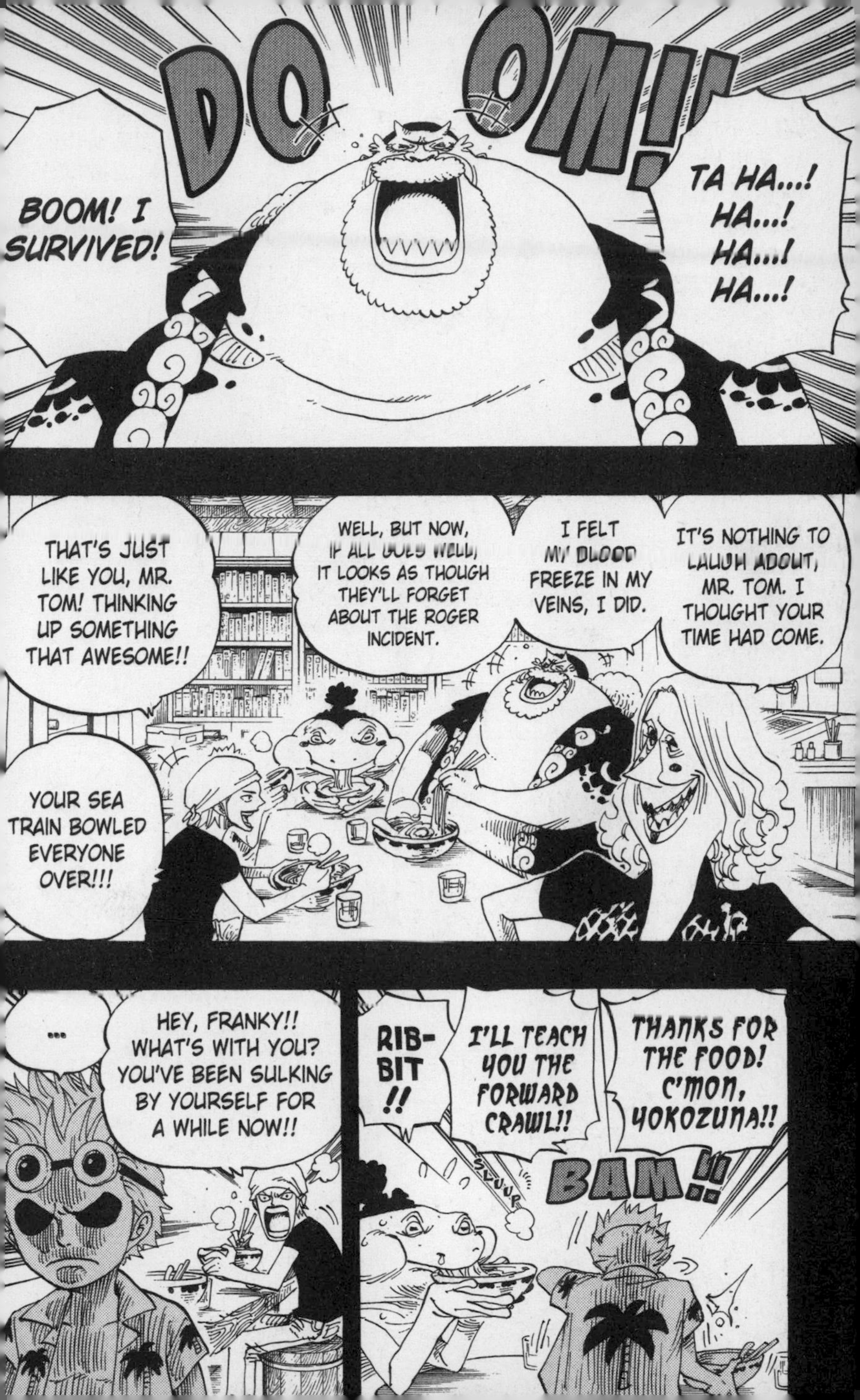
DOOM!!
TA HA...! HA...! HA...! HA...!
BOOM! I SURVIVED!
IT'S NOTHING TO LAUGH ABOUT, MR. TOM. I THOUGHT YOUR TIME HAD COME.
I FELT MY BLOOD FREEZE IN MY VEINS, I DID.
WELL, BUT NOW, IF ALL GOES WELL, IT LOOKS AS THOUGH THEY'LL FORGET ABOUT THE ROGER INCIDENT.
THAT'S JUST LIKE YOU, MR. TOM! THINKING UP SOMETHING THAT AWESOME!!
YOUR SEA TRAIN BOWLED EVERYONE OVER!!!
THANKS FOR THE FOOD! C'MON, YOKOZUNA!!
I'LL TEACH YOU THE FORWARD CRAWL!!
RIB-BIT!!
SLUUURP
BAM!!
HEY, FRANKY!! WHAT'S WITH YOU? YOU'VE BEEN SULKING BY YOURSELF FOR A WHILE NOW!!
...

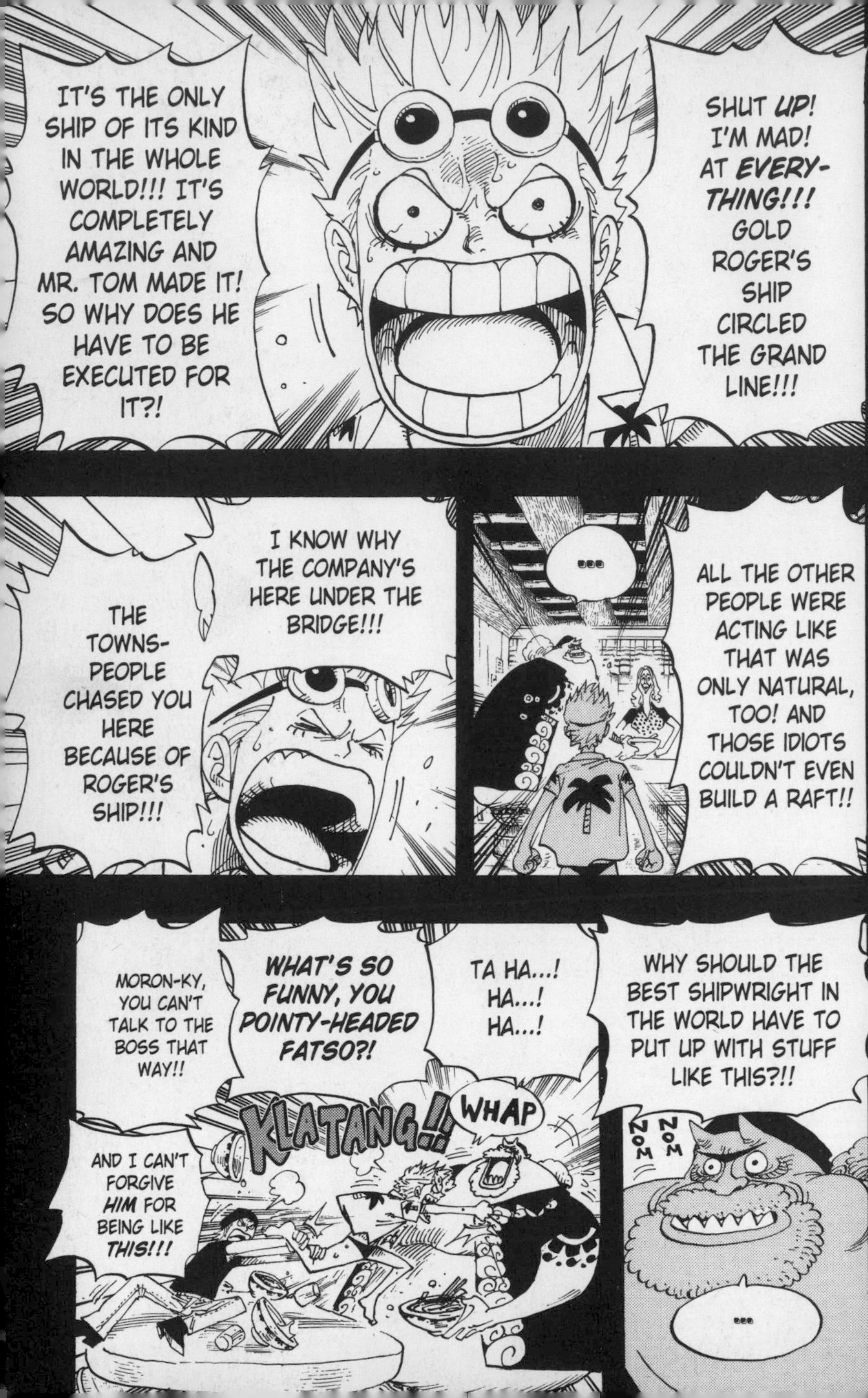
SHUT UP! I'M MAD! AT EVERY-THING!!! GOLD ROGER'S SHIP CIRCLED THE GRAND LINE!!!
IT'S THE ONLY SHIP OF ITS KIND IN THE WHOLE WORLD!!! IT'S COMPLETELY AMAZING AND MR. TOM MADE IT! SO WHY DOES HE HAVE TO BE EXECUTED FOR IT?!
ALL THE OTHER PEOPLE WERE ACTING LIKE THAT WAS ONLY NATURAL, TOO! AND THOSE IDIOTS COULDN'T EVEN BUILD A RAFT!!
...
I KNOW WHY THE COMPANY'S HERE UNDER THE BRIDGE!!!
THE TOWNS-PEOPLE CHASED YOU HERE BECAUSE OF ROGER'S SHIP!!!
WHY SHOULD THE BEST SHIPWRIGHT IN THE WORLD HAVE TO PUT UP WITH STUFF LIKE THIS?!!
NOM NOM
...
TA HA...! HA...! HA...!
WHAT'S SO FUNNY, YOU POINTY-HEADED FATSO?!
MORON-KY, YOU CAN'T TALK TO THE BOSS THAT WAY!!
WHAP
KLATANG!!
AND I CAN'T FORGIVE HIM FOR BEING LIKE THIS!!!

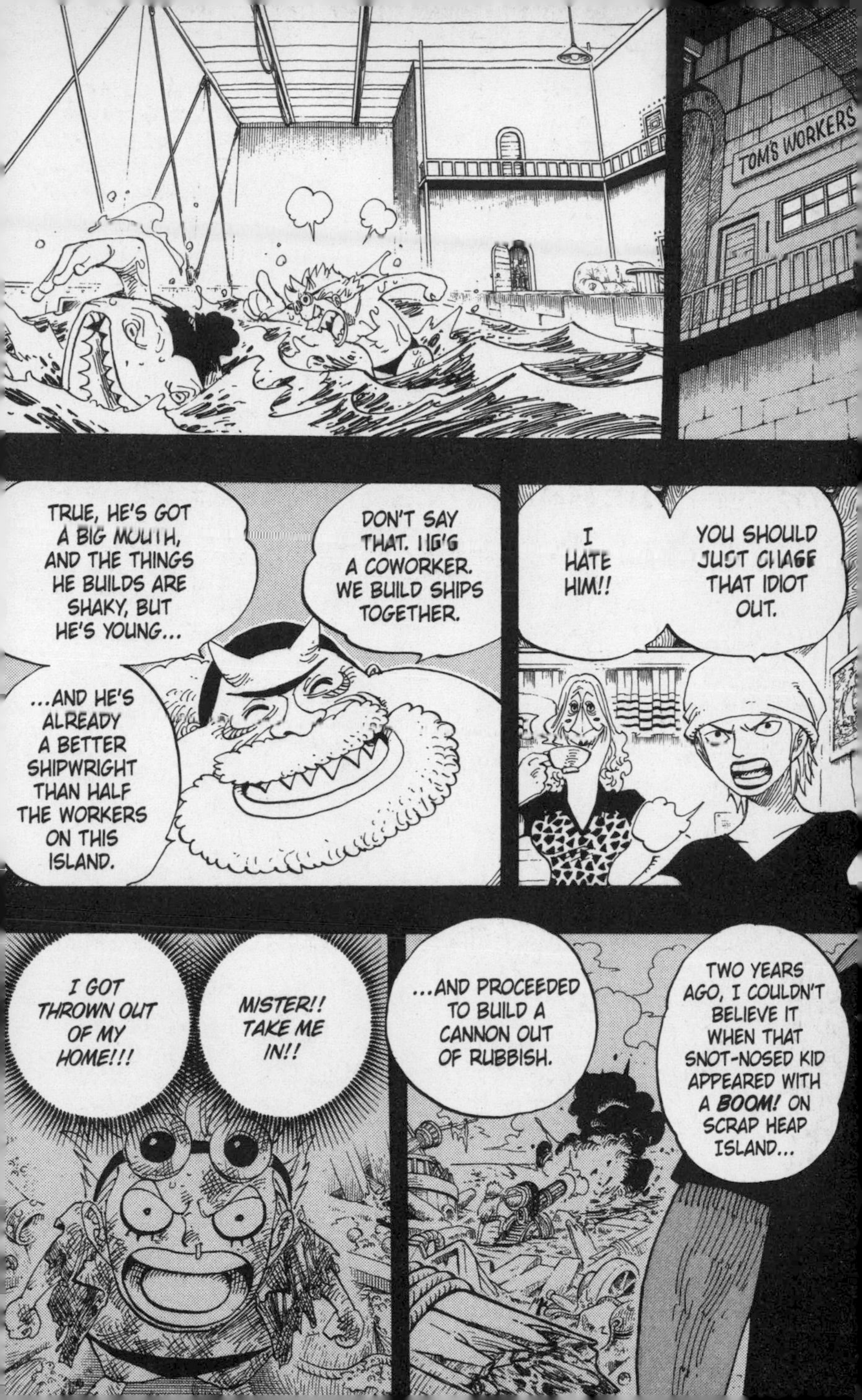
TOM'S WORKERS
YOU SHOULD JUST CHASE THAT IDIOT OUT.
I HATE HIM!!
DON'T SAY THAT. HE'S A COWORKER. WE BUILD SHIPS TOGETHER.
TRUE, HE'S GOT A BIG MOUTH, AND THE THINGS HE BUILDS ARE SHAKY, BUT HE'S YOUNG...
...AND HE'S ALREADY A BETTER SHIPWRIGHT THAN HALF THE WORKERS ON THIS ISLAND.
TWO YEARS AGO, I COULDN'T BELIEVE IT WHEN THAT SNOT-NOSED KID APPEARED WITH A **BOOM!** ON SCRAP HEAP ISLAND...
...AND PROCEEDED TO BUILD A CANNON OUT OF RUBBISH.
MISTER!! TAKE ME IN!!
I GOT THROWN OUT OF MY HOME!!!

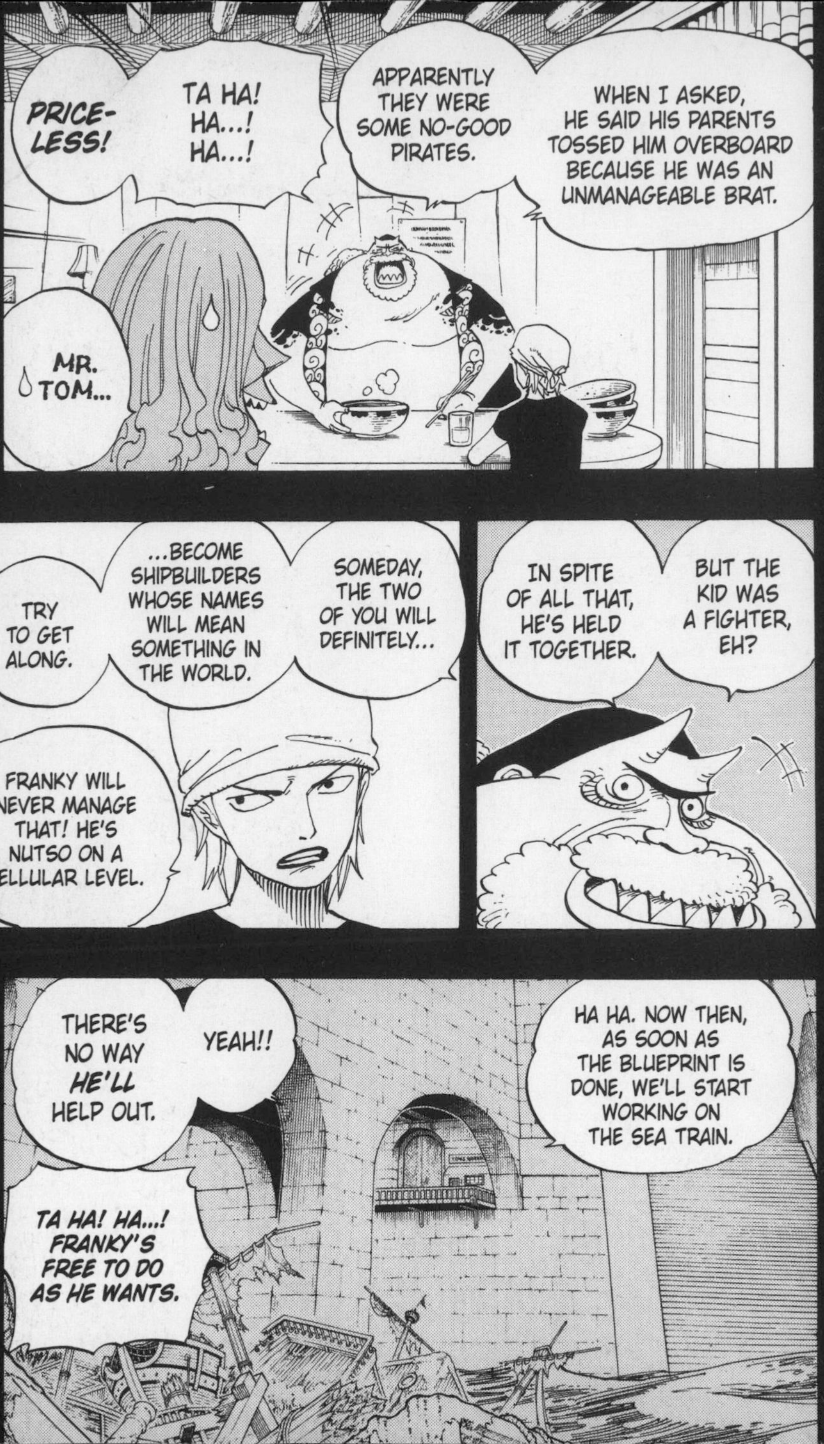
WHEN I ASKED, HE SAID HIS PARENTS TOSSED HIM OVERBOARD BECAUSE HE WAS AN UNMANAGEABLE BRAT.
APPARENTLY THEY WERE SOME NO-GOOD PIRATES.
TA HA! HA...! HA...!
PRICE-LESS!
MR. TOM...
BUT THE KID WAS A FIGHTER, EH?
IN SPITE OF ALL THAT, HE'S HELD IT TOGETHER.
SOMEDAY, THE TWO OF YOU WILL DEFINITELY...
...BECOME SHIPBUILDERS WHOSE NAMES WILL MEAN SOMETHING IN THE WORLD.
TRY TO GET ALONG.
FRANKY WILL NEVER MANAGE THAT! HE'S NUTSO ON A CELLULAR LEVEL.
HA HA. NOW THEN, AS SOON AS THE BLUEPRINT IS DONE, WE'LL START WORKING ON THE SEA TRAIN.
YEAH!!
THERE'S NO WAY HE'LL HELP OUT.
TA HA! HA...! FRANKY'S FREE TO DO AS HE WANTS.

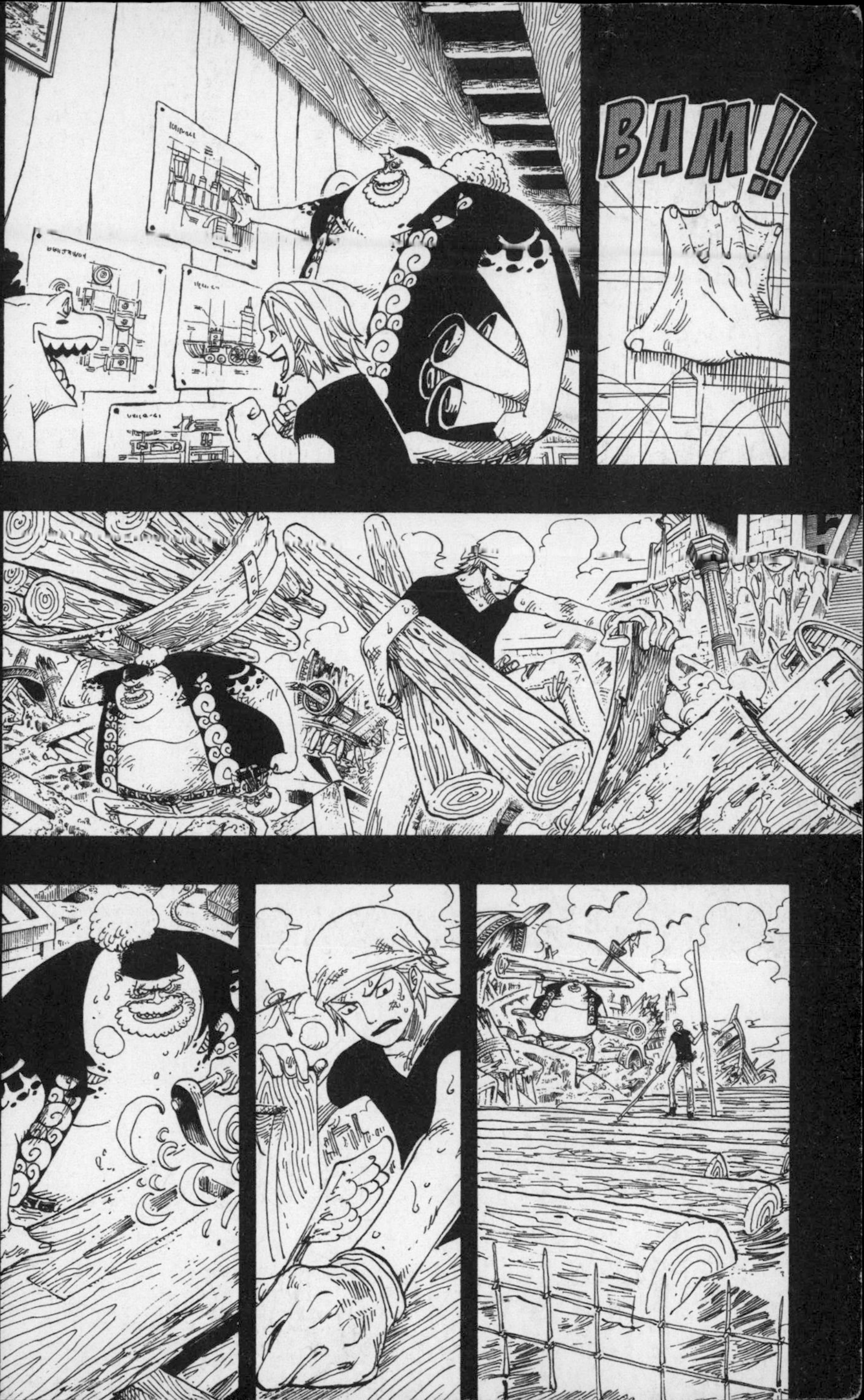
BAM!!

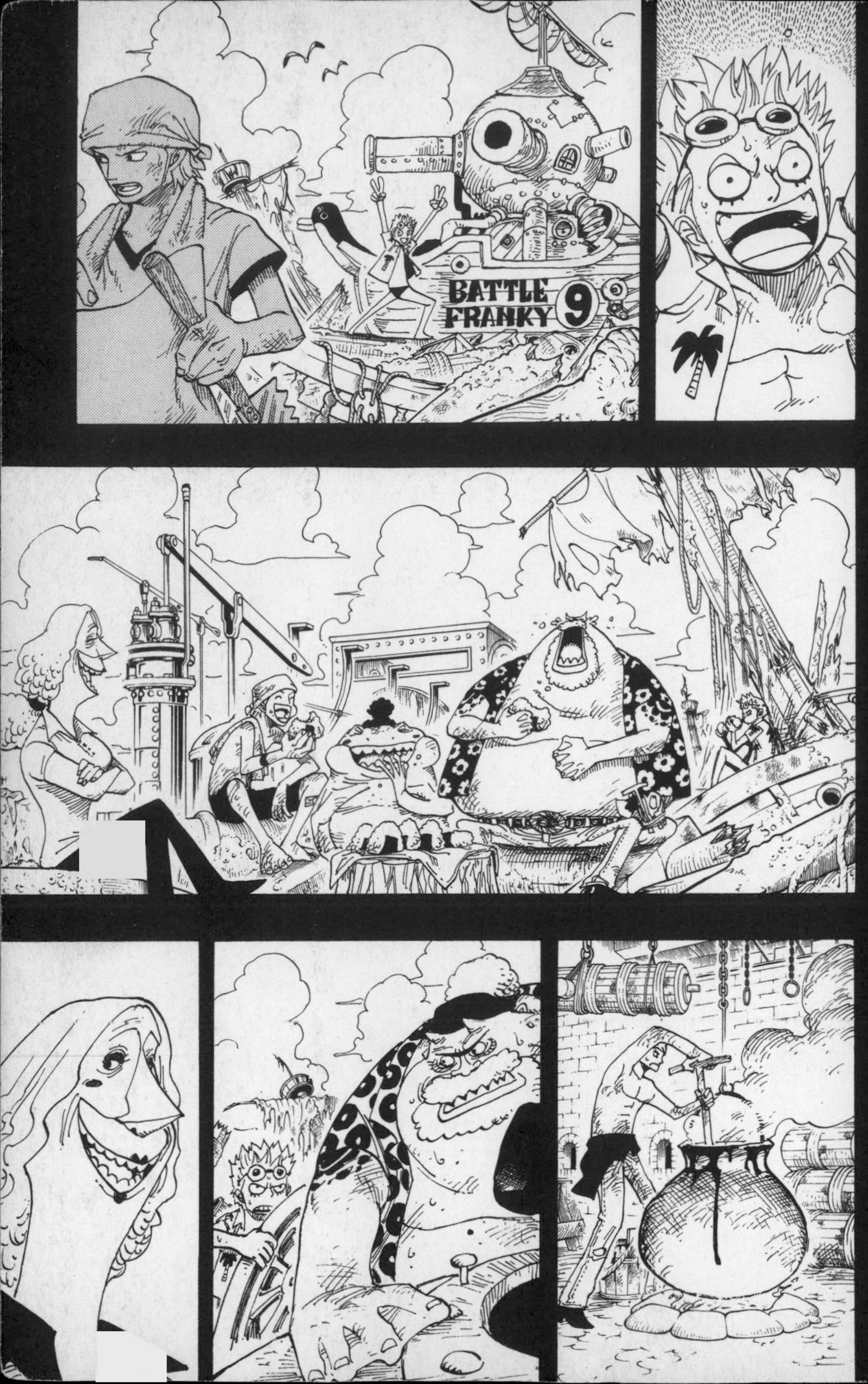
BATTLE FRANKY 9

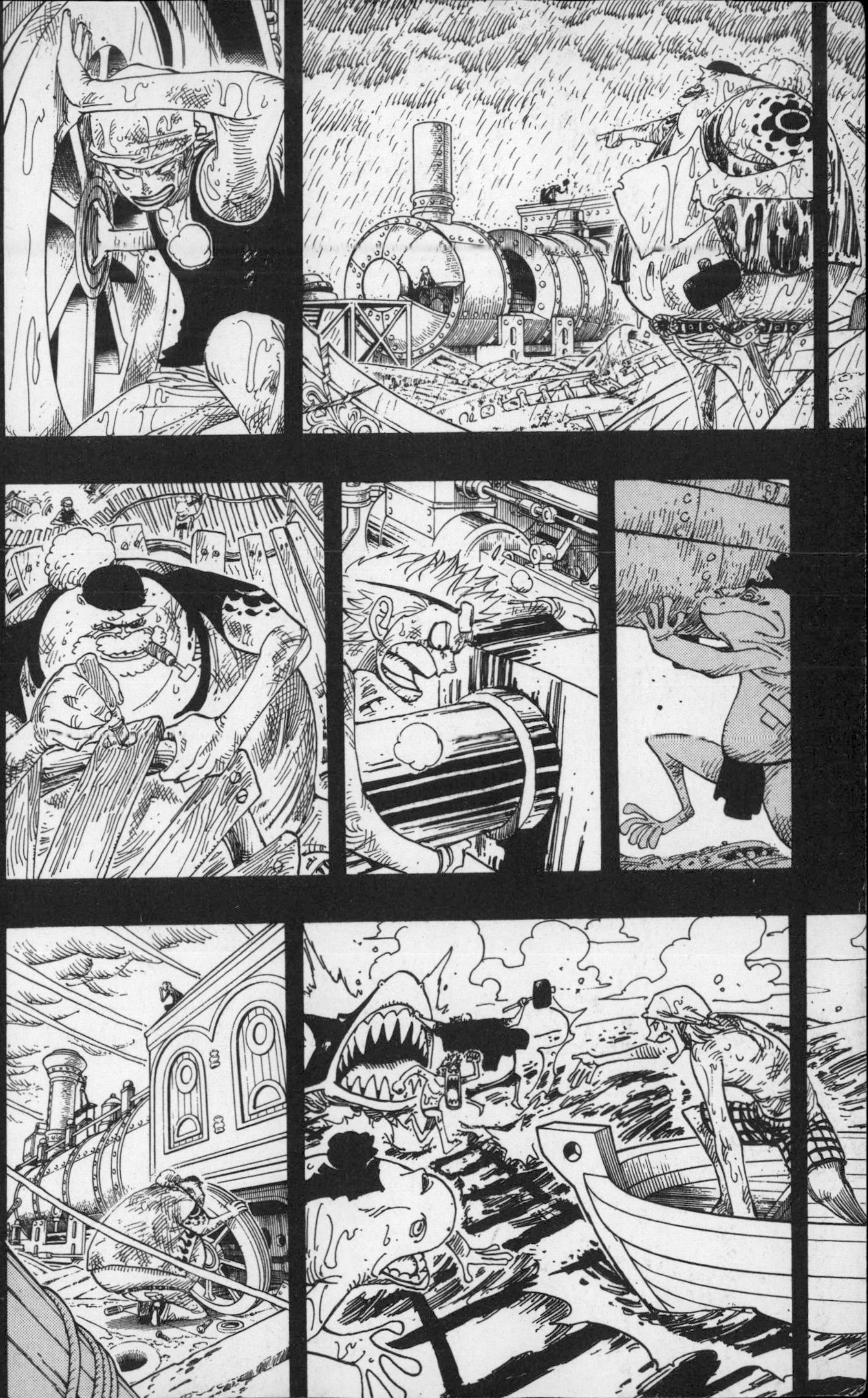

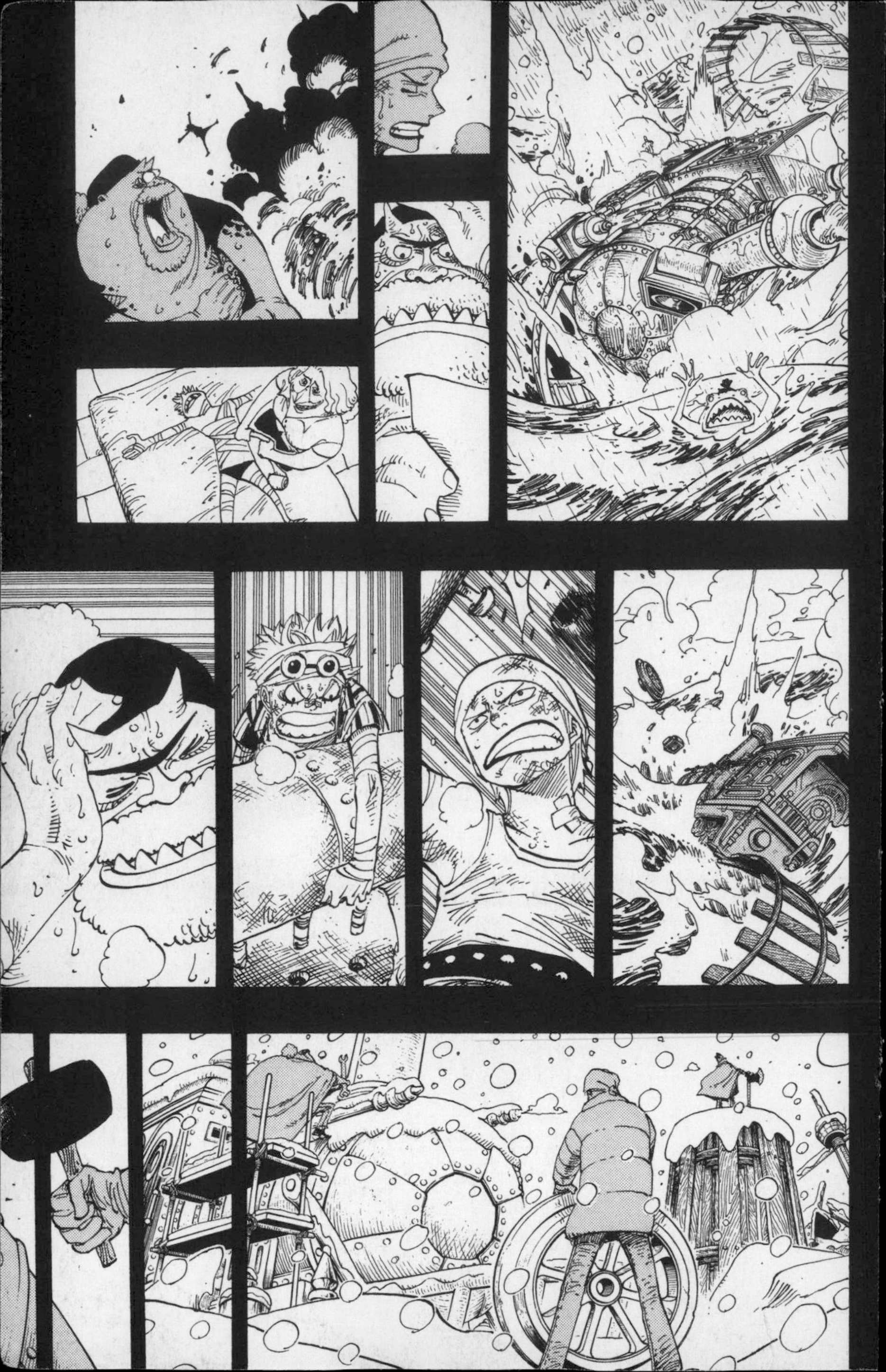

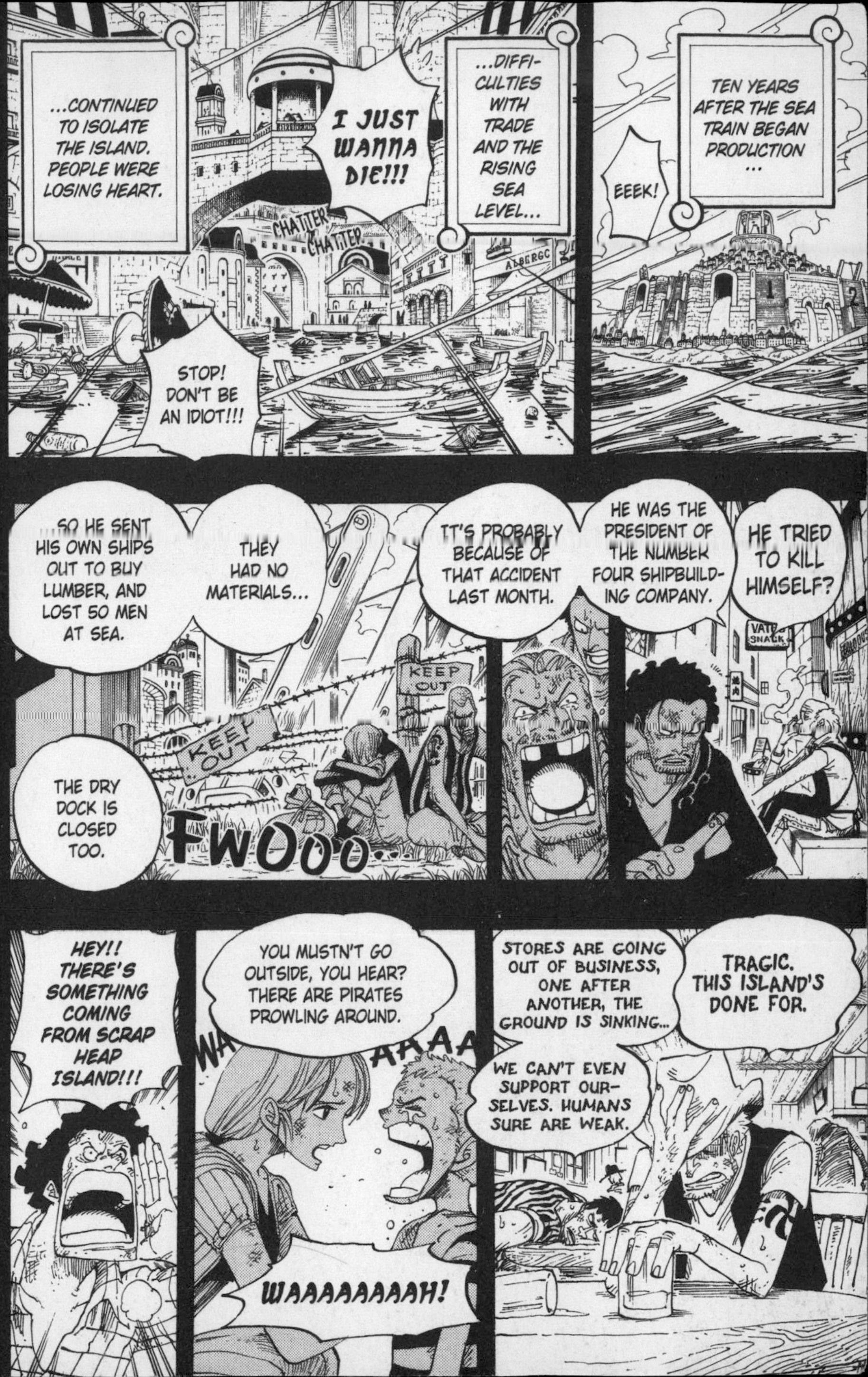
TEN YEARS AFTER THE SEA TRAIN BEGAN PRODUCTION ...
EEEK!
...DIFFI-CULTIES WITH TRADE AND THE RISING SEA LEVEL...
I JUST WANNA DIE!!!
...CONTINUED TO ISOLATE THE ISLAND. PEOPLE WERE LOSING HEART.
CHATTER CHATTER
STOP! DON'T BE AN IDIOT!!!
HE TRIED TO KILL HIMSELF?
HE WAS THE PRESIDENT OF THE NUMBER FOUR SHIPBUILD-ING COMPANY.
IT'S PROBABLY BECAUSE OF THAT ACCIDENT LAST MONTH.
SNACK
THEY HAD NO MATERIALS...
SO HE SENT HIS OWN SHIPS OUT TO BUY LUMBER, AND LOST 50 MEN AT SEA.
KEEP OUT
KEEP OUT
THE DRY DOCK IS CLOSED TOO.
FWOOO...
TRAGIC. THIS ISLAND'S DONE FOR.
STORES ARE GOING OUT OF BUSINESS, ONE AFTER ANOTHER, THE GROUND IS SINKING...
WE CAN'T EVEN SUPPORT OUR-SELVES. HUMANS SURE ARE WEAK.
YOU MUSTN'T GO OUTSIDE, YOU HEAR? THERE ARE PIRATES PROWLING AROUND.
AAAA
WAAAAAAAAH!
HEY!! THERE'S SOMETHING COMING FROM SCRAP HEAP ISLAND!!!

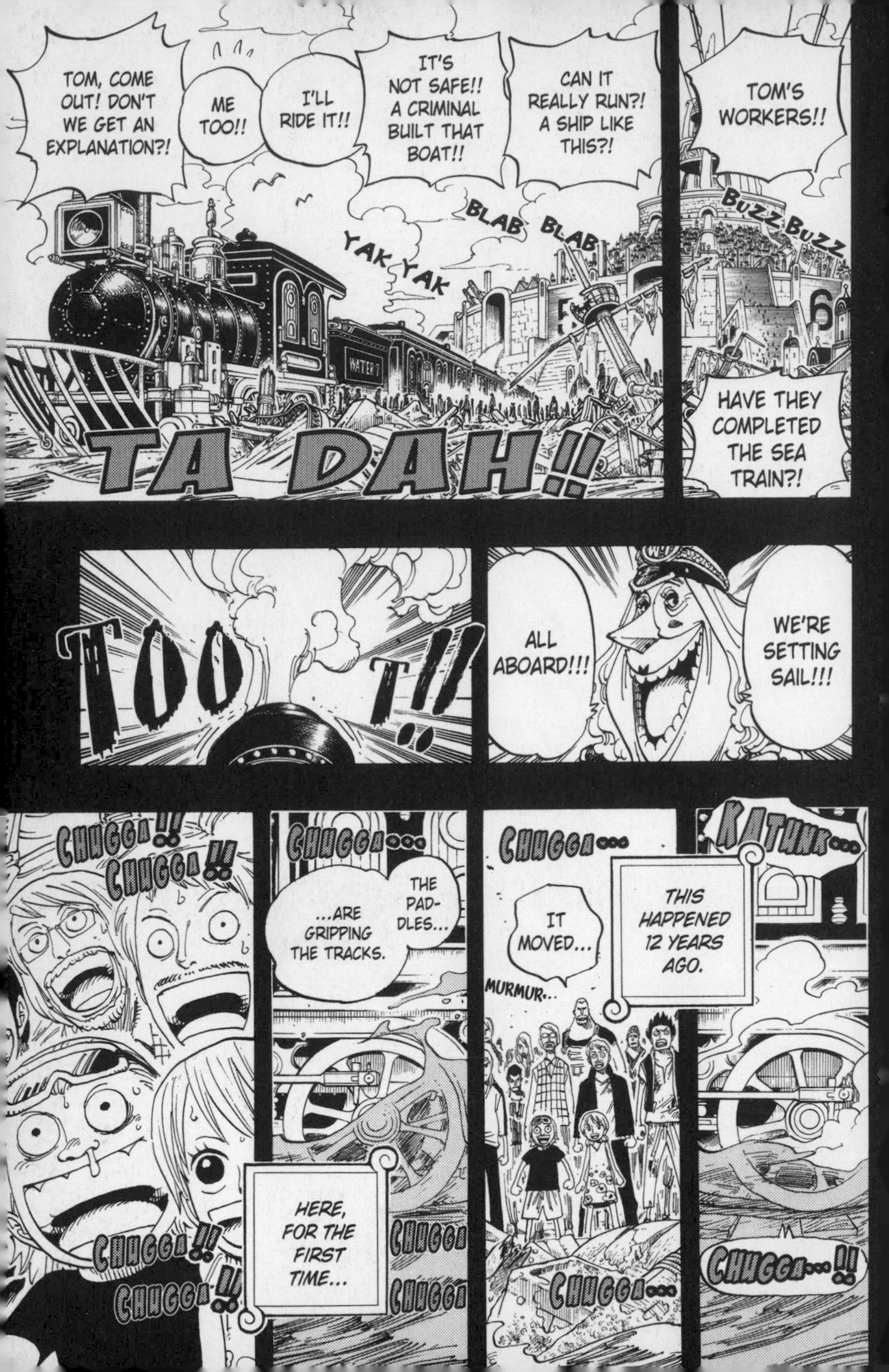
TOM'S WORKERS!!
BUZZ BUZZ
HAVE THEY COMPLETED THE SEA TRAIN?!
CAN IT REALLY RUN?! A SHIP LIKE THIS?!
IT'S NOT SAFE!! A CRIMINAL BUILT THAT BOAT!!
I'LL RIDE IT!!
ME TOO!!
TOM, COME OUT! DON'T WE GET AN EXPLANATION?!
BLAB BLAB
YAK YAK
WATER 7
TA DAH!!
WE'RE SETTING SAIL!!!
ALL ABOARD!!!
TOOT!!
KATUNK...
CHUGGA...!!
THIS HAPPENED 12 YEARS AGO.
CHUGGA...
IT MOVED...
MURMUR...
CHUGGI...
CHUGGA...
THE PADDLES...
...ARE GRIPPING THE TRACKS.
CHUGGI
CHUGGI
CHUGGA!!
CHUGGA!!
HERE, FOR THE FIRST TIME...
CHUGGA!!
CHUGGA!!

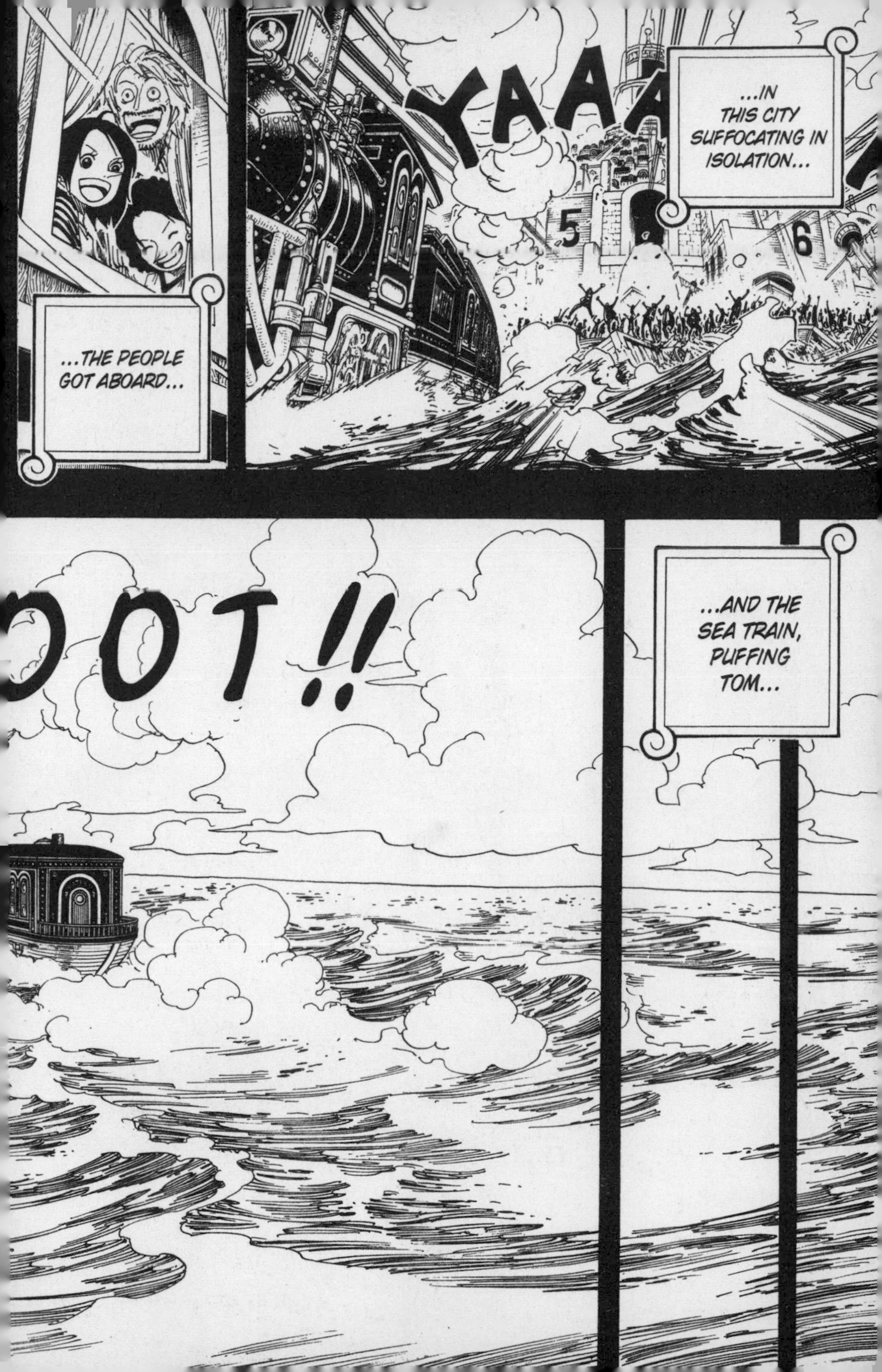
YAAA
...IN THIS CITY SUFFOCATING IN ISOLATION...
5
6
...THE PEOPLE GOT ABOARD...
...AND THE SEA TRAIN, PUFFING TOM...
OOT!!

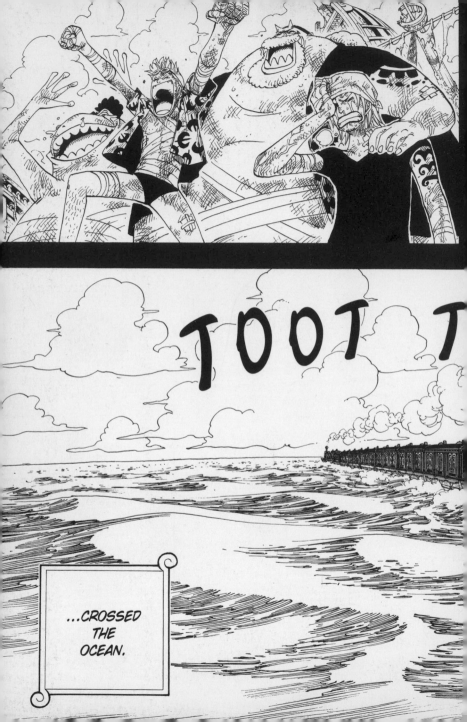

TOOT T

...CROSSED
THE
OCEAN.

Chapter 355:
SPANDAM

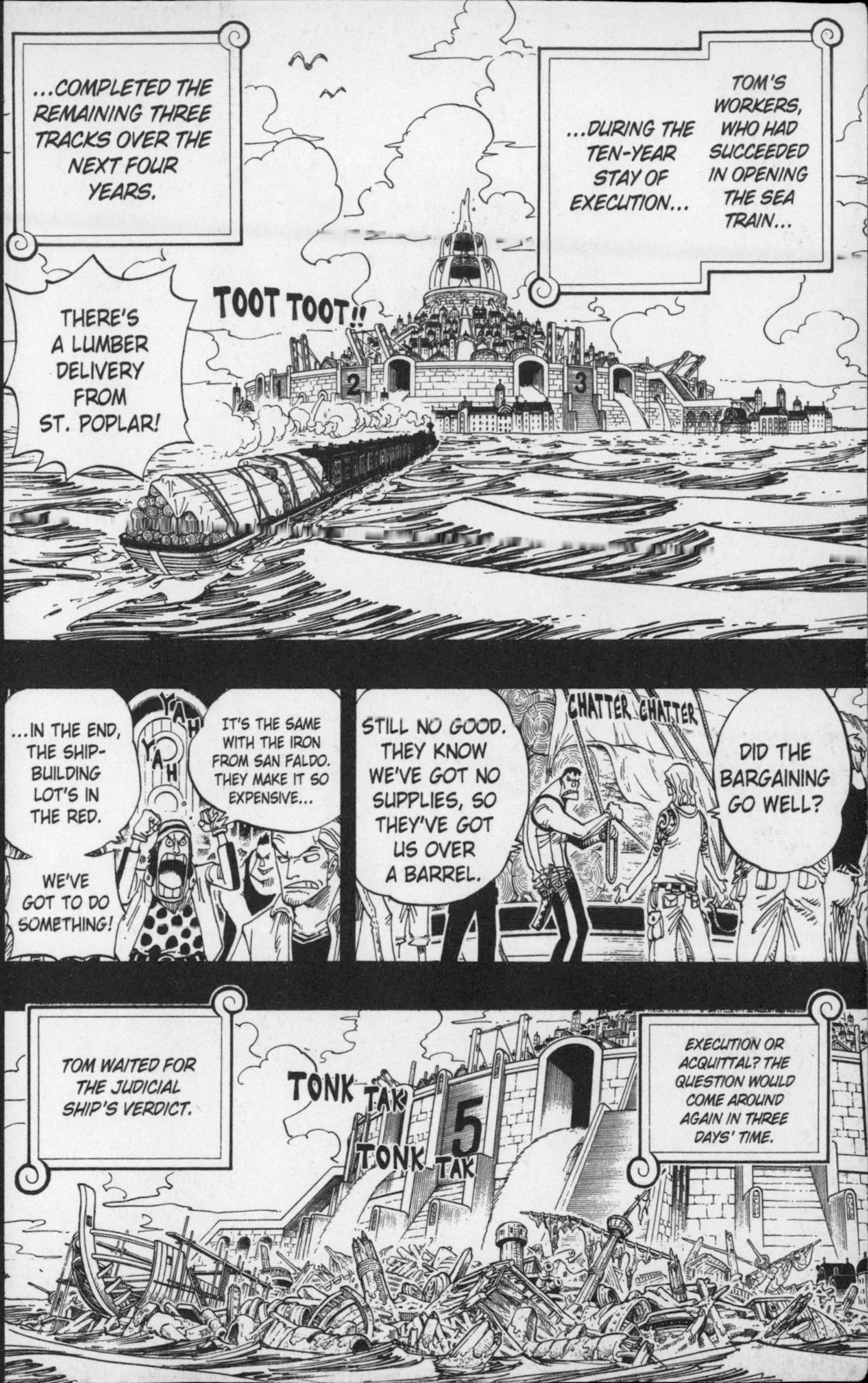
TOM'S WORKERS, WHO HAD SUCCEEDED IN OPENING THE SEA TRAIN...
...DURING THE TEN-YEAR STAY OF EXECUTION...
...COMPLETED THE REMAINING THREE TRACKS OVER THE NEXT FOUR YEARS.
TOOT TOOT!!
THERE'S A LUMBER DELIVERY FROM ST. POPLAR!
DID THE BARGAINING GO WELL?
CHATTER CHATTER
STILL NO GOOD. THEY KNOW WE'VE GOT NO SUPPLIES, SO THEY'VE GOT US OVER A BARREL.
IT'S THE SAME WITH THE IRON FROM SAN FALDO. THEY MAKE IT SO EXPENSIVE...
YAH YAH
...IN THE END, THE SHIP-BUILDING LOT'S IN THE RED.
WE'VE GOT TO DO SOMETHING!
EXECUTION OR ACQUITTAL? THE QUESTION WOULD COME AROUND AGAIN IN THREE DAYS' TIME.
TONK TAK
TONK TAK
TOM WAITED FOR THE JUDICIAL SHIP'S VERDICT.

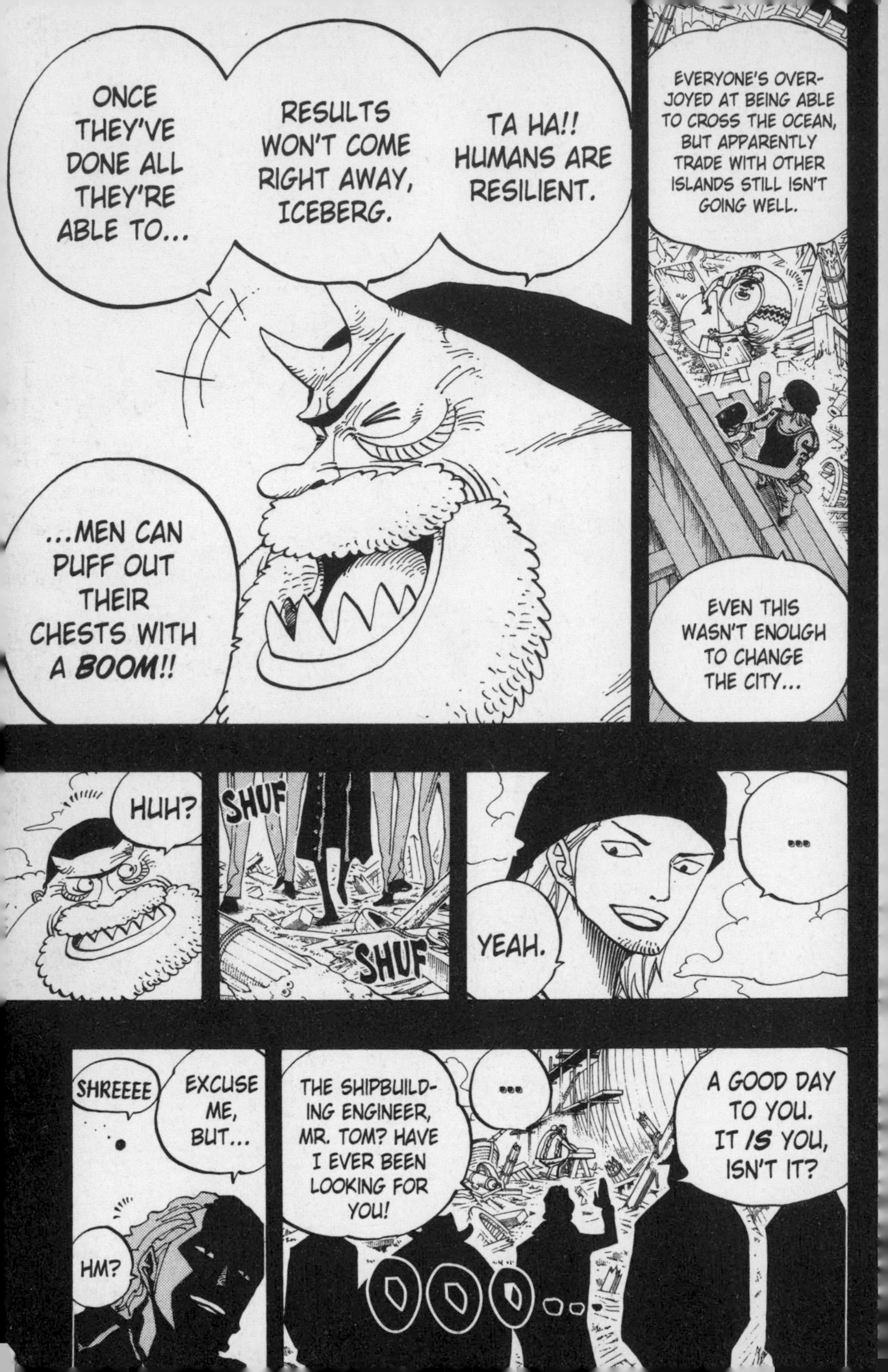
EVERYONE'S OVER-JOYED AT BEING ABLE TO CROSS THE OCEAN, BUT APPARENTLY TRADE WITH OTHER ISLANDS STILL ISN'T GOING WELL.
EVEN THIS WASN'T ENOUGH TO CHANGE THE CITY...
TA HA!! HUMANS ARE RESILIENT.
RESULTS WON'T COME RIGHT AWAY, ICEBERG.
ONCE THEY'VE DONE ALL THEY'RE ABLE TO...
...MEN CAN PUFF OUT THEIR CHESTS WITH A *BOOM*!!
...
YEAH.
SHUF
SHUF
HUH?
A GOOD DAY TO YOU. IT *IS* YOU, ISN'T IT?
...
THE SHIPBUILDING ENGINEER, MR. TOM? HAVE I EVER BEEN LOOKING FOR YOU!
EXCUSE ME, BUT...
SHREEEE
HM?

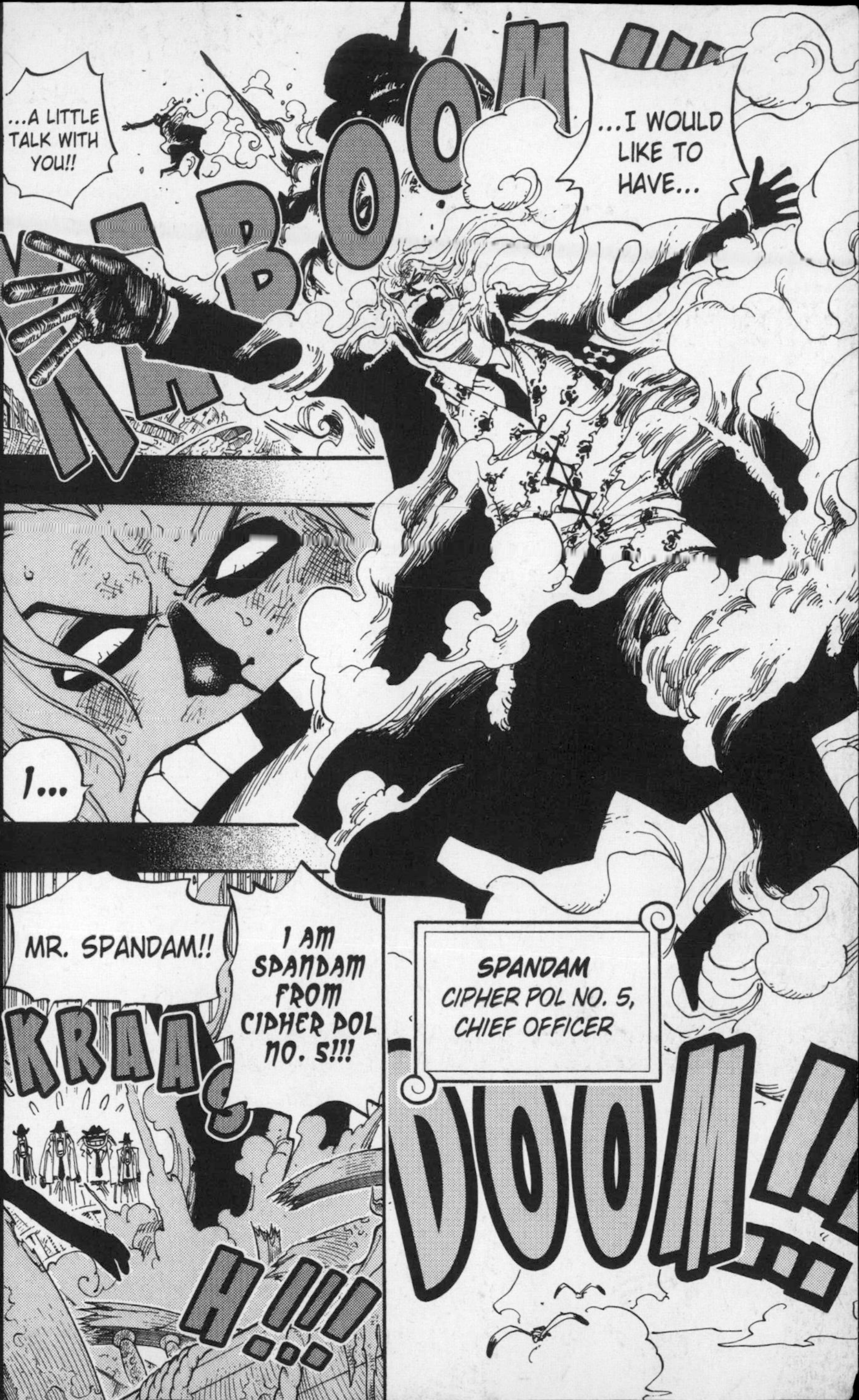
...I WOULD LIKE TO HAVE...
...A LITTLE TALK WITH YOU!!
KABOOOM
SPANDAM CIPHER POL NO. 5, CHIEF OFFICER
DOOM!!...
I...
I AM SPANDAM FROM CIPHER POL NO. 5!!!
MR. SPANDAM!!
KRAASH!!!...

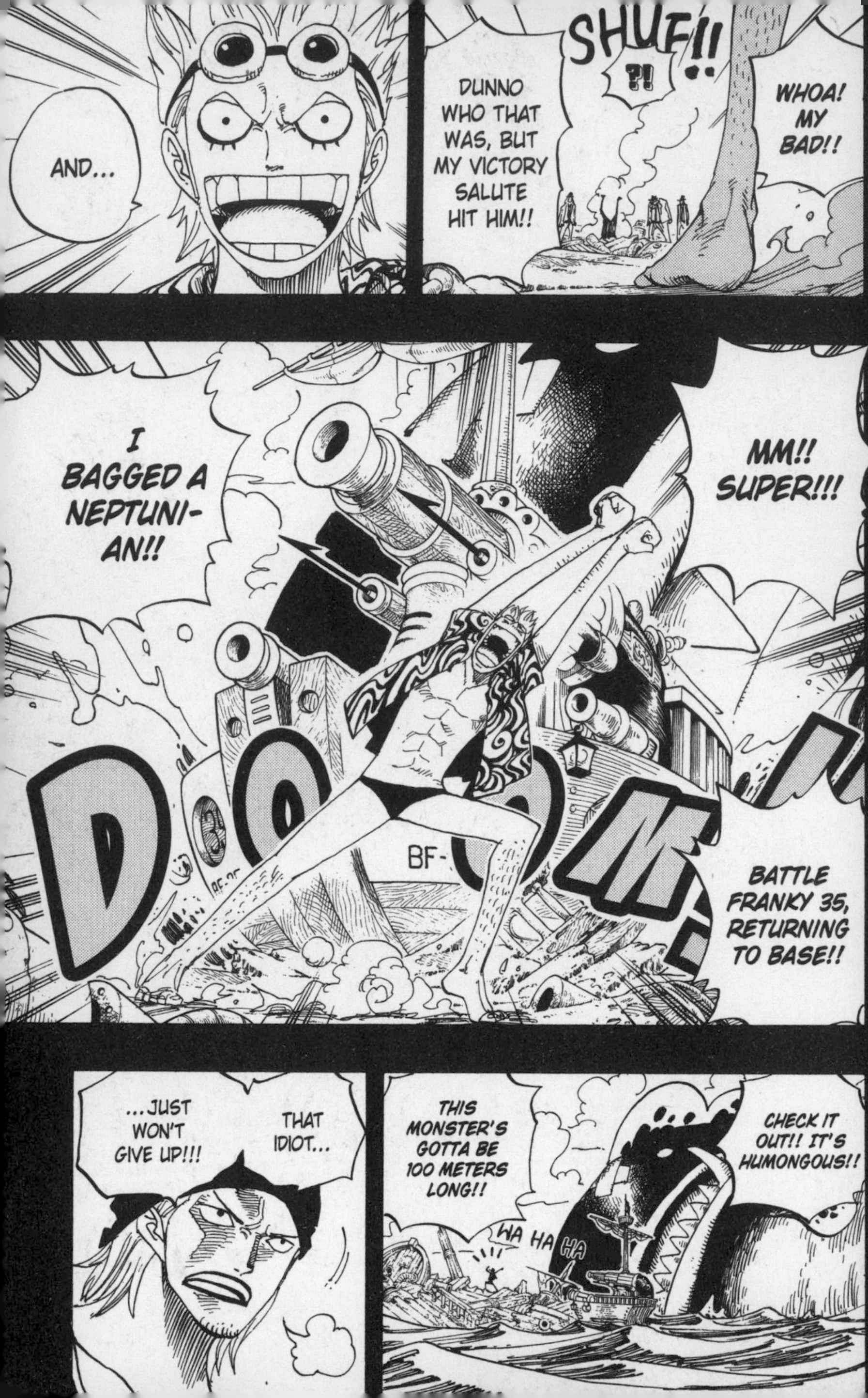

WHOA! MY BAD!!
SHUF!!
?!
DUNNO WHO THAT WAS, BUT MY VICTORY SALUTE HIT HIM!!
AND...
MM!! SUPER!!!
I BAGGED A NEPTUNI-AN!!
DOOM
BF-
BATTLE FRANKY 35, RETURNING TO BASE!!
CHECK IT OUT!! IT'S HUMONGOUS!!
THIS MONSTER'S GOTTA BE 100 METERS LONG!!
WA HA HA
THAT IDIOT...
...JUST WON'T GIVE UP!!!

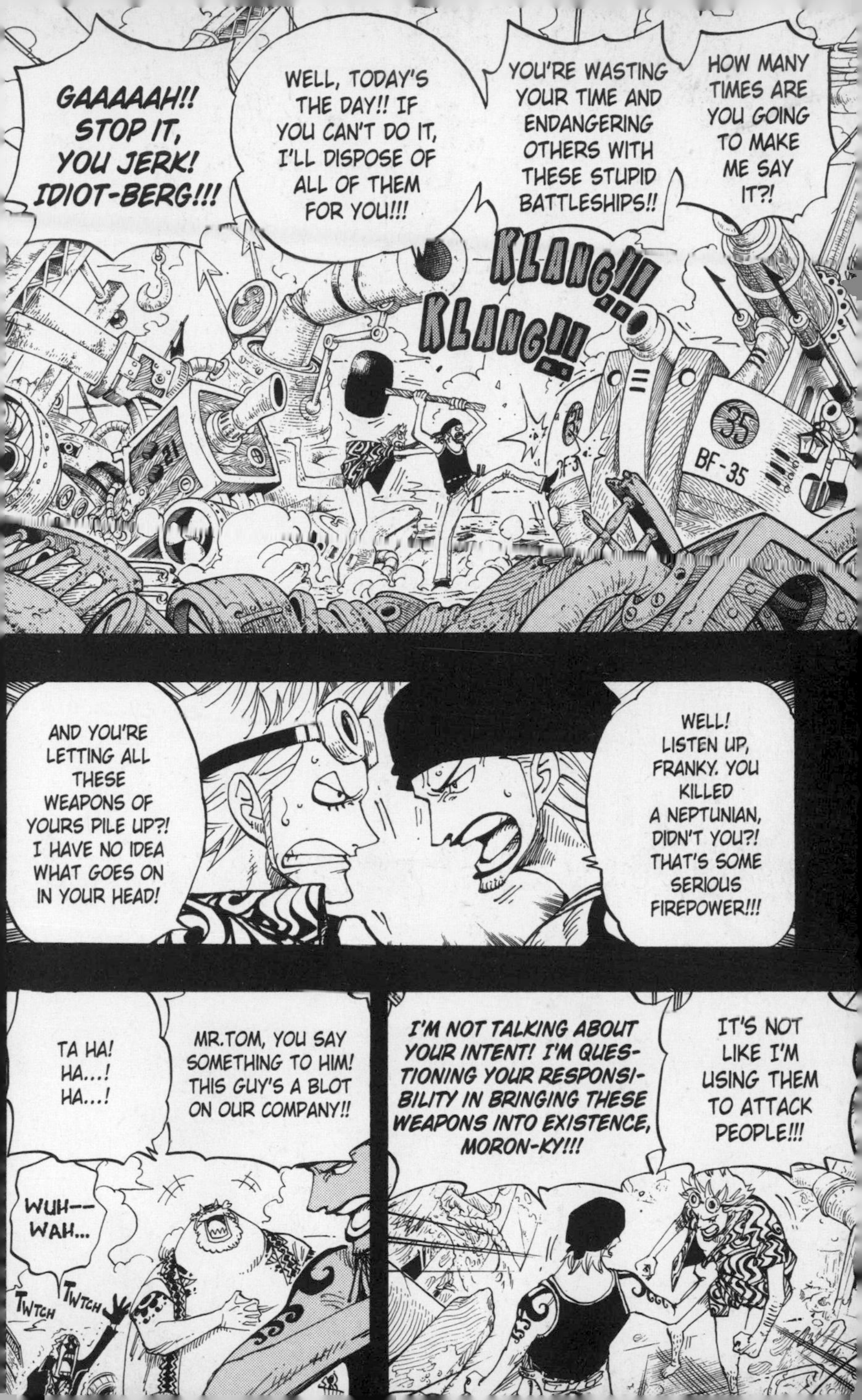
HOW MANY TIMES ARE YOU GOING TO MAKE ME SAY IT?!
YOU'RE WASTING YOUR TIME AND ENDANGERING OTHERS WITH THESE STUPID BATTLESHIPS!!
WELL, TODAY'S THE DAY!! IF YOU CAN'T DO IT, I'LL DISPOSE OF ALL OF THEM FOR YOU!!!
GAAAAAH!! STOP IT, YOU JERK! IDIOT-BERG!!!
KLANG!!
KLANG!!
BF-35
WELL! LISTEN UP, FRANKY. YOU KILLED A NEPTUNIAN, DIDN'T YOU?! THAT'S SOME SERIOUS FIREPOWER!!!
AND YOU'RE LETTING ALL THESE WEAPONS OF YOURS PILE UP?! I HAVE NO IDEA WHAT GOES ON IN YOUR HEAD!
IT'S NOT LIKE I'M USING THEM TO ATTACK PEOPLE!!!
I'M NOT TALKING ABOUT YOUR INTENT! I'M QUESTIONING YOUR RESPONSIBILITY IN BRINGING THESE WEAPONS INTO EXISTENCE, MORON-KY!!!
MR.TOM, YOU SAY SOMETHING TO HIM! THIS GUY'S A BLOT ON OUR COMPANY!!
TA HA! HA...! HA...!
WUH-- WAH...
TWTCH
TWTCH

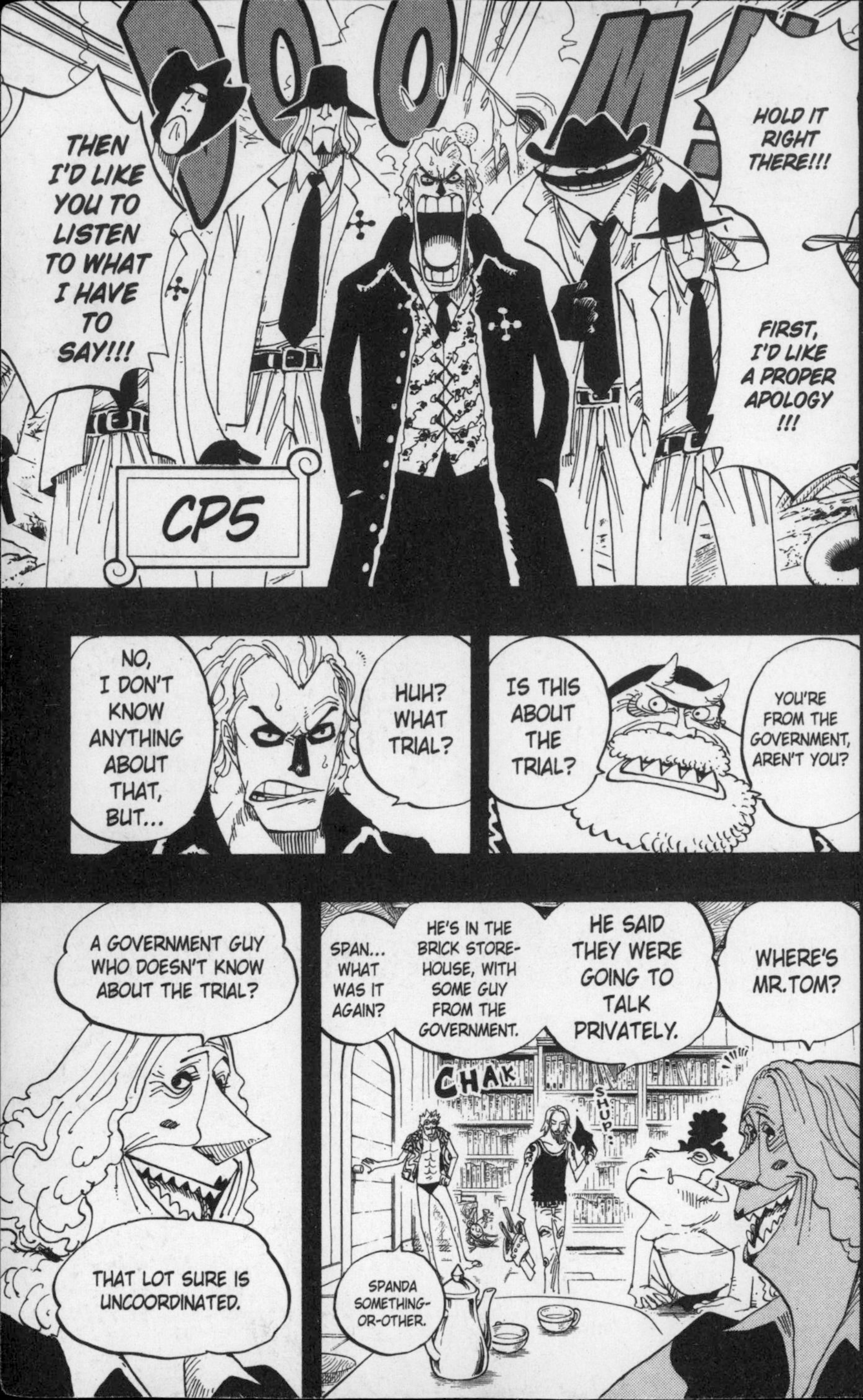
HOLD IT RIGHT THERE!!!
FIRST, I'D LIKE A PROPER APOLOGY !!!
THEN I'D LIKE YOU TO LISTEN TO WHAT I HAVE TO SAY!!!
CP5
YOU'RE FROM THE GOVERNMENT, AREN'T YOU?
IS THIS ABOUT THE TRIAL?
HUH? WHAT TRIAL?
NO, I DON'T KNOW ANYTHING ABOUT THAT, BUT...
WHERE'S MR.TOM?
HE SAID THEY WERE GOING TO TALK PRIVATELY.
HE'S IN THE BRICK STORE-HOUSE, WITH SOME GUY FROM THE GOVERNMENT.
SPAN... WHAT WAS IT AGAIN?
CHAK
SHUP
SPANDA SOMETHING-OR-OTHER.
A GOVERNMENT GUY WHO DOESN'T KNOW ABOUT THE TRIAL?
THAT LOT SURE IS UNCOORDINATED.

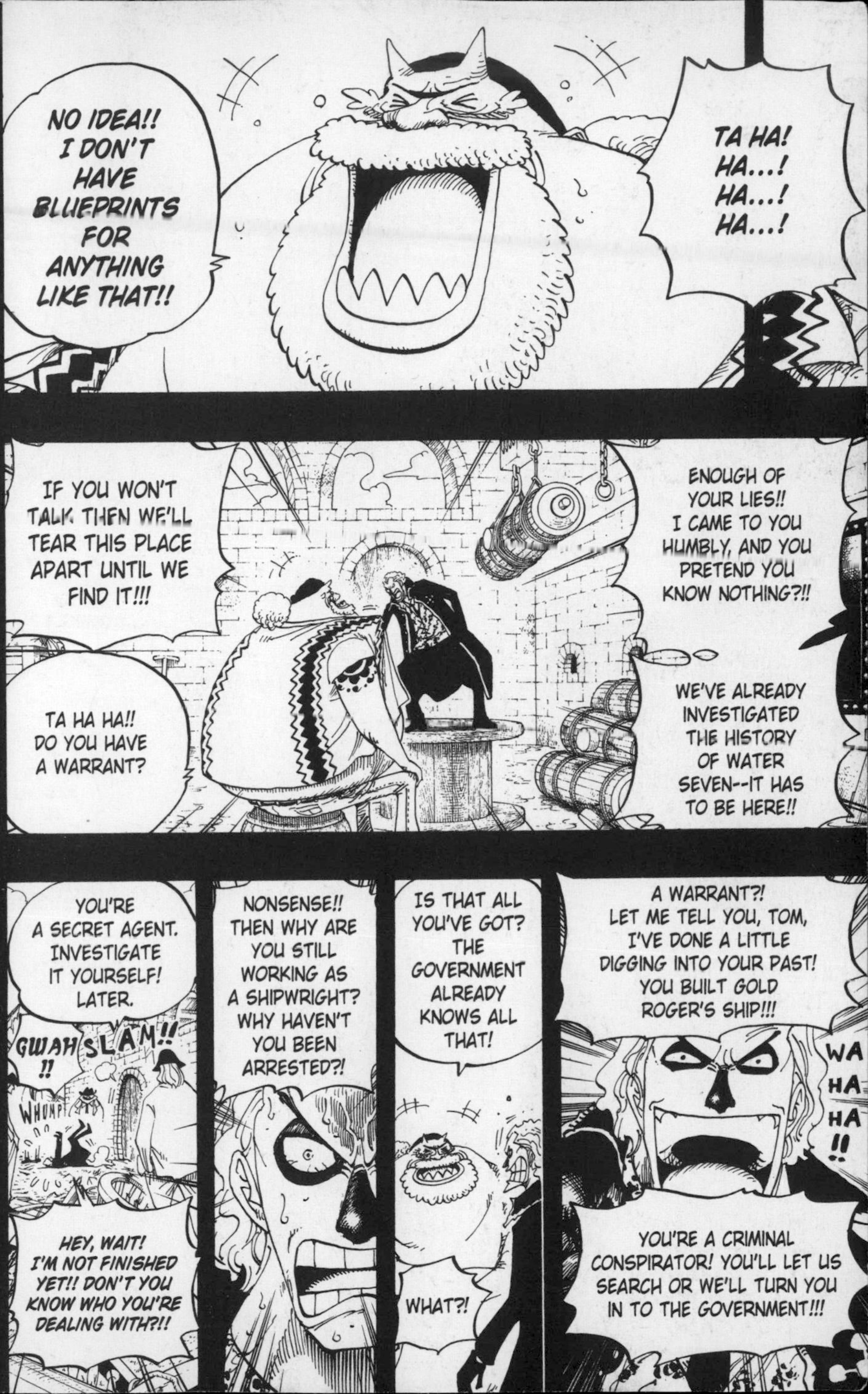
TA HA! HA...! HA...! HA...!
NO IDEA!! I DON'T HAVE BLUEPRINTS FOR ANYTHING LIKE THAT!!
ENOUGH OF YOUR LIES!! I CAME TO YOU HUMBLY, AND YOU PRETEND YOU KNOW NOTHING?!!
WE'VE ALREADY INVESTIGATED THE HISTORY OF WATER SEVEN--IT HAS TO BE HERE!!
IF YOU WON'T TALK THEN WE'LL TEAR THIS PLACE APART UNTIL WE FIND IT!!!
TA HA HA!! DO YOU HAVE A WARRANT?
A WARRANT?! LET ME TELL YOU, TOM, I'VE DONE A LITTLE DIGGING INTO YOUR PAST! YOU BUILT GOLD ROGER'S SHIP!!!
WA HA HA!!
YOU'RE A CRIMINAL CONSPIRATOR! YOU'LL LET US SEARCH OR WE'LL TURN YOU IN TO THE GOVERNMENT!!!
IS THAT ALL YOU'VE GOT? THE GOVERNMENT ALREADY KNOWS ALL THAT!
WHAT?!
NONSENSE!! THEN WHY ARE YOU STILL WORKING AS A SHIPWRIGHT? WHY HAVEN'T YOU BEEN ARRESTED?!
YOU'RE A SECRET AGENT. INVESTIGATE IT YOURSELF! LATER.
SLAM!!
GWAH!!
WHUMP
HEY, WAIT! I'M NOT FINISHED YET!! DON'T YOU KNOW WHO YOU'RE DEALING WITH?!!

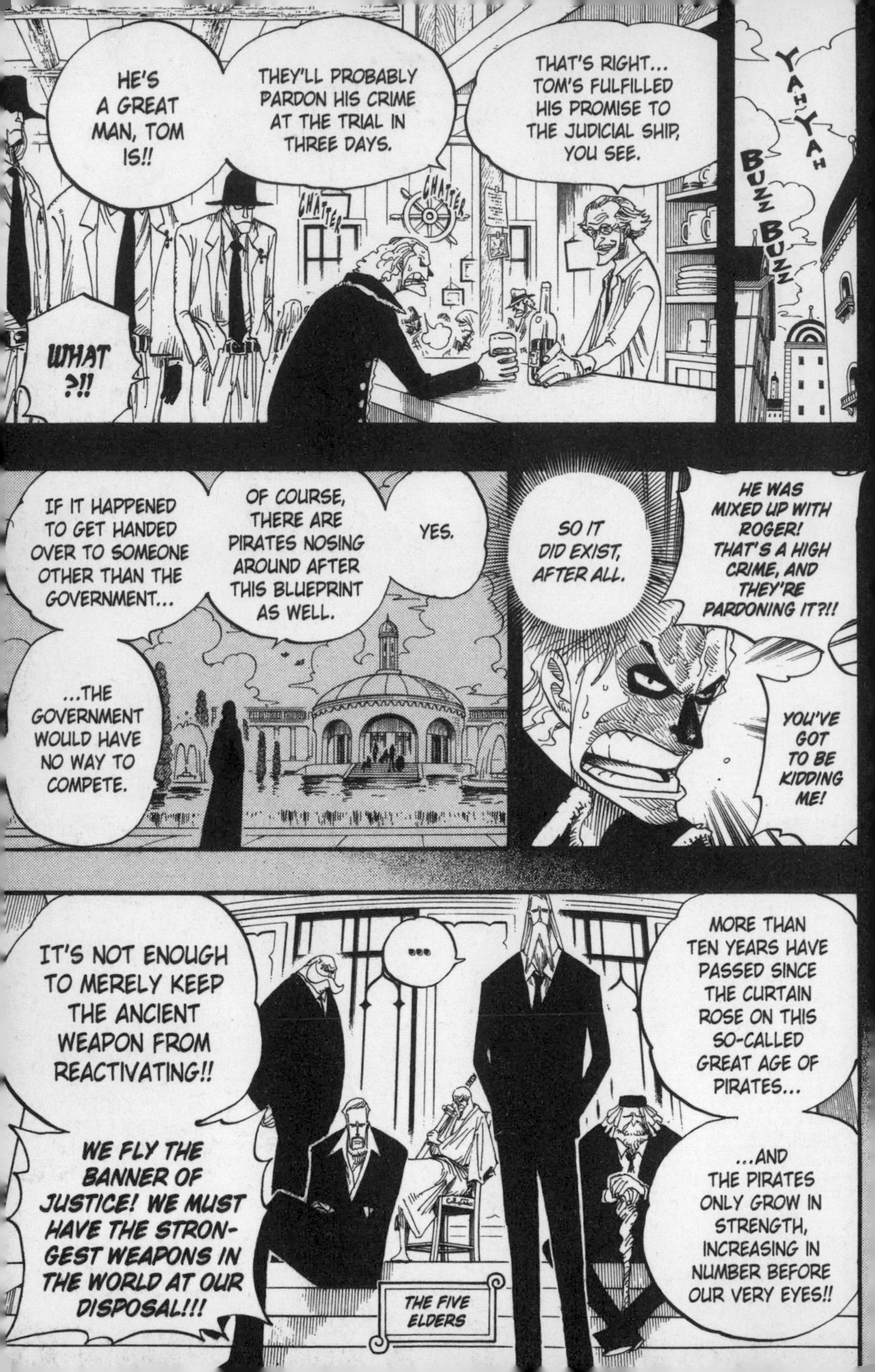

YAH YAH
BUZZ BUZZ
THAT'S RIGHT... TOM'S FULFILLED HIS PROMISE TO THE JUDICIAL SHIP, YOU SEE.
THEY'LL PROBABLY PARDON HIS CRIME AT THE TRIAL IN THREE DAYS.
HE'S A GREAT MAN, TOM IS!!
CHATTER
CHATTER
WHAT ?!!
HE WAS MIXED UP WITH ROGER! THAT'S A HIGH CRIME, AND THEY'RE PARDONING IT?!!
SO IT DID EXIST, AFTER ALL.
YOU'VE GOT TO BE KIDDING ME!
YES.
OF COURSE, THERE ARE PIRATES NOSING AROUND AFTER THIS BLUEPRINT AS WELL.
IF IT HAPPENED TO GET HANDED OVER TO SOMEONE OTHER THAN THE GOVERNMENT...
...THE GOVERNMENT WOULD HAVE NO WAY TO COMPETE.
MORE THAN TEN YEARS HAVE PASSED SINCE THE CURTAIN ROSE ON THIS SO-CALLED GREAT AGE OF PIRATES...
...
IT'S NOT ENOUGH TO MERELY KEEP THE ANCIENT WEAPON FROM REACTIVATING!!
...AND THE PIRATES ONLY GROW IN STRENGTH, INCREASING IN NUMBER BEFORE OUR VERY EYES!!
WE FLY THE BANNER OF JUSTICE! WE MUST HAVE THE STRONGEST WEAPONS IN THE WORLD AT OUR DISPOSAL!!!
THE FIVE ELDERS

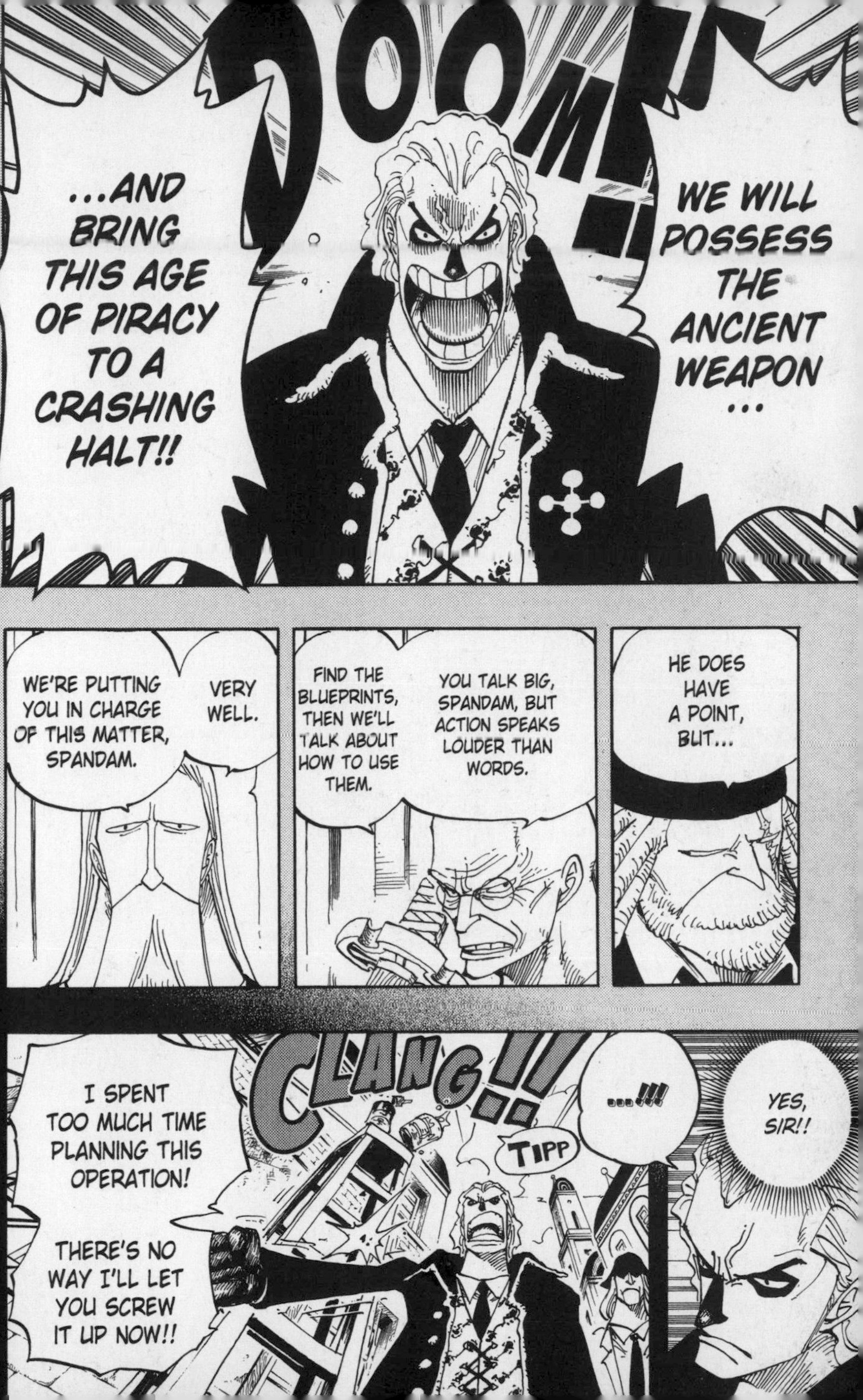
WE WILL POSSESS THE ANCIENT WEAPON ...
DOOM!!
...AND BRING THIS AGE OF PIRACY TO A CRASHING HALT!!
HE DOES HAVE A POINT, BUT...
YOU TALK BIG, SPANDAM, BUT ACTION SPEAKS LOUDER THAN WORDS.
FIND THE BLUEPRINTS, THEN WE'LL TALK ABOUT HOW TO USE THEM.
VERY WELL.
WE'RE PUTTING YOU IN CHARGE OF THIS MATTER, SPANDAM.
YES, SIR!!
...!!!
TIPP
CLANG!!
I SPENT TOO MUCH TIME PLANNING THIS OPERATION!
THERE'S NO WAY I'LL LET YOU SCREW IT UP NOW!!

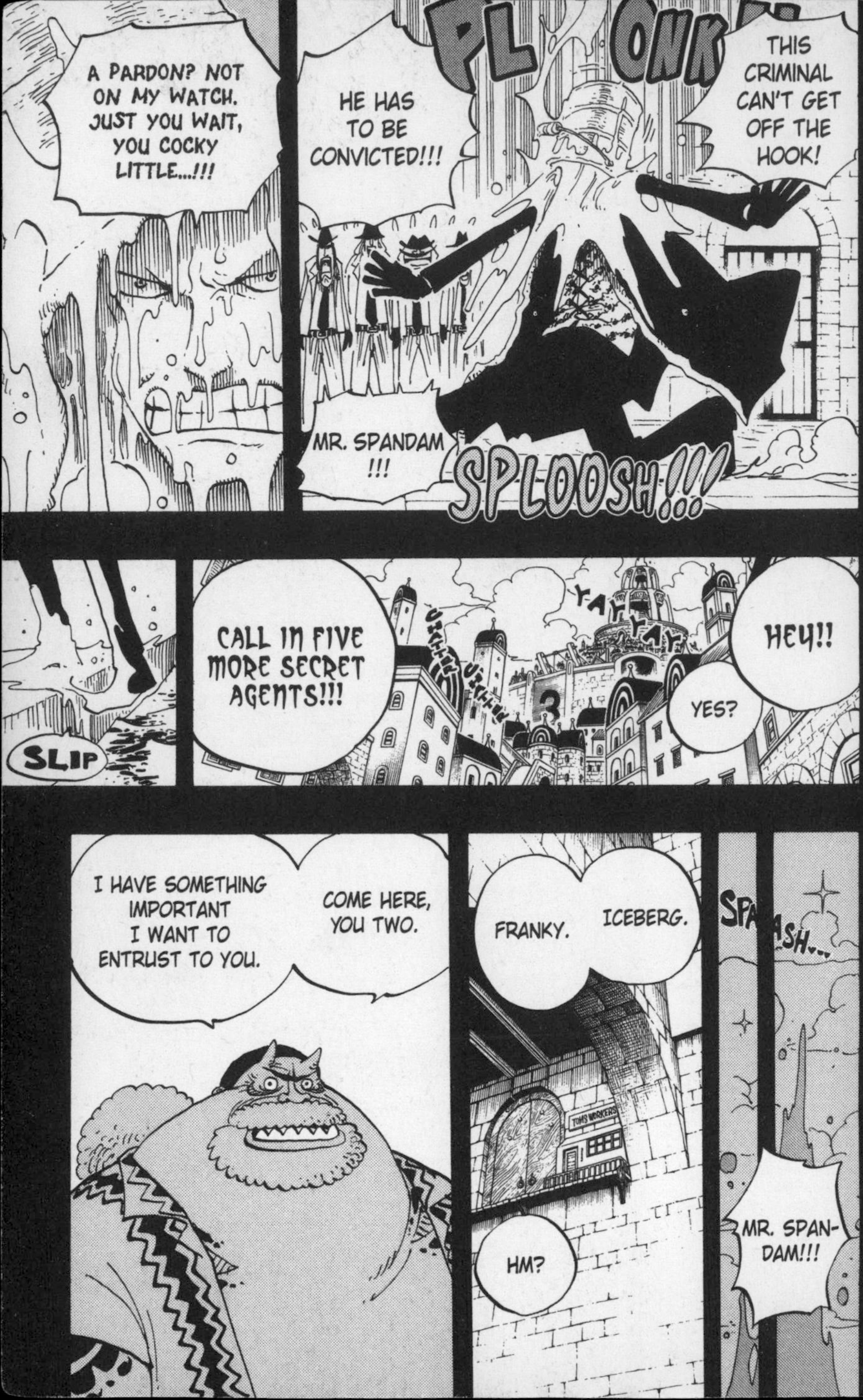
THIS CRIMINAL CAN'T GET OFF THE HOOK!
PLONK
HE HAS TO BE CONVICTED!!!
MR. SPANDAM !!!
SPLOOSH!!!
A PARDON? NOT ON MY WATCH. JUST YOU WAIT, YOU COCKY LITTLE...!!!
HEY!!
YES?
YAY YAY
CALL IN FIVE MORE SECRET AGENTS!!!
SLIP
SPLASH...
MR. SPAN-DAM!!!
ICEBERG.
FRANKY.
TOM'S WORKERS
HM?
COME HERE, YOU TWO.
I HAVE SOMETHING IMPORTANT I WANT TO ENTRUST TO YOU.

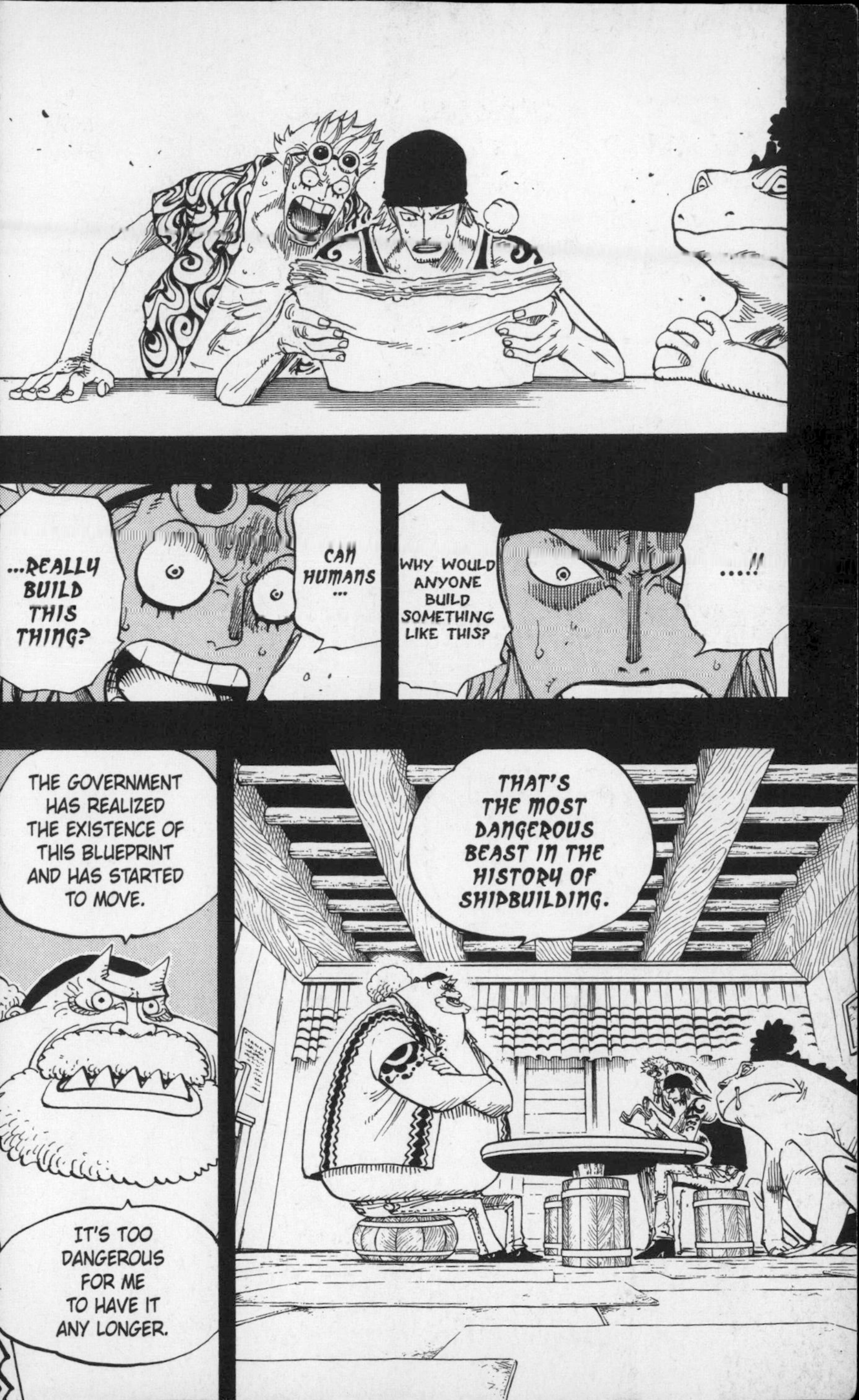
....!!
WHY WOULD ANYONE BUILD SOMETHING LIKE THIS?
CAN HUMANS ...
...REALLY BUILD THIS THING?
THAT'S THE MOST DANGEROUS BEAST IN THE HISTORY OF SHIPBUILDING.
THE GOVERNMENT HAS REALIZED THE EXISTENCE OF THIS BLUEPRINT AND HAS STARTED TO MOVE.
IT'S TOO DANGEROUS FOR ME TO HAVE IT ANY LONGER.

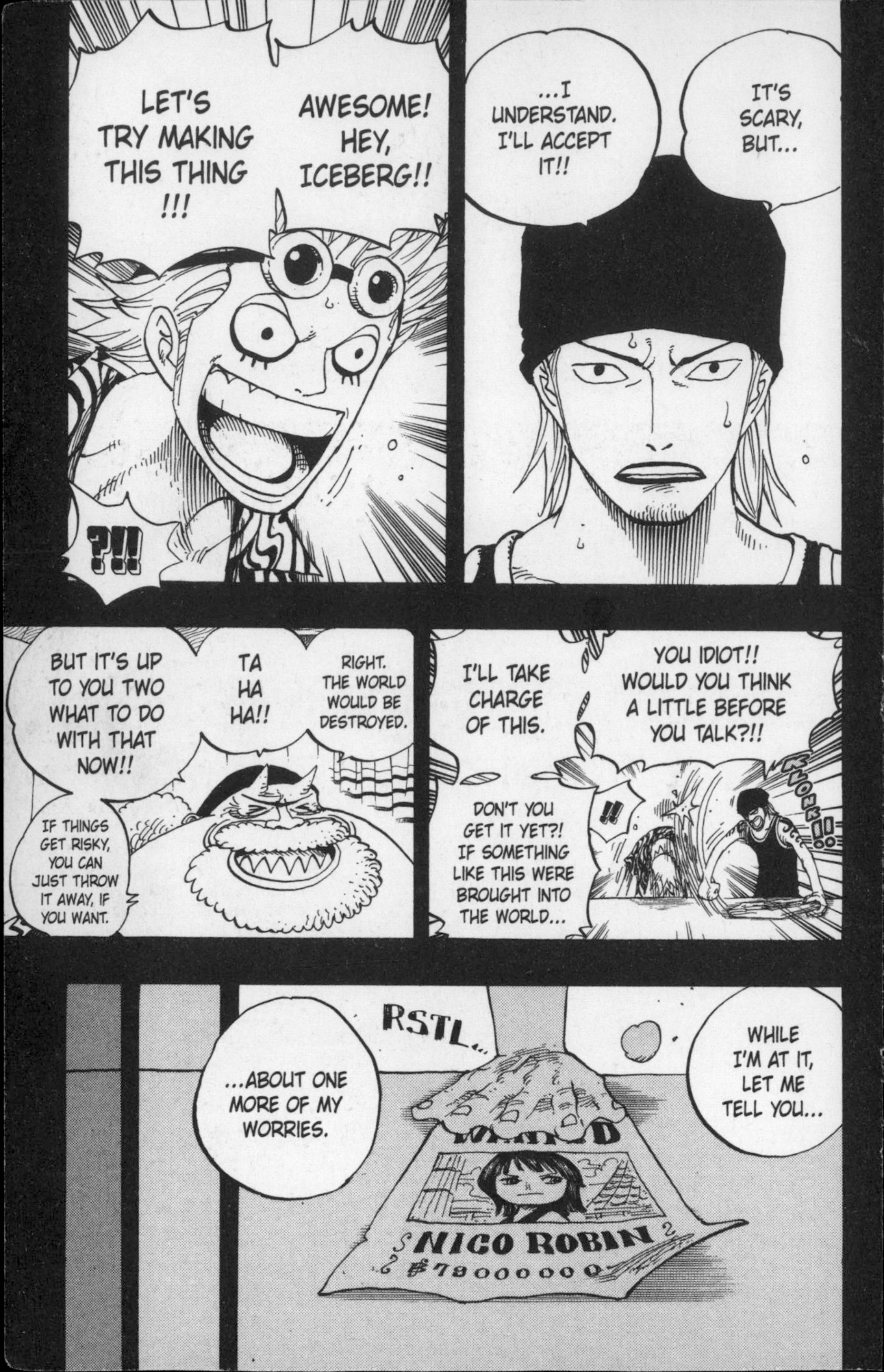
IT'S SCARY, BUT...
...I UNDERSTAND. I'LL ACCEPT IT!!
AWESOME! HEY, ICEBERG!!
LET'S TRY MAKING THIS THING !!!
?!!
YOU IDIOT!! WOULD YOU THINK A LITTLE BEFORE YOU TALK?!!
KWONK!!
I'LL TAKE CHARGE OF THIS.
!!
DON'T YOU GET IT YET?! IF SOMETHING LIKE THIS WERE BROUGHT INTO THE WORLD...
RIGHT. THE WORLD WOULD BE DESTROYED.
TA HA HA!!
BUT IT'S UP TO YOU TWO WHAT TO DO WITH THAT NOW!!
IF THINGS GET RISKY, YOU CAN JUST THROW IT AWAY, IF YOU WANT.
WHILE I'M AT IT, LET ME TELL YOU...
RSTL...
...ABOUT ONE MORE OF MY WORRIES.
NICO ROBIN
79000000

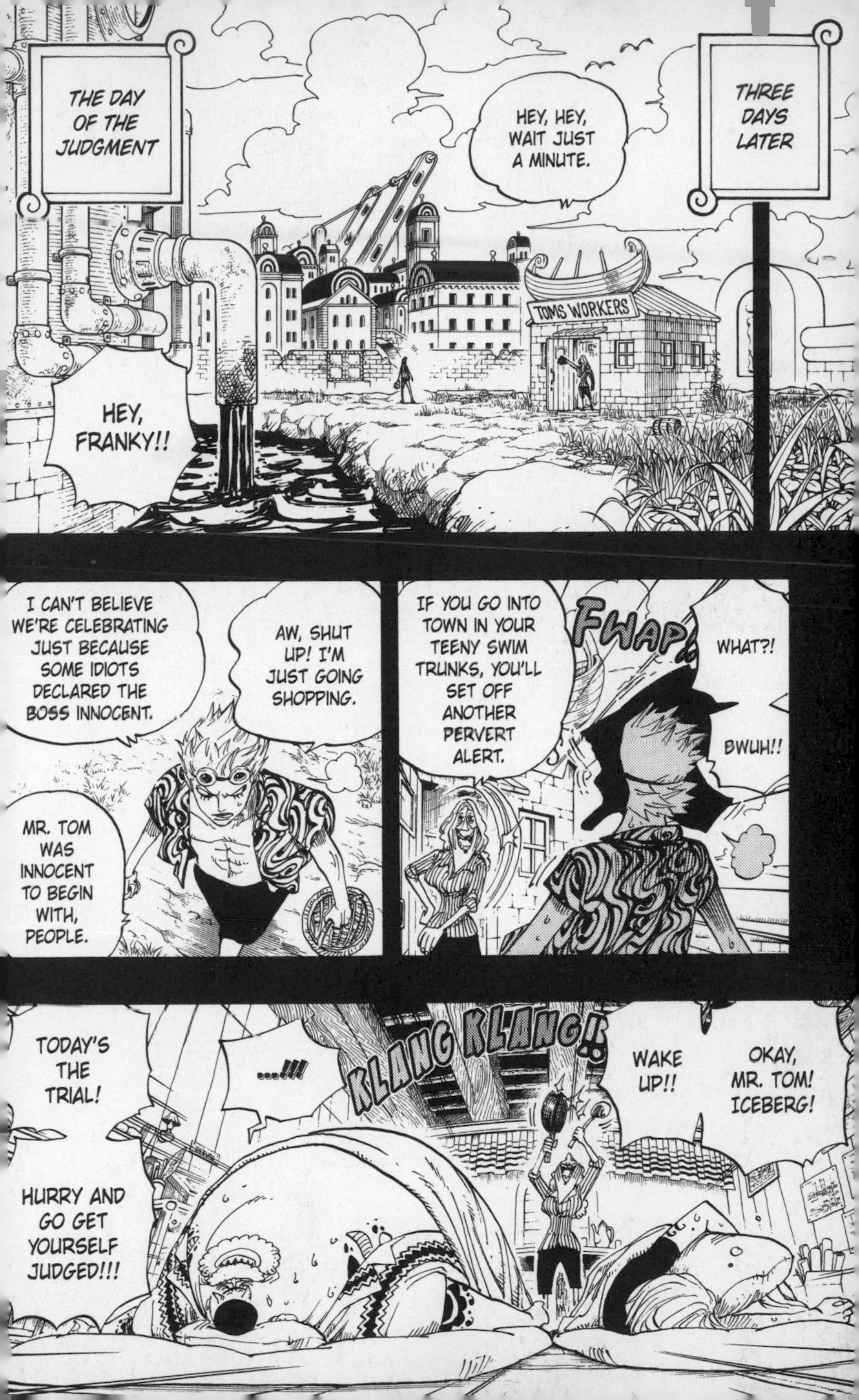
THREE DAYS LATER
HEY, HEY, WAIT JUST A MINUTE.
TOMS WORKERS
THE DAY OF THE JUDGMENT
HEY, FRANKY!!
WHAT?!
FWAP
IF YOU GO INTO TOWN IN YOUR TEENY SWIM TRUNKS, YOU'LL SET OFF ANOTHER PERVERT ALERT.
BWUH!!
AW, SHUT UP! I'M JUST GOING SHOPPING.
I CAN'T BELIEVE WE'RE CELEBRATING JUST BECAUSE SOME IDIOTS DECLARED THE BOSS INNOCENT.
MR. TOM WAS INNOCENT TO BEGIN WITH, PEOPLE.
OKAY, MR. TOM! ICEBERG!
WAKE UP!!
KLANG KLANG!!
...!!!
TODAY'S THE TRIAL!
HURRY AND GO GET YOURSELF JUDGED!!!

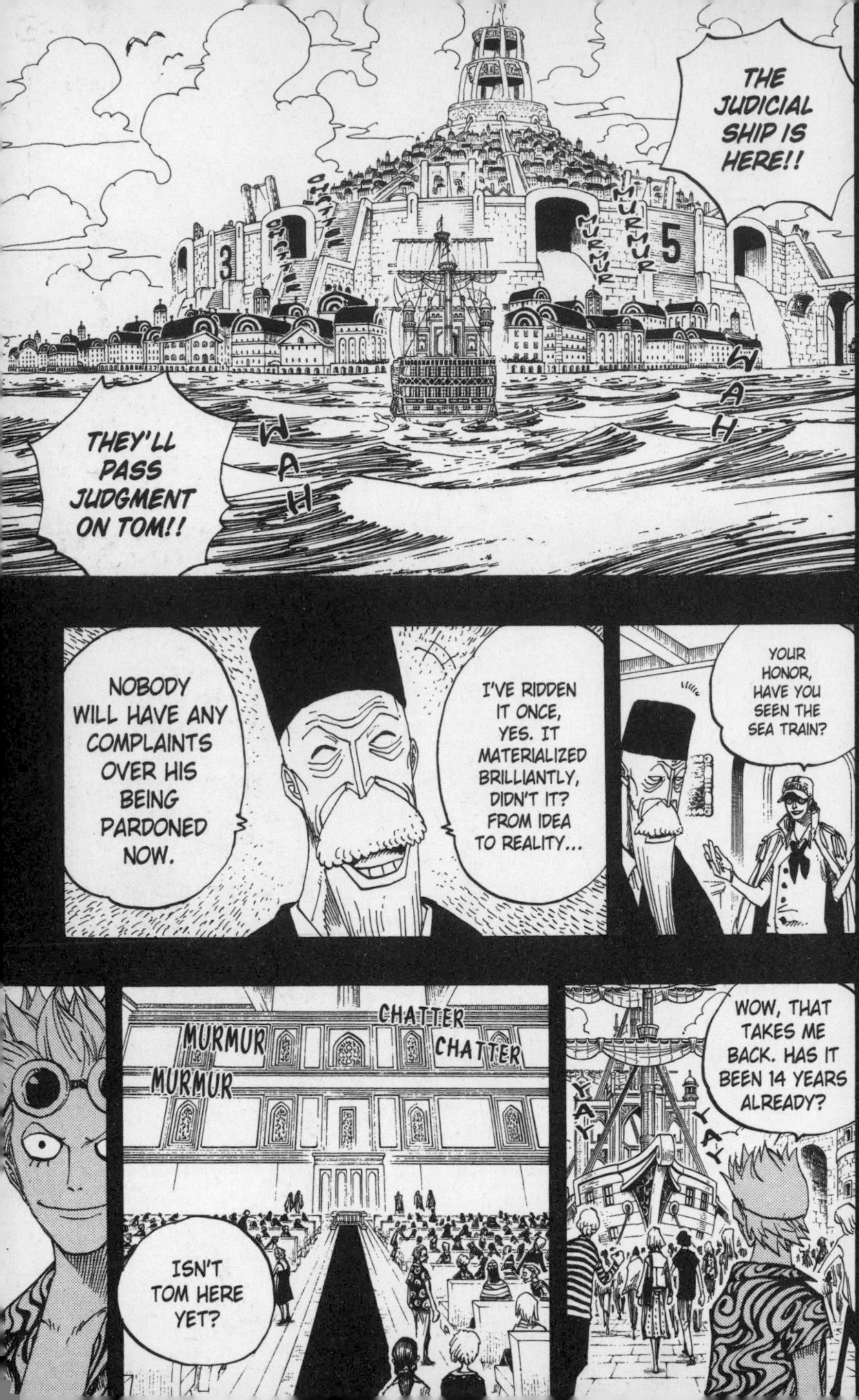
THE JUDICIAL SHIP IS HERE!!
MURMUR MURMUR
5
WAH
CHATTER CHATTER
3
THEY'LL PASS JUDGMENT ON TOM!!
WAH
YOUR HONOR, HAVE YOU SEEN THE SEA TRAIN?
I'VE RIDDEN IT ONCE, YES. IT MATERIALIZED BRILLIANTLY, DIDN'T IT? FROM IDEA TO REALITY...
NOBODY WILL HAVE ANY COMPLAINTS OVER HIS BEING PARDONED NOW.
WOW, THAT TAKES ME BACK. HAS IT BEEN 14 YEARS ALREADY?
YAY
YAY
CHATTER
CHATTER
MURMUR
MURMUR
ISN'T TOM HERE YET?

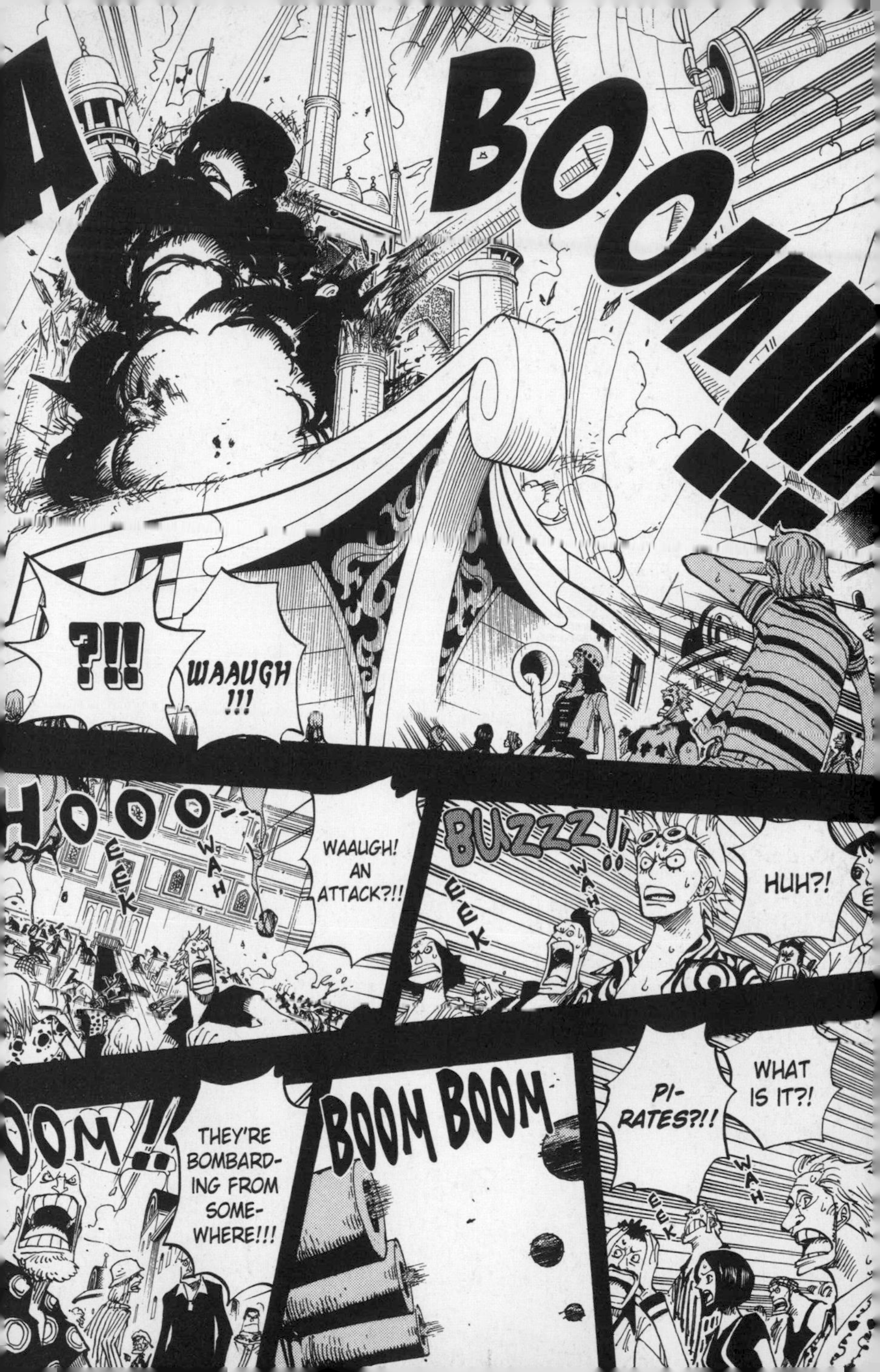
A BOOM!!!!
WAAUGH !!!
?!!
HUH?!
BUZZZ!!
WAH
EEEK
WAAUGH! AN ATTACK?!!
HOOO-
WAH
EEEK
WHAT IS IT?!
PI-RATES?!!
WAH
EEEK
BOOM BOOM
THEY'RE BOMBARD-ING FROM SOME-WHERE!!!
OOM!!

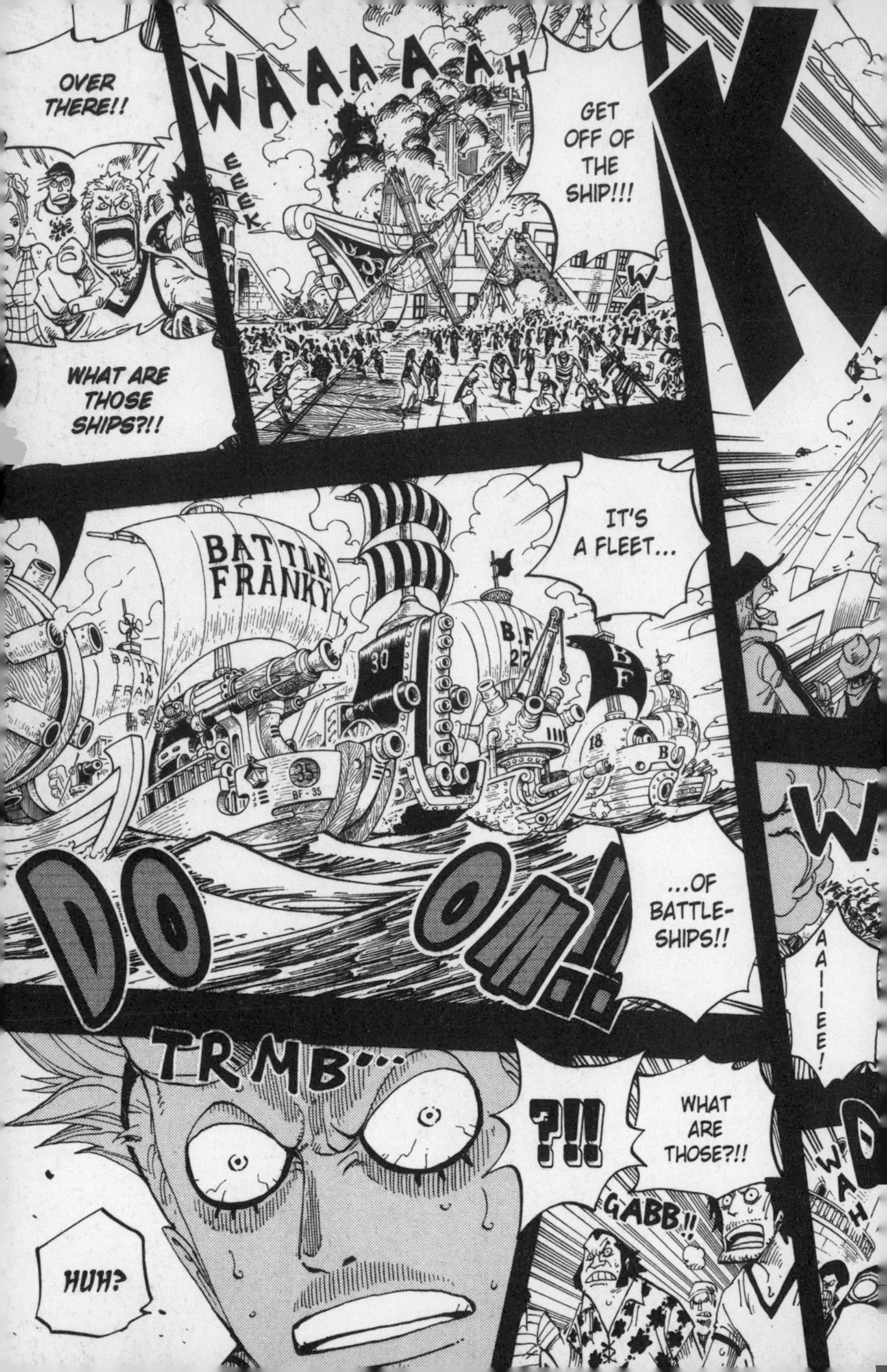
K
WAAAAAH
EEEEK
GET OFF OF THE SHIP!!!
WAH
OVER THERE!!
WHAT ARE THOSE SHIPS?!!
W
AAIIEE!
IT'S A FLEET...
BATTLE FRANKY
B.F 27
BF-35
...OF BATTLE-SHIPS!!
DOOM..
WAH
WHAT ARE THOSE?!!
GABB!!
?!!
TRMB...
HUH?

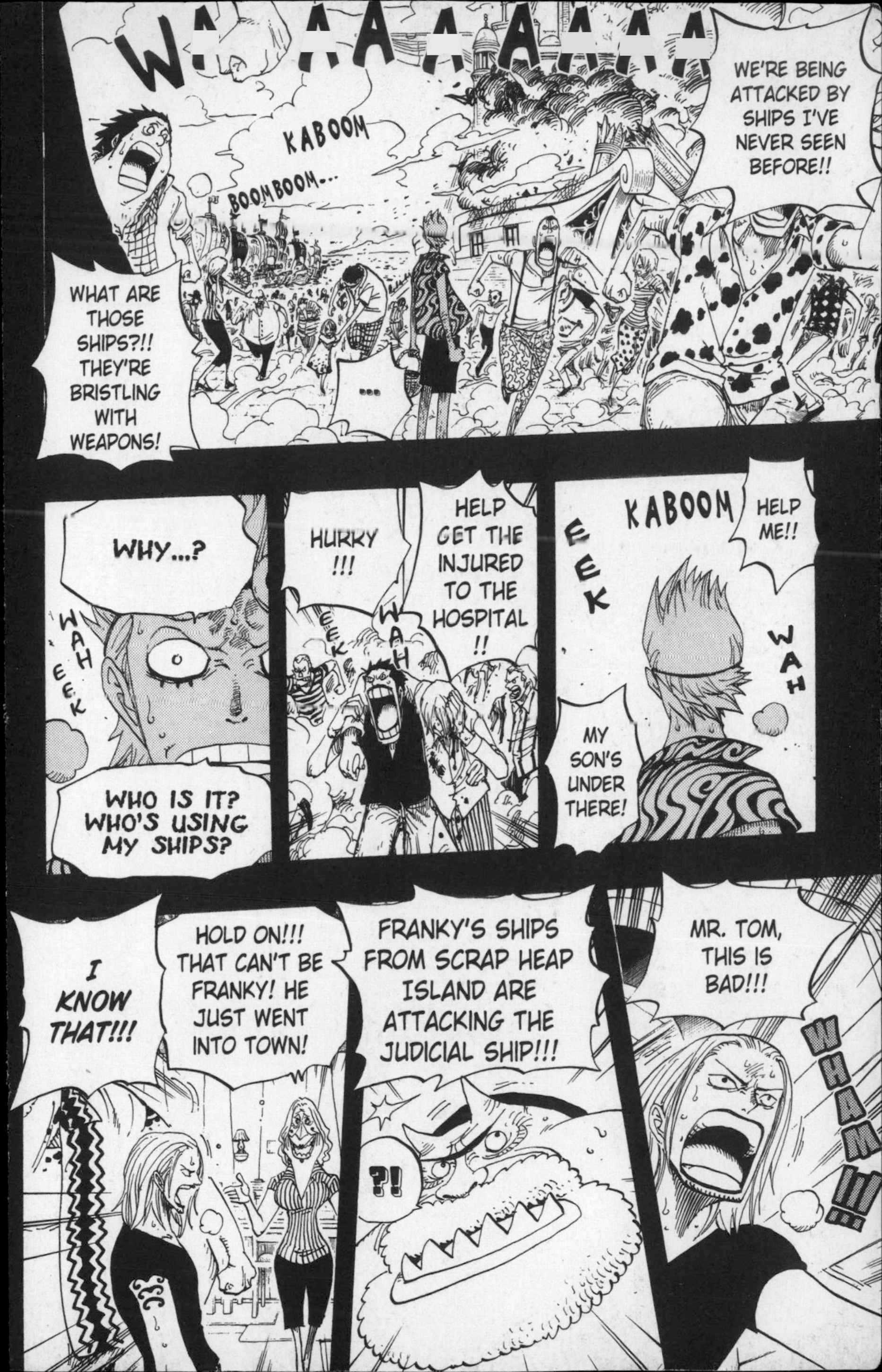
WE'RE BEING ATTACKED BY SHIPS I'VE NEVER SEEN BEFORE!!
KABOOM
BOOMBOOM...
WHAT ARE THOSE SHIPS?!! THEY'RE BRISTLING WITH WEAPONS!
...
KABOOM
HELP ME!!
EEK
WAH
MY SON'S UNDER THERE!
HELP GET THE INJURED TO THE HOSPITAL!!
HURRY!!!
WAH
EEK
WHY...?
WAH
EEK
WHO IS IT? WHO'S USING MY SHIPS?
MR. TOM, THIS IS BAD!!!
WHAM!!!
FRANKY'S SHIPS FROM SCRAP HEAP ISLAND ARE ATTACKING THE JUDICIAL SHIP!!!
?!
HOLD ON!!! THAT CAN'T BE FRANKY! HE JUST WENT INTO TOWN!
I KNOW THAT!!!

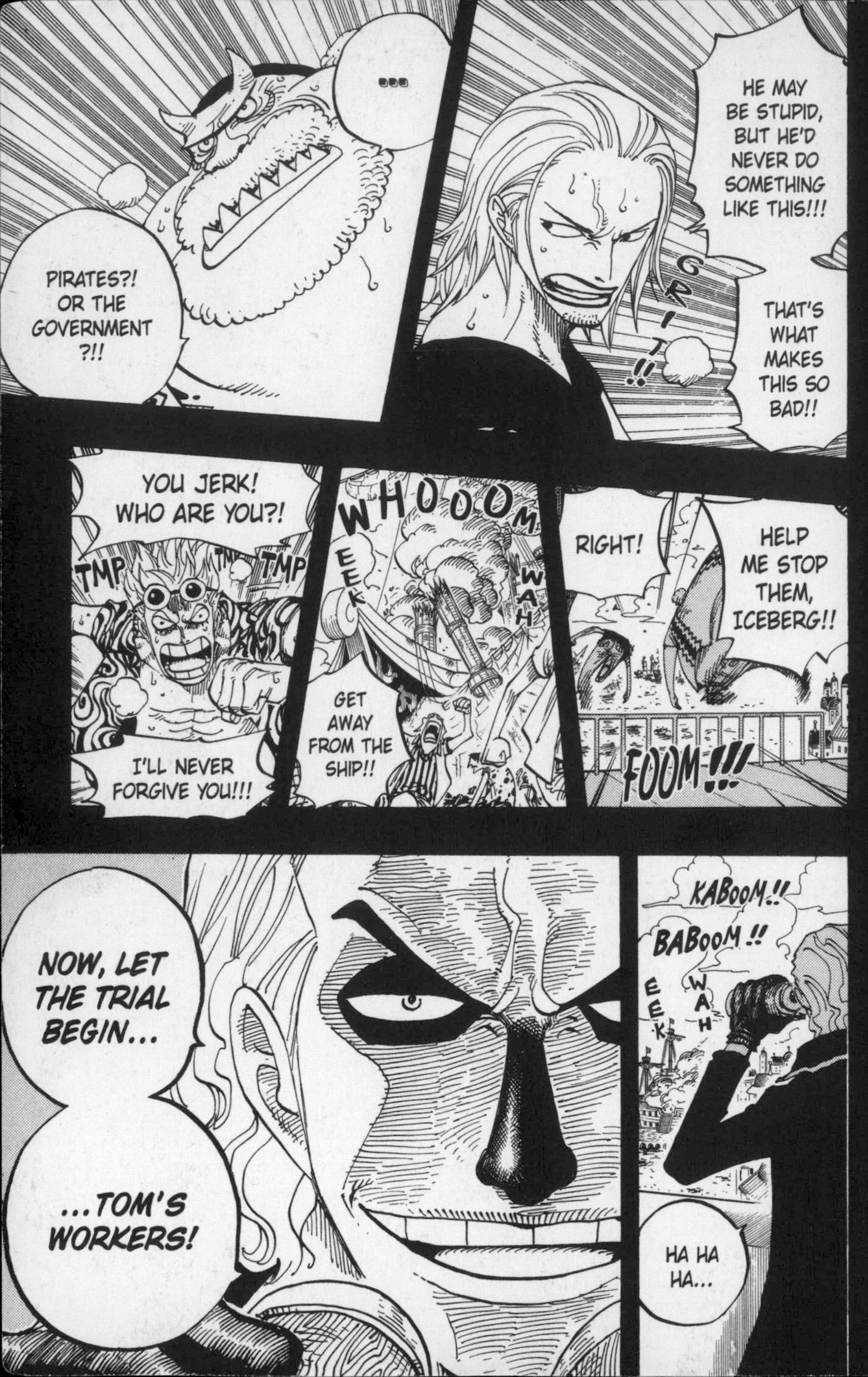
HE MAY BE STUPID, BUT HE'D NEVER DO SOMETHING LIKE THIS!!!
GRIT!!
THAT'S WHAT MAKES THIS SO BAD!!
...
PIRATES?! OR THE GOVERNMENT ?!!
HELP ME STOP THEM, ICEBERG!!
RIGHT!
FOOM!!!
WHOOOM
WAH
EEK
GET AWAY FROM THE SHIP!!
YOU JERK! WHO ARE YOU?!
TMP TMP TMP
I'LL NEVER FORGIVE YOU!!!
KABOOM!!
BABOOM!!
WAH
EEK
HA HA HA...
NOW, LET THE TRIAL BEGIN...
...TOM'S WORKERS!

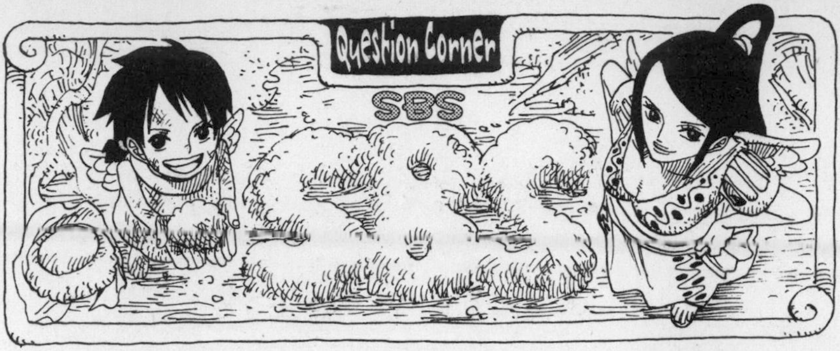
Question Corner
SBS

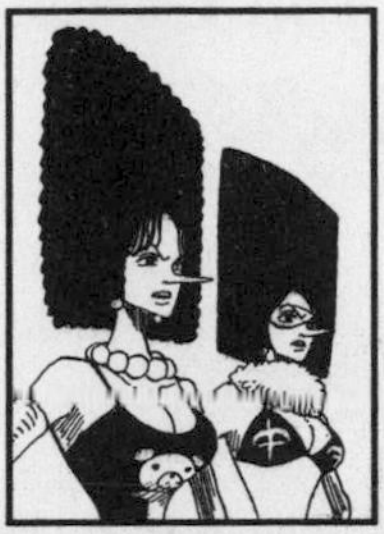

Reader: Hello, Oda-chan! Um, are Kiwi and Mozu's hairstyles natural? Or are they man-made styles born as the result of a perfected, groovy fashion sense? Also, I'd really love to see the two of them in profile. Thank you!

--Afro Zoro = Natural Monument

Oda: Yeah. Of course they're there to look snazzy! The name of that hairstyle is "Squ-hair." Pronounce it as though you were saying "square," please. Ready, set: "Squ-hair." Right, relax your shoulders, speak more lazily! "Squ-hair."

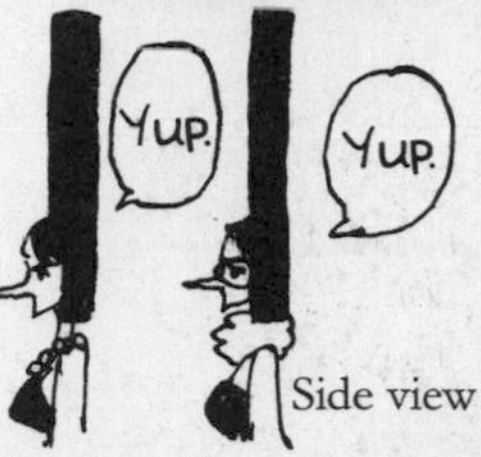
Yup.
Yup.
Side view

Reader: Odacchi! Don't say anything, please just accept this: WHUMP (A huge backlog of homework). So, that's how it is, and, um, thanks. STOMP STOMP STOMP…

--Iijima-kun

Oda: Okay, homework! I'll do my best! Um, 16 divided by 4 is... 16/4. 999 divided by 9 is 999/9... Wow, I'm pretty good at this stuff, huh? Division's my specialty, see. I'll keep going and solve all the problems like this! Scribble-scribble-scribble... (One hour later) scribble-scribble-scribble... (Three hours later) ...scribble-scribble... Crunch-crunch-munch-munch. Oops! That's no good; I mistakenly ate a pickle. Homework, homework! Scribble-scribble-scribble-scribble-Kalifa-Kalifa... Ack! No, not good, I accidentally turned into the beautiful secretary... Hey. HEEEEEEY! Don't shove your homework off on me! (Wildly successful delayed comeback.)

And this is as far as the Question Corner goes! We're done! See you next volume!

Chapter 356:
MR. TOM

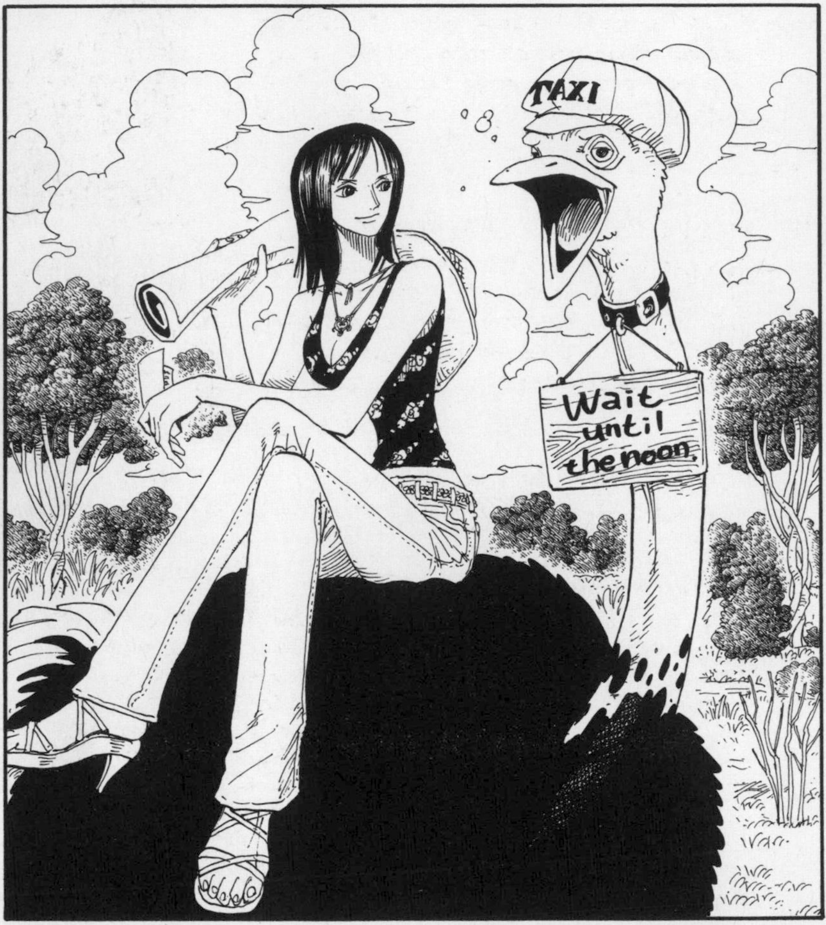
TAXI
Wait until the noon.

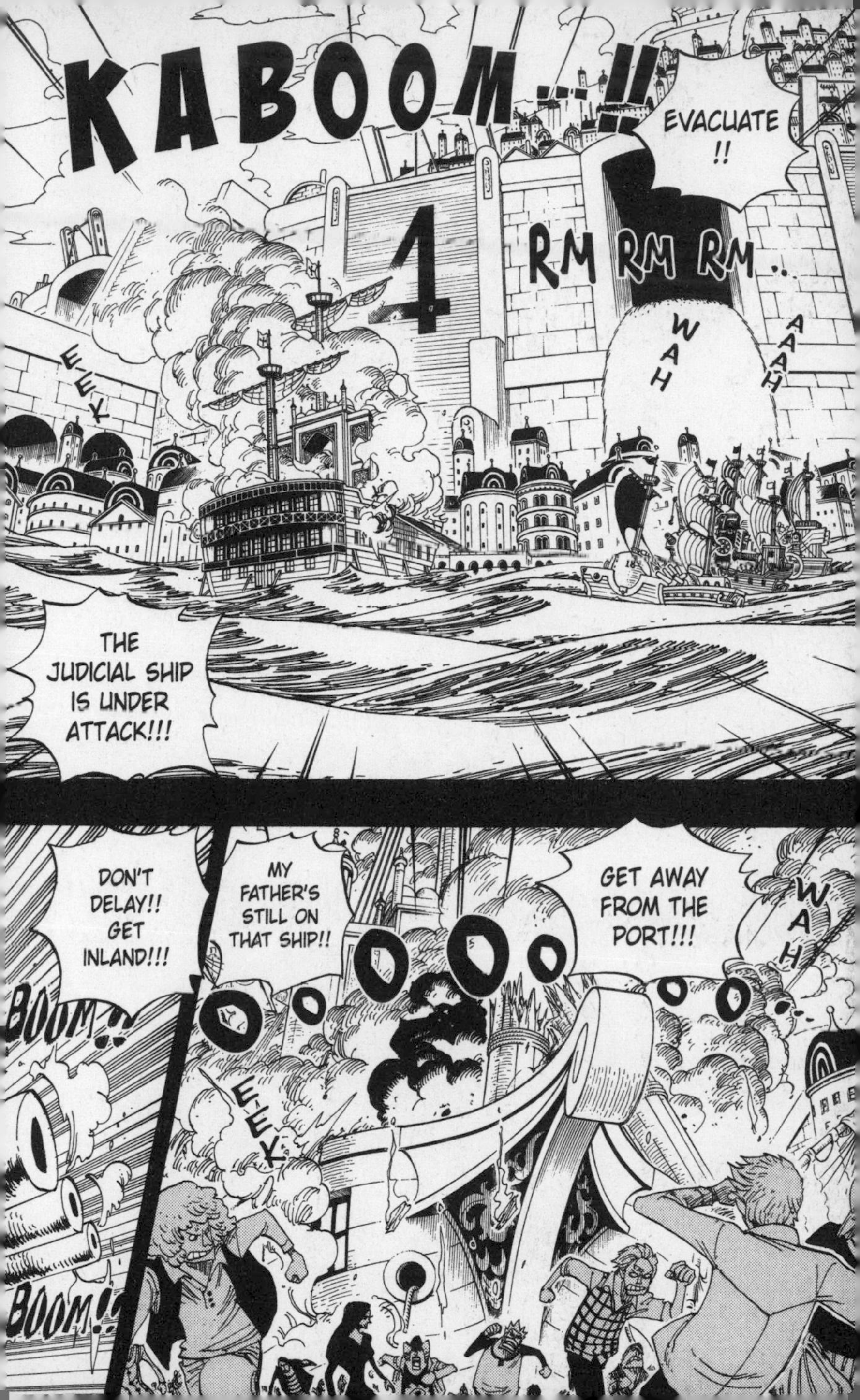
KABOOM...!!
EVACUATE!!
RM RM RM..
AAAAH
WAH
EEK
THE JUDICIAL SHIP IS UNDER ATTACK!!!
GET AWAY FROM THE PORT!!!
WAH
MY FATHER'S STILL ON THAT SHIP!!
OOOOOOO
EEK
DON'T DELAY!! GET INLAND!!!
BOOM..
BOOM!!

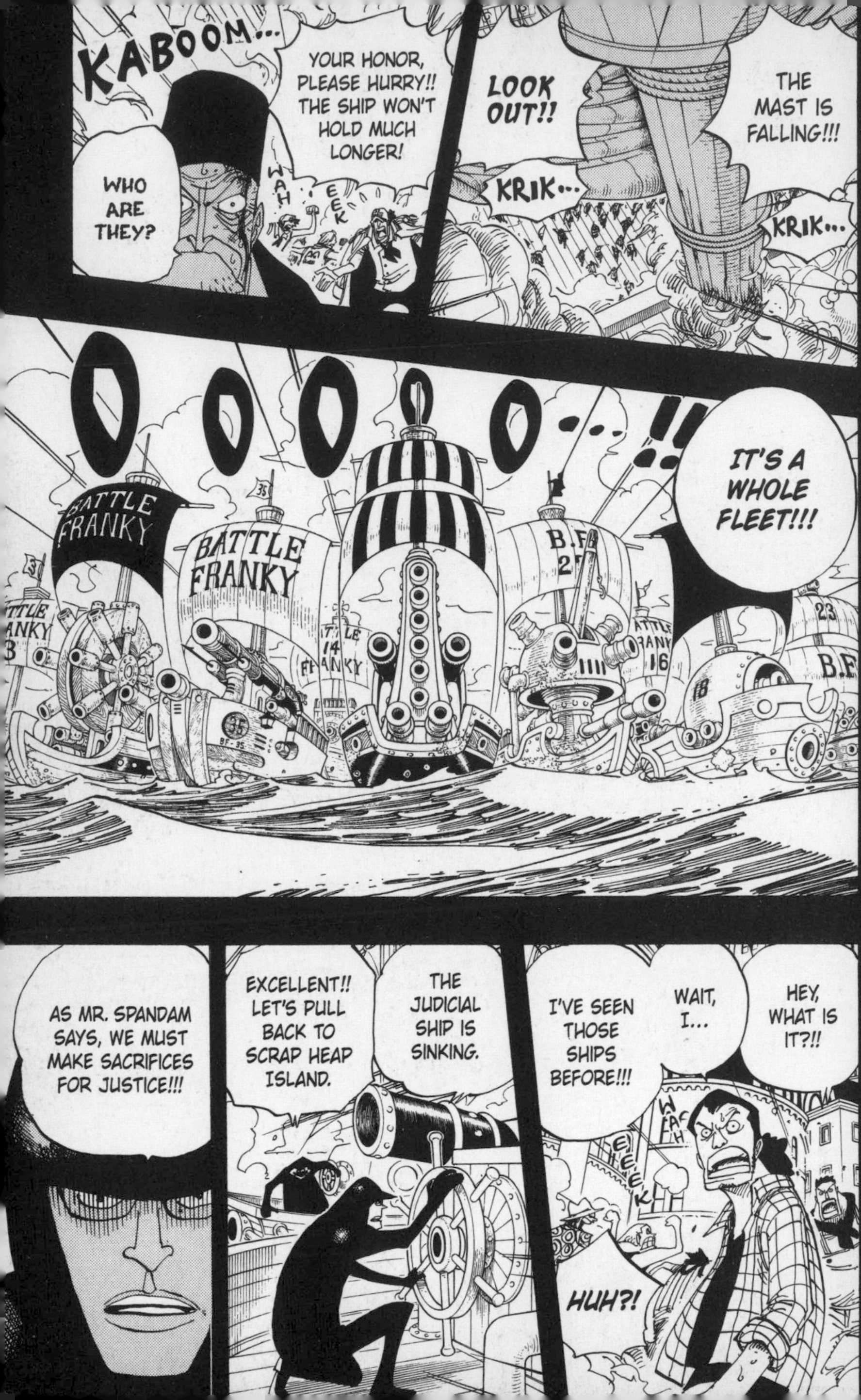
THE MAST IS FALLING!!!
LOOK OUT!!
KRIK...
KRIK...
YOUR HONOR, PLEASE HURRY!! THE SHIP WON'T HOLD MUCH LONGER!
KABOOM...
WAH
EEEK
WHO ARE THEY?
OOOOO...!!
IT'S A WHOLE FLEET!!!
BATTLE FRANKY
BATTLE FRANKY
HEY, WHAT IS IT?!!
WAIT, I...
I'VE SEEN THOSE SHIPS BEFORE!!!
WAAAH
EEEEK
HUH?!
THE JUDICIAL SHIP IS SINKING.
EXCELLENT!! LET'S PULL BACK TO SCRAP HEAP ISLAND.
AS MR. SPANDAM SAYS, WE MUST MAKE SACRIFICES FOR JUSTICE!!!

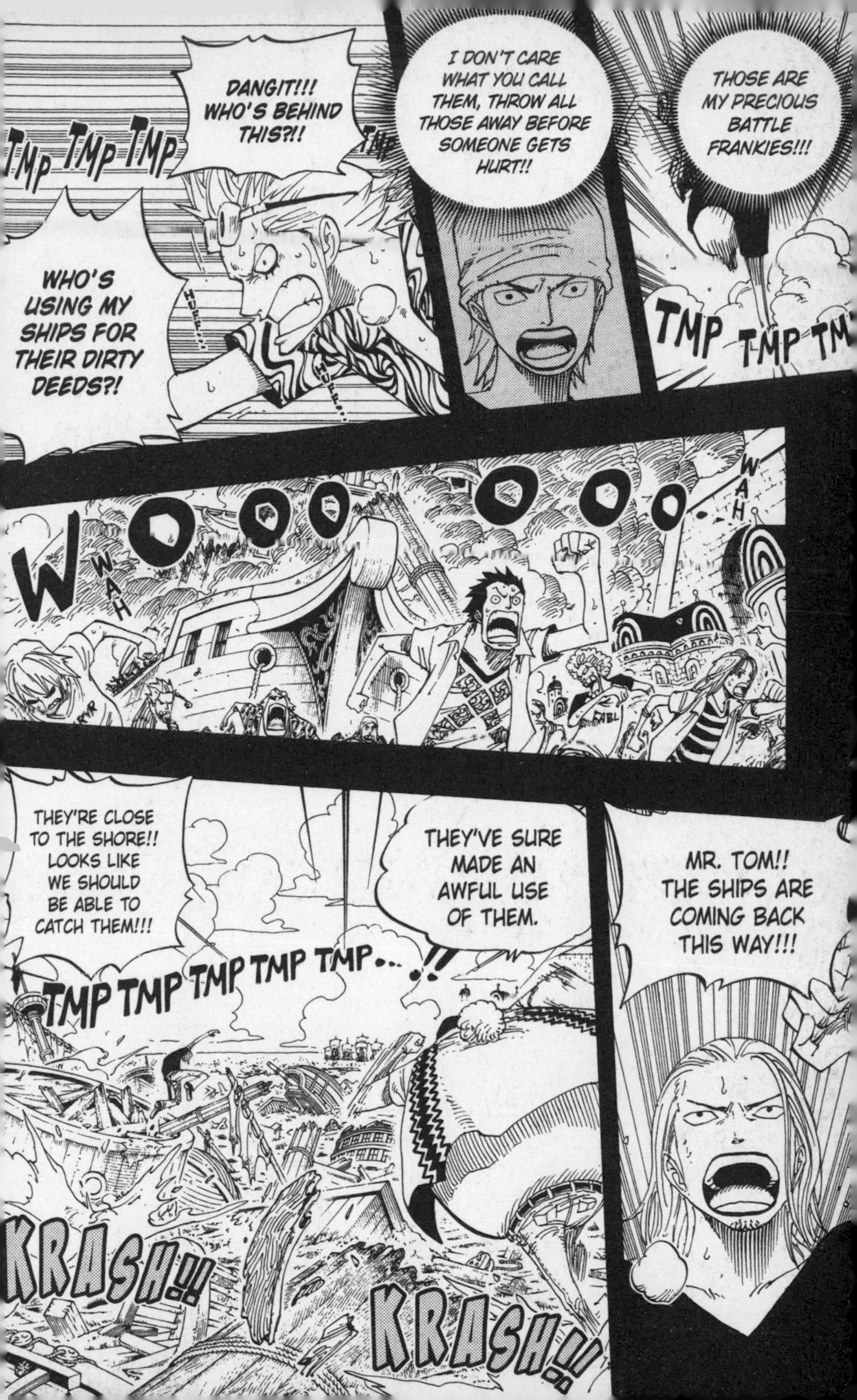
THOSE ARE MY PRECIOUS BATTLE FRANKIES!!!
TMP TMP TM
I DON'T CARE WHAT YOU CALL THEM, THROW ALL THOSE AWAY BEFORE SOMEONE GETS HURT!!
DANGIT!!! WHO'S BEHIND THIS?!!
TMP TMP TMP
WHO'S USING MY SHIPS FOR THEIR DIRTY DEEDS?!
HUFF...
HUFF...
WOOOOOOO
WAH
WAH
MR. TOM!! THE SHIPS ARE COMING BACK THIS WAY!!!
THEY'VE SURE MADE AN AWFUL USE OF THEM.
THEY'RE CLOSE TO THE SHORE!! LOOKS LIKE WE SHOULD BE ABLE TO CATCH THEM!!!
TMP TMP TMP TMP TMP...
!!
KRASH!!
KRASH!!!

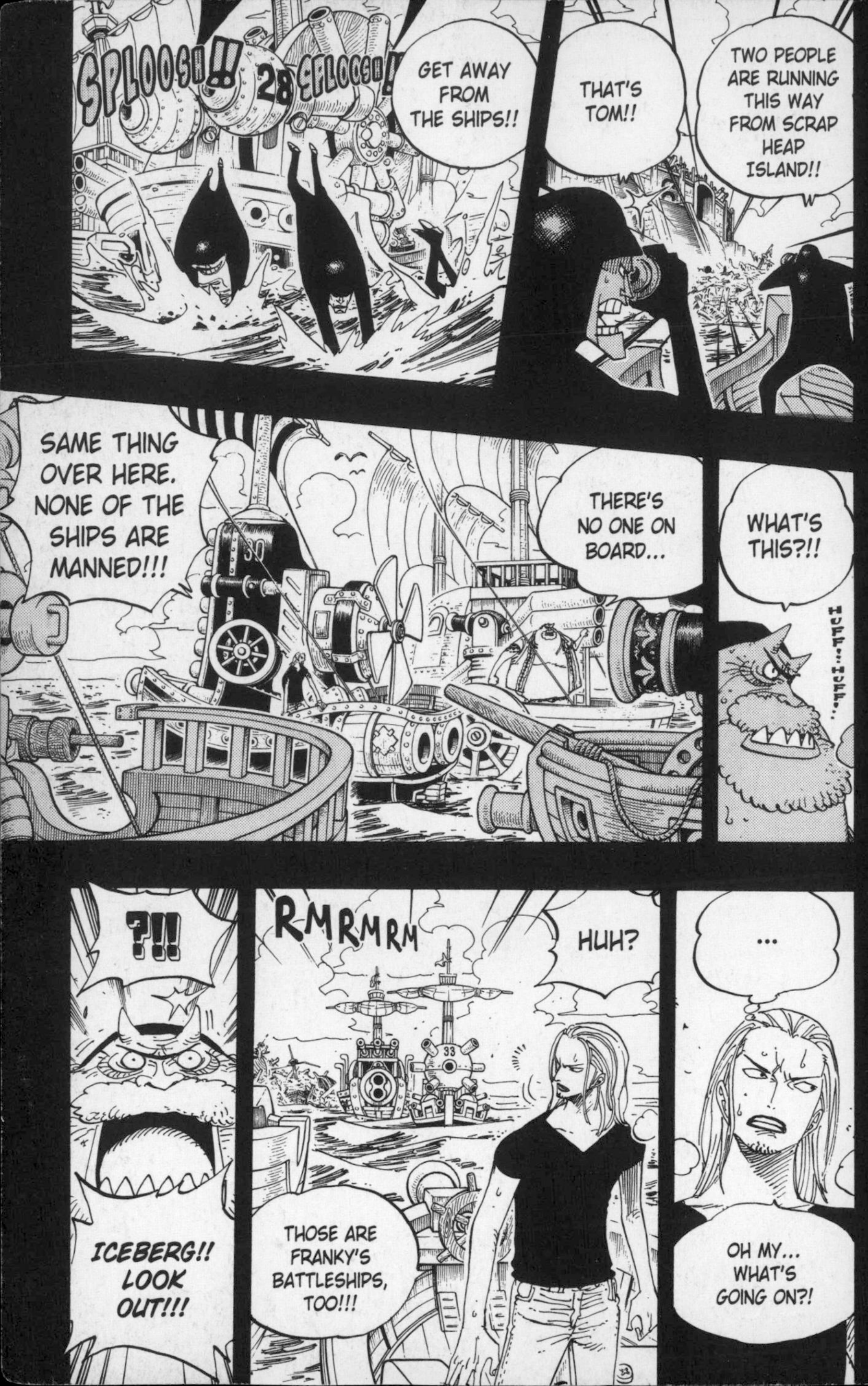
TWO PEOPLE ARE RUNNING THIS WAY FROM SCRAP HEAP ISLAND!!
THAT'S TOM!!
GET AWAY FROM THE SHIPS!!
SPLOOSH!!
SPLOOSH!!
WHAT'S THIS?!!
HUFF!! HUFF!!...
THERE'S NO ONE ON BOARD...
SAME THING OVER HERE. NONE OF THE SHIPS ARE MANNED!!!
...
OH MY... WHAT'S GOING ON?!
HUH?
RMRMRM
THOSE ARE FRANKY'S BATTLESHIPS, TOO!!!
?!!
ICEBERG!! LOOK OUT!!!

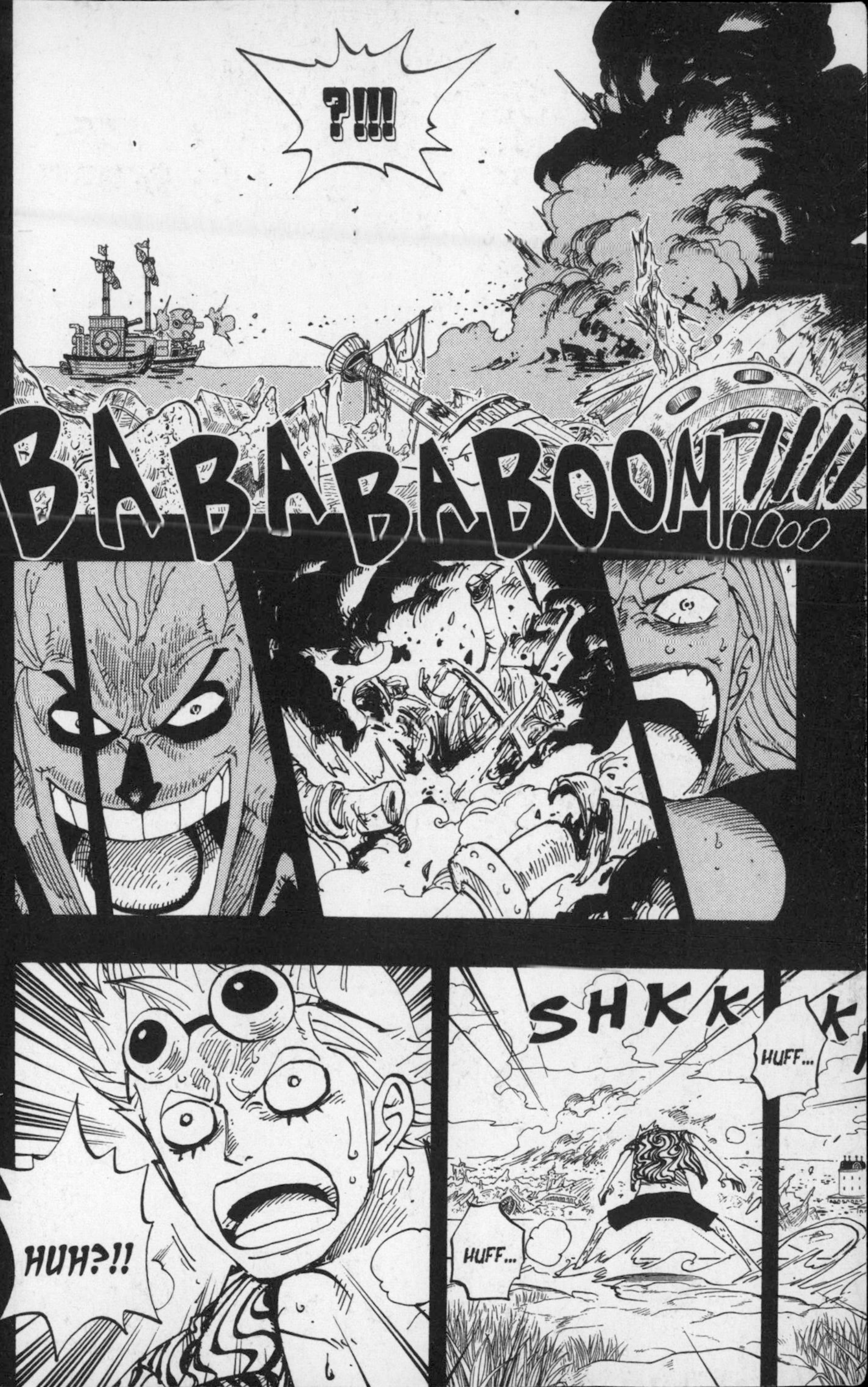
?!!!
BABABABOOM!!!!
SHKK K
HUFF...
HUFF...
HUH?!!

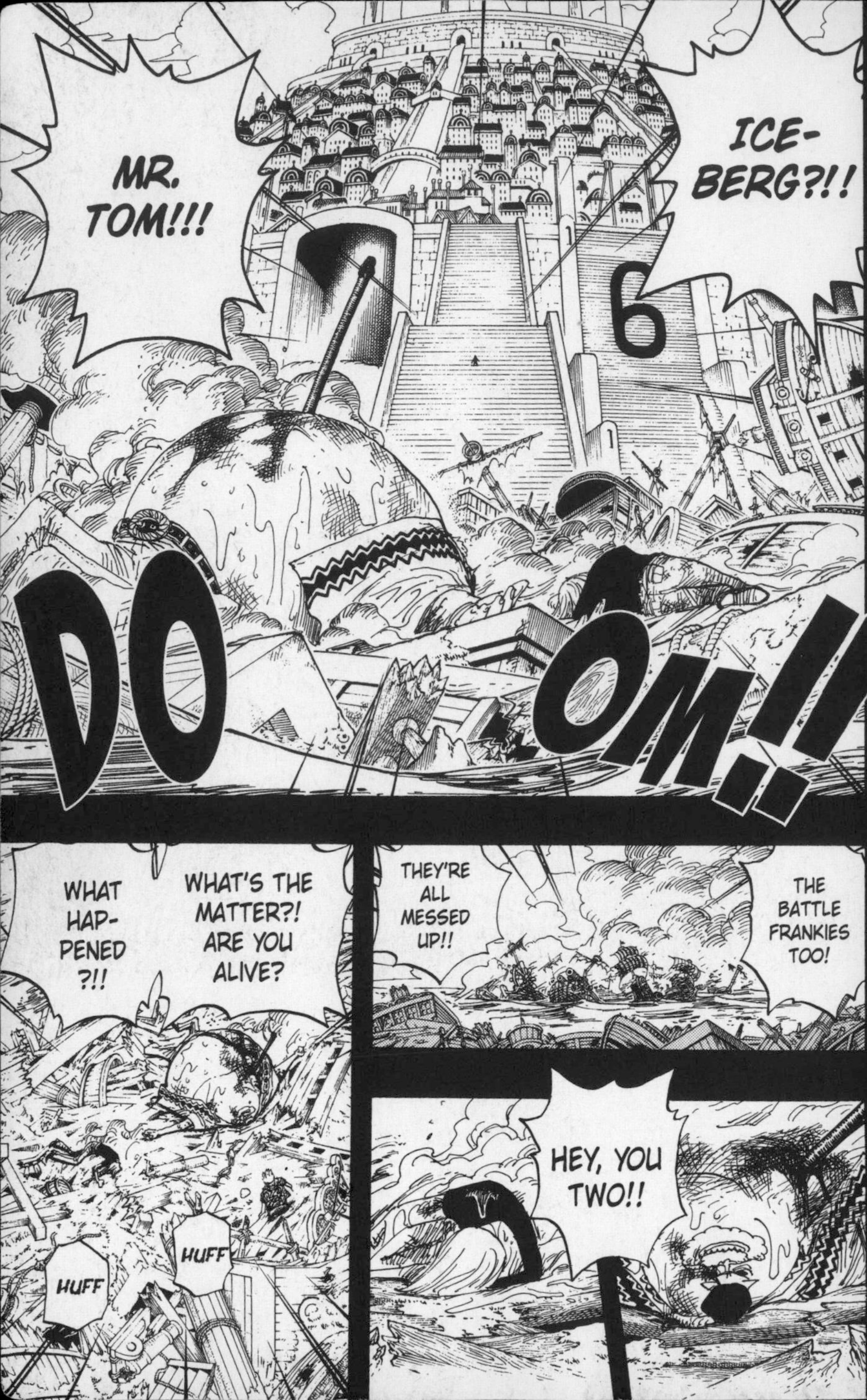
ICE-BERG?!!
MR. TOM!!!
6
DOOM!!
THE BATTLE FRANKIES TOO!
THEY'RE ALL MESSED UP!!
HEY, YOU TWO!!
WHAT'S THE MATTER?! ARE YOU ALIVE?
WHAT HAPPENED?!!
HUFF
HUFF

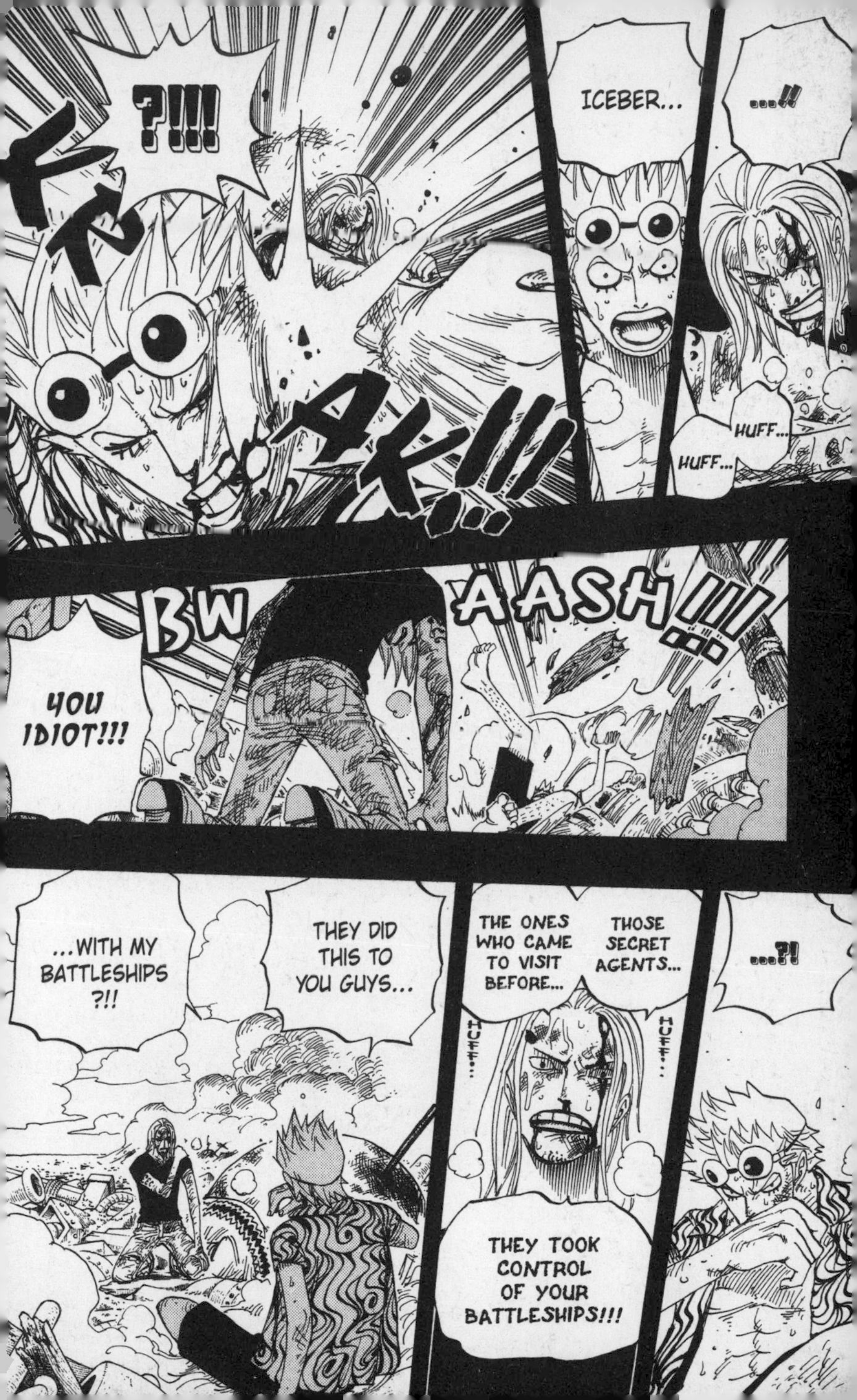
...!!
HUFF... HUFF...
ICEBER...
?!!!
AK!!!
BW AASH!!!
YOU IDIOT!!!
...?!
THOSE SECRET AGENTS...
THE ONES WHO CAME TO VISIT BEFORE...
HUFF...
HUFF...
THEY TOOK CONTROL OF YOUR BATTLESHIPS!!!
THEY DID THIS TO YOU GUYS...
...WITH MY BATTLESHIPS ?!!

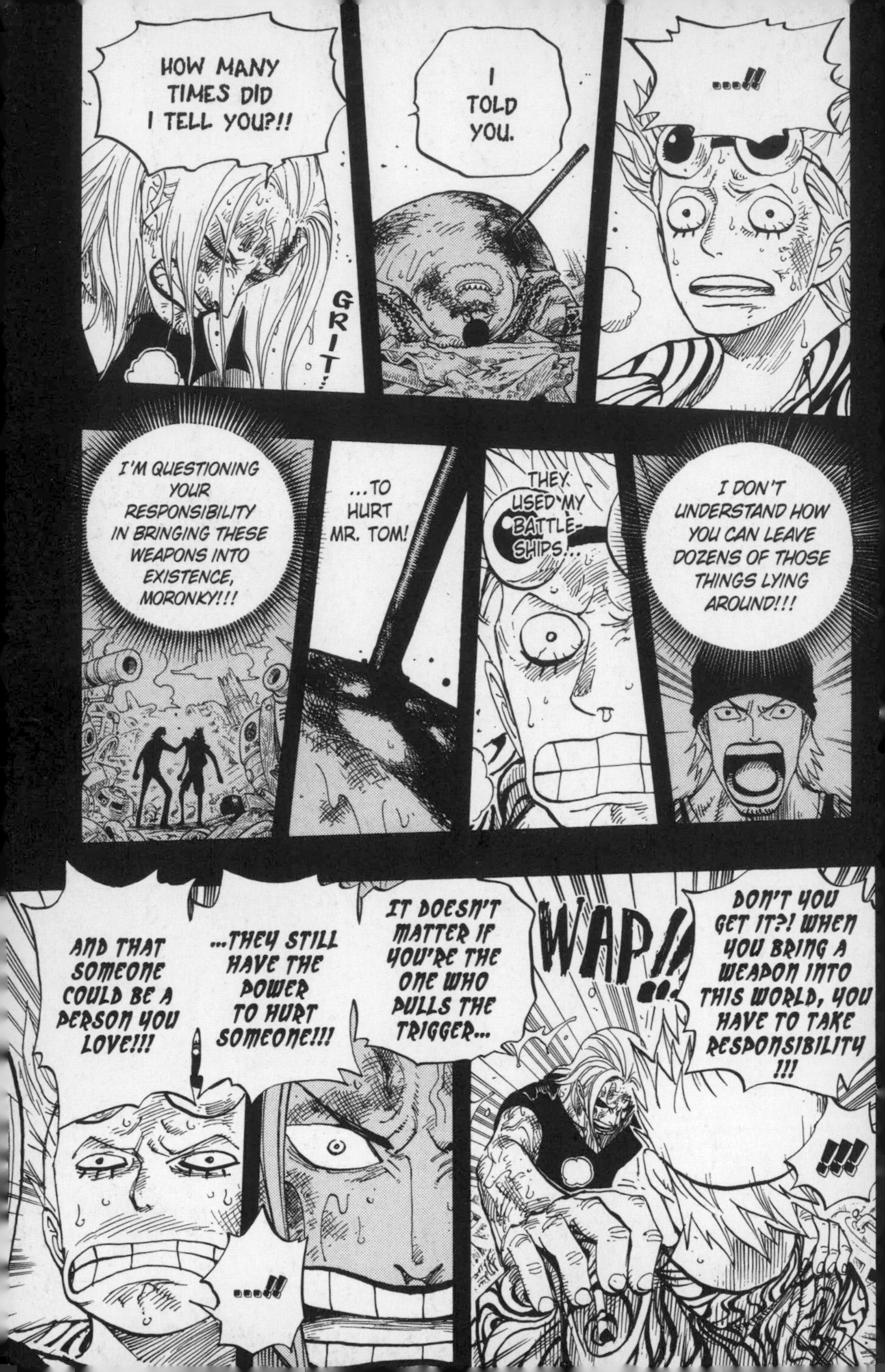
...!!
I TOLD YOU.
HOW MANY TIMES DID I TELL YOU?!!
GRIT!!
I DON'T UNDERSTAND HOW YOU CAN LEAVE DOZENS OF THOSE THINGS LYING AROUND!!!
THEY USED MY BATTLESHIPS...
...TO HURT MR. TOM!
I'M QUESTIONING YOUR RESPONSIBILITY IN BRINGING THESE WEAPONS INTO EXISTENCE, MORONKY!!!
DON'T YOU GET IT?! WHEN YOU BRING A WEAPON INTO THIS WORLD, YOU HAVE TO TAKE RESPONSIBILITY!!!
WAP!!
!!!
IT DOESN'T MATTER IF YOU'RE THE ONE WHO PULLS THE TRIGGER...
...THEY STILL HAVE THE POWER TO HURT SOMEONE!!!
AND THAT SOMEONE COULD BE A PERSON YOU LOVE!!!
...!!

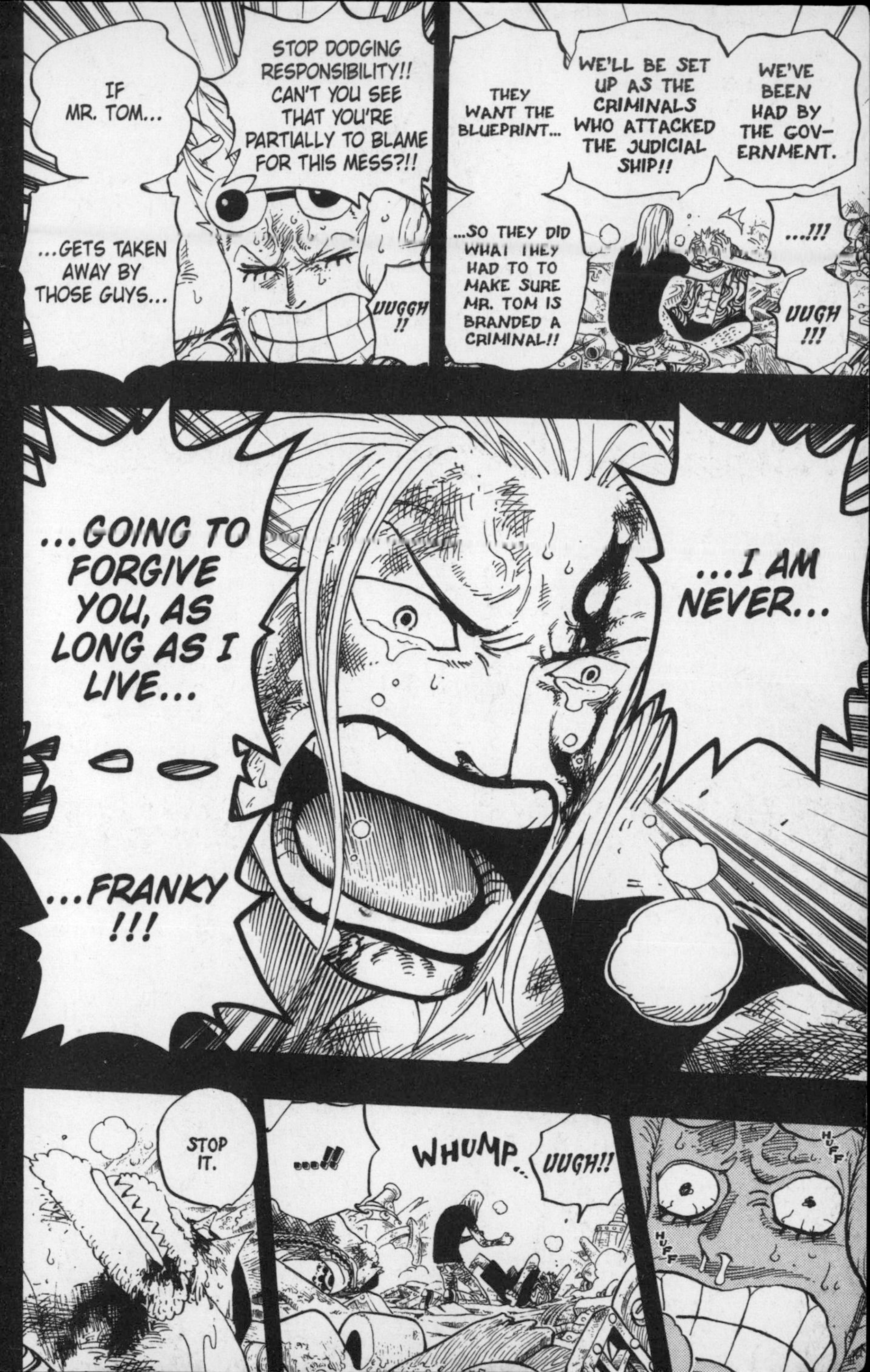
WE'VE BEEN HAD BY THE GOVERNMENT.
WE'LL BE SET UP AS THE CRIMINALS WHO ATTACKED THE JUDICIAL SHIP!!
THEY WANT THE BLUEPRINT...
...!!!
UUGH !!!
...SO THEY DID WHAT THEY HAD TO TO MAKE SURE MR. TOM IS BRANDED A CRIMINAL!!
STOP DODGING RESPONSIBILITY!! CAN'T YOU SEE THAT YOU'RE PARTIALLY TO BLAME FOR THIS MESS?!!
IF MR. TOM...
UUGGH !!
...GETS TAKEN AWAY BY THOSE GUYS...
...I AM NEVER...
...GOING TO FORGIVE YOU, AS LONG AS I LIVE...
...FRANKY !!!
HUFF
HUFF
UUGH!!
WHUMP
...!!
STOP IT.

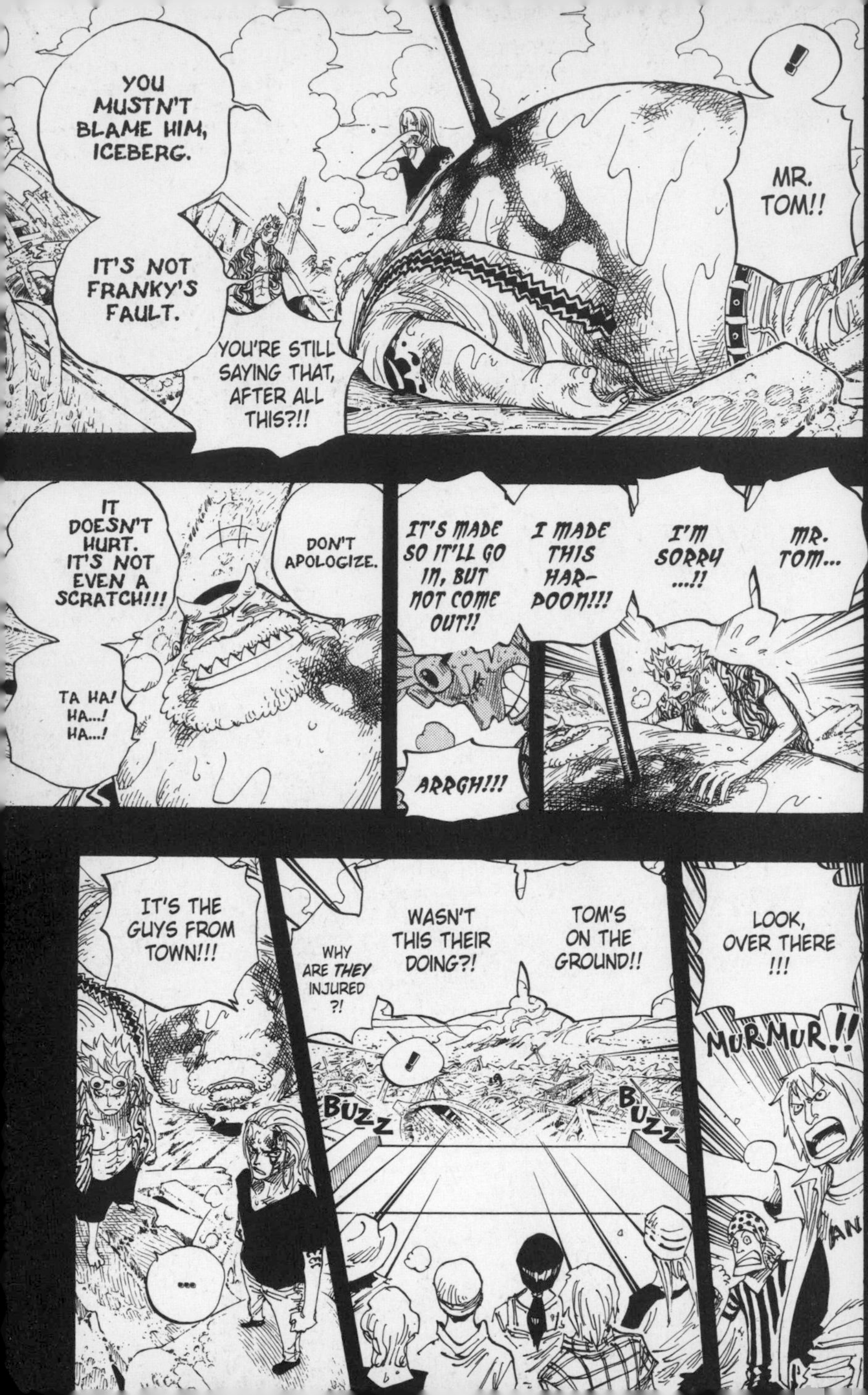
!
MR. TOM!!
YOU MUSTN'T BLAME HIM, ICEBERG.
IT'S NOT FRANKY'S FAULT.
YOU'RE STILL SAYING THAT, AFTER ALL THIS?!!
MR. TOM...
I'M SORRY ...!!
I MADE THIS HAR-POON!!!
IT'S MADE SO IT'LL GO IN, BUT NOT COME OUT!!
ARRGH!!!
DON'T APOLOGIZE.
IT DOESN'T HURT. IT'S NOT EVEN A SCRATCH!!!
TA HA! HA...! HA...!
LOOK, OVER THERE !!!
MURMUR!!
TOM'S ON THE GROUND!!
WASN'T THIS THEIR DOING?!
WHY ARE THEY INJURED ?!
!
BUZZ
BUZZ
IT'S THE GUYS FROM TOWN!!!
...

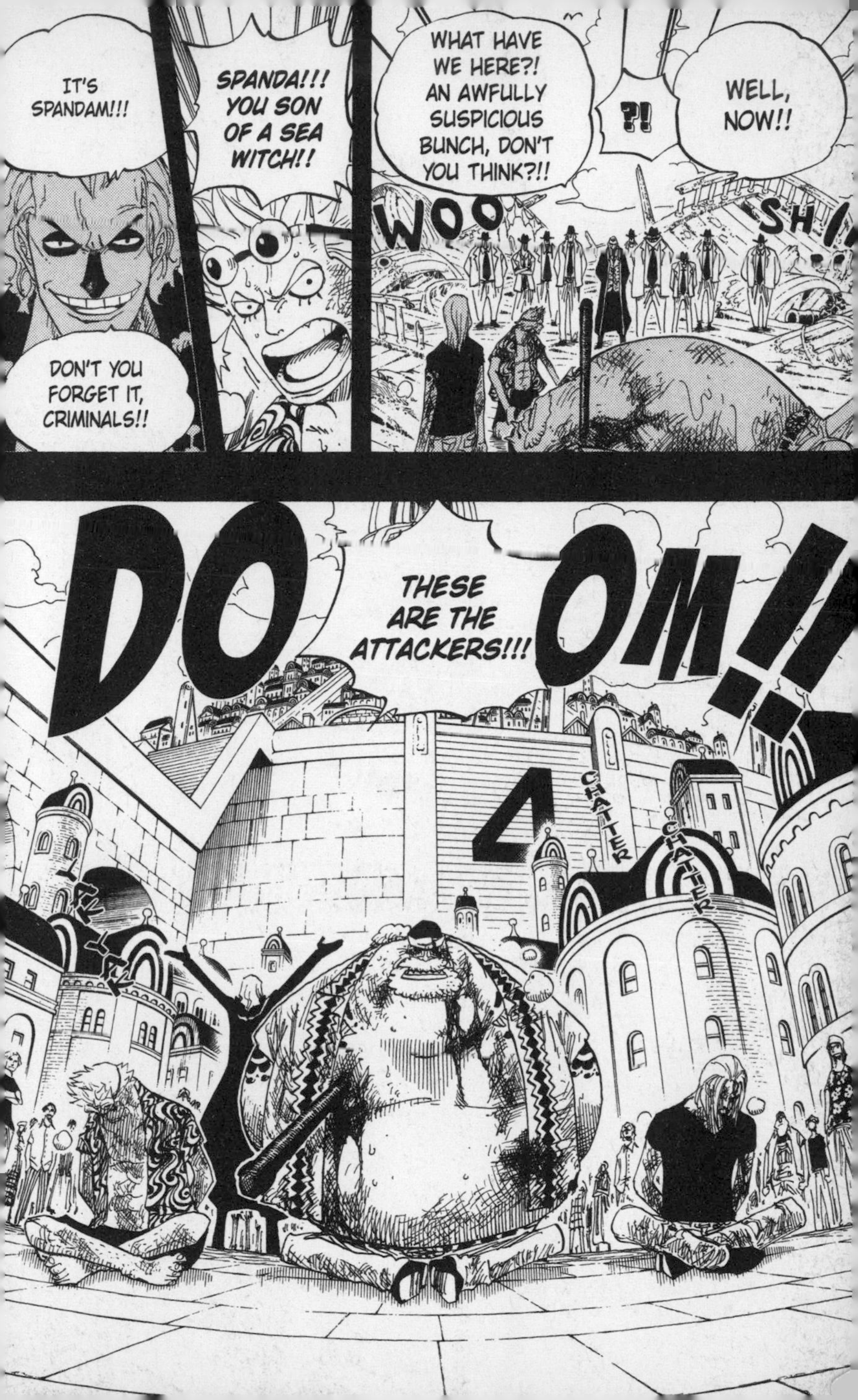
WELL, NOW!!
?!
WHAT HAVE WE HERE?! AN AWFULLY SUSPICIOUS BUNCH, DON'T YOU THINK?!!
WOO
SH
SPANDA!!! YOU SON OF A SEA WITCH!!
IT'S SPANDAM!!!
DON'T YOU FORGET IT, CRIMINALS!!
DO
OM!!
THESE ARE THE ATTACKERS!!!
4
CHATTER
CHATTER

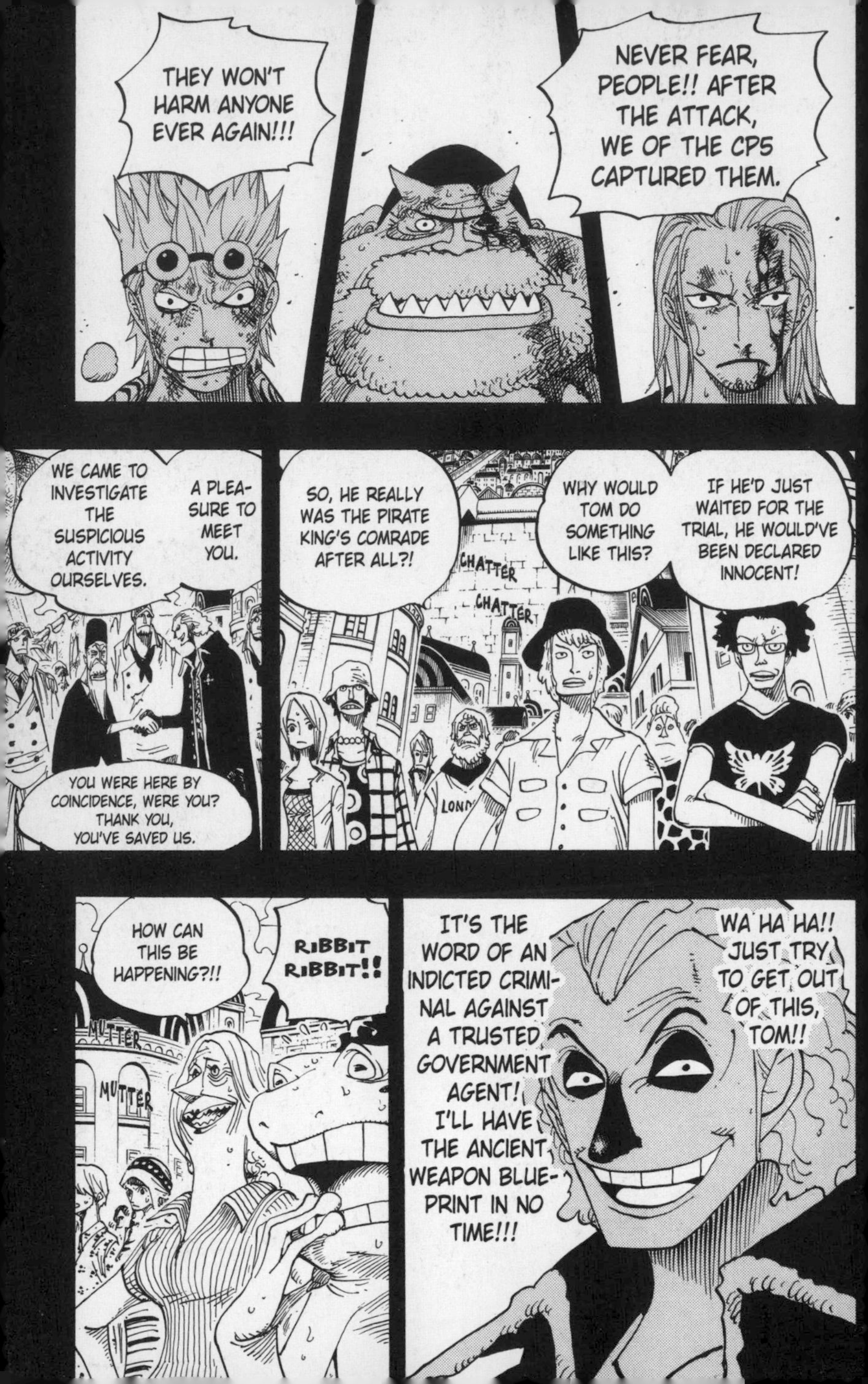
NEVER FEAR, PEOPLE!! AFTER THE ATTACK, WE OF THE CP5 CAPTURED THEM.
THEY WON'T HARM ANYONE EVER AGAIN!!!
IF HE'D JUST WAITED FOR THE TRIAL, HE WOULD'VE BEEN DECLARED INNOCENT!
WHY WOULD TOM DO SOMETHING LIKE THIS?
CHATTER
CHATTER
SO, HE REALLY WAS THE PIRATE KING'S COMRADE AFTER ALL?!
A PLEASURE TO MEET YOU.
WE CAME TO INVESTIGATE THE SUSPICIOUS ACTIVITY OURSELVES.
YOU WERE HERE BY COINCIDENCE, WERE YOU? THANK YOU, YOU'VE SAVED US.
WA HA HA!! JUST TRY TO GET OUT OF THIS, TOM!!
IT'S THE WORD OF AN INDICTED CRIMINAL AGAINST A TRUSTED GOVERNMENT AGENT! I'LL HAVE THE ANCIENT WEAPON BLUEPRINT IN NO TIME!!!
RIBBIT RIBBIT!!
HOW CAN THIS BE HAPPENING?!!
MUTTER
MUTTER

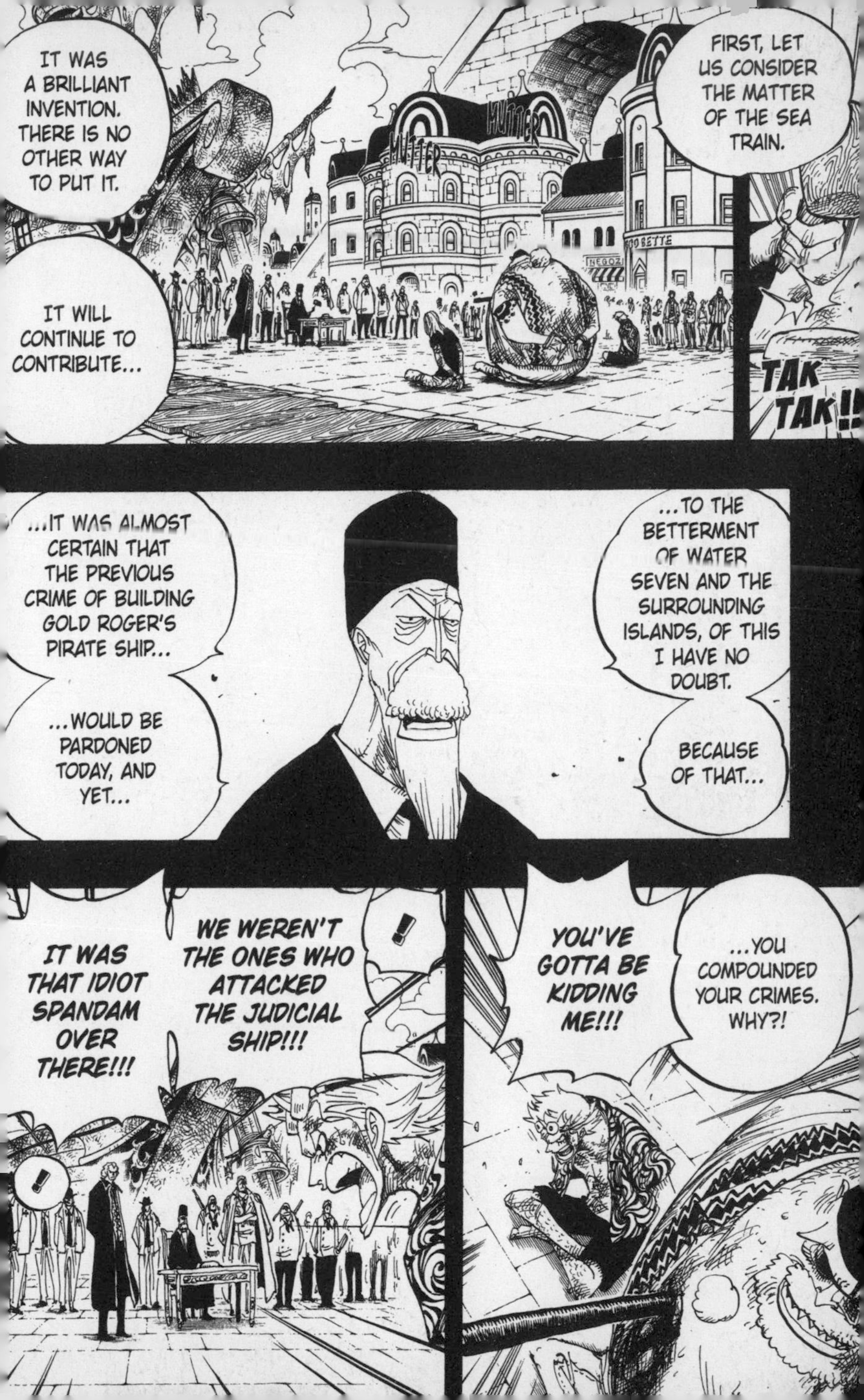
FIRST, LET US CONSIDER THE MATTER OF THE SEA TRAIN.
TAK TAK!!
IT WAS A BRILLIANT INVENTION. THERE IS NO OTHER WAY TO PUT IT.
IT WILL CONTINUE TO CONTRIBUTE...
...TO THE BETTERMENT OF WATER SEVEN AND THE SURROUNDING ISLANDS, OF THIS I HAVE NO DOUBT.
BECAUSE OF THAT...
...IT WAS ALMOST CERTAIN THAT THE PREVIOUS CRIME OF BUILDING GOLD ROGER'S PIRATE SHIP...
...WOULD BE PARDONED TODAY, AND YET...
...YOU COMPOUNDED YOUR CRIMES. WHY?!
YOU'VE GOTTA BE KIDDING ME!!!
!
WE WEREN'T THE ONES WHO ATTACKED THE JUDICIAL SHIP!!!
IT WAS THAT IDIOT SPANDAM OVER THERE!!!
!

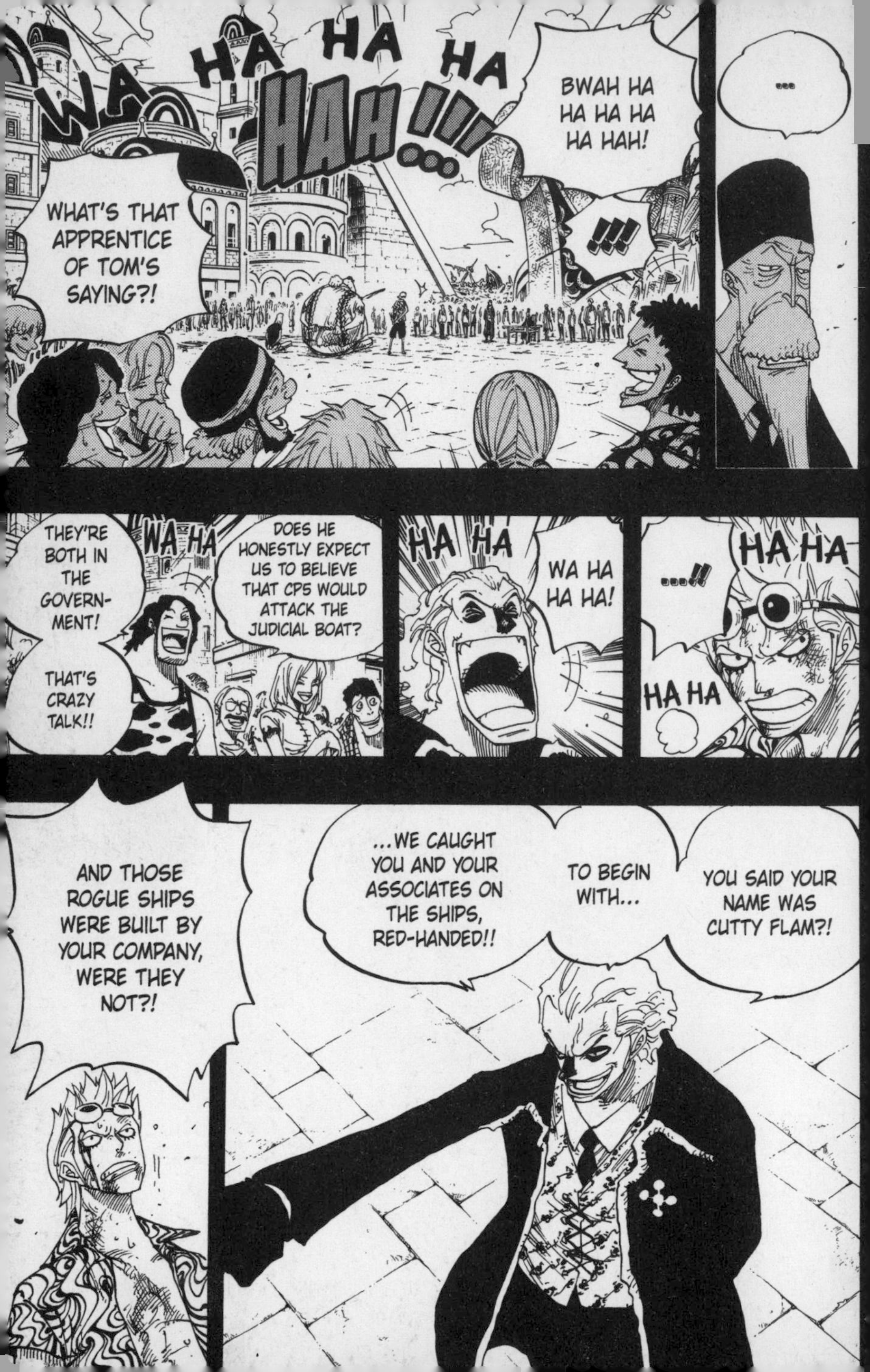
...
BWAH HA HA HA HA HA HAH!
WA HA HA HA HAH!!!...
!!!
WHAT'S THAT APPRENTICE OF TOM'S SAYING?!
HA HA
...!!
HA HA
HA HA
WA HA HA HA!
DOES HE HONESTLY EXPECT US TO BELIEVE THAT CP5 WOULD ATTACK THE JUDICIAL BOAT?
WA HA
THEY'RE BOTH IN THE GOVERNMENT!
THAT'S CRAZY TALK!!
YOU SAID YOUR NAME WAS CUTTY FLAM?!
TO BEGIN WITH...
...WE CAUGHT YOU AND YOUR ASSOCIATES ON THE SHIPS, RED-HANDED!!
AND THOSE ROGUE SHIPS WERE BUILT BY YOUR COMPANY, WERE THEY NOT?!

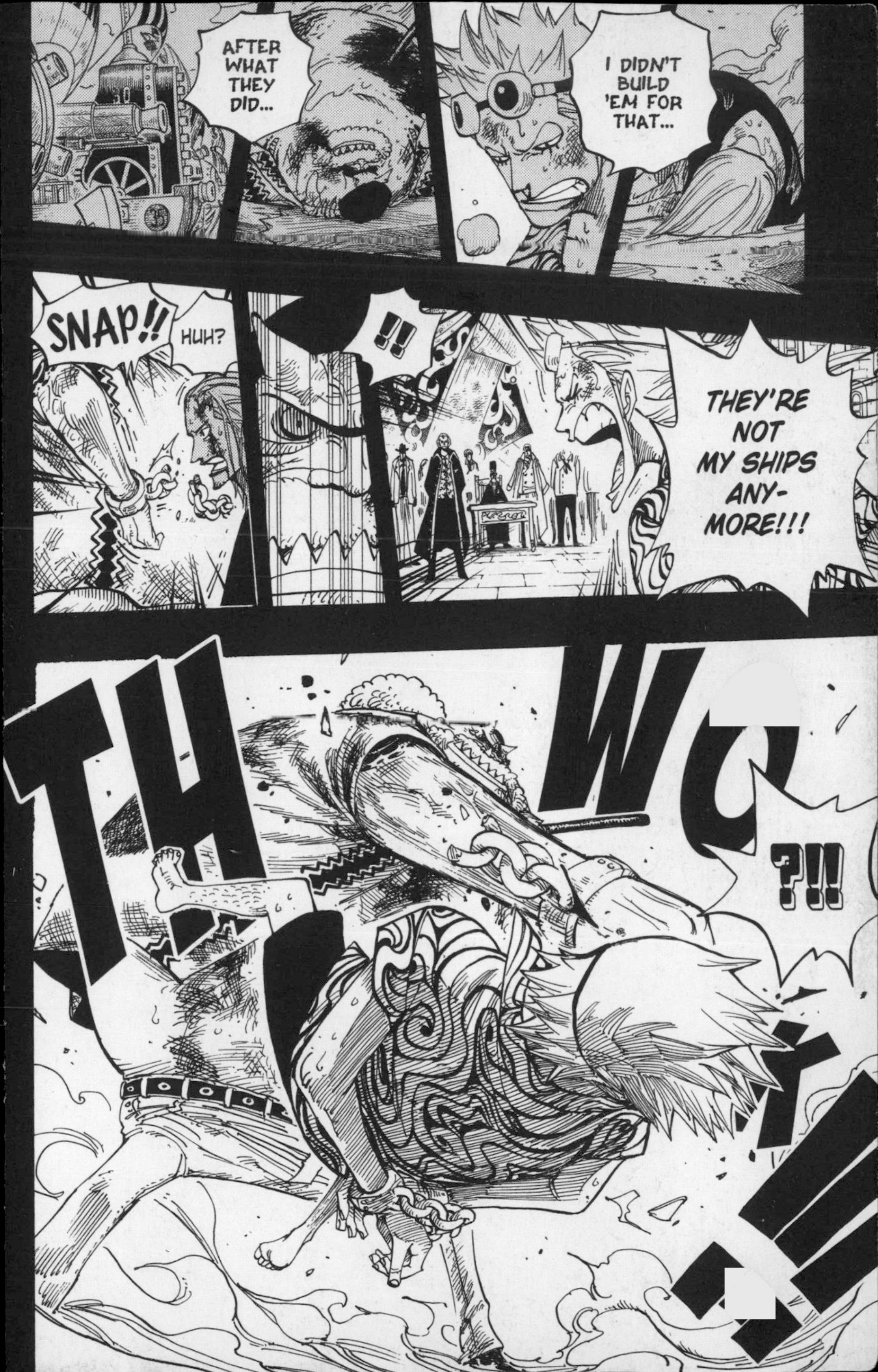
I DIDN'T BUILD 'EM FOR THAT...
AFTER WHAT THEY DID...
THEY'RE NOT MY SHIPS ANY-MORE!!!
!!
SNAP!!
HUH?
?!!

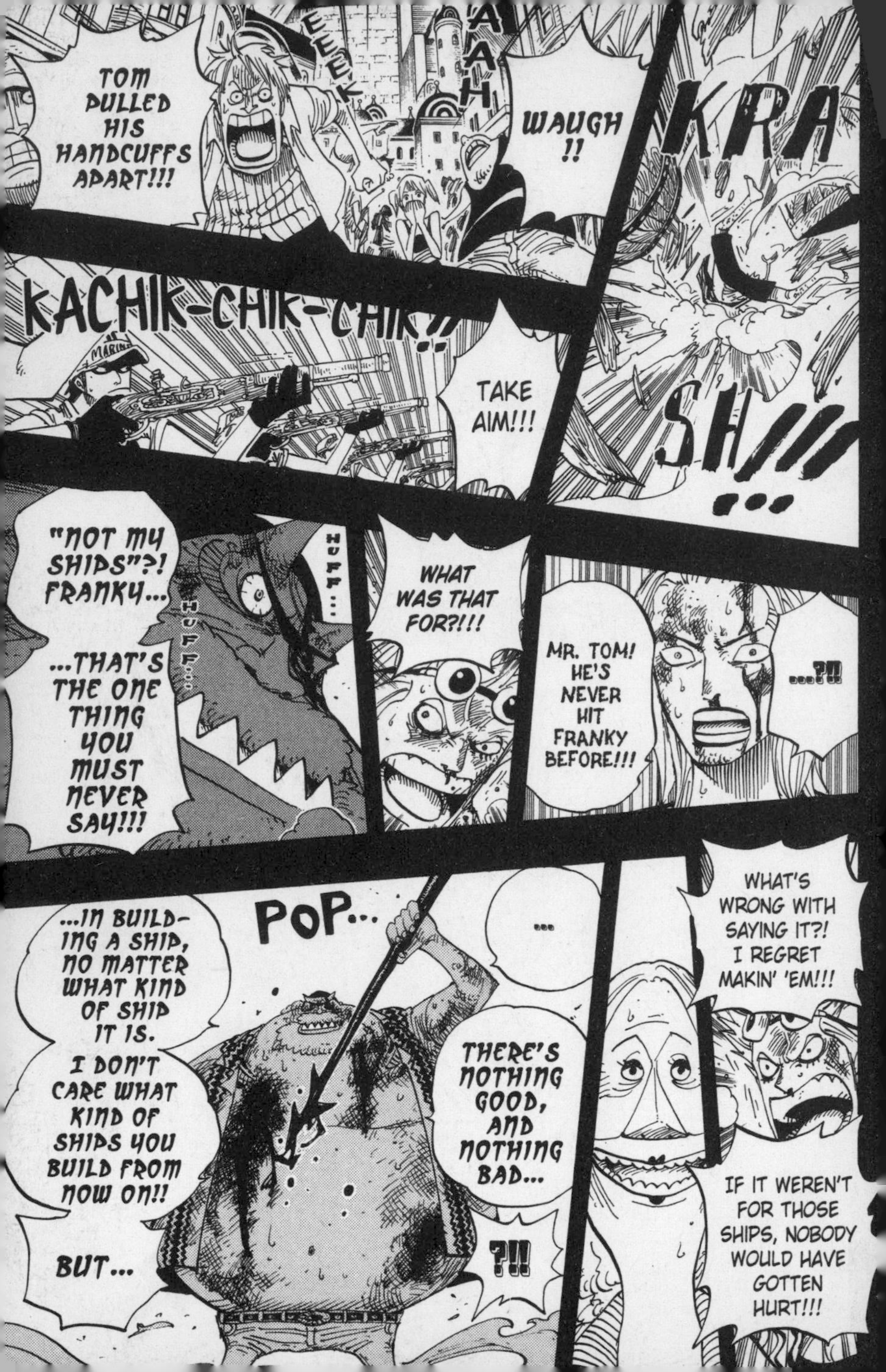
KRA
SH!!!
...
WAUGH!!
AAAH
EEEEK
TOM PULLED HIS HANDCUFFS APART!!!
TAKE AIM!!!
KACHIK-CHIK-CHIK!!
...?!!
MR. TOM! HE'S NEVER HIT FRANKY BEFORE!!!
WHAT WAS THAT FOR?!!!
HUFF...
HUFF...
"NOT MY SHIPS"?! FRANKY...
...THAT'S THE ONE THING YOU MUST NEVER SAY!!!
WHAT'S WRONG WITH SAYING IT?! I REGRET MAKIN' 'EM!!!
IF IT WEREN'T FOR THOSE SHIPS, NOBODY WOULD HAVE GOTTEN HURT!!!
...
THERE'S NOTHING GOOD, AND NOTHING BAD...
?!!
POP...
...IN BUILDING A SHIP, NO MATTER WHAT KIND OF SHIP IT IS.
I DON'T CARE WHAT KIND OF SHIPS YOU BUILD FROM NOW ON!!
BUT...

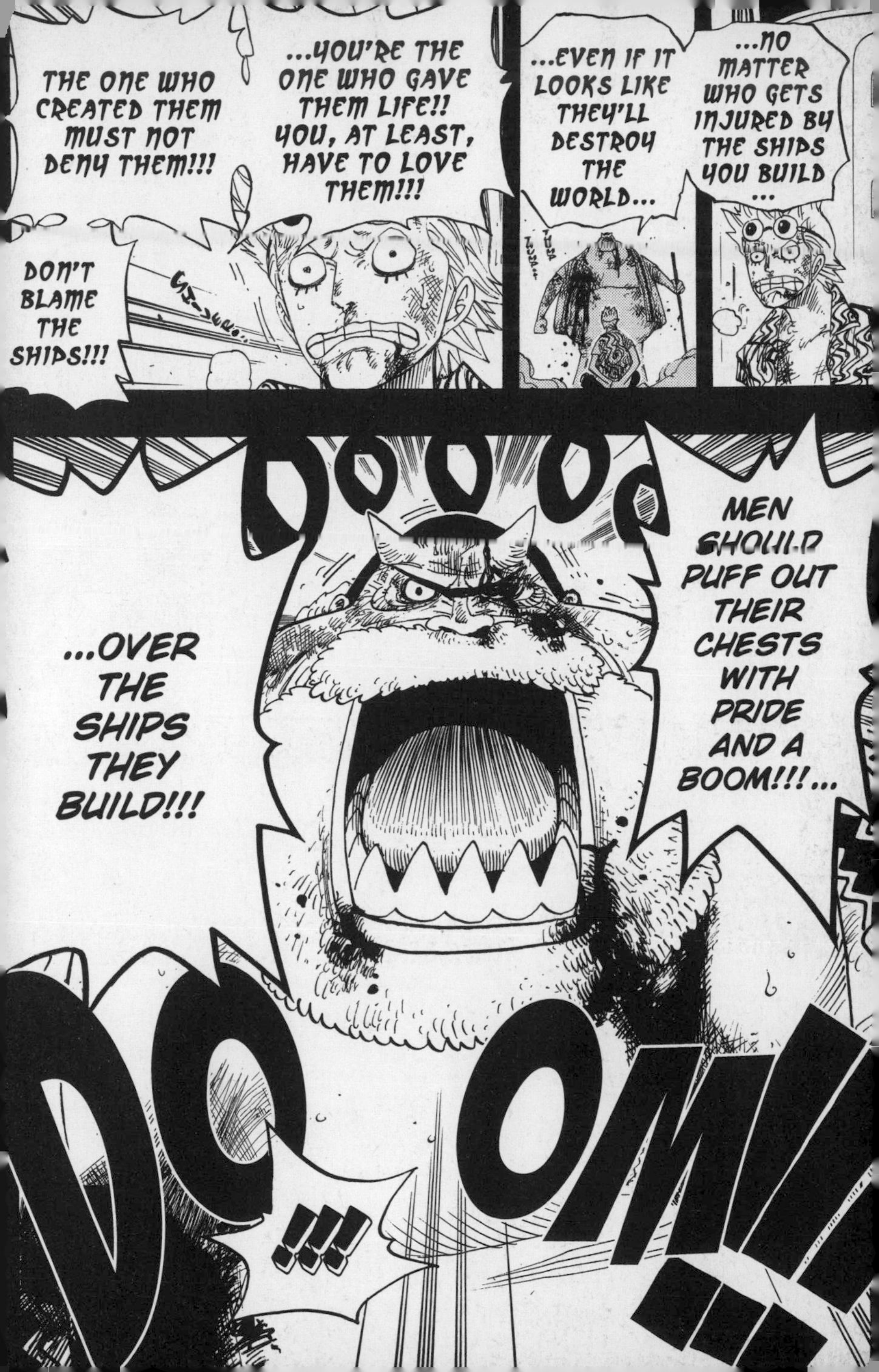
...NO MATTER WHO GETS INJURED BY THE SHIPS YOU BUILD ...
...EVEN IF IT LOOKS LIKE THEY'LL DESTROY THE WORLD...
...YOU'RE THE ONE WHO GAVE THEM LIFE!! YOU, AT LEAST, HAVE TO LOVE THEM!!!
THE ONE WHO CREATED THEM MUST NOT DENY THEM!!!
DON'T BLAME THE SHIPS!!!
MEN SHOULD PUFF OUT THEIR CHESTS WITH PRIDE AND A BOOM!!! ...
...OVER THE SHIPS THEY BUILD!!!

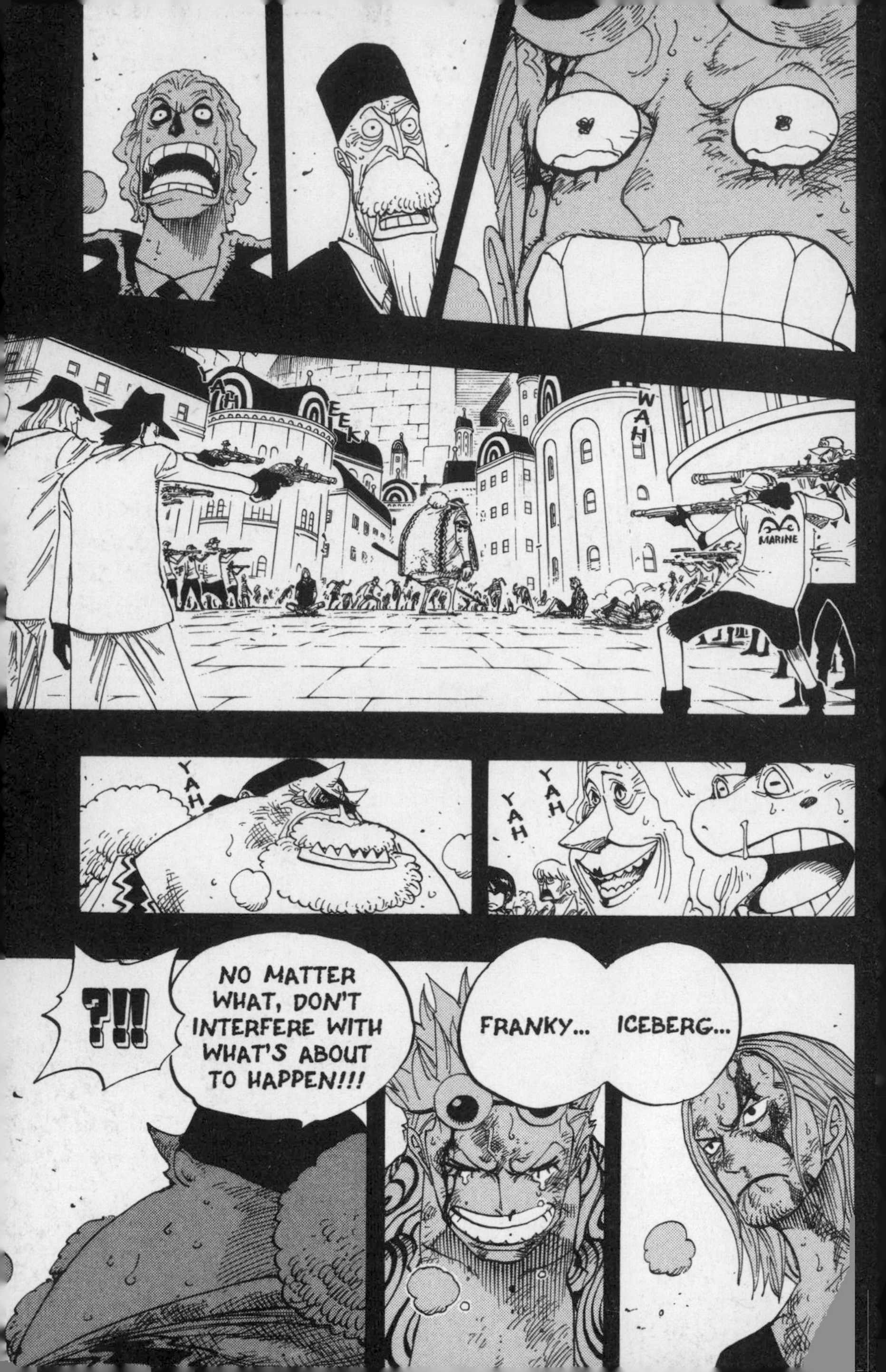
WAH
EEK
YAH
YAH
YAH
YAH
FRANKY... ICEBERG...
NO MATTER WHAT, DON'T INTERFERE WITH WHAT'S ABOUT TO HAPPEN!!!
?!!

Chapter 357: CUTTY FLAM

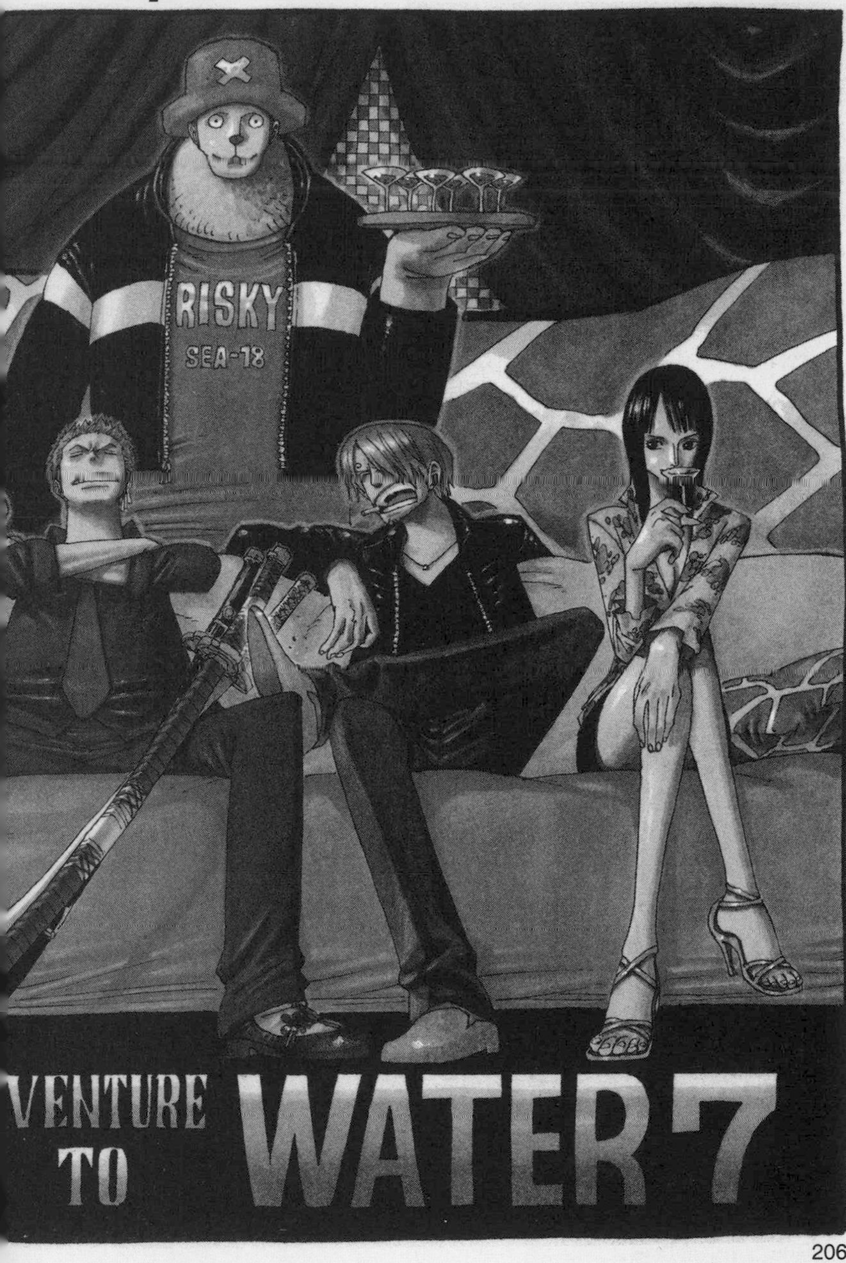
RISKY
SEA-18
VENTURE
TO
WATER 7

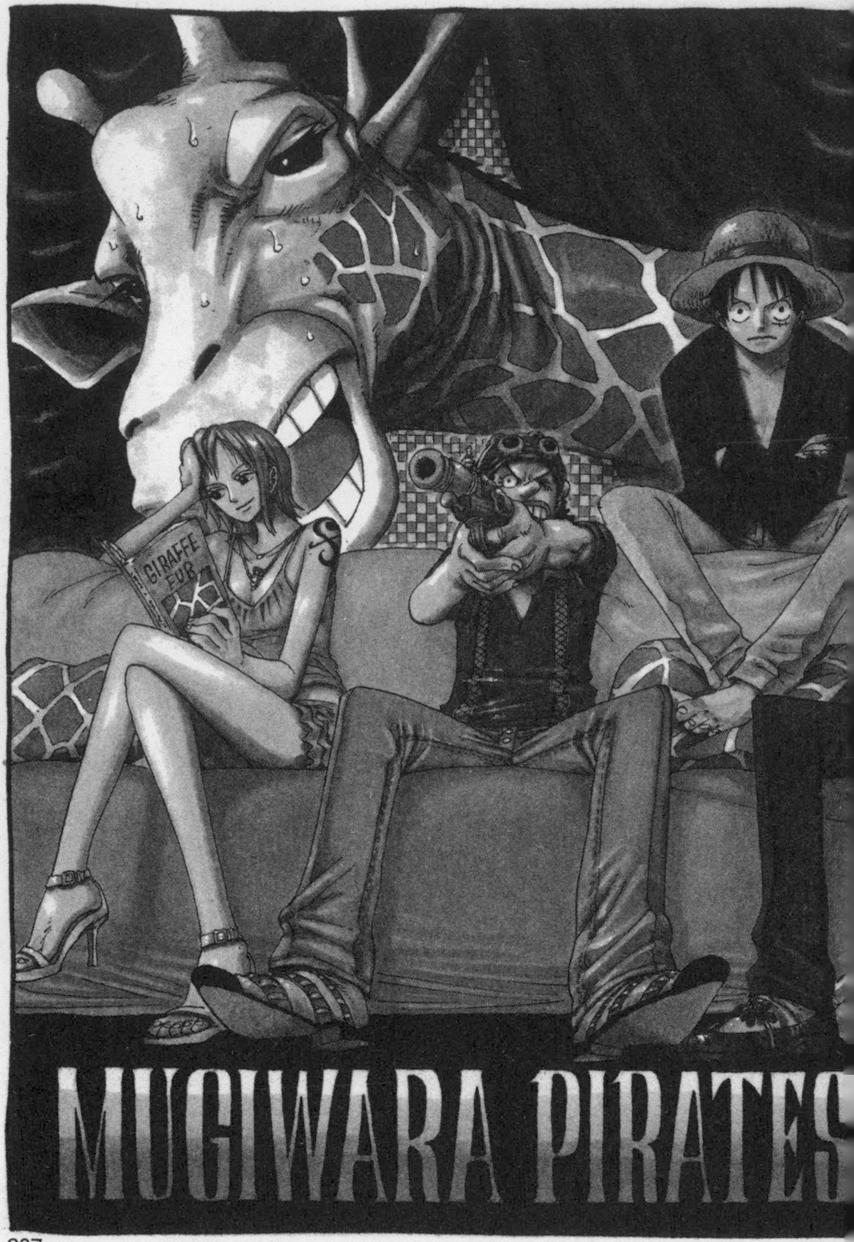
GIRAFFE
MUGIWARA PIRATES

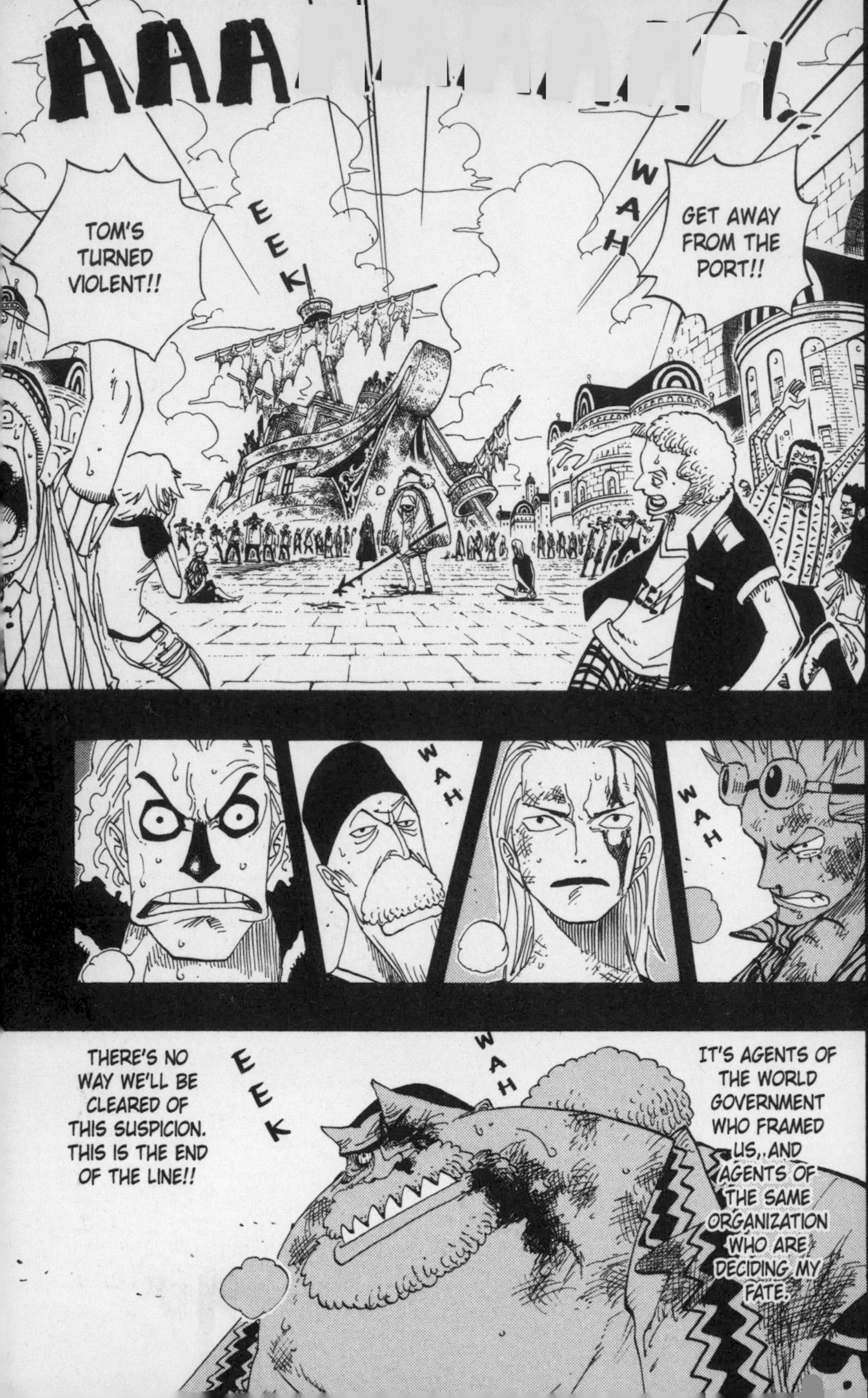
AAA
GET AWAY FROM THE PORT!!
WAH
EEK
TOM'S TURNED VIOLENT!!
WAH
WAH
IT'S AGENTS OF THE WORLD GOVERNMENT WHO FRAMED US, AND AGENTS OF THE SAME ORGANIZATION WHO ARE DECIDING MY FATE.
WAH
EEK
THERE'S NO WAY WE'LL BE CLEARED OF THIS SUSPICION. THIS IS THE END OF THE LINE!!

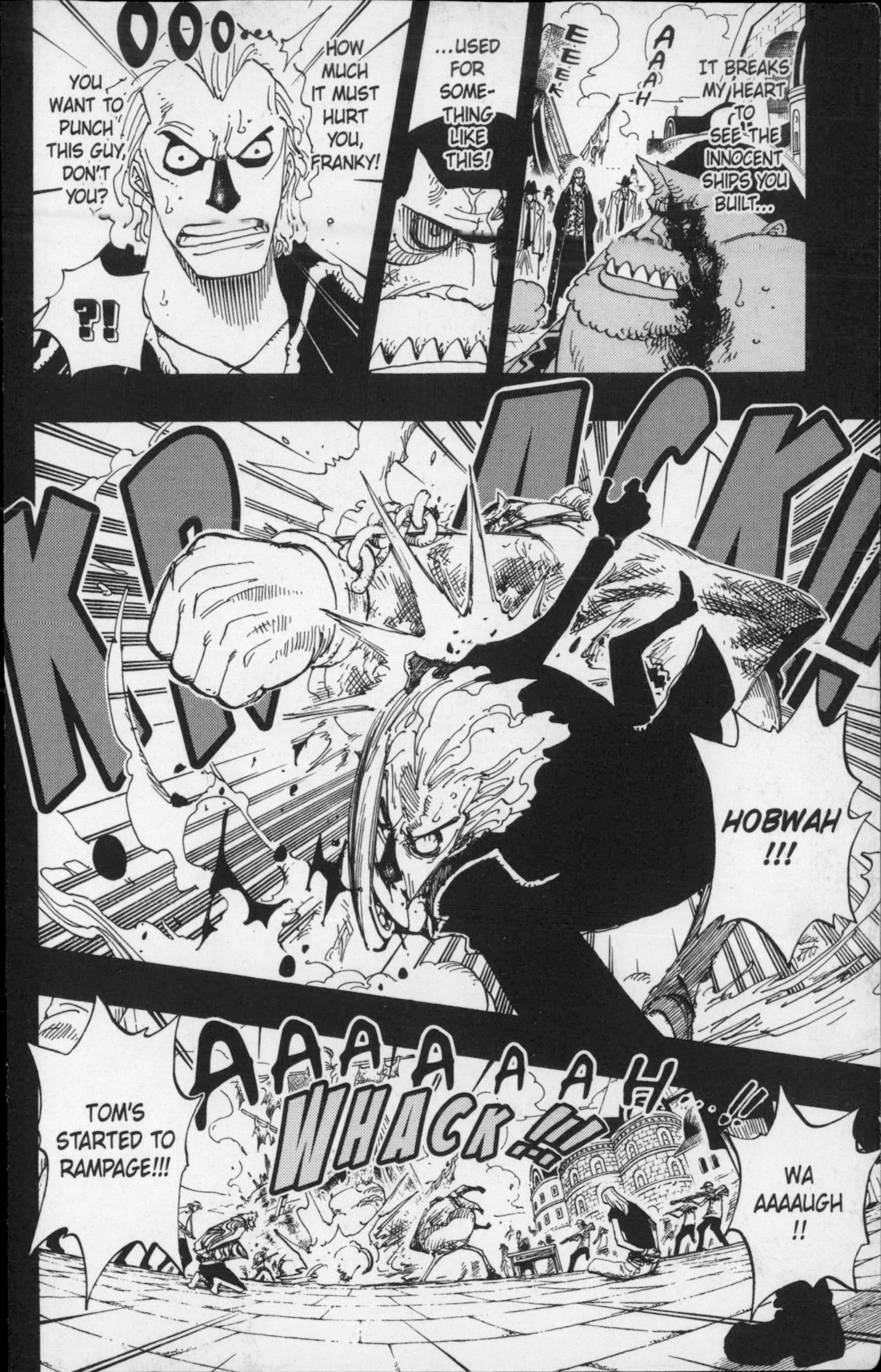
IT BREAKS MY HEART TO SEE THE INNOCENT SHIPS YOU BUILT...
AAAAH
EEEEK
...USED FOR SOMETHING LIKE THIS!
HOW MUCH IT MUST HURT YOU, FRANKY!
OOO
YOU WANT TO PUNCH THIS GUY, DON'T YOU?
?!
HOBWAH !!!
WA AAAAUGH !!
AAAAAAAH..!!
WHACK!!!
TOM'S STARTED TO RAMPAGE!!!

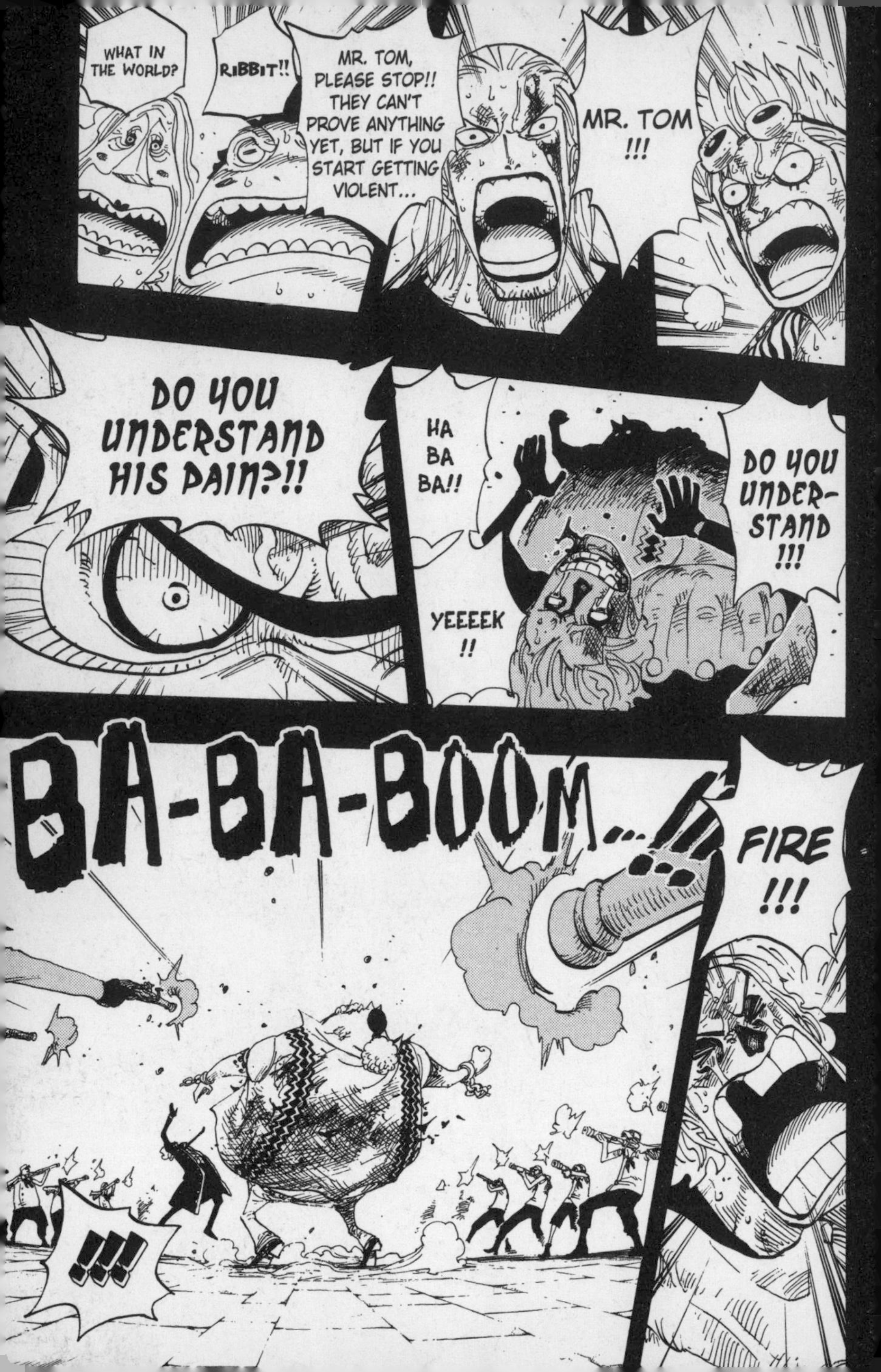

MR. TOM !!!
MR. TOM, PLEASE STOP!! THEY CAN'T PROVE ANYTHING YET, BUT IF YOU START GETTING VIOLENT...
RIBBIT!!
WHAT IN THE WORLD?
DO YOU UNDER-STAND !!!
HA BA BA!!
YEEEEK !!
DO YOU UNDERSTAND HIS PAIN?!!
FIRE !!!
BA-BA-BOOM...!!
!!!

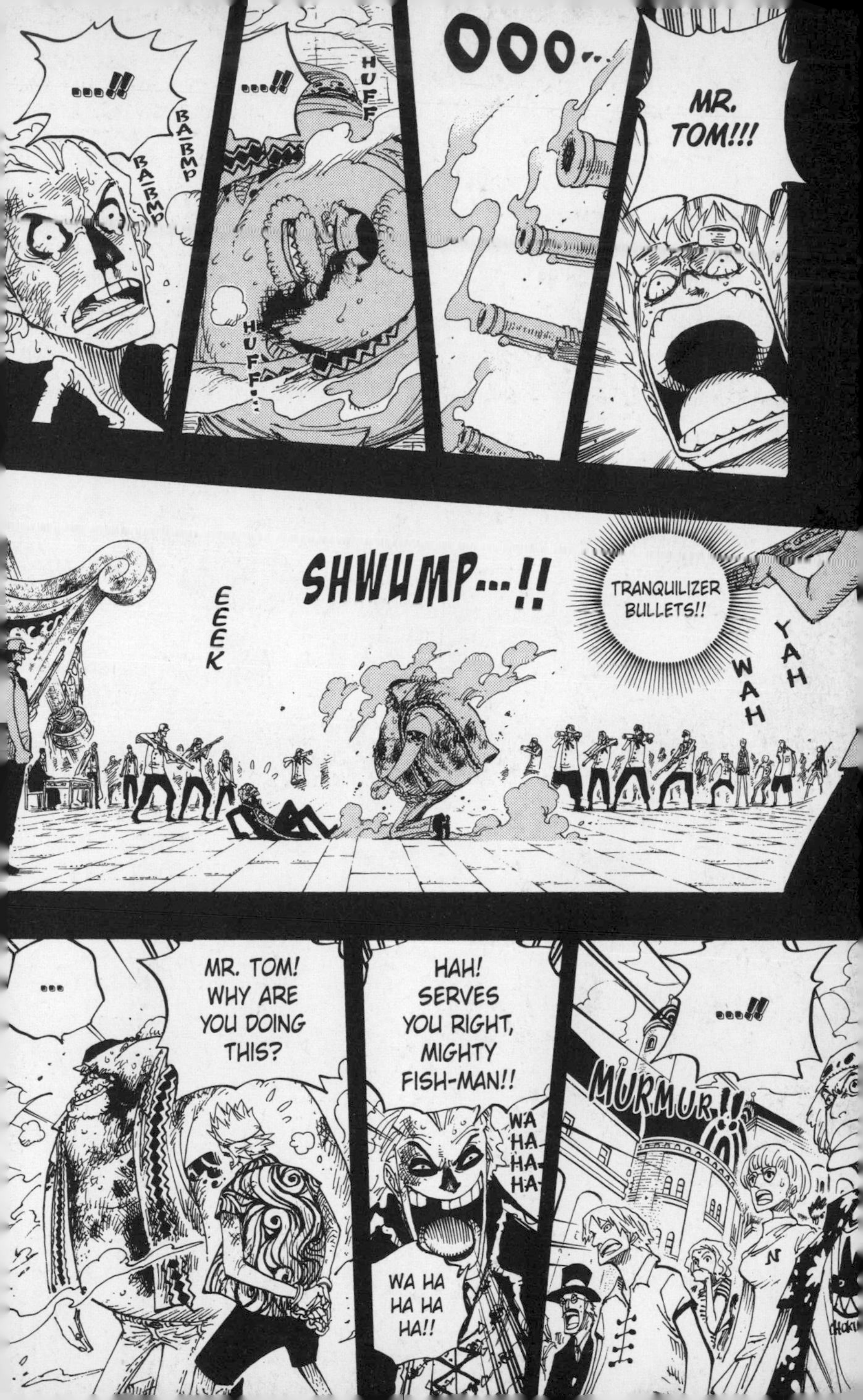
MR. TOM!!!
OOO...
...!!
HUFF
HUFF...
...!!
BA-BMP
BA-BMP
TRANQUILIZER BULLETS!!
YAH
WAH
SHWUMP...!!
EEEK
...!!
MURMUR!!
HAH! SERVES YOU RIGHT, MIGHTY FISH-MAN!!
WA HA HA HA
WA HA HA HA HA!!
MR. TOM! WHY ARE YOU DOING THIS?
...

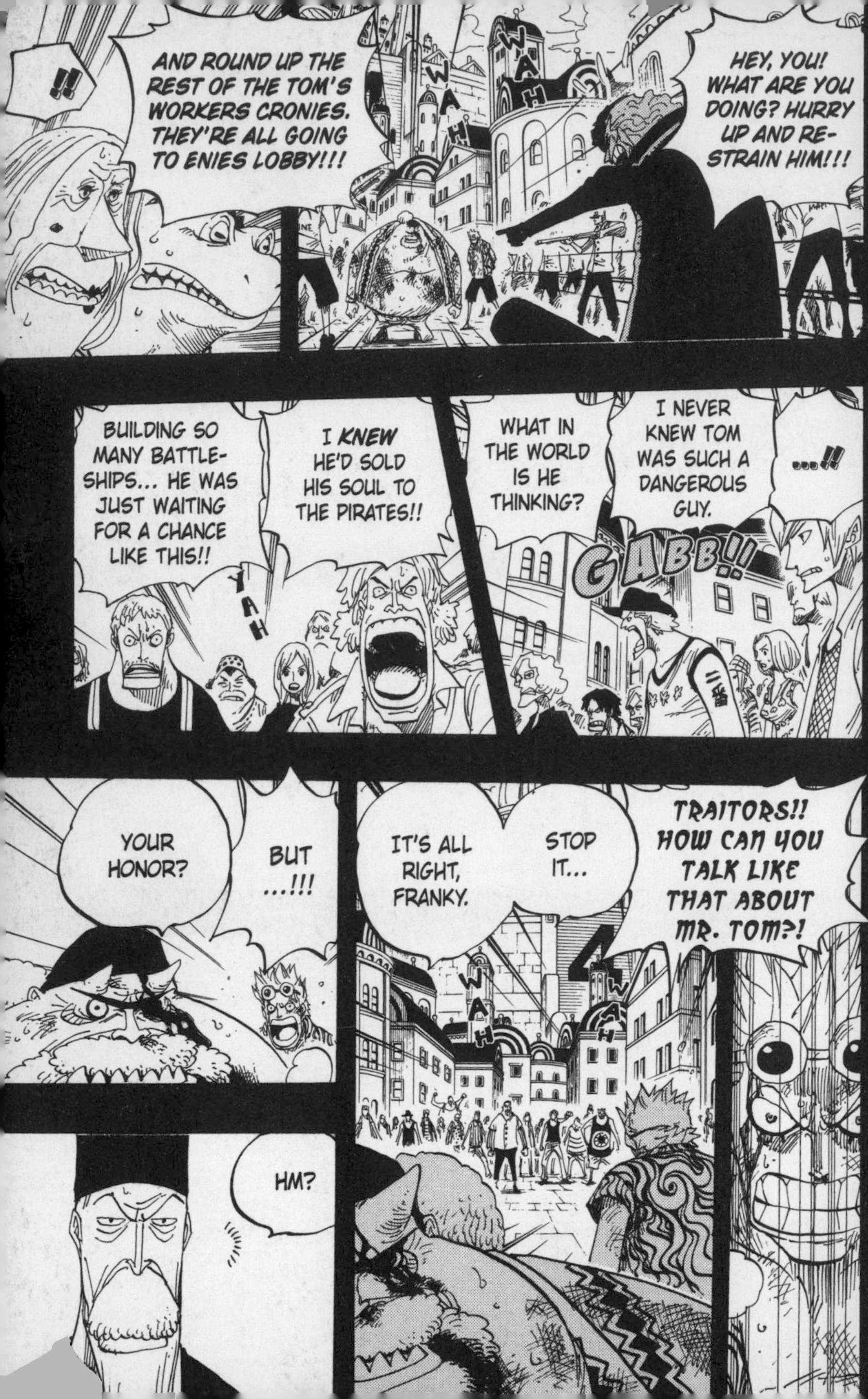
HEY, YOU! WHAT ARE YOU DOING? HURRY UP AND RE-STRAIN HIM!!!
AND ROUND UP THE REST OF THE TOM'S WORKERS CRONIES. THEY'RE ALL GOING TO ENIES LOBBY!!!
WAH
WAH
!!
...!!
I NEVER KNEW TOM WAS SUCH A DANGEROUS GUY.
WHAT IN THE WORLD IS HE THINKING?
GABB!!
I *KNEW* HE'D SOLD HIS SOUL TO THE PIRATES!!
BUILDING SO MANY BATTLE-SHIPS... HE WAS JUST WAITING FOR A CHANCE LIKE THIS!!
YAH
TRAITORS!! HOW CAN YOU TALK LIKE THAT ABOUT MR. TOM?!
STOP IT...
IT'S ALL RIGHT, FRANKY.
WAH
WAH
BUT ...!!!
YOUR HONOR?
HM?

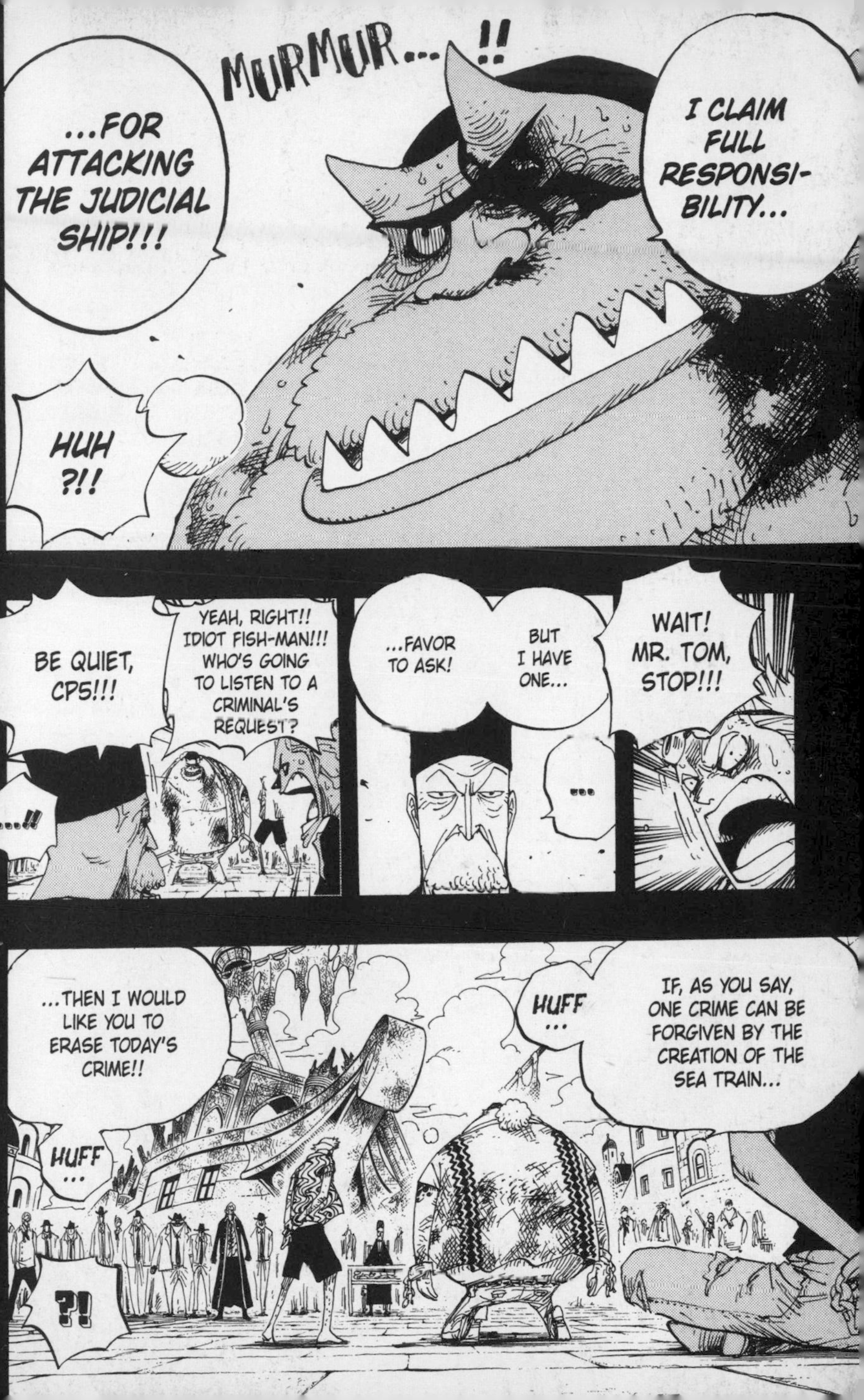

I CLAIM FULL RESPONSIBILITY...
...FOR ATTACKING THE JUDICIAL SHIP!!!
MURMUR...!!
HUH ?!!
WAIT! MR. TOM, STOP!!!
BUT I HAVE ONE...
...FAVOR TO ASK!
...
YEAH, RIGHT!! IDIOT FISH-MAN!!! WHO'S GOING TO LISTEN TO A CRIMINAL'S REQUEST?
BE QUIET, CP5!!!
...!!
IF, AS YOU SAY, ONE CRIME CAN BE FORGIVEN BY THE CREATION OF THE SEA TRAIN...
HUFF...
...THEN I WOULD LIKE YOU TO ERASE TODAY'S CRIME!!
HUFF...
?!

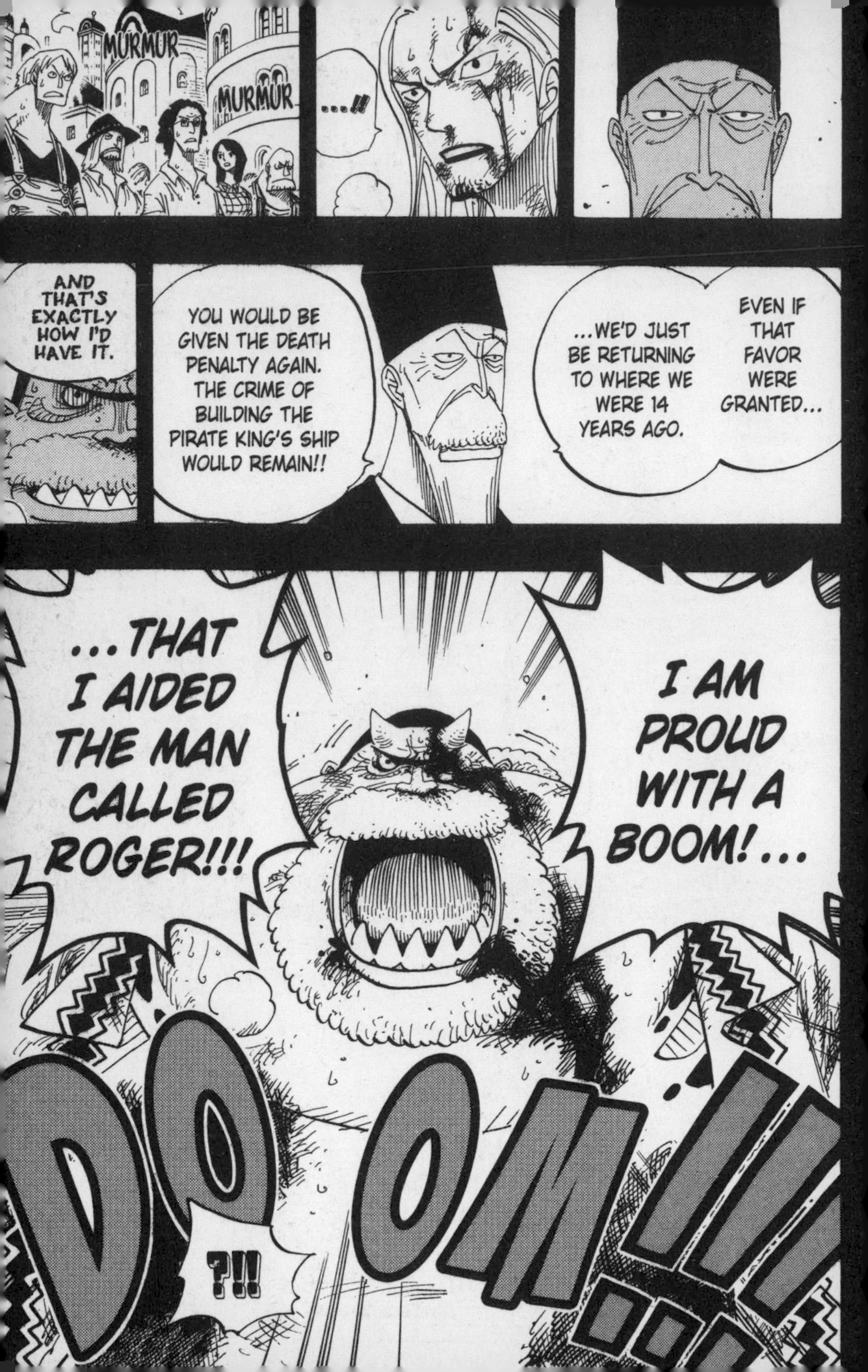
...!!
MURMUR
MURMUR
EVEN IF THAT FAVOR WERE GRANTED...
...WE'D JUST BE RETURNING TO WHERE WE WERE 14 YEARS AGO.
YOU WOULD BE GIVEN THE DEATH PENALTY AGAIN. THE CRIME OF BUILDING THE PIRATE KING'S SHIP WOULD REMAIN!!
AND THAT'S EXACTLY HOW I'D HAVE IT.
I AM PROUD WITH A BOOM!...
...THAT I AIDED THE MAN CALLED ROGER!!!
?!!

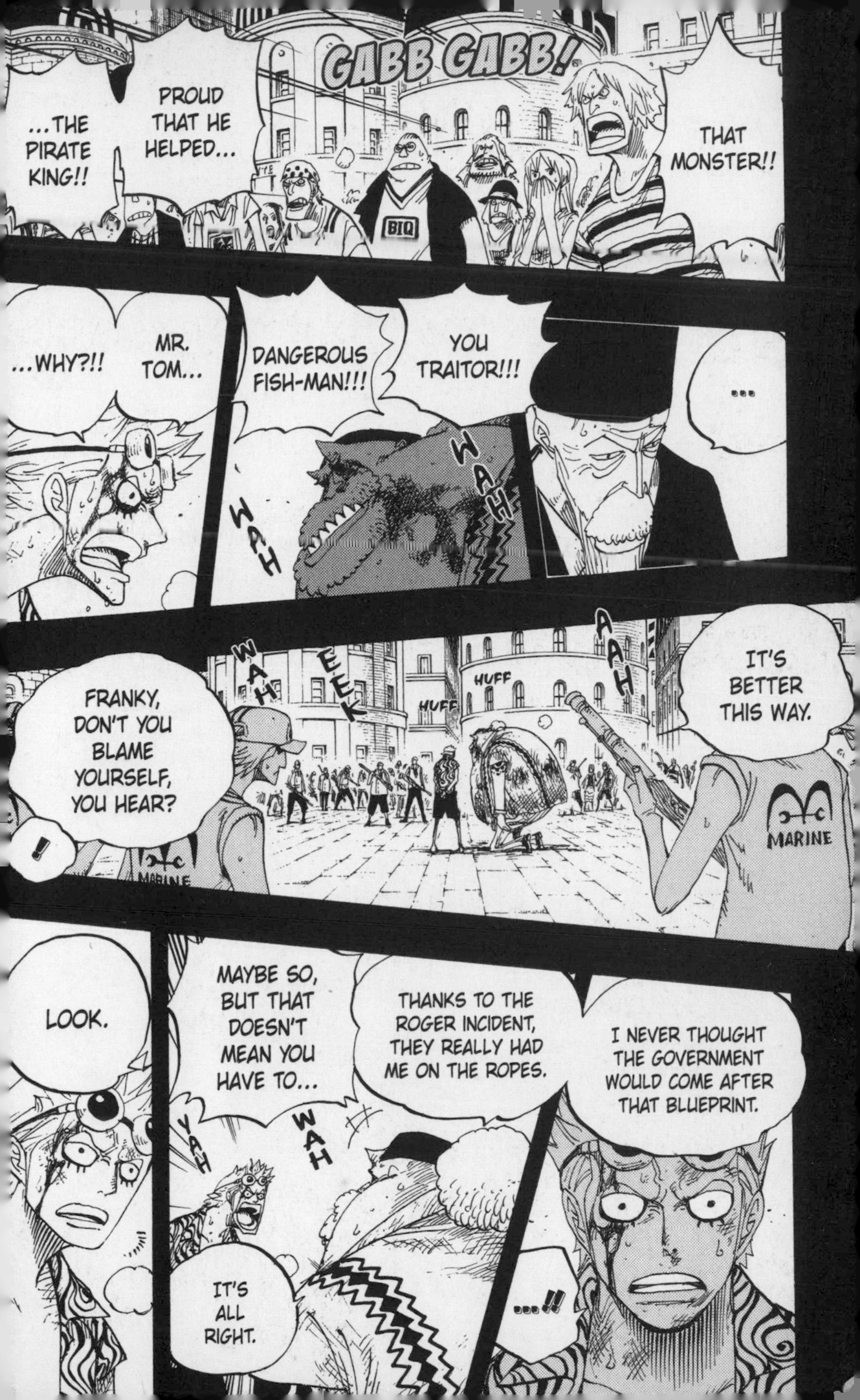
THAT MONSTER!!
GABB GABB!
PROUD THAT HE HELPED...
...THE PIRATE KING!!
...
YOU TRAITOR!!!
WAH
DANGEROUS FISH-MAN!!!
WAH
MR. TOM...
...WHY?!!
IT'S BETTER THIS WAY.
AAH
HUFF
HUFF
EEK
WAH
FRANKY, DON'T YOU BLAME YOURSELF, YOU HEAR?
!
I NEVER THOUGHT THE GOVERNMENT WOULD COME AFTER THAT BLUEPRINT.
...!!
THANKS TO THE ROGER INCIDENT, THEY REALLY HAD ME ON THE ROPES.
MAYBE SO, BUT THAT DOESN'T MEAN YOU HAVE TO...
WAH
YAH
IT'S ALL RIGHT.
LOOK.

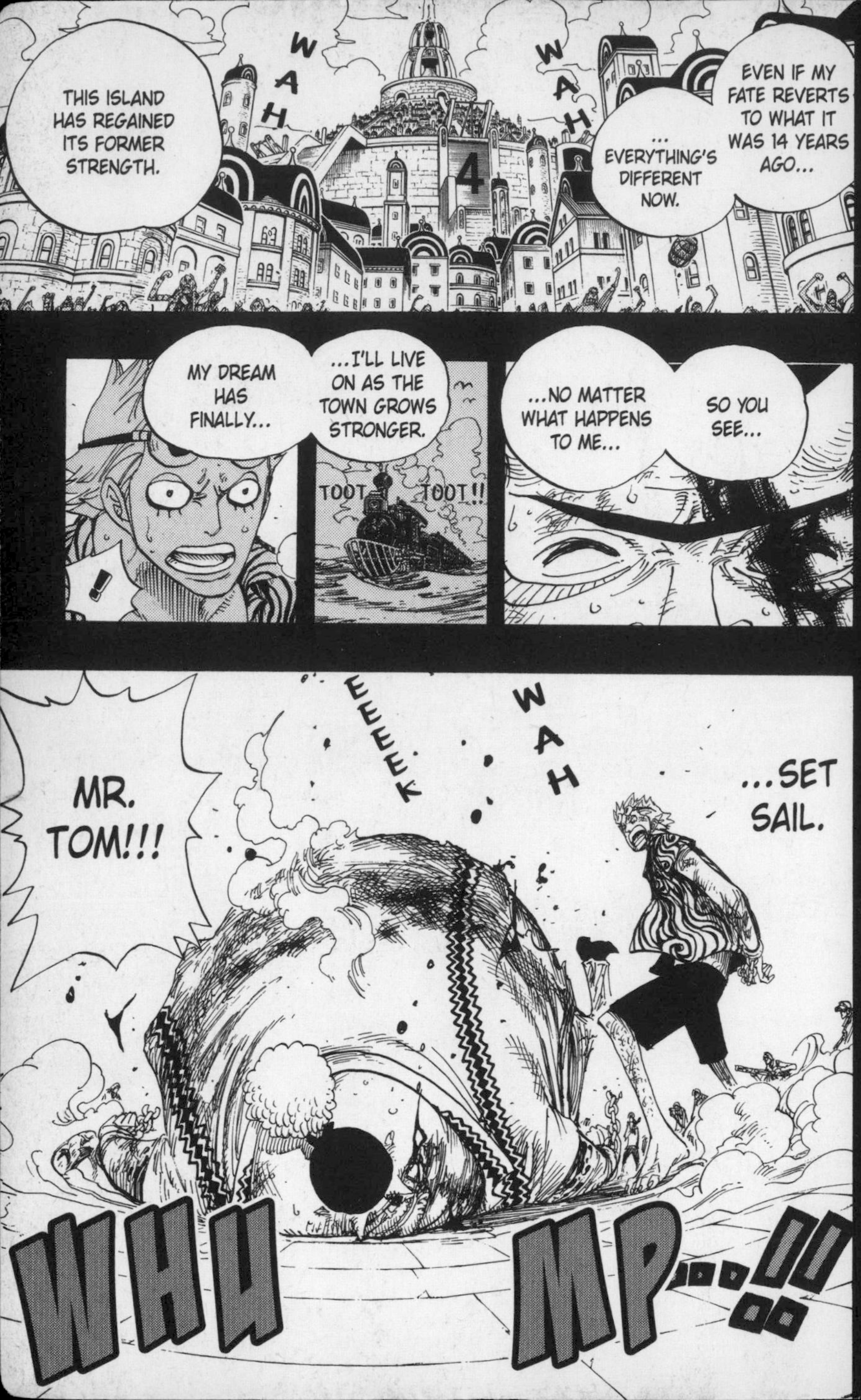
EVEN IF MY FATE REVERTS TO WHAT IT WAS 14 YEARS AGO...
... EVERYTHING'S DIFFERENT NOW.
WAH
WAH
THIS ISLAND HAS REGAINED ITS FORMER STRENGTH.
SO YOU SEE...
...NO MATTER WHAT HAPPENS TO ME...
...I'LL LIVE ON AS THE TOWN GROWS STRONGER.
TOOT TOOT!!
MY DREAM HAS FINALLY...
!
...SET SAIL.
WAH
EEEEK
MR. TOM!!!
WHUMP..!!

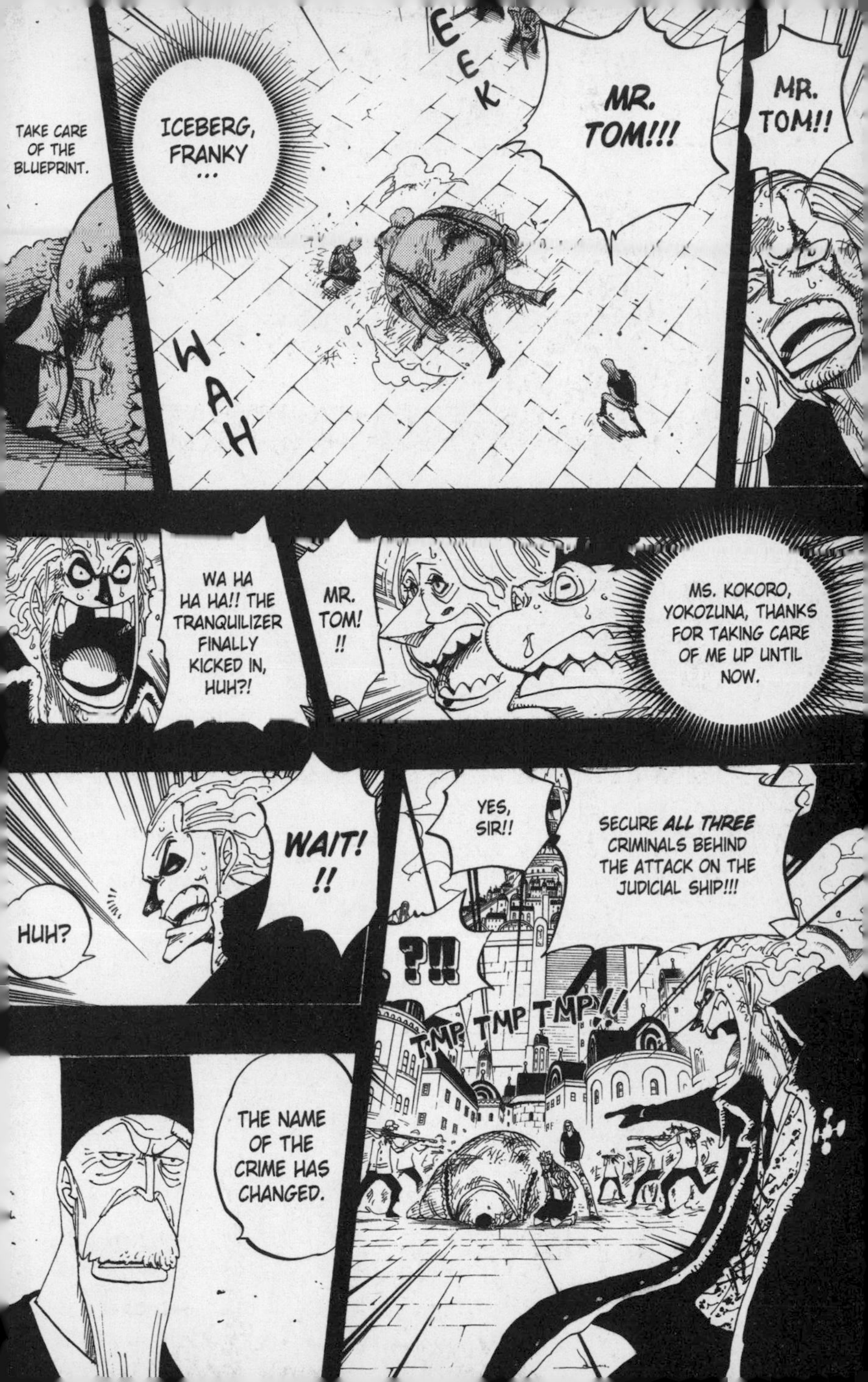
MR. TOM!!
MR. TOM!!!
EEEK
ICEBERG, FRANKY ...
WAH
TAKE CARE OF THE BLUEPRINT.
MS. KOKORO, YOKOZUNA, THANKS FOR TAKING CARE OF ME UP UNTIL NOW.
MR. TOM! !!
WA HA HA HA!! THE TRANQUILIZER FINALLY KICKED IN, HUH?!
SECURE *ALL THREE* CRIMINALS BEHIND THE ATTACK ON THE JUDICIAL SHIP!!!
YES, SIR!!
?!!
TMP TMP TMP!!
WAIT! !!
HUH?
THE NAME OF THE CRIME HAS CHANGED.

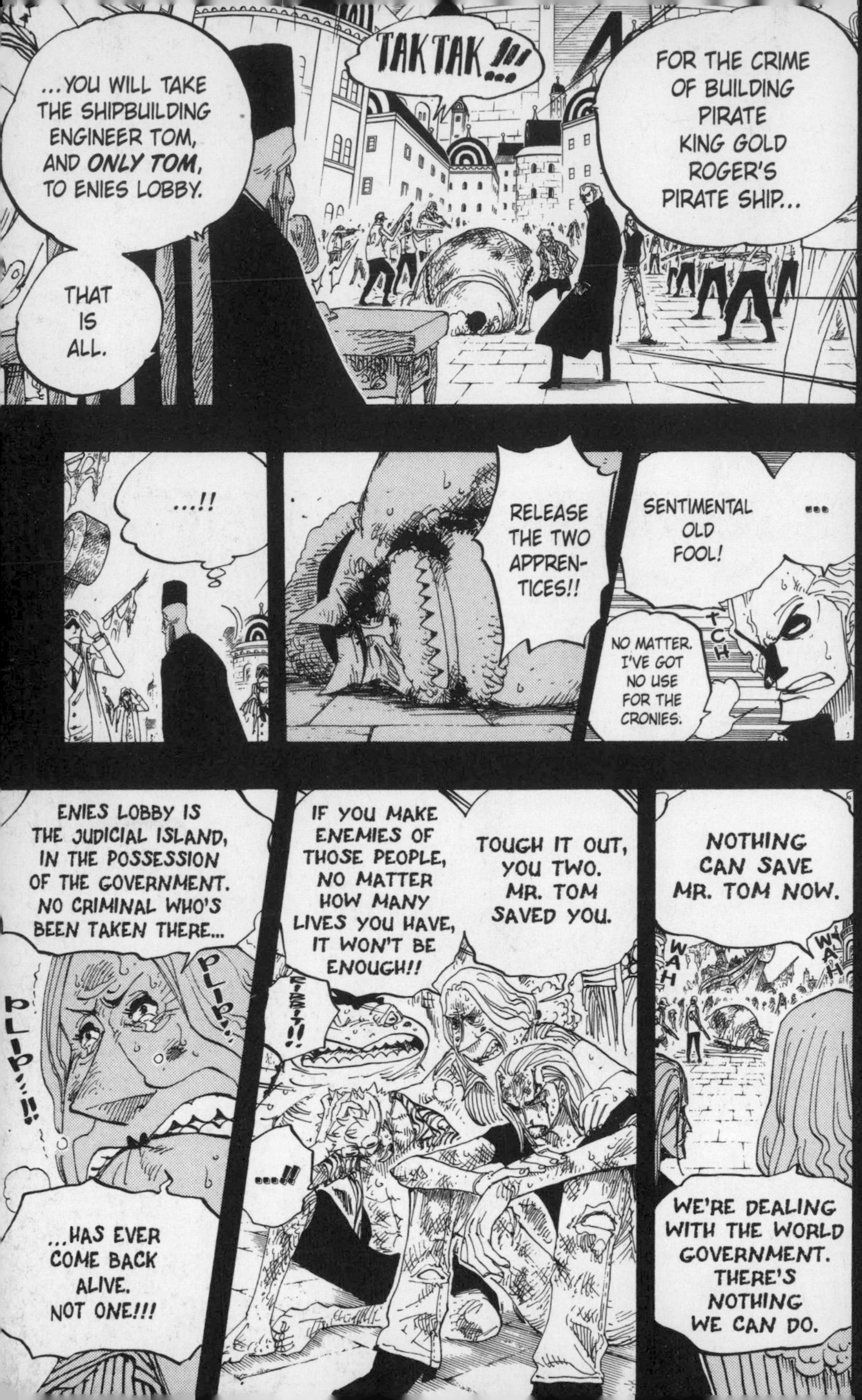
FOR THE CRIME OF BUILDING PIRATE KING GOLD ROGER'S PIRATE SHIP...
TAK TAK!!!...
...YOU WILL TAKE THE SHIPBUILDING ENGINEER TOM, AND ONLY TOM, TO ENIES LOBBY.
THAT IS ALL.
SENTIMENTAL OLD FOOL!
...
TCH
NO MATTER. I'VE GOT NO USE FOR THE CRONIES.
RELEASE THE TWO APPRENTICES!!
...!!
NOTHING CAN SAVE MR. TOM NOW.
WAH
WAH
WE'RE DEALING WITH THE WORLD GOVERNMENT. THERE'S NOTHING WE CAN DO.
TOUGH IT OUT, YOU TWO. MR. TOM SAVED YOU.
IF YOU MAKE ENEMIES OF THOSE PEOPLE, NO MATTER HOW MANY LIVES YOU HAVE, IT WON'T BE ENOUGH!!
RIBBIT!!
...!!
ENIES LOBBY IS THE JUDICIAL ISLAND, IN THE POSSESSION OF THE GOVERNMENT. NO CRIMINAL WHO'S BEEN TAKEN THERE...
PLIP..
PLIP...!!
...HAS EVER COME BACK ALIVE. NOT ONE!!!

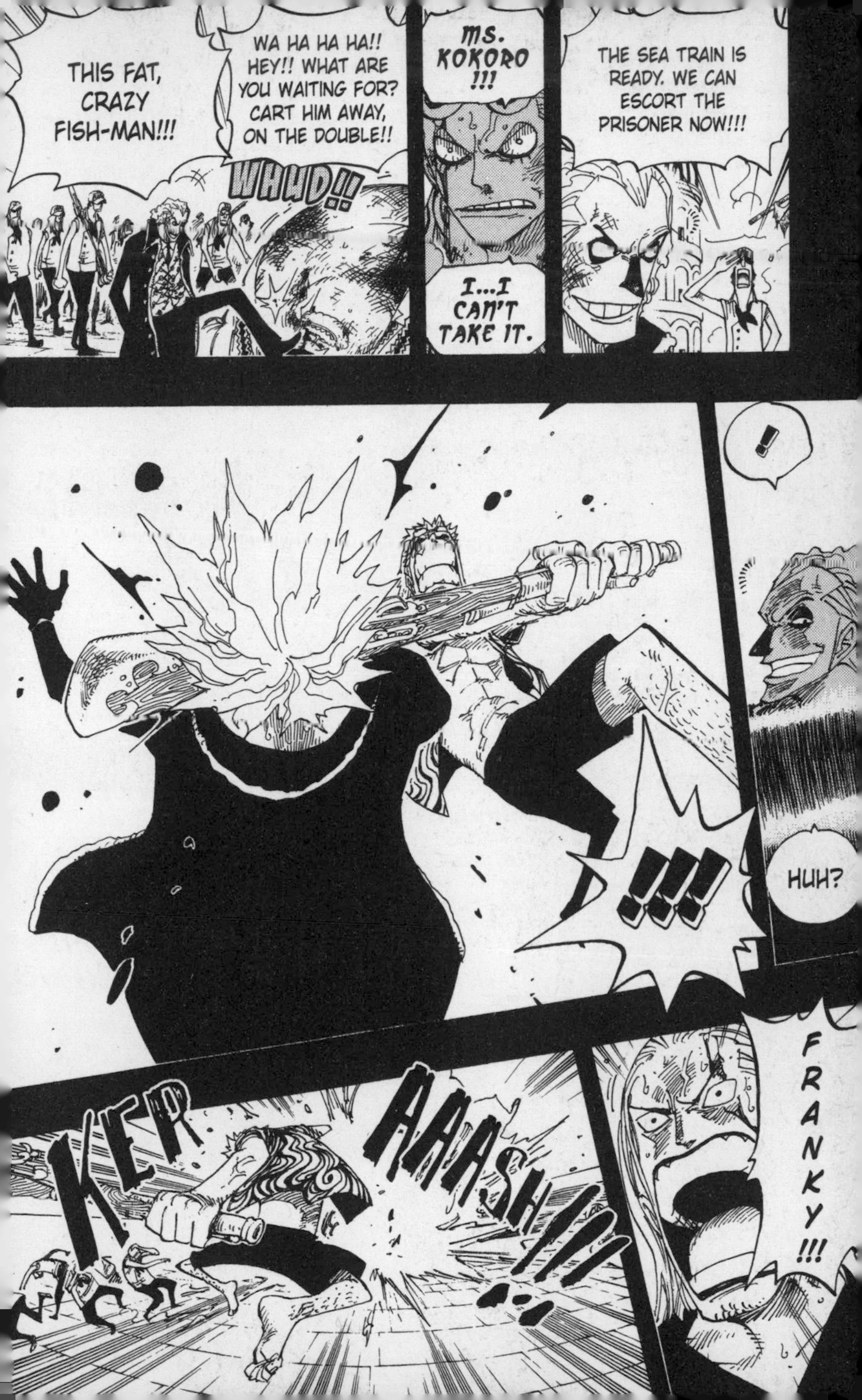

THE SEA TRAIN IS READY. WE CAN ESCORT THE PRISONER NOW!!!
MS. KOKORO!!!
I...I CAN'T TAKE IT.
WA HA HA HA!! HEY!! WHAT ARE YOU WAITING FOR? CART HIM AWAY, ON THE DOUBLE!!
THIS FAT, CRAZY FISH-MAN!!!
WHUD!!
!
HUH?
!!!
FRANKY!!!
KERAAASH!!!

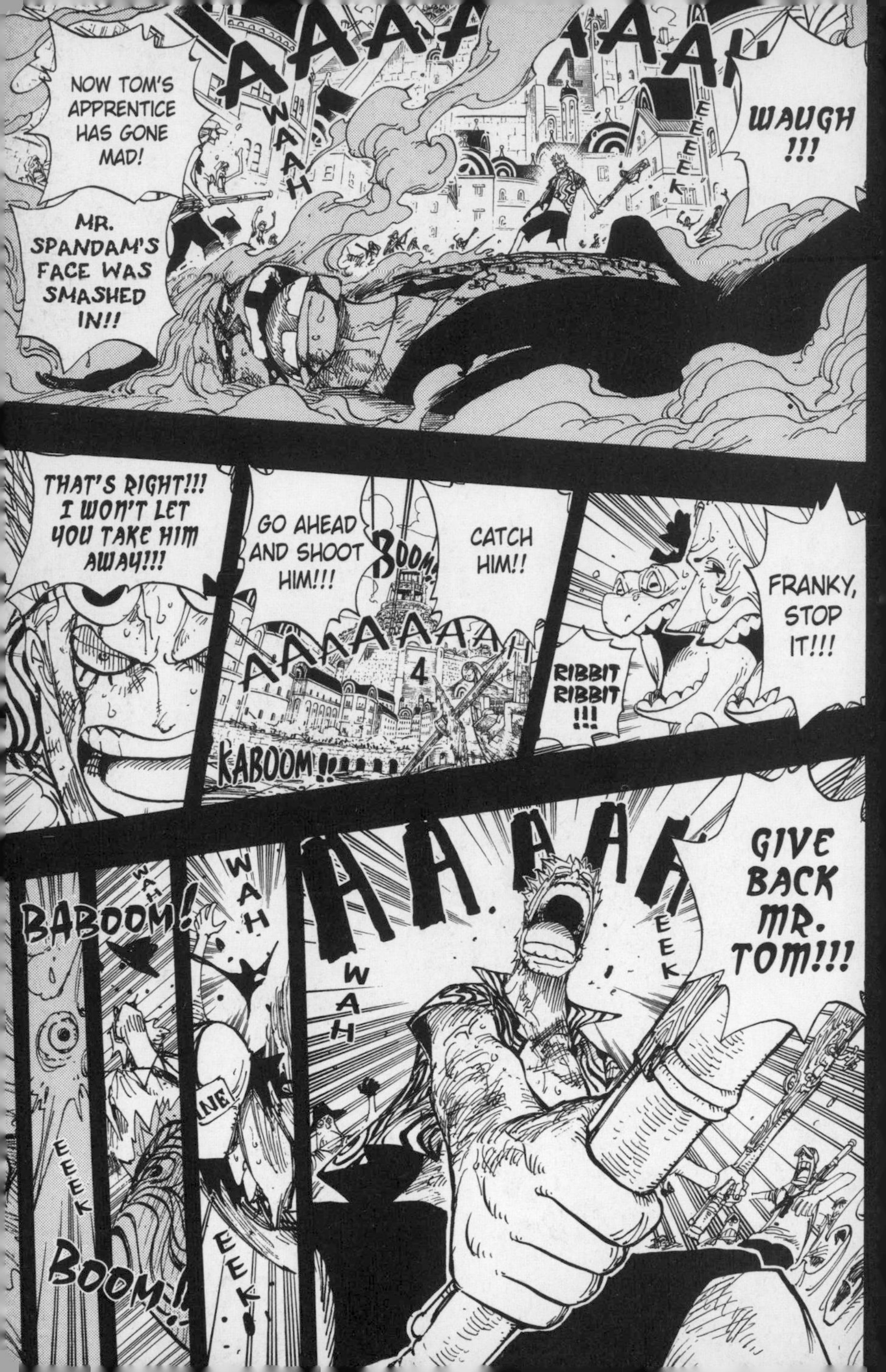
WAUGH!!!
EEEEEK
WAAAH
NOW TOM'S APPRENTICE HAS GONE MAD!
MR. SPANDAM'S FACE WAS SMASHED IN!!
FRANKY, STOP IT!!!
RIBBIT RIBBIT !!!
CATCH HIM!!
BOOM
GO AHEAD AND SHOOT HIM!!!
AAAAAAAAH
KABOOM!!
THAT'S RIGHT!!! I WON'T LET YOU TAKE HIM AWAY!!!
GIVE BACK MR. TOM!!!
EEEK
WAAH
WAAH
WAH
BABOOM!
EEEK
EEEK
BOOM!!

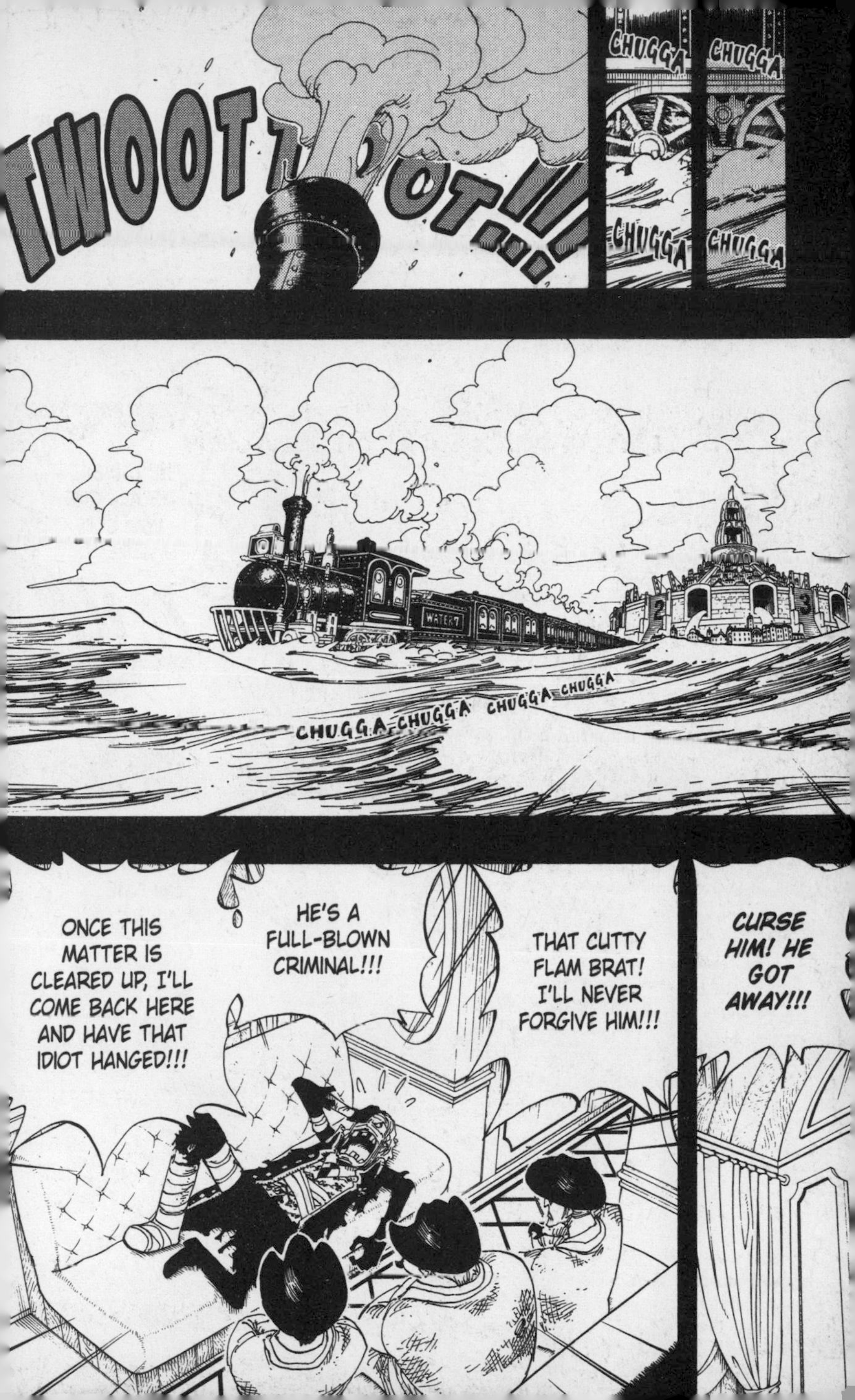
CHUGGA
CHUGGA
CHUGGA
CHUGGA
TWOOT TOOT!!!
CHUGGA CHUGGA CHUGGA CHUGGA
CURSE HIM! HE GOT AWAY!!!
THAT CUTTY FLAM BRAT! I'LL NEVER FORGIVE HIM!!!
HE'S A FULL-BLOWN CRIMINAL!!!
ONCE THIS MATTER IS CLEARED UP, I'LL COME BACK HERE AND HAVE THAT IDIOT HANGED!!!

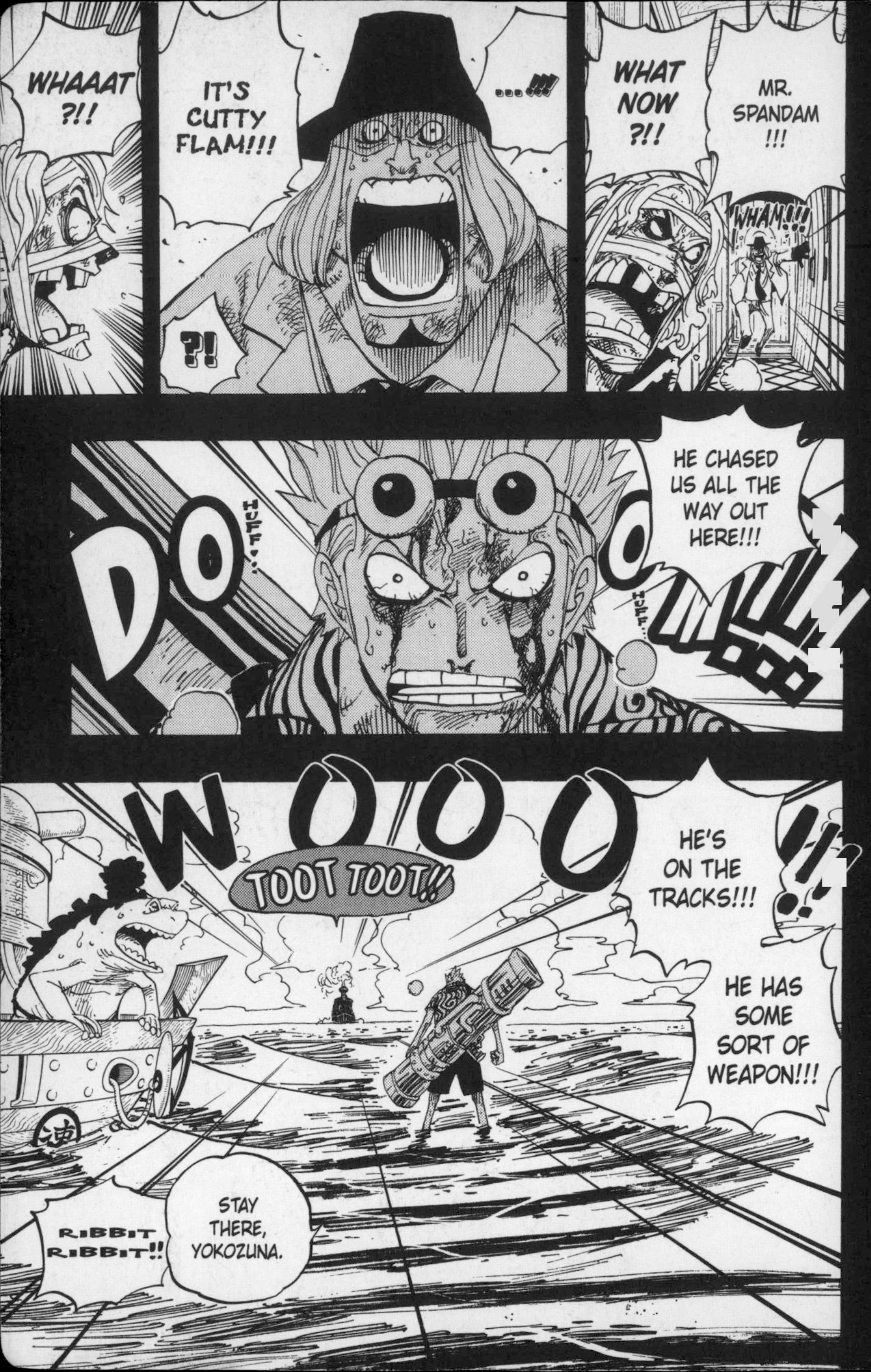
MR. SPANDAM!!!
WHAT NOW?!!
WHAM!!!
...!!!
IT'S CUTTY FLAM!!!
?!
WHAAAT?!!
HE CHASED US ALL THE WAY OUT HERE!!!
HUFF...
HUFF...
WOOOO!!
TOOT TOOT!!
HE'S ON THE TRACKS!!!
HE HAS SOME SORT OF WEAPON!!!
STAY THERE, YOKOZUNA.
RIBBIT RIBBIT!!

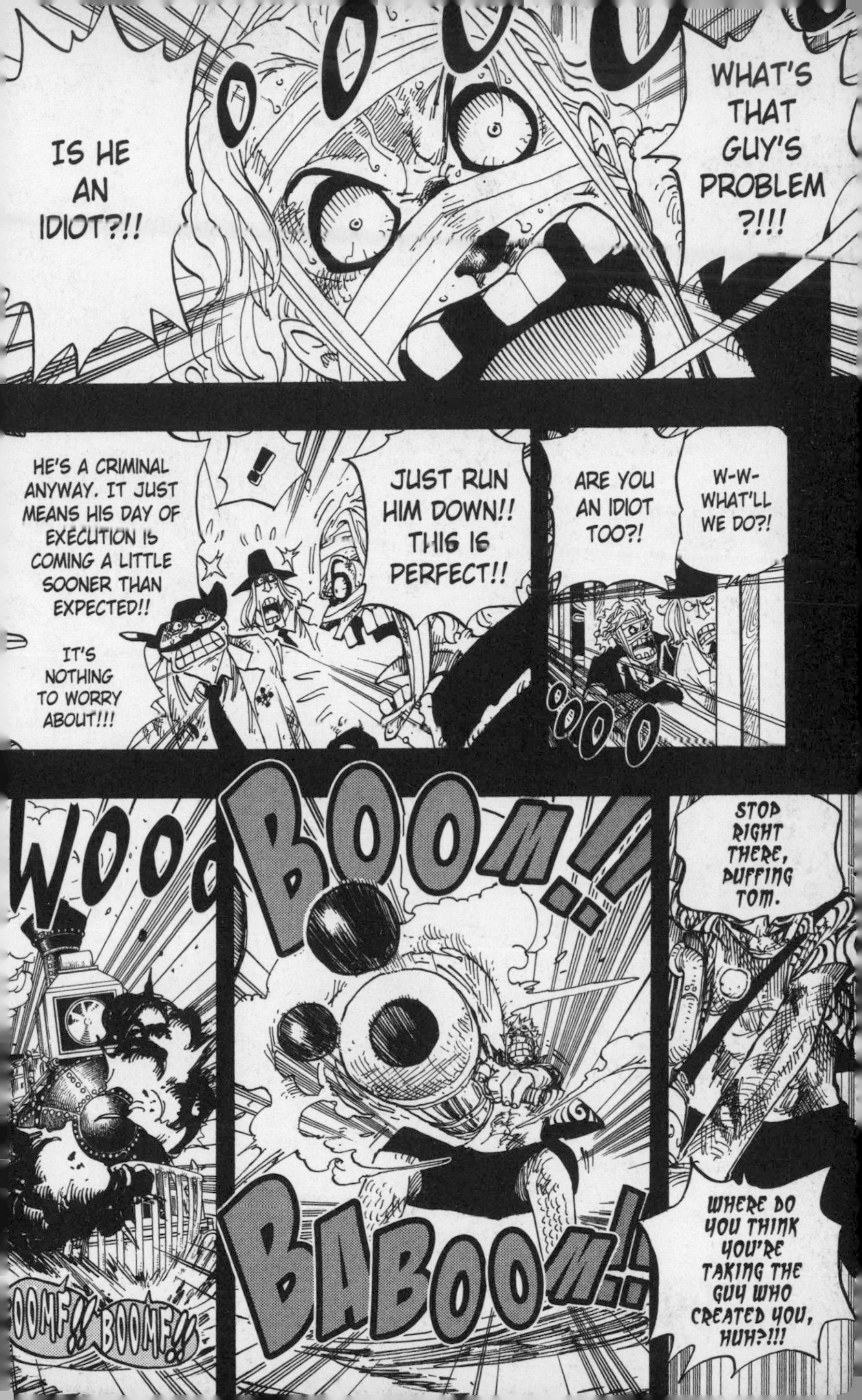

WHAT'S THAT GUY'S PROBLEM ?!!!
IS HE AN IDIOT?!!
W-W-WHAT'LL WE DO?!
ARE YOU AN IDIOT TOO?!
!
JUST RUN HIM DOWN!! THIS IS PERFECT!!
HE'S A CRIMINAL ANYWAY. IT JUST MEANS HIS DAY OF EXECUTION IS COMING A LITTLE SOONER THAN EXPECTED!!
IT'S NOTHING TO WORRY ABOUT!!!
STOP RIGHT THERE, PUFFING TOM.
WHERE DO YOU THINK YOU'RE TAKING THE GUY WHO CREATED YOU, HUH?!!!
BOOM!!
BABOOM!!
WOO
BOOMF!! BOOMF!!

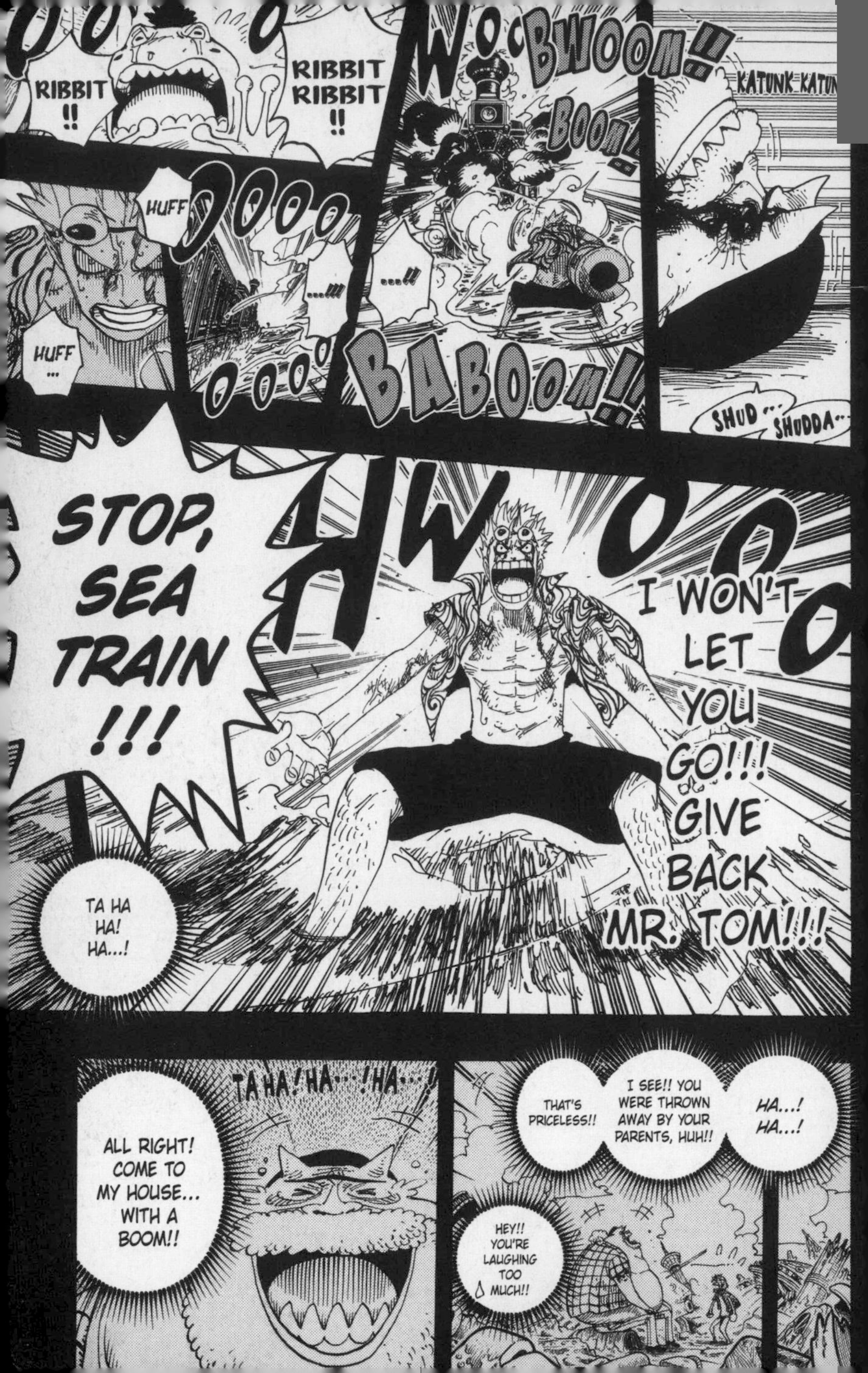
KATUNK KATUN
SHUD... SHUDDA...
WOO
BWOOM!!
BOOM!!
...!!
BABOOM!!!
RIBBIT RIBBIT!!
RIBBIT!!
...!!!
HUFF
HUFF...
AWOOO
I WON'T LET YOU GO!!! GIVE BACK MR. TOM!!!
STOP, SEA TRAIN!!!
TA HA HA! HA...!
HA...! HA...!
I SEE!! YOU WERE THROWN AWAY BY YOUR PARENTS, HUH!!
THAT'S PRICELESS!!
HEY!! YOU'RE LAUGHING TOO MUCH!!
TA HA! HA...!HA...!
ALL RIGHT! COME TO MY HOUSE... WITH A BOOM!!

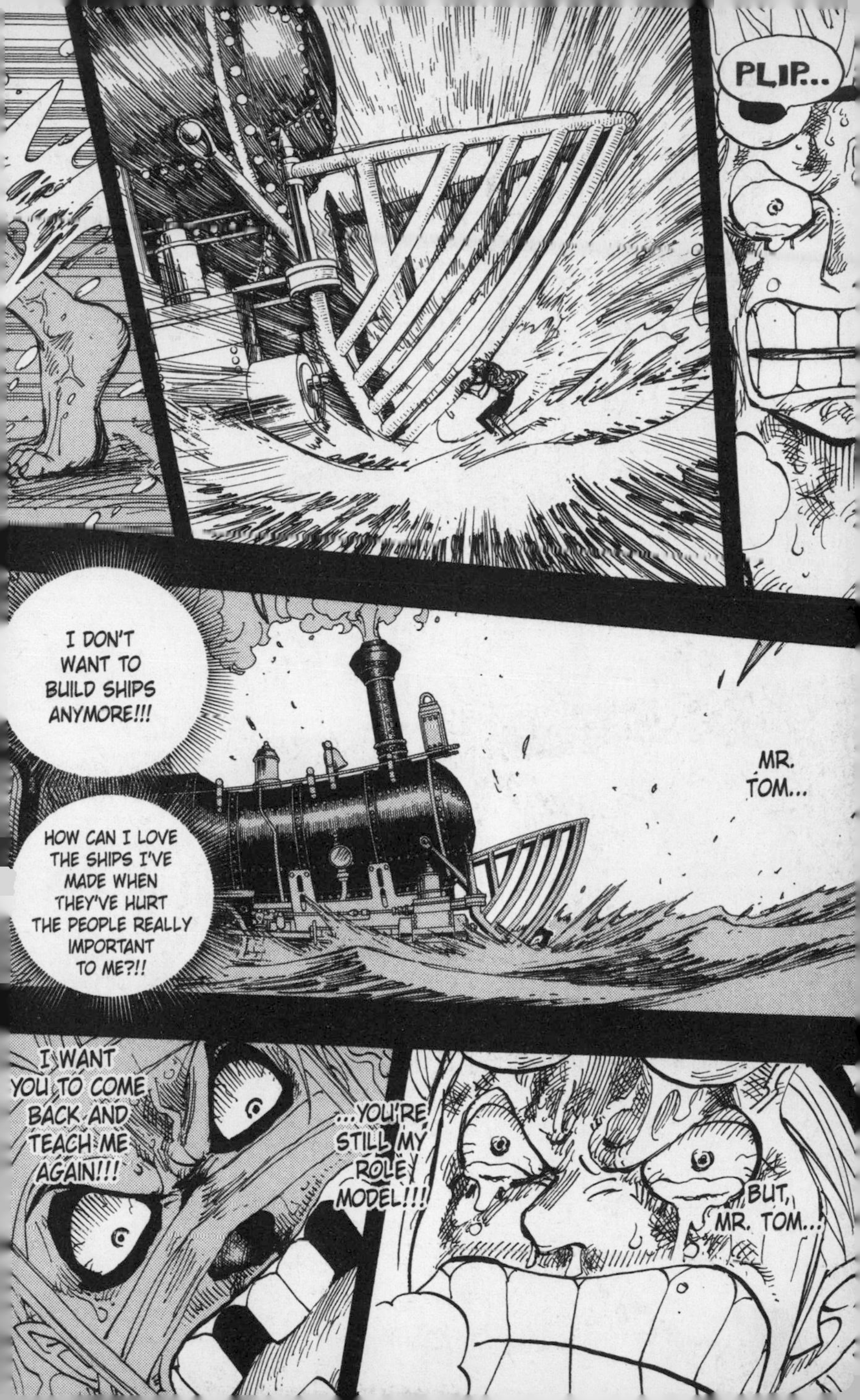
PLIP...
MR. TOM...
I DON'T WANT TO BUILD SHIPS ANYMORE!!!
HOW CAN I LOVE THE SHIPS I'VE MADE WHEN THEY'VE HURT THE PEOPLE REALLY IMPORTANT TO ME?!!
BUT, MR. TOM...
...YOU'RE STILL MY ROLE MODEL!!!
I WANT YOU TO COME BACK AND TEACH ME AGAIN!!!

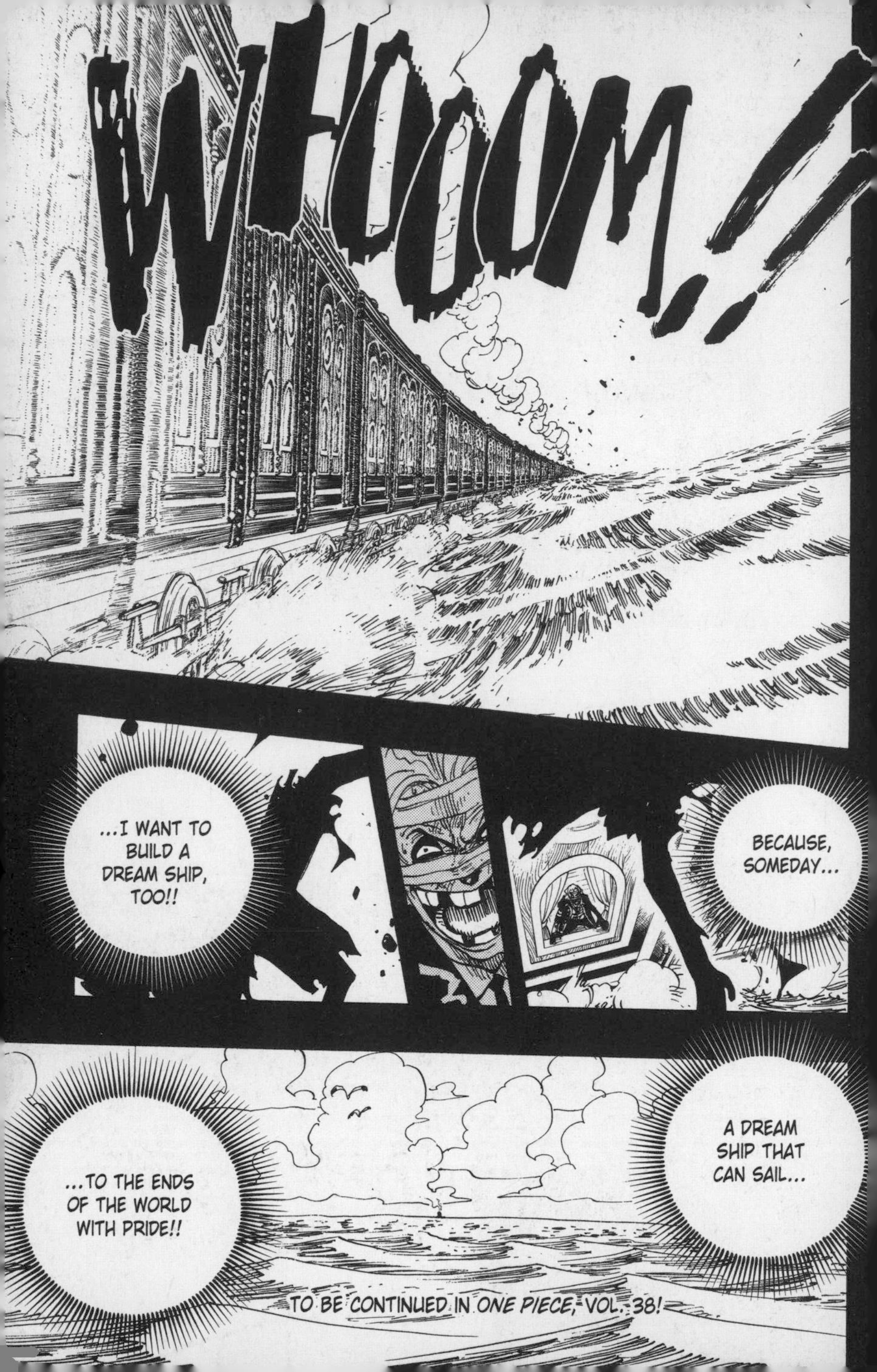
WHOOOM!!
BECAUSE, SOMEDAY...
...I WANT TO BUILD A DREAM SHIP, TOO!!
A DREAM SHIP THAT CAN SAIL...
...TO THE ENDS OF THE WORLD WITH PRIDE!!
TO BE CONTINUED IN ONE PIECE, VOL. 38!

COMING NEXT VOLUME:

After finding out the real reason behind Robin's betrayal, the Straw Hats are in a madcap race to rescue her from CP9, the Navy's elite assassin gang. But first they'll have to find a way to sail through the tidal wave known as Aqua Laguna. Will the Rocketman be seaworthy for the task at hand, or will it be a runaway train to catastrophe?!

ON SALE NOW!

Set Sail with

Read all about **MONKEY D. LUFFY**'s adventures as he sails around the world assembling a motley crew to join him on his search for the legendary treasure **"ONE PIECE."** For more information, check out **onepiece.viz.com**.

EAST BLUE
(Vols. 1-12)
Available now!

See where it all began! One man, a dinghy and a dream. Or rather… a rubber man who can't swim, setting out in a tiny boat on the vast seas without any navigational skills. What are the odds that his dream of becoming King of the Pirates will ever come true?

BAROQUE WORKS
(Vols. 12-24)
Available now!

Friend or foe? Ms. Wednesday is part of a group of bounty hunters—or isn't she? The Straw Hats get caught up in a civil war when they find a princess in their midst. But can they help her stop the revolution in her home country before the evil Crocodile gets his way?!

SKYPIEA
(Vols. 24-32)
Available now!

Luffy's quest to become King of the Pirates and find the elusive treasure known as "One Piece" continues…in the sky! The Straw Hats sail to Skypiea, an airborne island in the midst of a territorial war and ruled by a short-fused megalomaniac!

WATER SEVEN
(Vols. 32-46)
Available from February 2010!

The *Merry Go* has been a stalwart for the Straw Hats since the beginning, but countless battles have taken their toll on the ship. Luckily, their next stop is Water Seven, where a rough-and-tumble crew of shipwrights awaits their arrival!

THRILLER BARK
(Vols. 46-50)
Available from May 2010!

Luffy and crew get more than they bargained for when their ship is drawn toward haunted Thriller Bark. When Gecko Moria, one of the Warlords of the Sea, steals the crew's shadows, they'll have to get them back before the sun rises or else they'll all turn into zombies!

SABAODY
(Vols. 50-54)
Available from June 2010!

On the way to Fish-Man Island, the Straw Hats disembark on the Sabaody archipelago to get soaped up for their undersea adventure! But it's not too long before they get caught up in trouble! Luffy's made an enemy of an exalted World Noble when he saves Camie the mermaid from being sold on the slave market, and now he's got the Navy after him too!

IMPEL DOWN
(from Vol. 54)
Available from July 2010!

Luffy's brother Ace is about to be executed! Held in the Navy's maximum security prison Impel Down, Luffy needs to find a way to break in to help Ace escape. But with murderous fiends for guards inside, the notorious prisoners start to seem not so bad. Some are even friendly enough to give Luffy a helping hand!

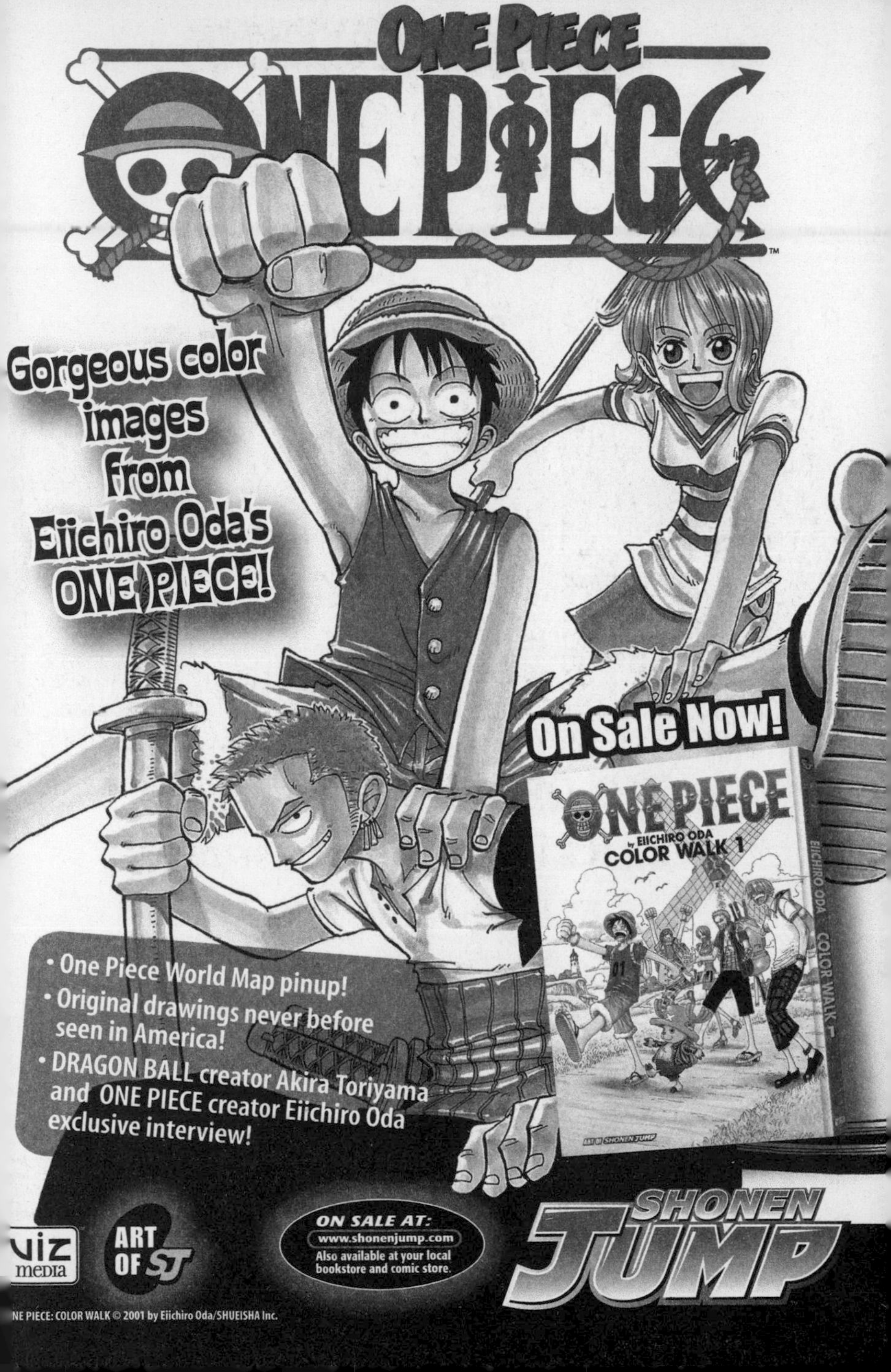
ONE PIECE
ONE PIECE
Gorgeous color images from Eiichiro Oda's ONE PIECE!
On Sale Now!
ONE PIECE
by EIICHIRO ODA
COLOR WALK 1
EIICHIRO ODA COLOR WALK 1
ART OF SHONEN JUMP
• One Piece World Map pinup!
• Original drawings never before seen in America!
• DRAGON BALL creator Akira Toriyama and ONE PIECE creator Eiichiro Oda exclusive interview!
viz media
ART OF SJ
ON SALE AT:
www.shonenjump.com
Also available at your local bookstore and comic store.
SHONEN JUMP
NE PIECE: COLOR WALK © 2001 by Eiichiro Oda/SHUEISHA Inc.

SAVE 50% OFF
THE COVER PRICE!

IT'S LIKE GETTING 6 ISSUES
FREE!

THE WORLD'S MOST POPULAR MANGA

OVER **350+** PAGES PER ISSUE

This monthly magazine contains 7 of the coolest manga available in the U.S., PLUS anime news, and info about video & card games, toys AND more!

❏ **I want 12 HUGE issues of SHONEN JUMP for only $29.95*!**

NAME

ADDRESS

CITY/STATE/ZIP

EMAIL ADDRESS   **DATE OF BIRTH**

❏ YES, send me via email information, advertising, offers, and promotions related to VIZ Media, SHONEN JUMP, and/or their business partners.

❏ **CHECK ENCLOSED** (payable to SHONEN JUMP)   ❏ **BILL ME LATER**

CREDIT CARD: ❏ **Visa** ❏ **Mastercard**

ACCOUNT NUMBER   **EXP. DATE**

SIGNATURE

CLIP&MAIL TO:

3 1901 04264 8107

Mount Morris, IL 61054-0515

P9GNC1

www.viz.com

P9-AGT-806